Touring After the Apocalypse

[1]

Sakae Saito

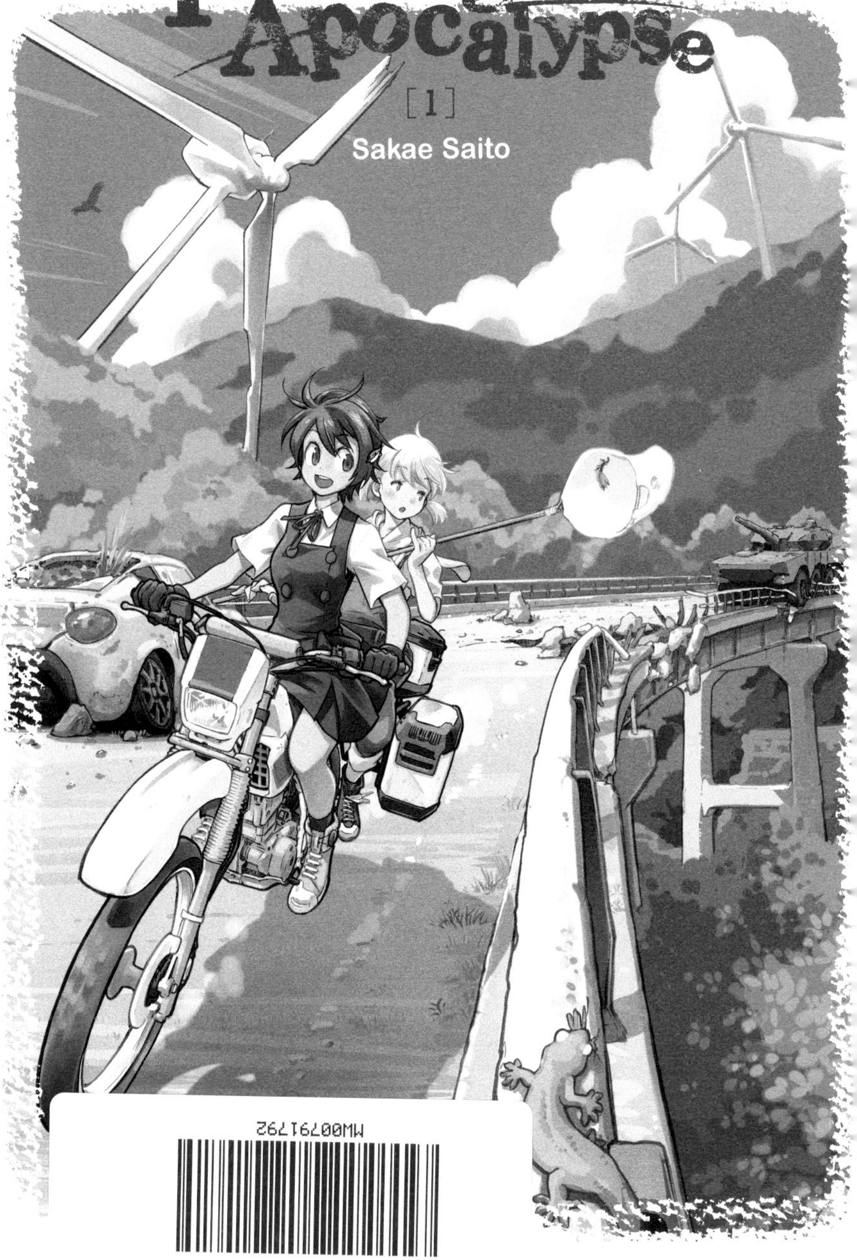

CONTENTS

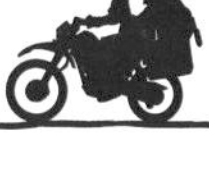

Touring After the Apocalypse

Chapter 1

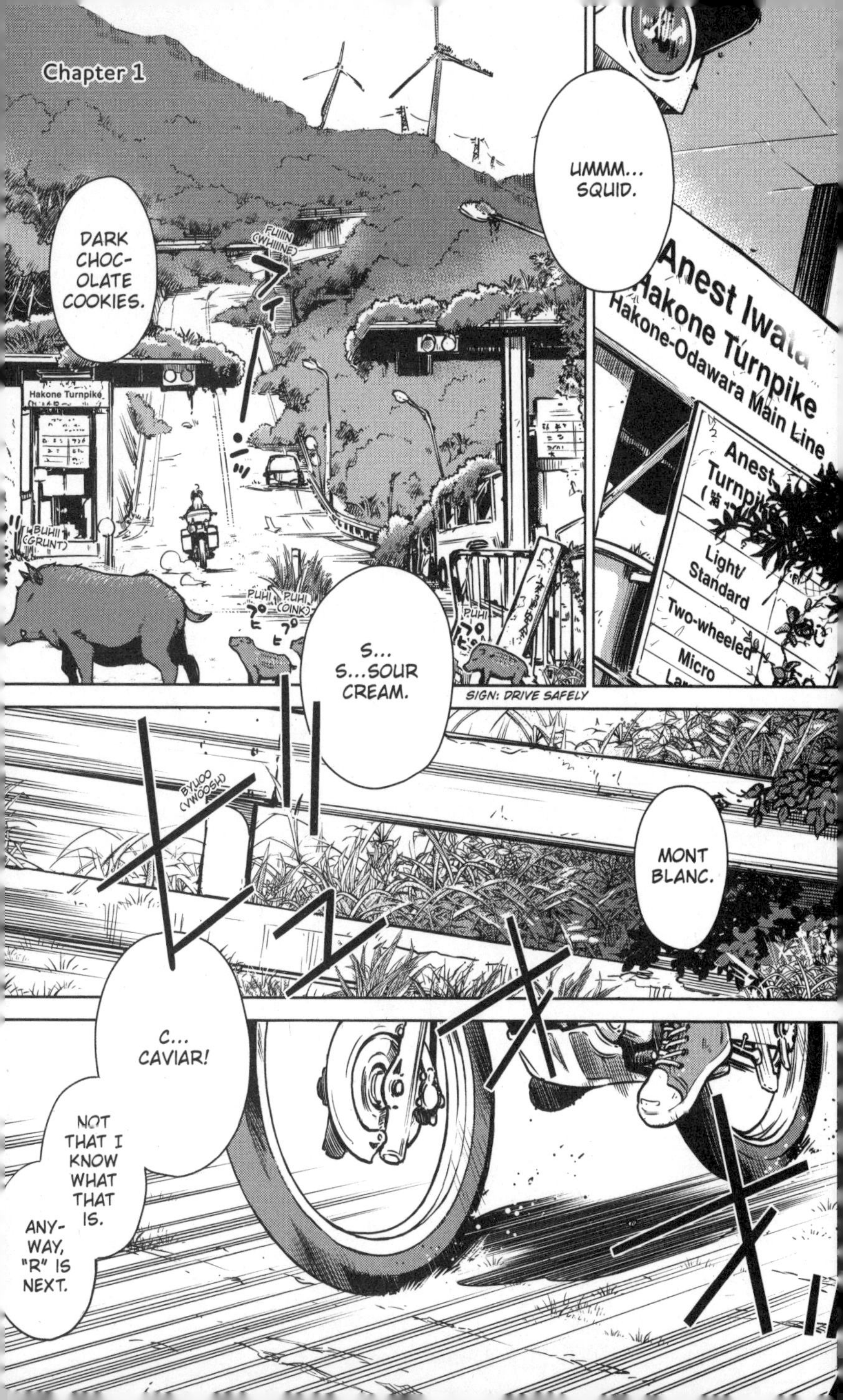
UMMM... SQUID.
Anest Iwata
Hakone Turnpike
Hakone-Odawara Main Line
Anest Turnpike
Light/ Standard
Two-wheeled
Micro
Hakone Turnpike
FUIIIN (WHIIINE)
DARK CHOC-OLATE COOKIES.
BUHII (GRUNT)
PUHI PUHI (OINK)
PUHI
SIGN: DRIVE SAFELY
MONT BLANC.
S... S...SOUR CREAM.
BYUOO (VWOOSH)
C... CAVIAR!
NOT THAT I KNOW WHAT THAT IS.
ANY-WAY, "R" IS NEXT.

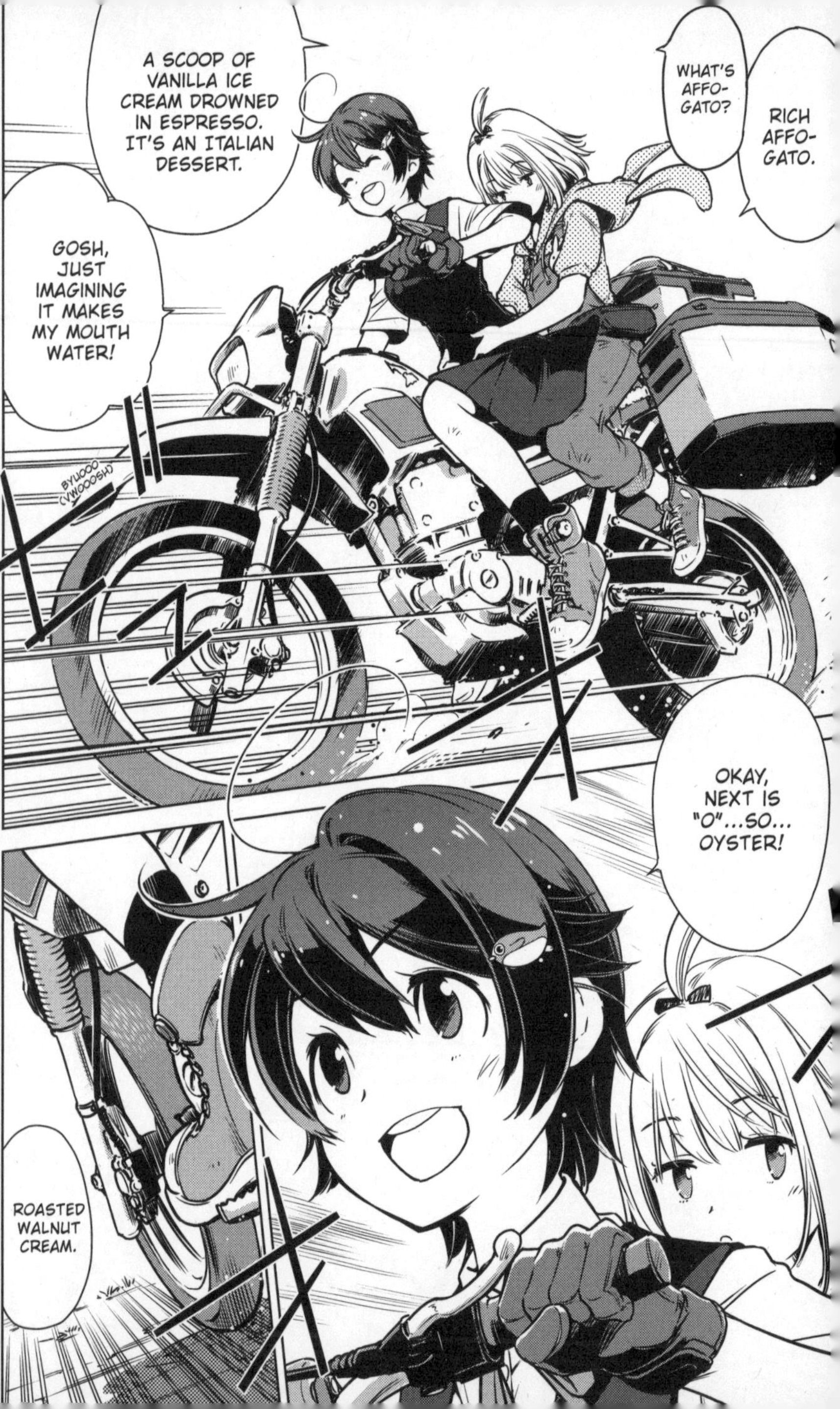
RICH AFFO-GATO.
WHAT'S AFFO-GATO?
A SCOOP OF VANILLA ICE CREAM DROWNED IN ESPRESSO. IT'S AN ITALIAN DESSERT.
GOSH, JUST IMAGINING IT MAKES MY MOUTH WATER!
BYUOOO (VWOOOSH)
OKAY, NEXT IS "O"...SO... OYSTER!
ROASTED WALNUT CREAM.

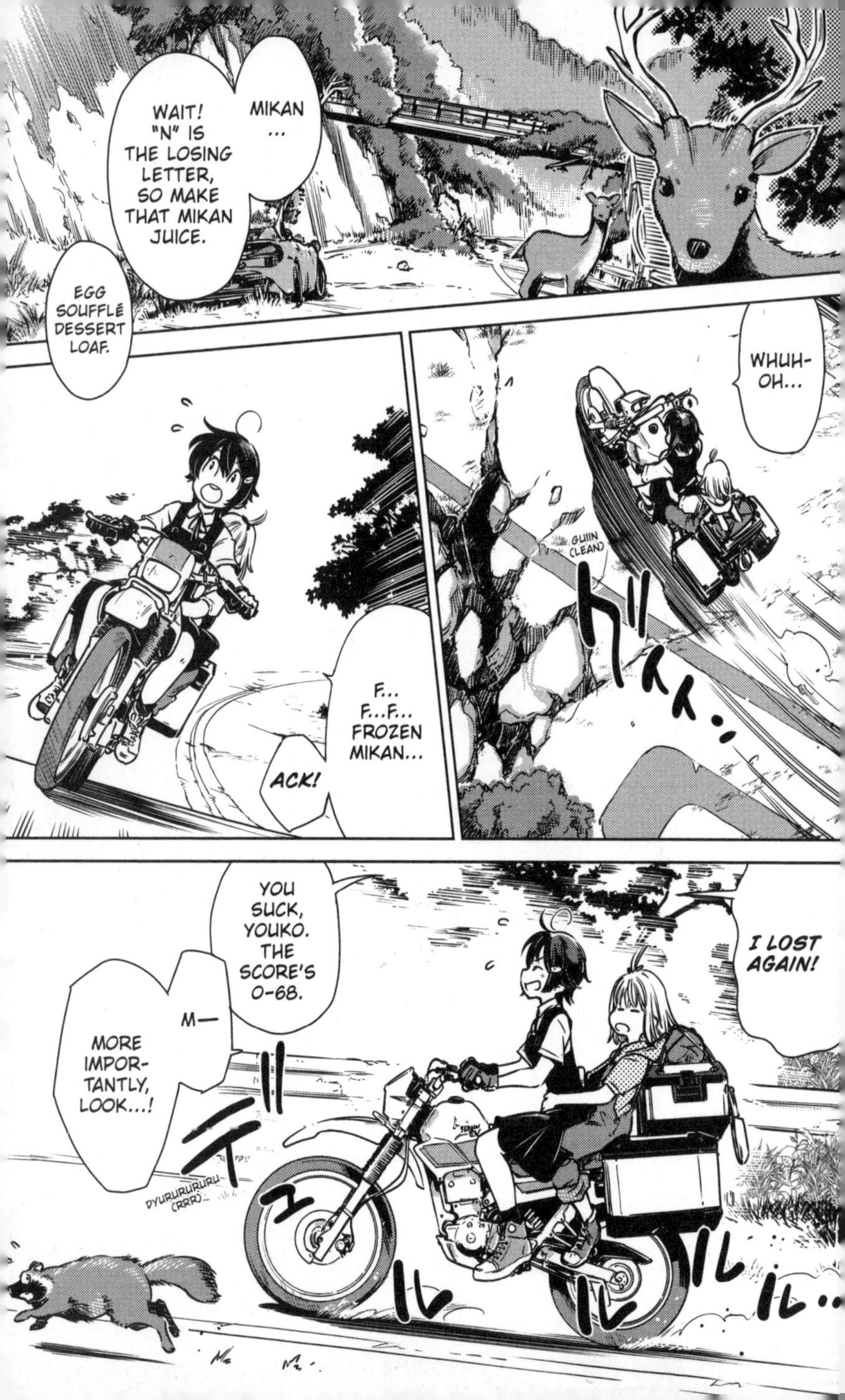
MIKAN ...
WAIT! "N" IS THE LOSING LETTER, SO MAKE THAT MIKAN JUICE.
EGG SOUFFLÉ DESSERT LOAF.
WHUH-OH...
GUIIN (LEAN)
F... F...F... FROZEN MIKAN...
ACK!
I LOST AGAIN!
YOU SUCK, YOUKO. THE SCORE'S 0-68.
M— MORE IMPORTANTLY, LOOK...!
DYURURURURU (RRR)

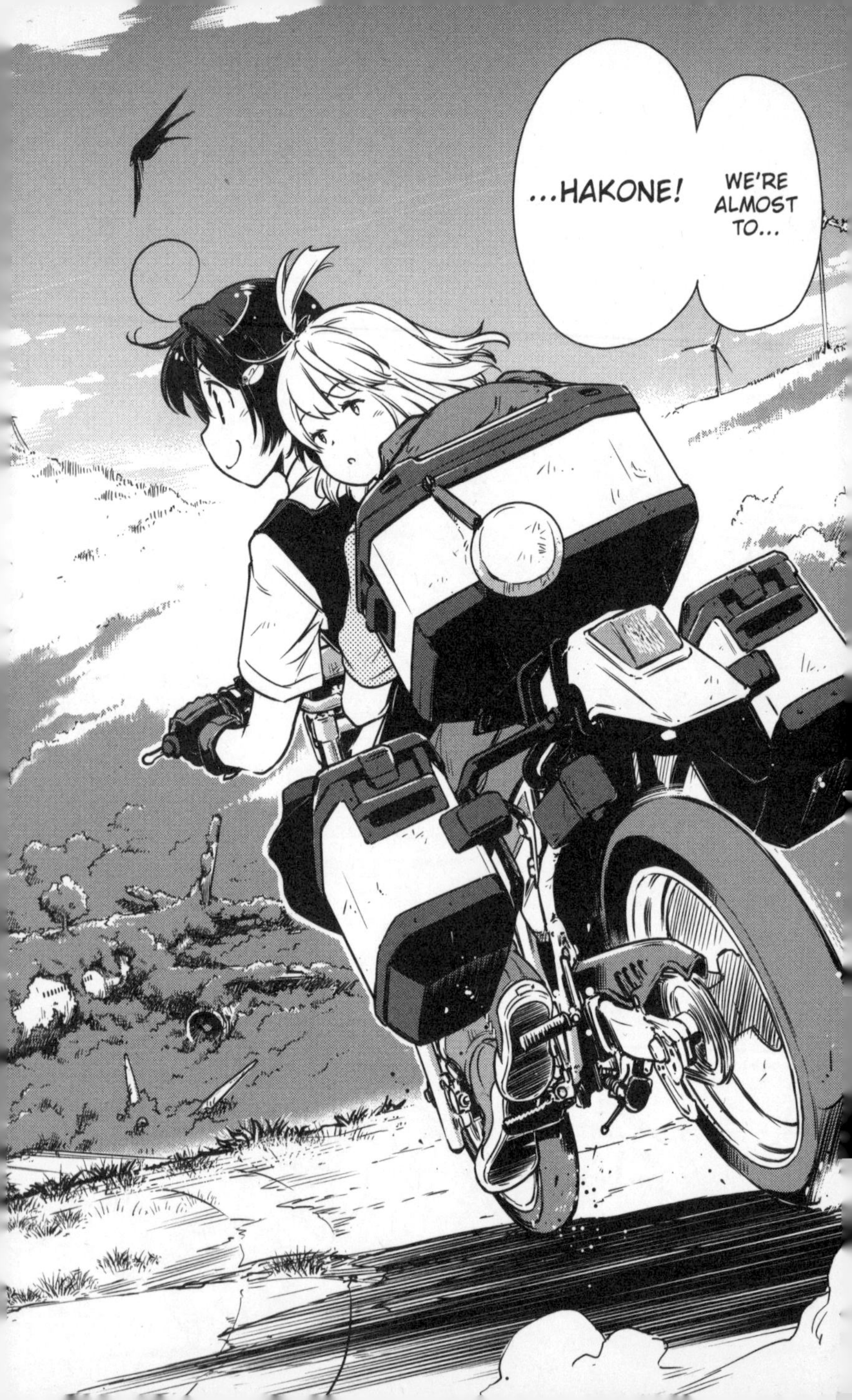
WE'RE ALMOST TO...
...HAKONE!

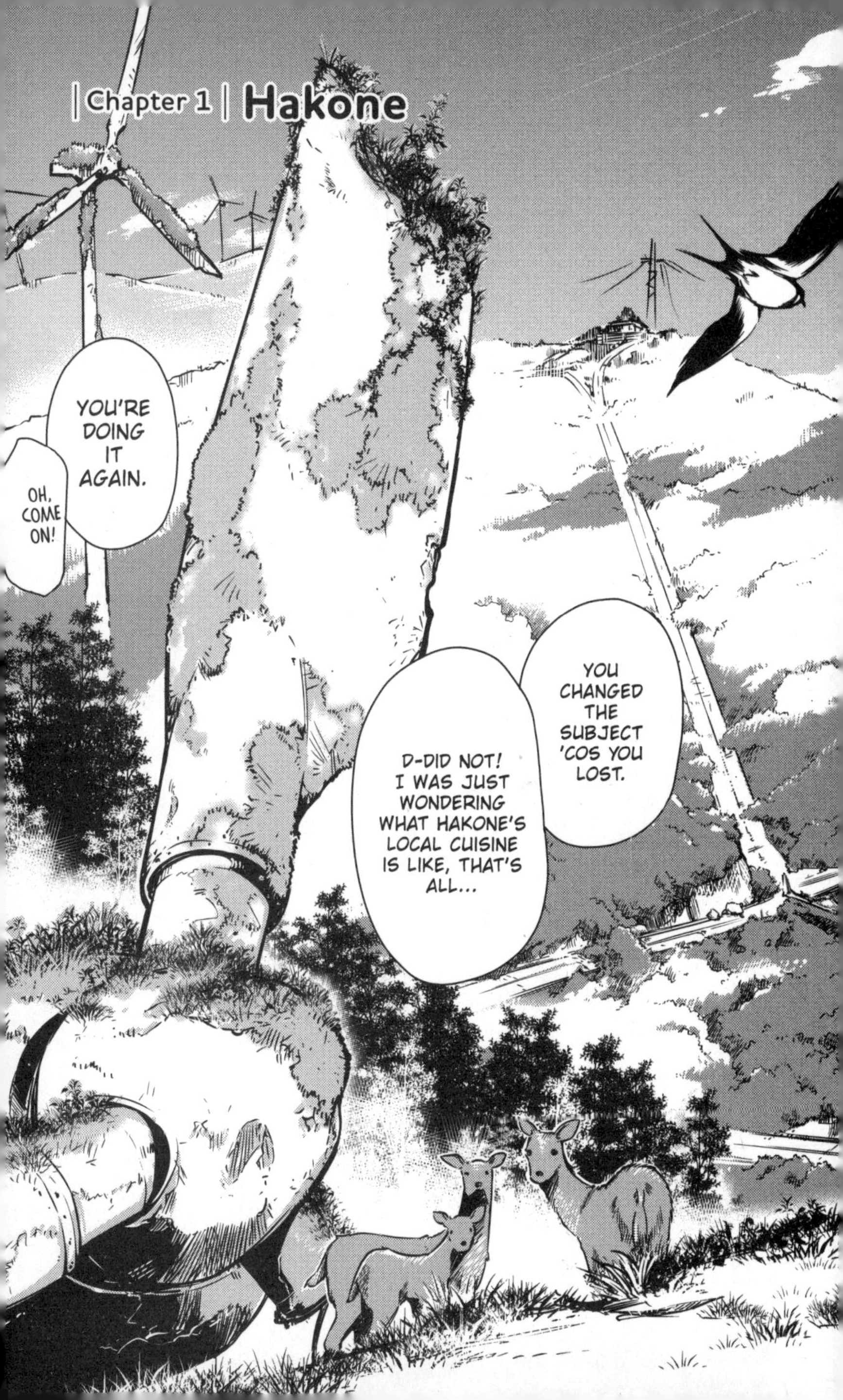
| Chapter 1 | Hakone
YOU'RE DOING IT AGAIN.
OH, COME ON!
YOU CHANGED THE SUBJECT 'COS YOU LOST.
D-DID NOT! I WAS JUST WONDERING WHAT HAKONE'S LOCAL CUISINE IS LIKE, THAT'S ALL...

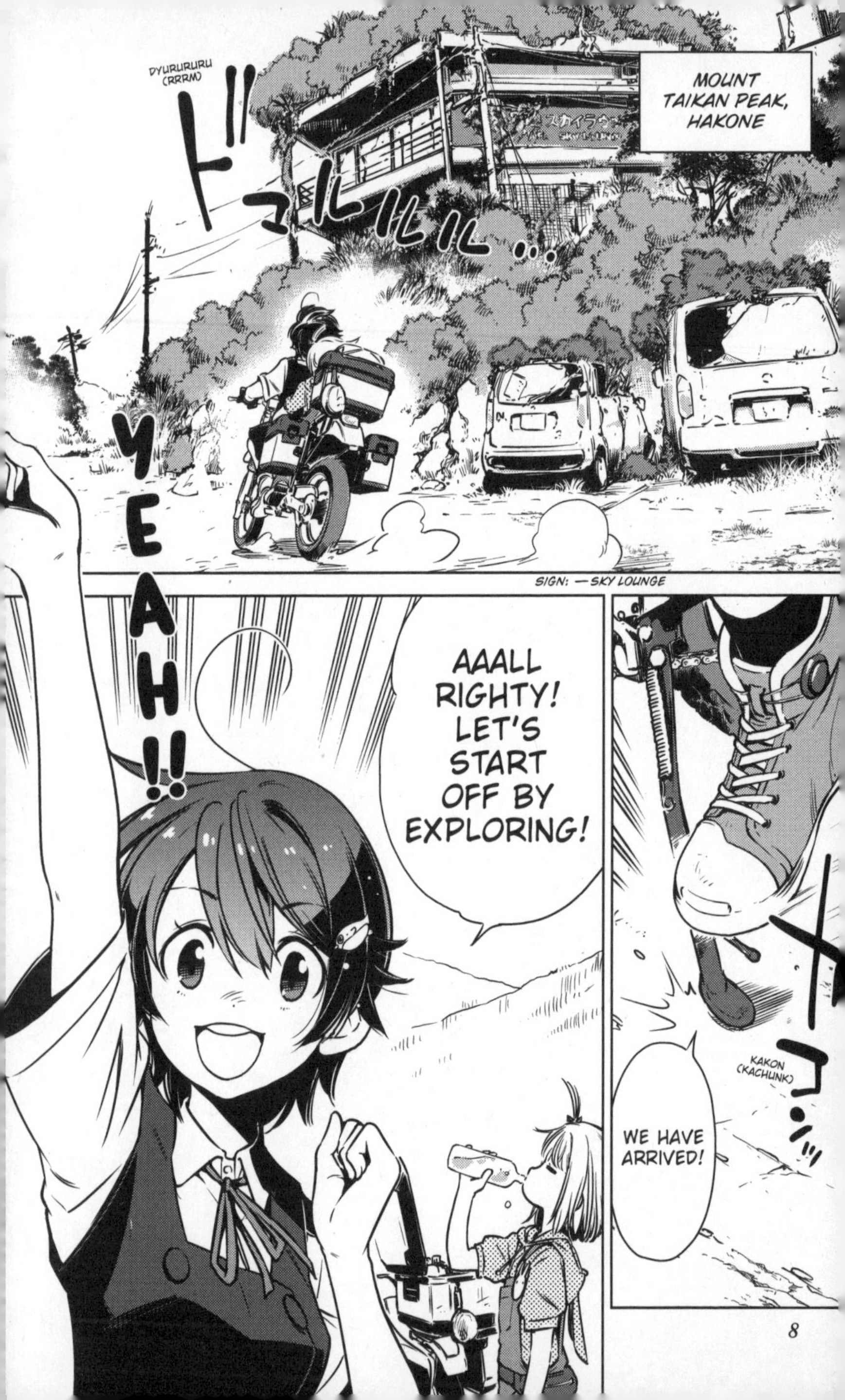
MOUNT TAIKAN PEAK, HAKONE
DYURURURU (RRRM)
SIGN: —SKY LOUNGE
KAKON (KACHUNK)
WE HAVE ARRIVED!
YEAH!!
AAALL RIGHTY! LET'S START OFF BY EXPLORING!

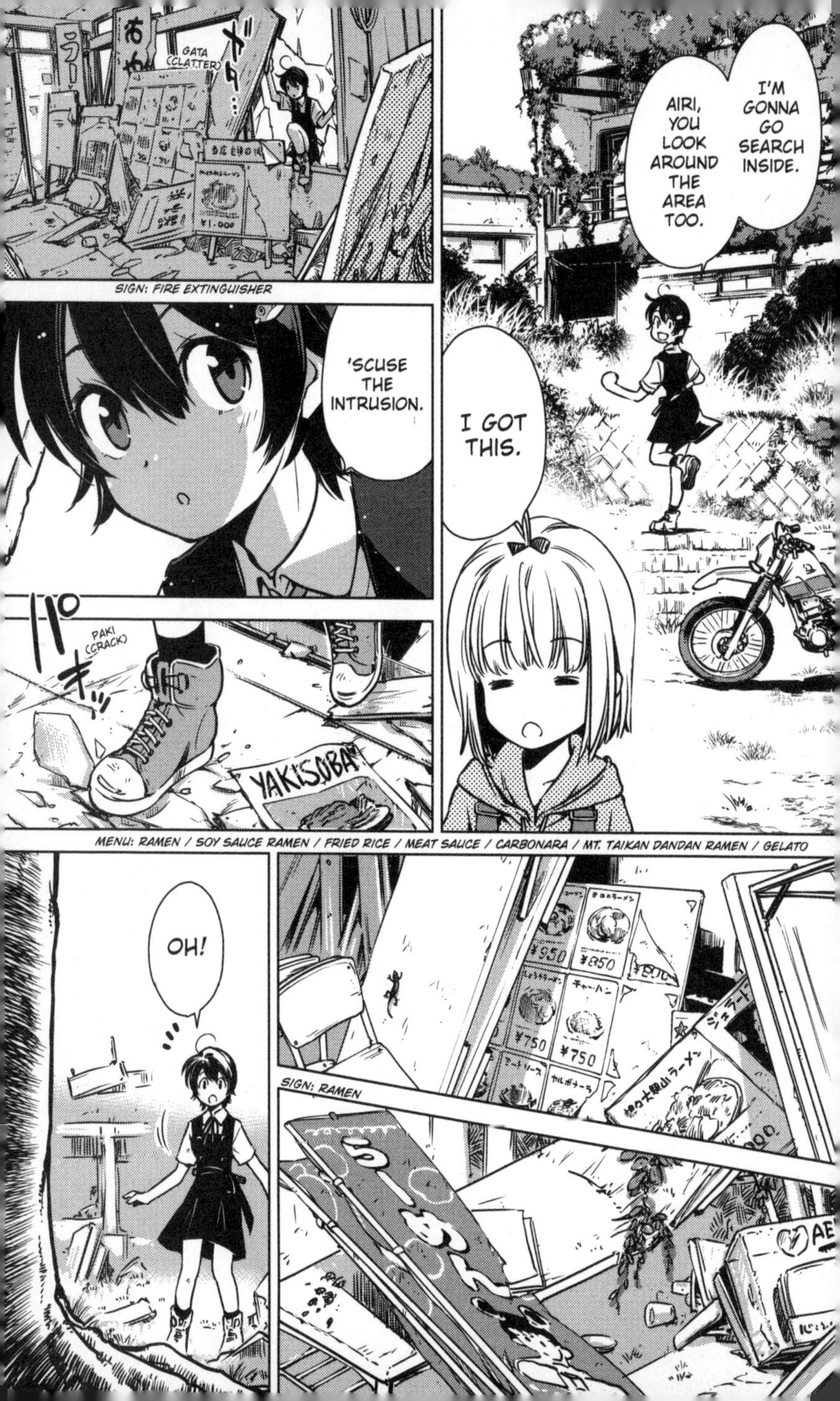
I'M GONNA GO SEARCH INSIDE.
AIRI, YOU LOOK AROUND THE AREA TOO.
I GOT THIS.
GATA (CLATTER)
SIGN: FIRE EXTINGUISHER
'SCUSE THE INTRUSION.
PAKI (CRACK)
YAKISOBA
MENU: RAMEN / SOY SAUCE RAMEN / FRIED RICE / MEAT SAUCE / CARBONARA / MT. TAIKAN DANDAN RAMEN / GELATO
¥950
¥850
¥750
¥750
SIGN: RAMEN
OH!

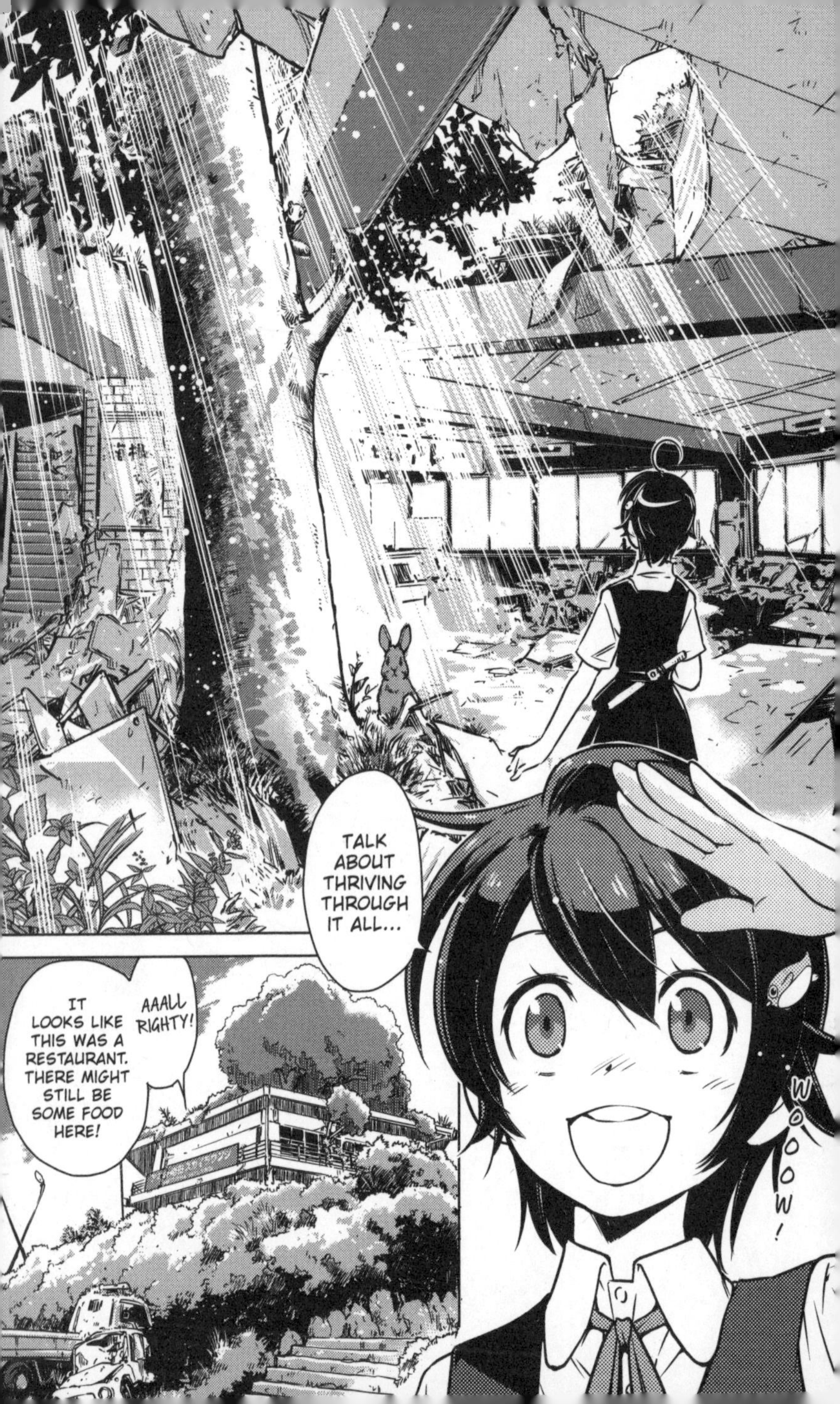
TALK ABOUT THRIVING THROUGH IT ALL...
WOOOOW!
AAALL RIGHTY!
IT LOOKS LIKE THIS WAS A RESTAURANT. THERE MIGHT STILL BE SOME FOOD HERE!

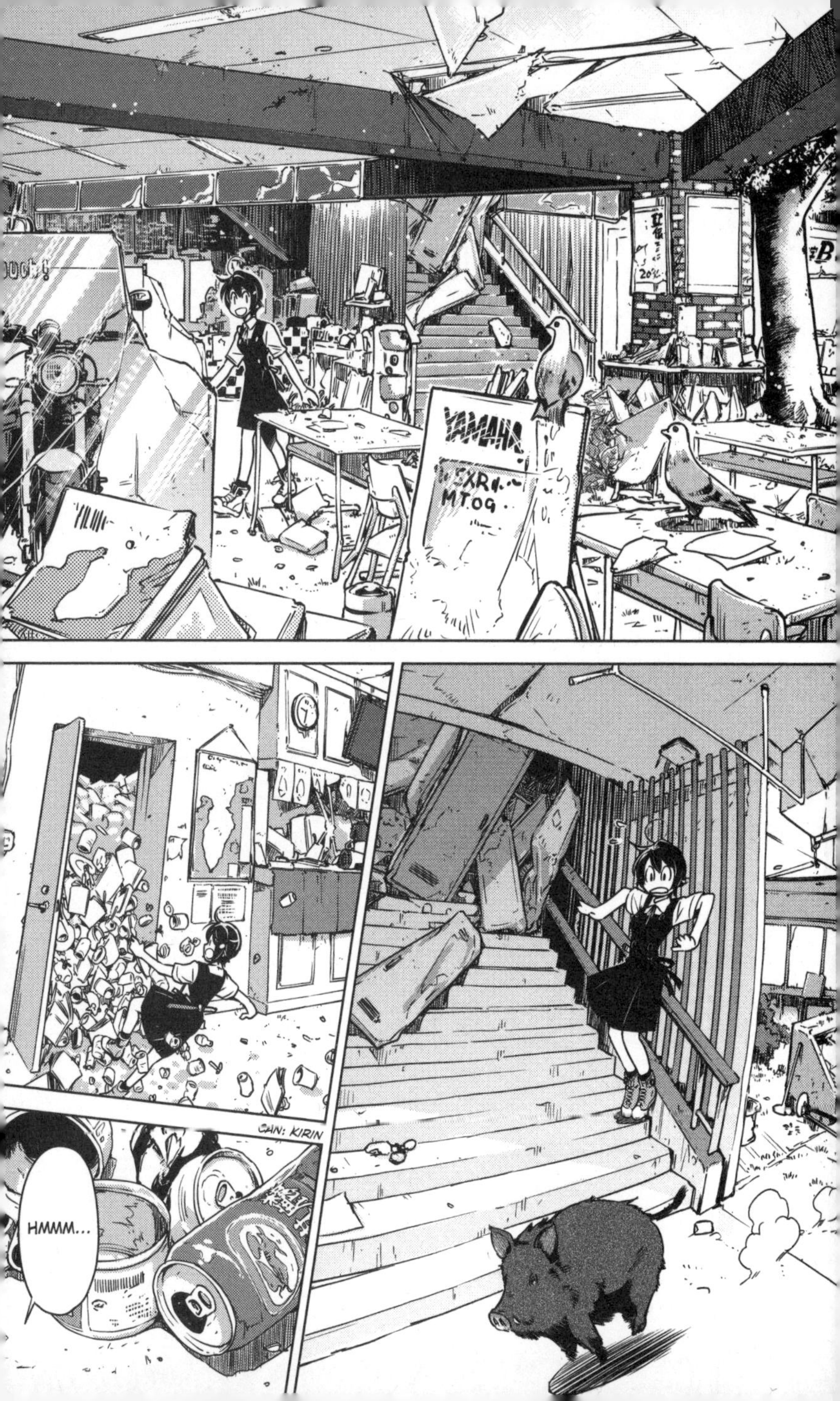
YAMAHA
SXR
MT.09
CAN: KIRIN
HMMM...

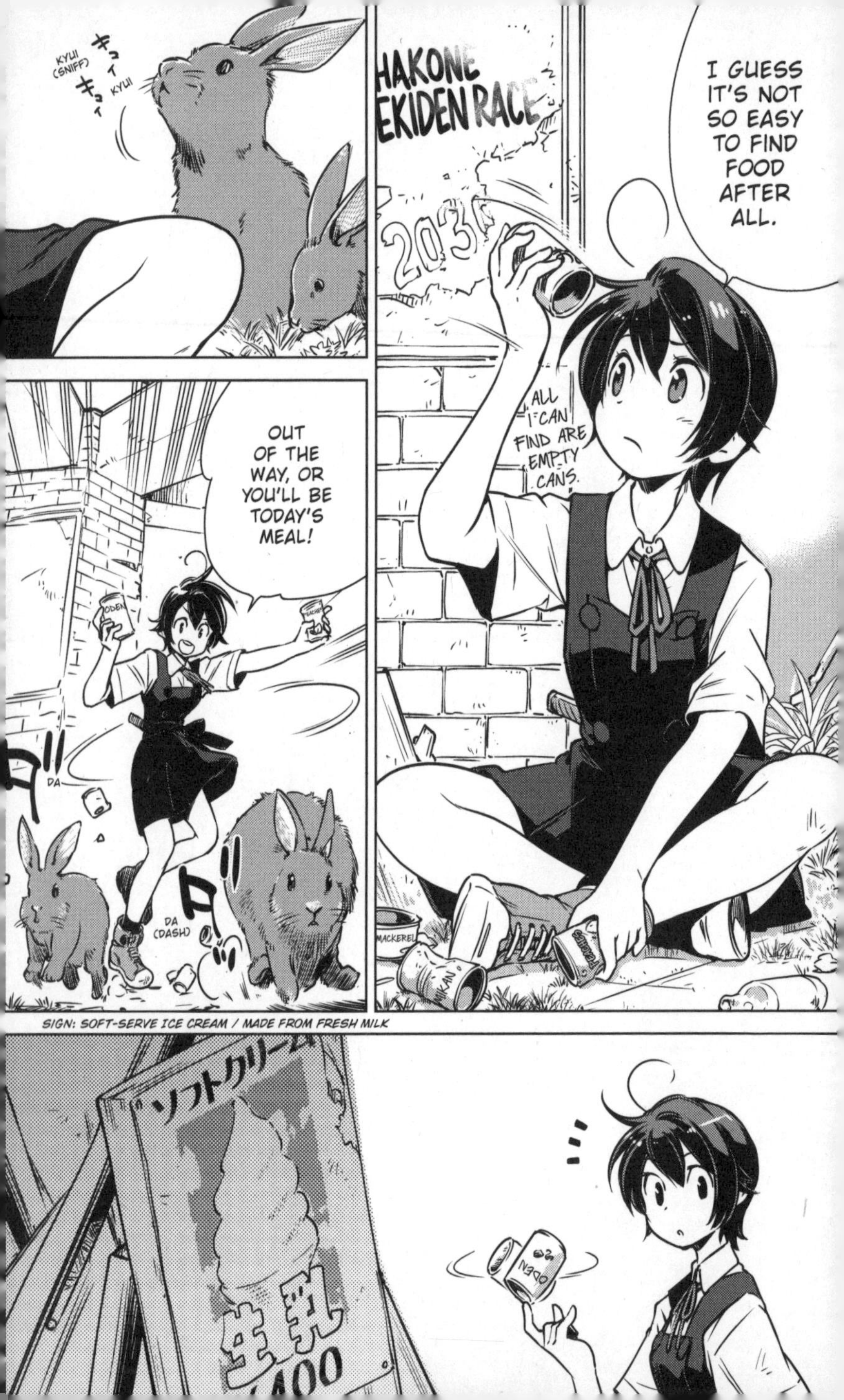
HAKONE EKIDEN RACE
2030
I GUESS IT'S NOT SO EASY TO FIND FOOD AFTER ALL.
ALL I CAN FIND ARE EMPTY CANS.
MACKEREL
MIKAN
PEACHES
キュイ
KYUI (SNIFF)
キュイ
KYUI
OUT OF THE WAY, OR YOU'LL BE TODAY'S MEAL!
ODEN
PEACHES
ダッ
DA
ダッ
DA (DASH)
SIGN: SOFT-SERVE ICE CREAM / MADE FROM FRESH MILK
ソフトクリーム
生乳
400
ODEN

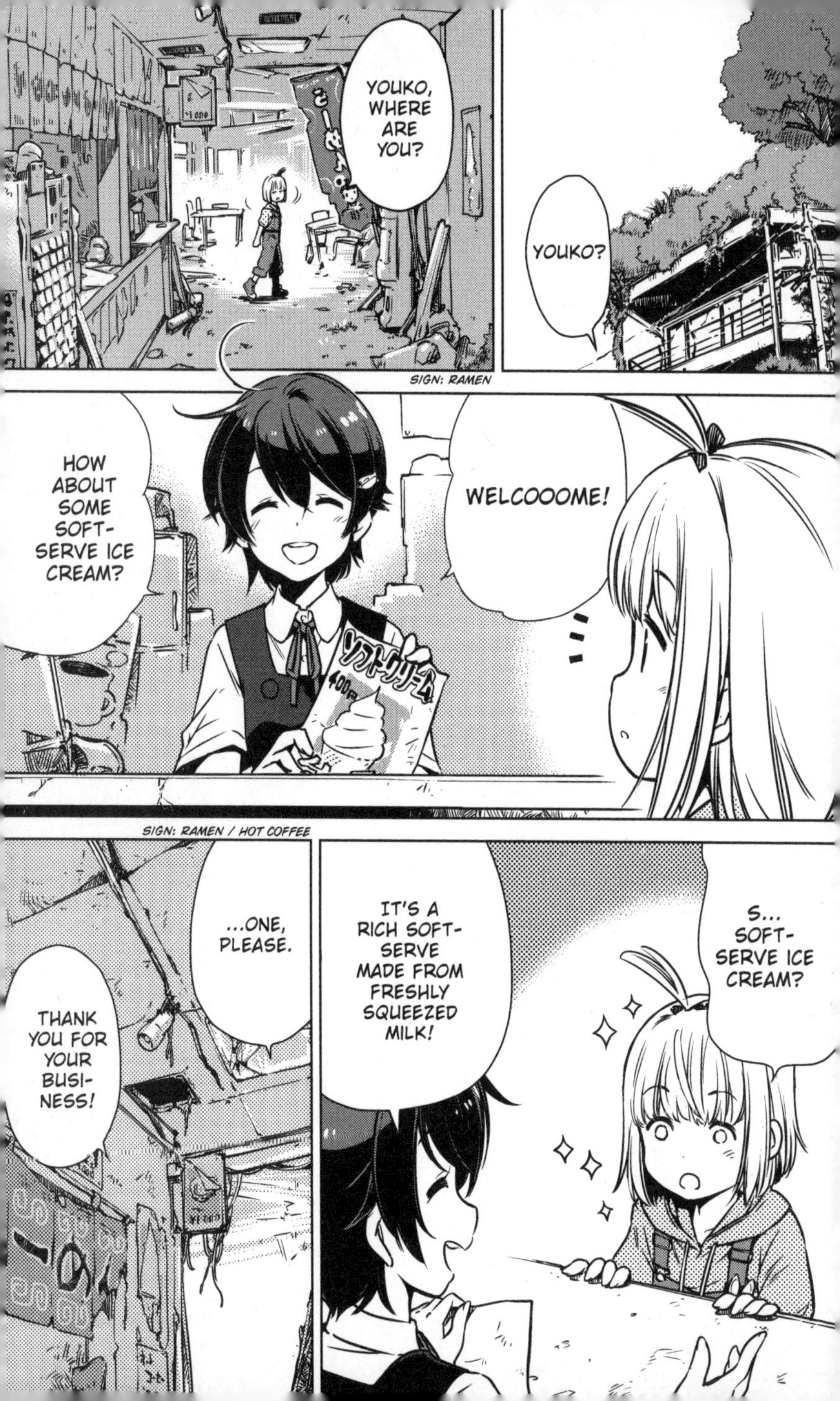
YOUKO?
YOUKO, WHERE ARE YOU?
SIGN: RAMEN
WELCOOOME!
HOW ABOUT SOME SOFT-SERVE ICE CREAM?
ソフトクリーム 400円
SIGN: RAMEN / HOT COFFEE
S... SOFT-SERVE ICE CREAM?
IT'S A RICH SOFT-SERVE MADE FROM FRESHLY SQUEEZED MILK!
...ONE, PLEASE.
THANK YOU FOR YOUR BUSINESS!

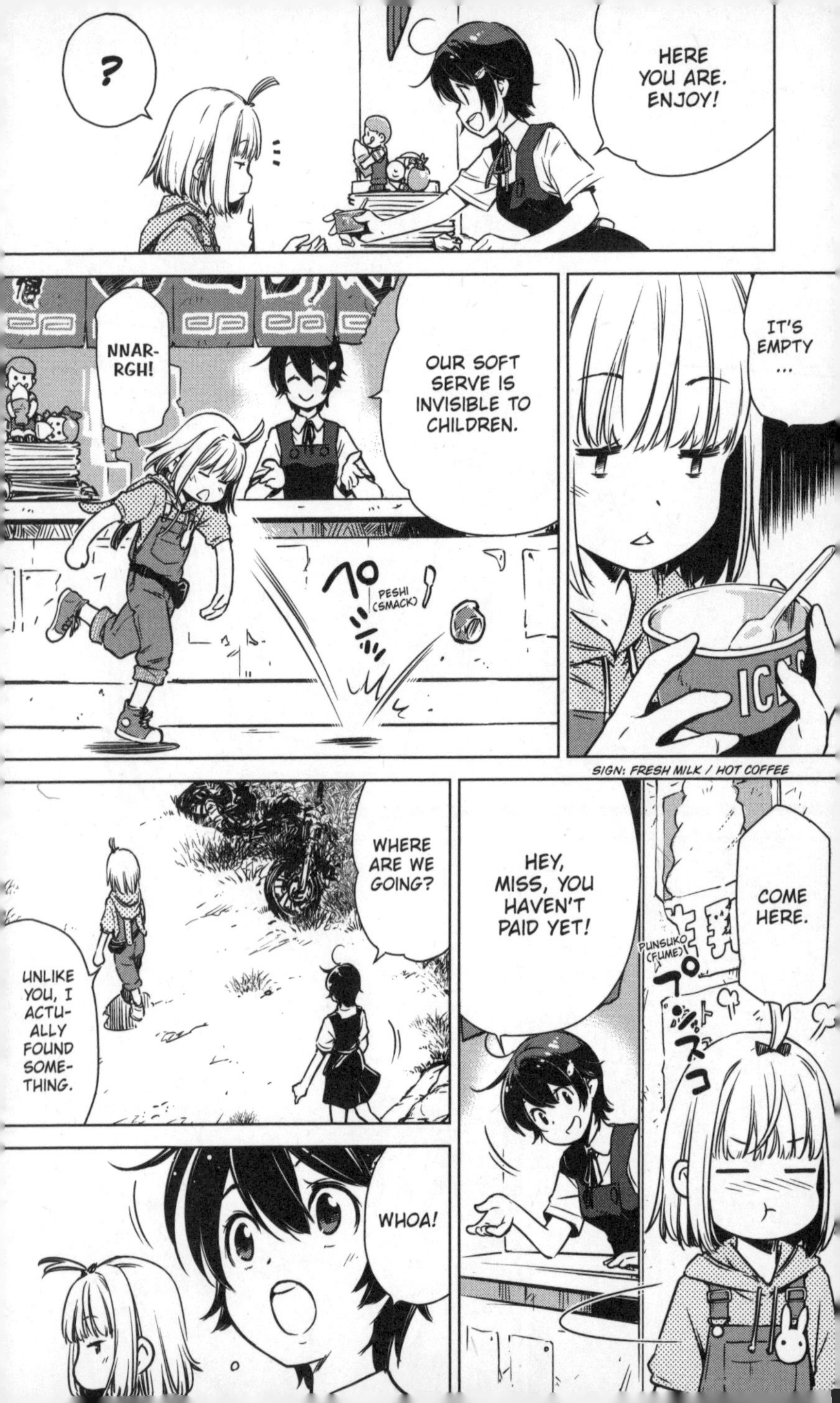
HERE YOU ARE. ENJOY!
?
IT'S EMPTY ...
OUR SOFT SERVE IS INVISIBLE TO CHILDREN.
NNARGH!
PESHI (SMACK)
SIGN: FRESH MILK / HOT COFFEE
COME HERE.
PUNSUKO (FUME)
HEY, MISS, YOU HAVEN'T PAID YET!
WHERE ARE WE GOING?
UNLIKE YOU, I ACTUALLY FOUND SOMETHING.
WHOA!

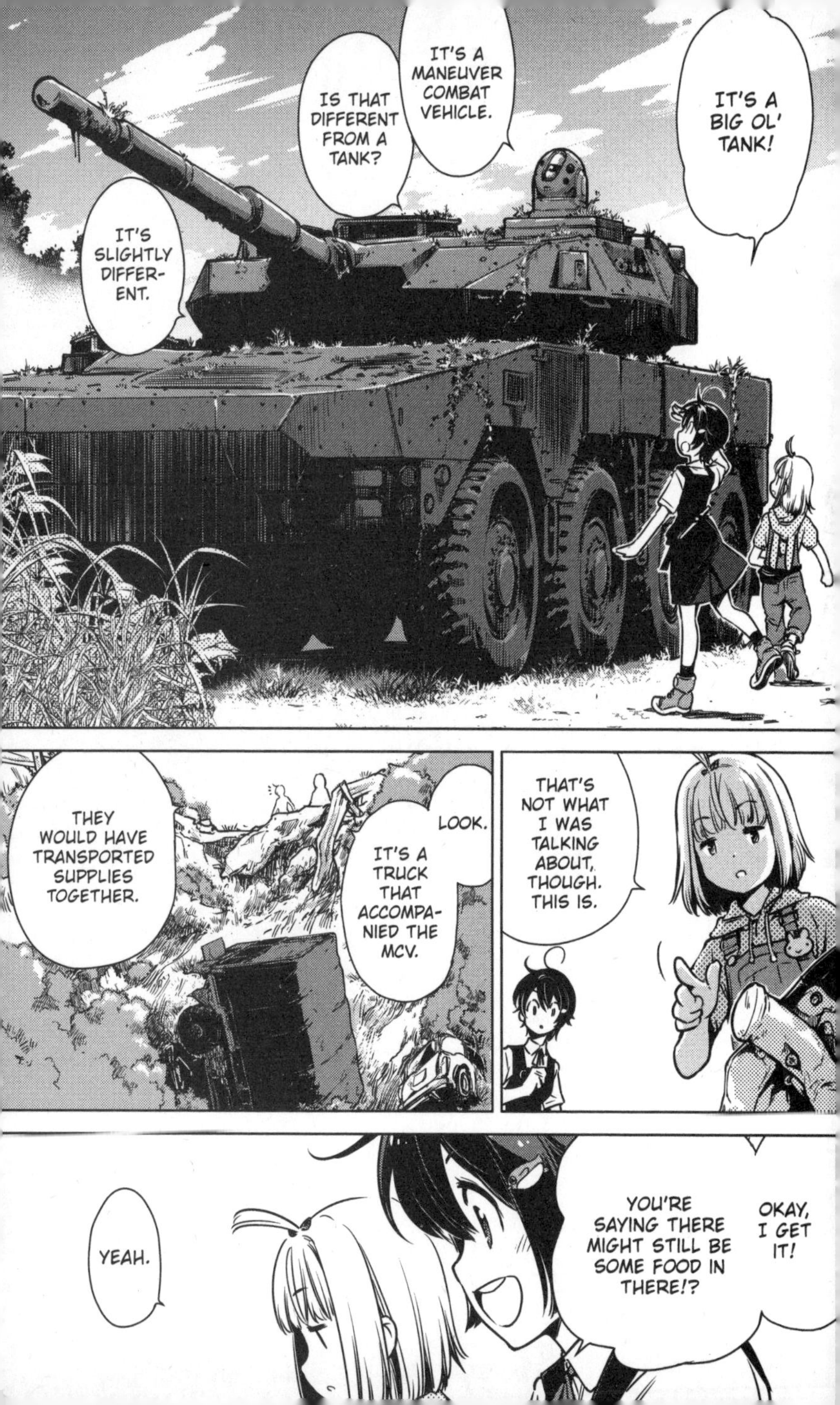
IT'S A BIG OL' TANK!
IT'S A MANEUVER COMBAT VEHICLE.
IS THAT DIFFERENT FROM A TANK?
IT'S SLIGHTLY DIFFER-ENT.
THAT'S NOT WHAT I WAS TALKING ABOUT, THOUGH. THIS IS.
LOOK.
IT'S A TRUCK THAT ACCOMPA-NIED THE MCV.
THEY WOULD HAVE TRANSPORTED SUPPLIES TOGETHER.
OKAY, I GET IT!
YOU'RE SAYING THERE MIGHT STILL BE SOME FOOD IN THERE!?
YEAH.

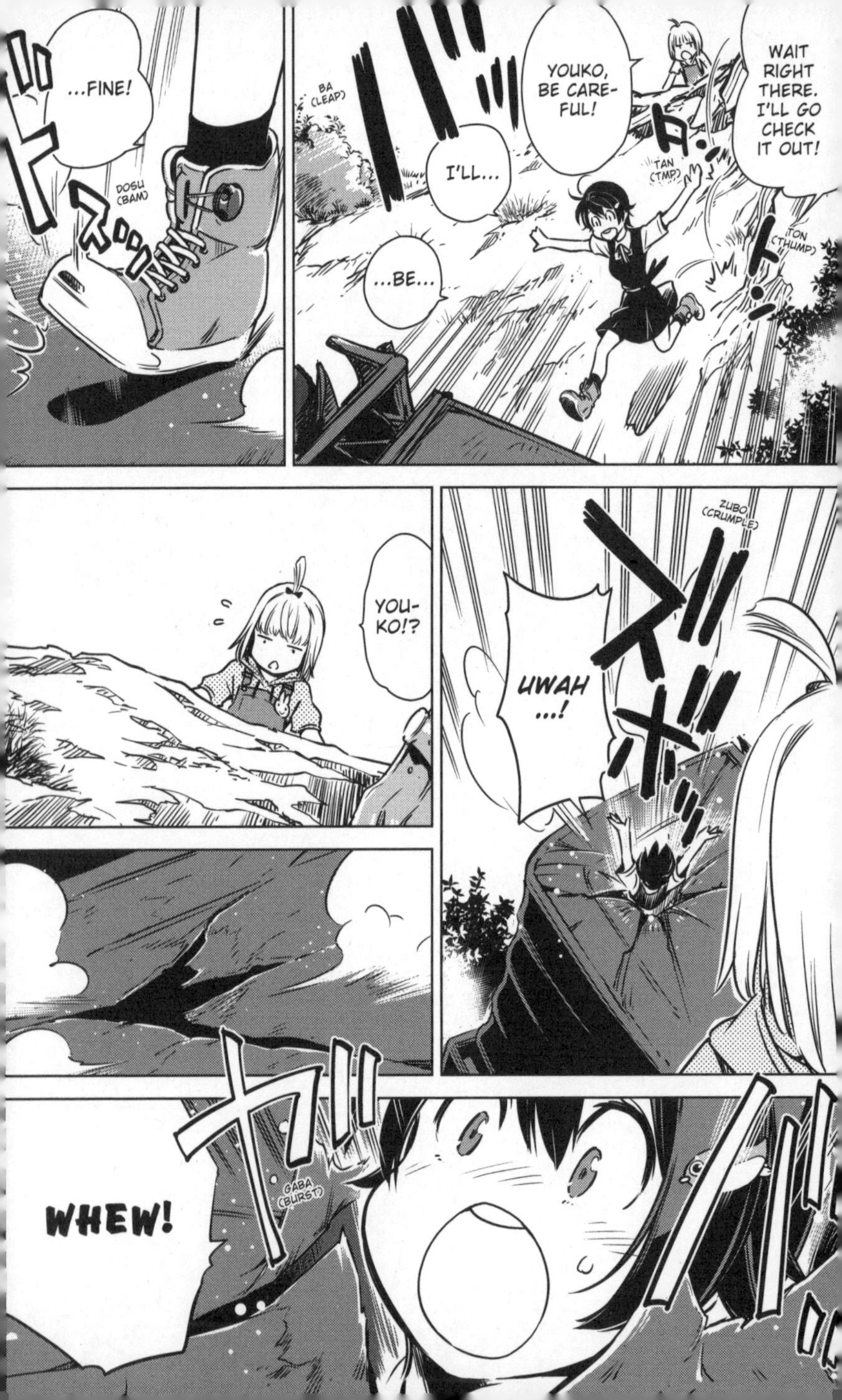
WAIT RIGHT THERE. I'LL GO CHECK IT OUT!
TON (THUMP)
YOUKO, BE CAREFUL!
TAN (TMP)
BA (LEAP)
I'LL...
...BE...
...FINE!
DOSU (BAM)
ZUBO (CRUMPLE)
UWAH ...!
YOU-KO!?
GABA (BURST)
WHEW!

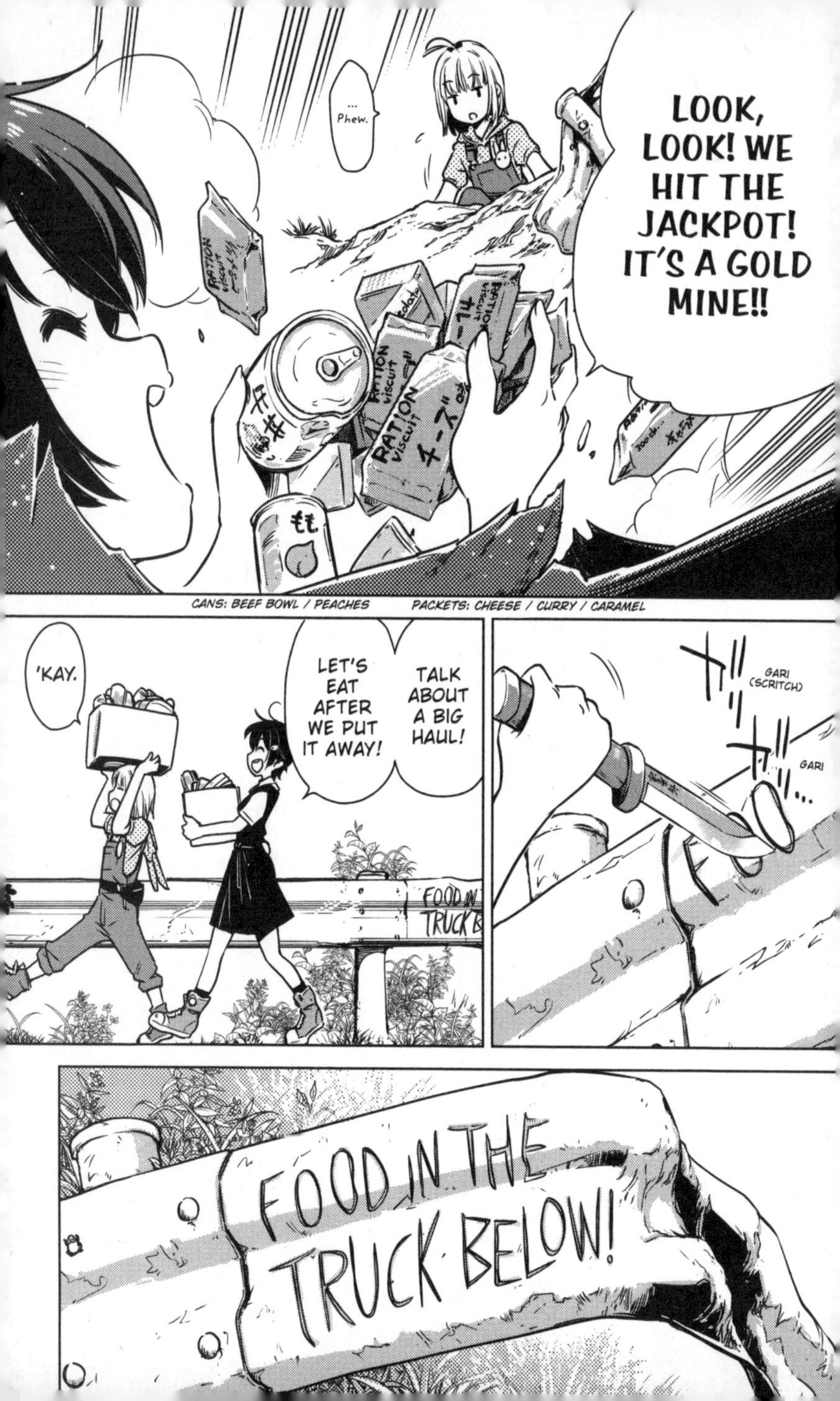
LOOK, LOOK! WE HIT THE JACKPOT! IT'S A GOLD MINE!!
... Phew.
CANS: BEEF BOWL / PEACHES PACKETS: CHEESE / CURRY / CARAMEL
GARI (SCRITCH)
GARI
TALK ABOUT A BIG HAUL!
LET'S EAT AFTER WE PUT IT AWAY!
'KAY.
FOOD IN THE TRUCK BELOW!

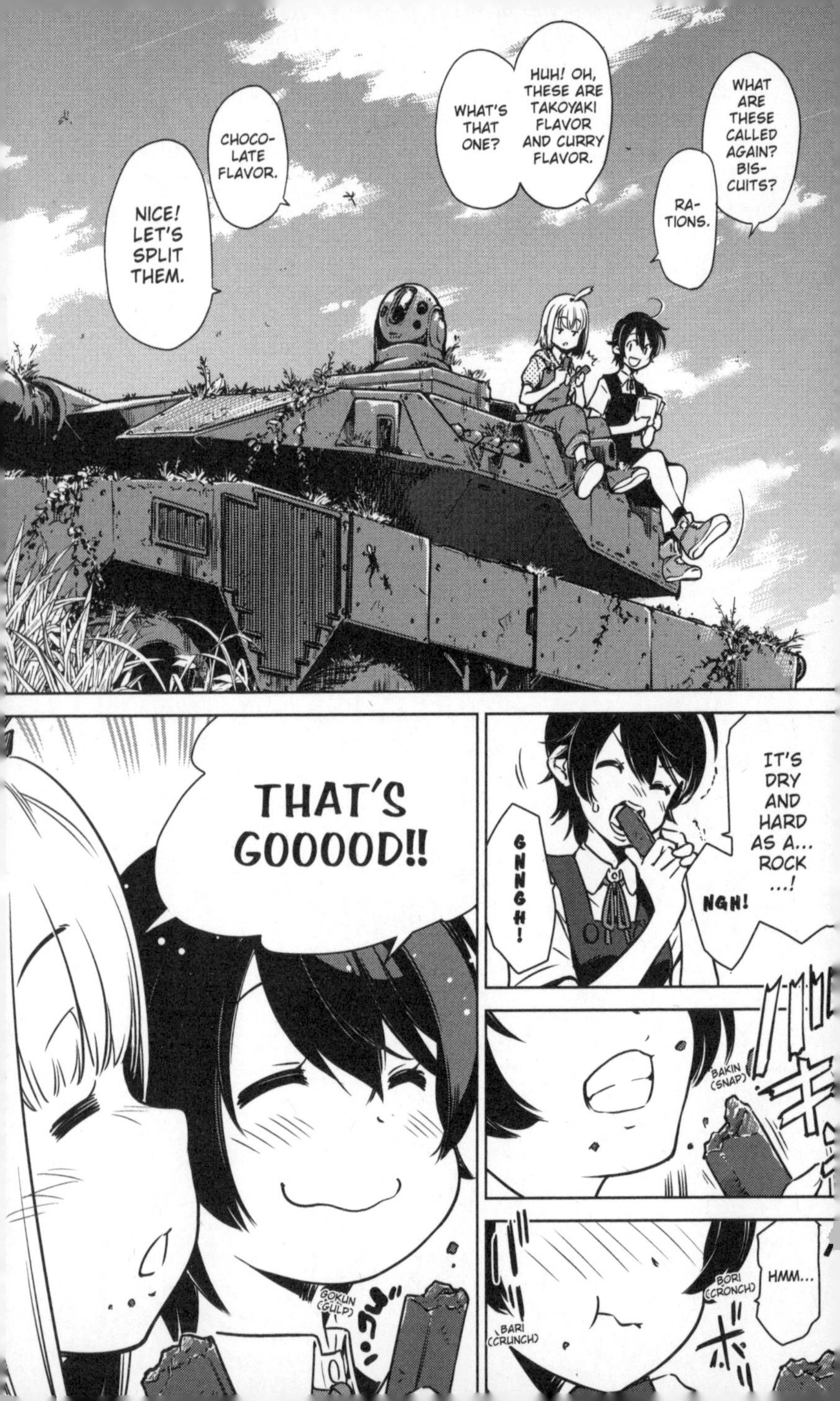
WHAT ARE THESE CALLED AGAIN? BIS-CUITS?
RA-TIONS.
HUH! OH, THESE ARE TAKOYAKI FLAVOR AND CURRY FLAVOR.
WHAT'S THAT ONE?
CHOCO-LATE FLAVOR.
NICE! LET'S SPLIT THEM.
IT'S DRY AND HARD AS A... ROCK ...!
NGH!
GNNGH!
BAKIN (SNAP)
HMM...
BORI (CRONCH)
BARI (CRUNCH)
THAT'S GOOOOD!!
GOKUN (GULP)

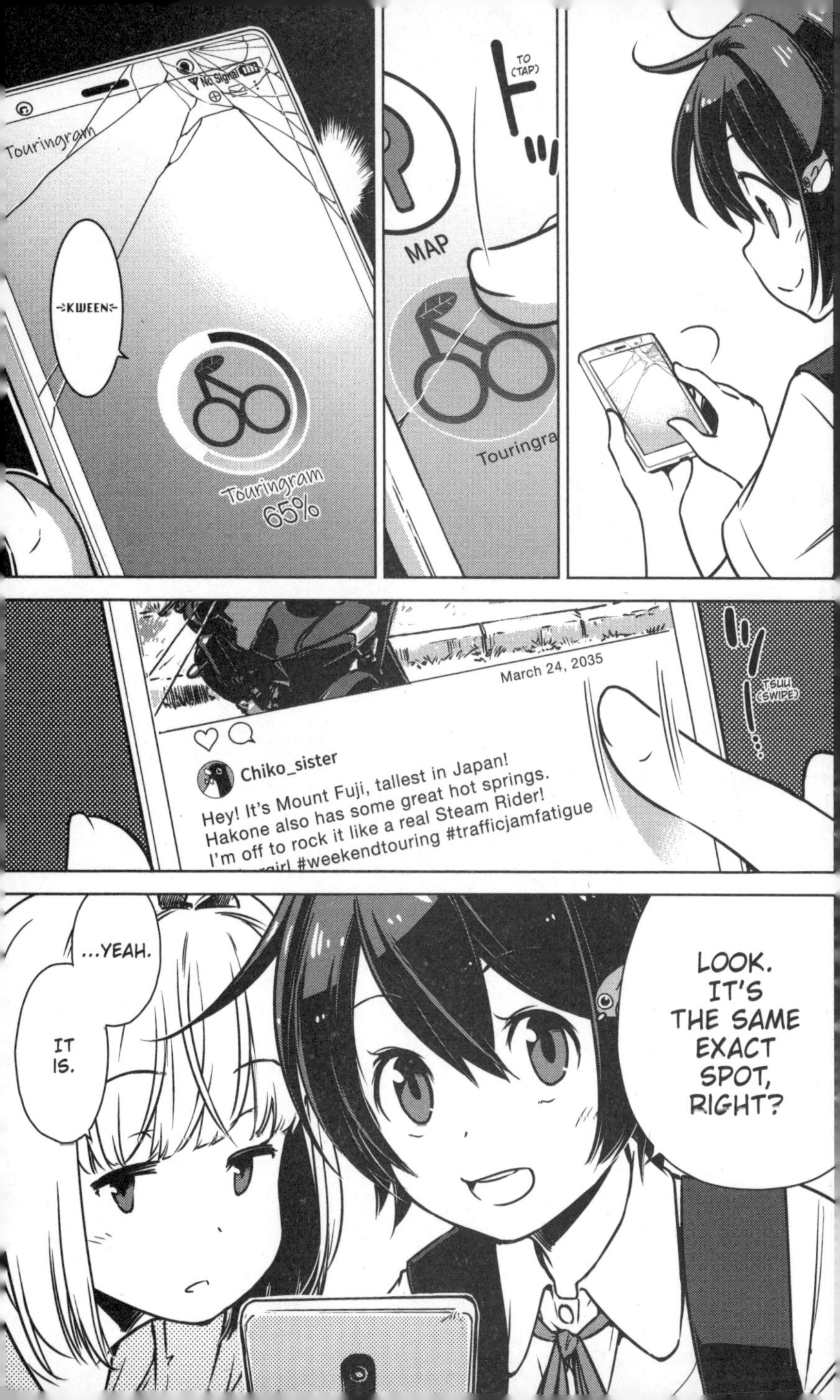

TO (TAP)
MAP
Touringra
No Signal
Touringram
KWEEN
Touringram 65%
TSUU (SWIPE)
March 24, 2035
Chiko_sister
Hey! It's Mount Fuji, tallest in Japan! Hakone also has some great hot springs. I'm off to rock it like a real Steam Rider! #trafficjamfatigue
#weekendtouring
LOOK. IT'S THE SAME EXACT SPOT, RIGHT?
...YEAH.
IT IS.

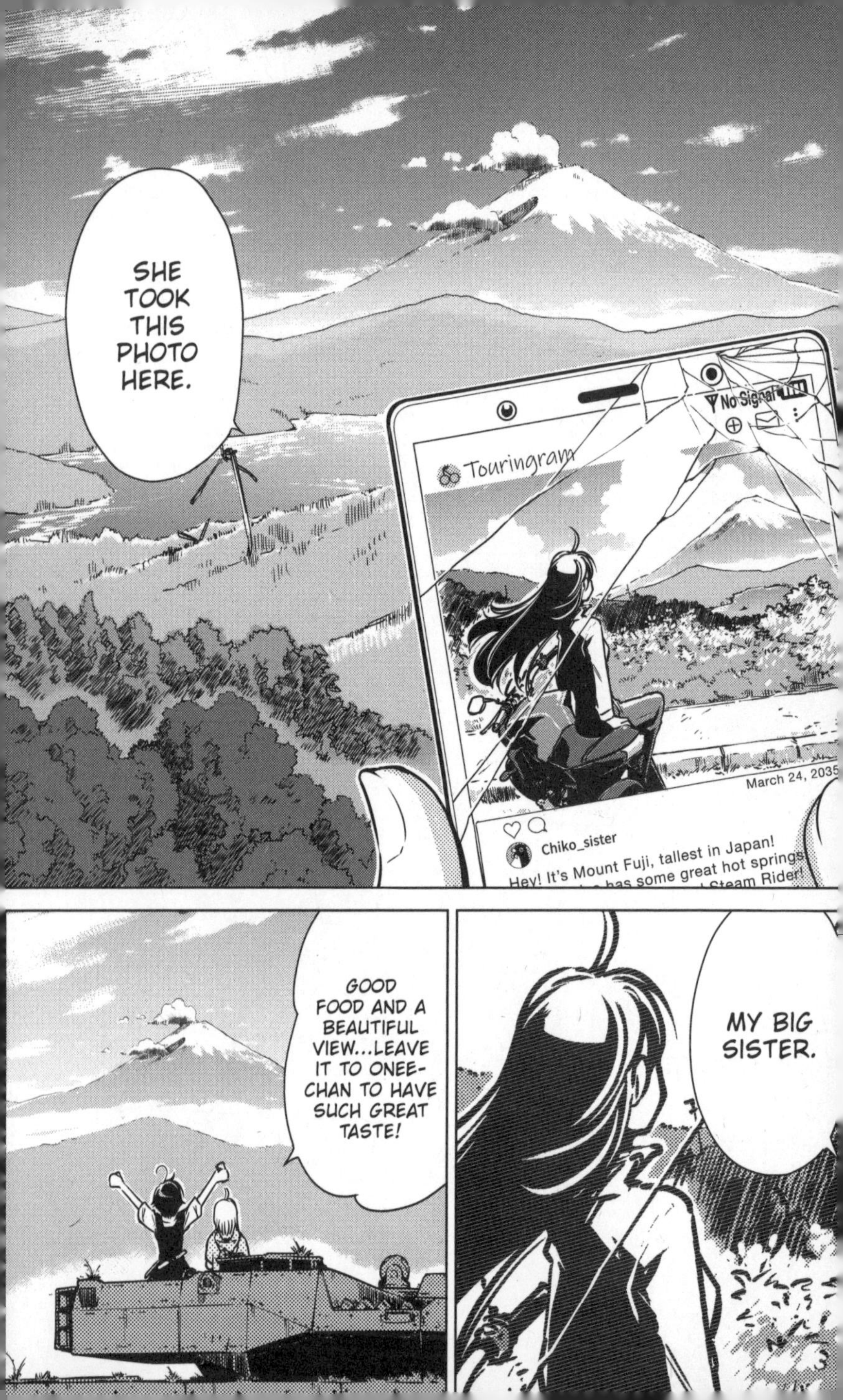
SHE TOOK THIS PHOTO HERE.
No Signal
Touringram
March 24, 2035
Chiko_sister
Hey! It's Mount Fuji, tallest in Japan!
MY BIG SISTER.
GOOD FOOD AND A BEAUTIFUL VIEW...LEAVE IT TO ONEE-CHAN TO HAVE SUCH GREAT TASTE!

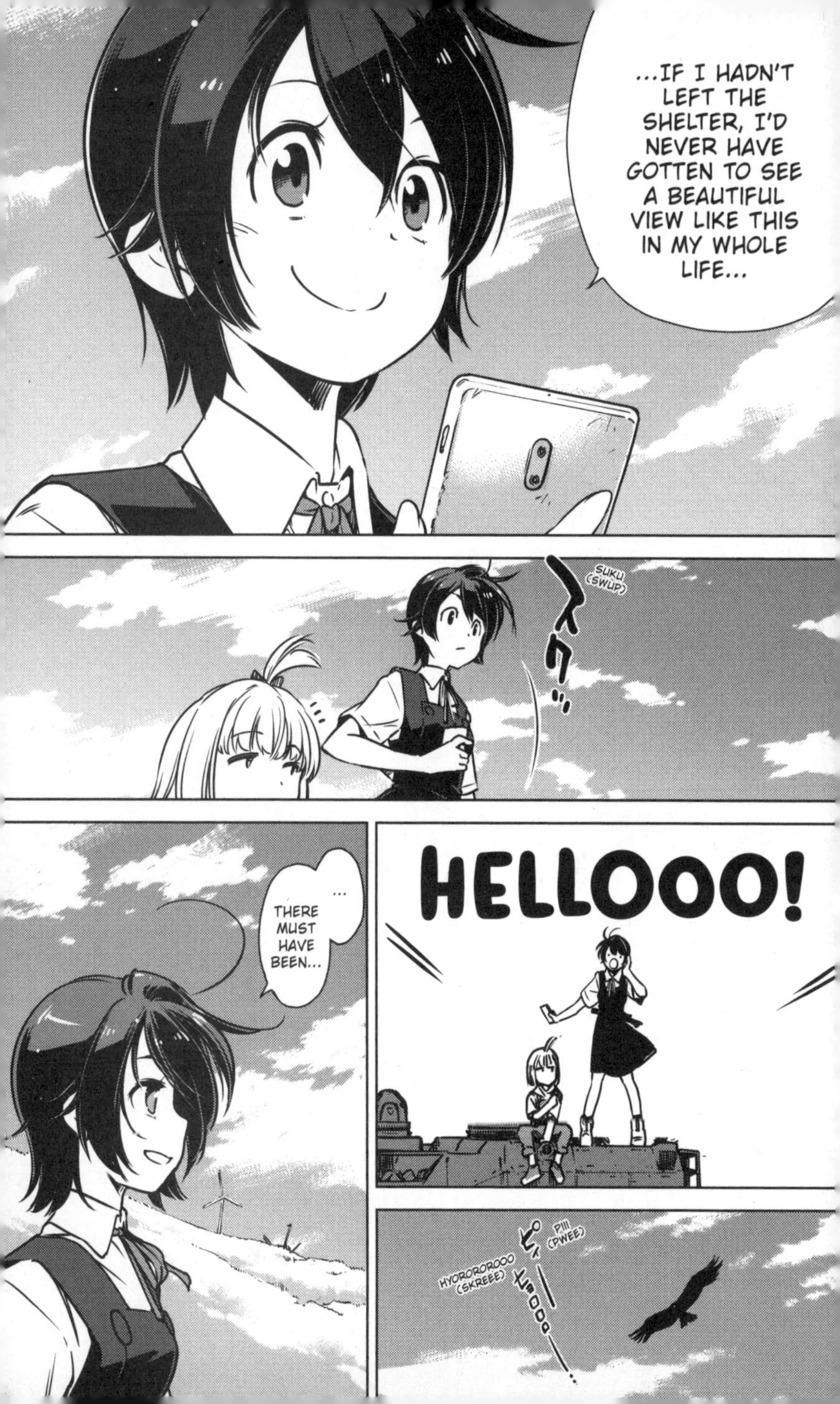
...IF I HADN'T LEFT THE SHELTER, I'D NEVER HAVE GOTTEN TO SEE A BEAUTIFUL VIEW LIKE THIS IN MY WHOLE LIFE...
SUKU (SWUP)
HELLOOO!
PIII (PWEE)
HYORORORΟOO (SKREEE)
...
THERE MUST HAVE BEEN...

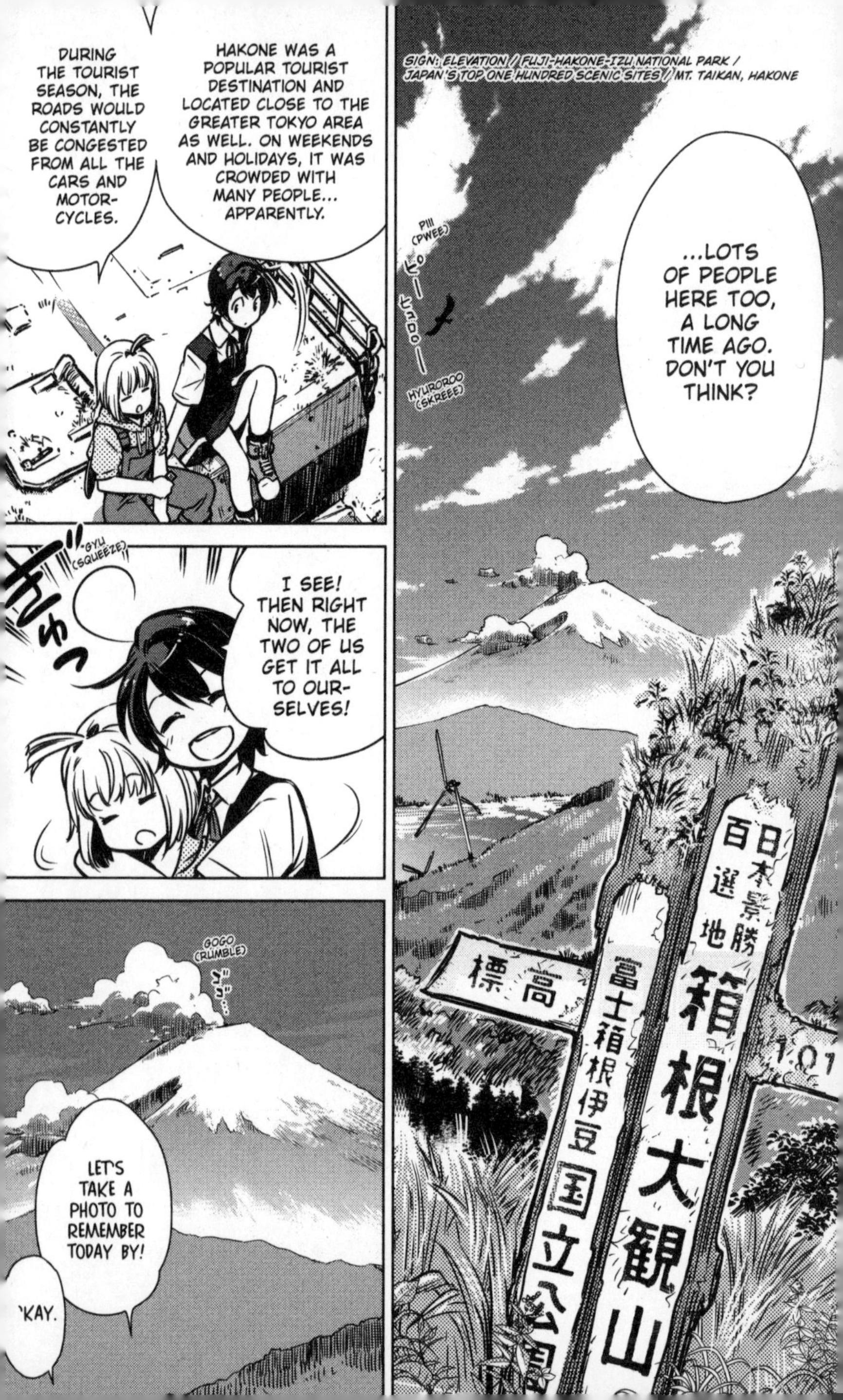
SIGN: ELEVATION / FUJI-HAKONE-IZU NATIONAL PARK / JAPAN'S TOP ONE HUNDRED SCENIC SITES / MT. TAIKAN, HAKONE
PIII (PWEE)
ピー
HYUROROO (SKREEE)
ヒュロロー
...LOTS OF PEOPLE HERE TOO, A LONG TIME AGO. DON'T YOU THINK?
日本景勝百選地
箱根大観山
富士箱根伊豆国立公
標高
HAKONE WAS A POPULAR TOURIST DESTINATION AND LOCATED CLOSE TO THE GREATER TOKYO AREA AS WELL. ON WEEKENDS AND HOLIDAYS, IT WAS CROWDED WITH MANY PEOPLE... APPARENTLY.
DURING THE TOURIST SEASON, THE ROADS WOULD CONSTANTLY BE CONGESTED FROM ALL THE CARS AND MOTOR-CYCLES.
GYU (SQUEEZE)
ぎゅっ
I SEE! THEN RIGHT NOW, THE TWO OF US GET IT ALL TO OUR-SELVES!
GOGO (RUMBLE)
ゴゴ…
LET'S TAKE A PHOTO TO REMEMBER TODAY BY!
'KAY.

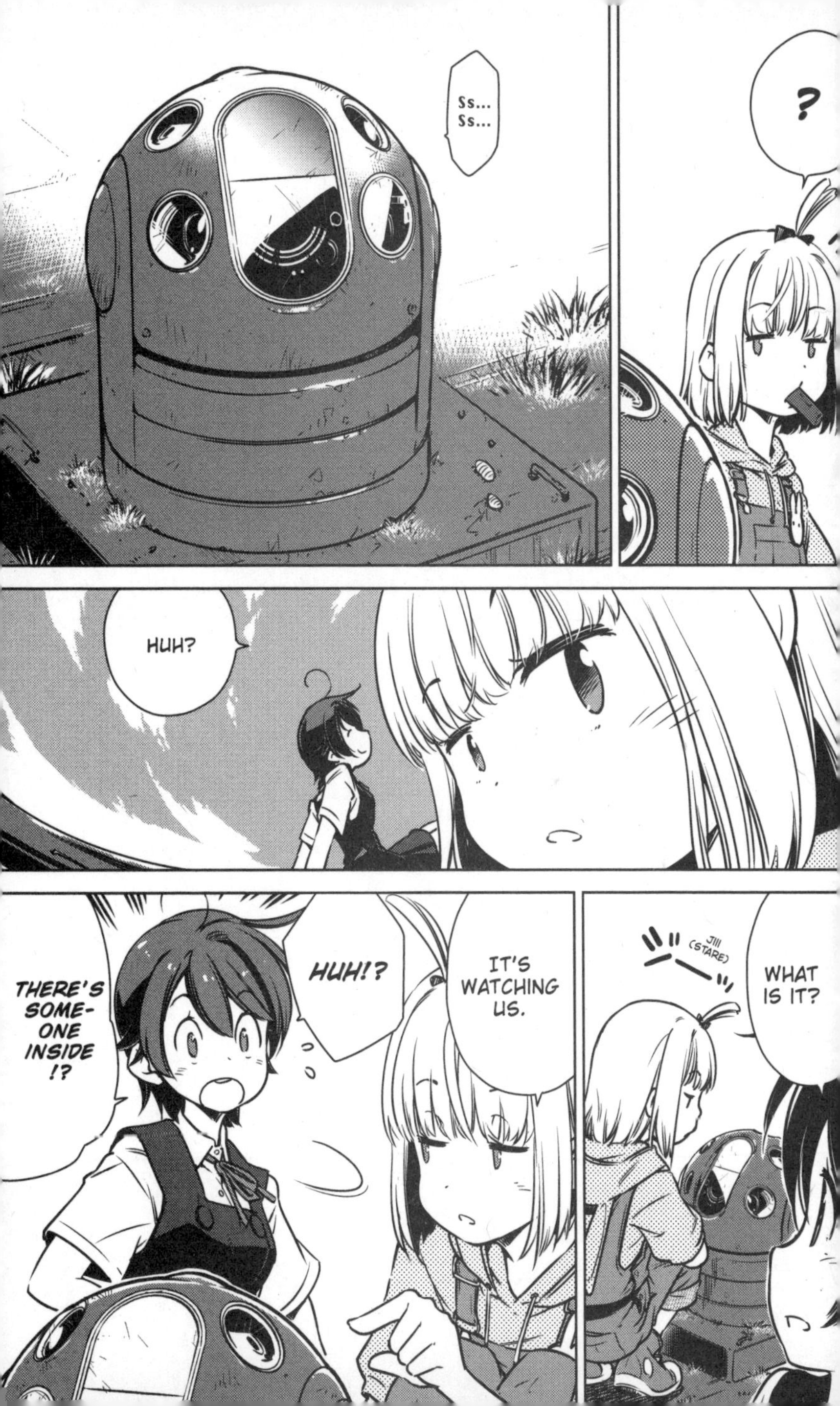
?
Ss...
Ss...
HUH?
WHAT IS IT?
JIII (STARE)
IT'S WATCHING US.
HUH!?
THERE'S SOME-ONE INSIDE !?

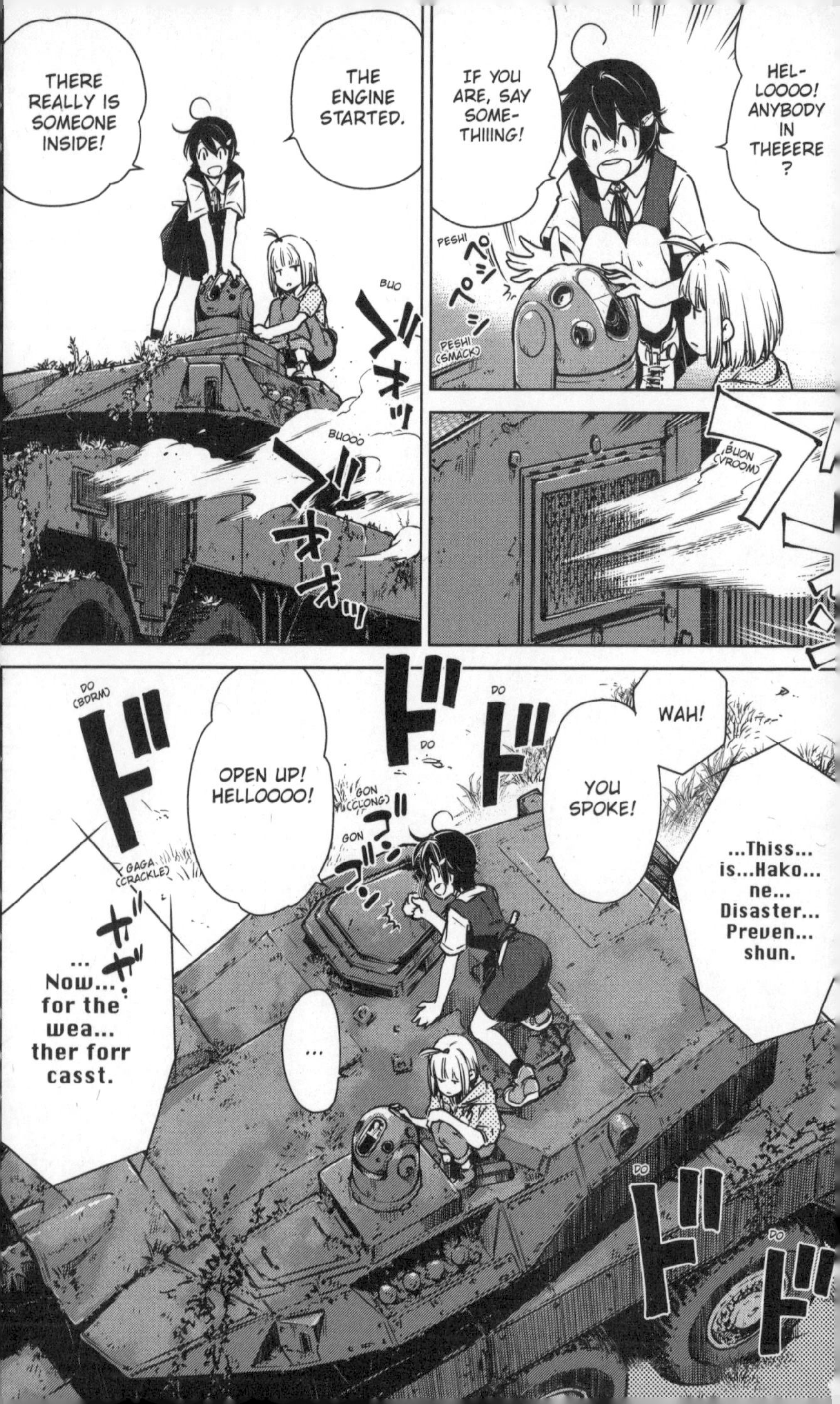
HEL-LOOOO! ANYBODY IN THEEERE?
IF YOU ARE, SAY SOME-THIIING!
PESHI
PESHI (SMACK)
BUON (VROOM)
THE ENGINE STARTED.
THERE REALLY IS SOMEONE INSIDE!
BUO
BUOOO
...Thiss... is...Hako... ne... Disaster... Preven... shun.
WAH!
YOU SPOKE!
DO
DO
OPEN UP! HELLOOOO!
GON (CLONG)
GON
DO (BDRM)
GAGA (CRACKLE)
... Now... for the wea... ther forr casst.
...
DO
DO

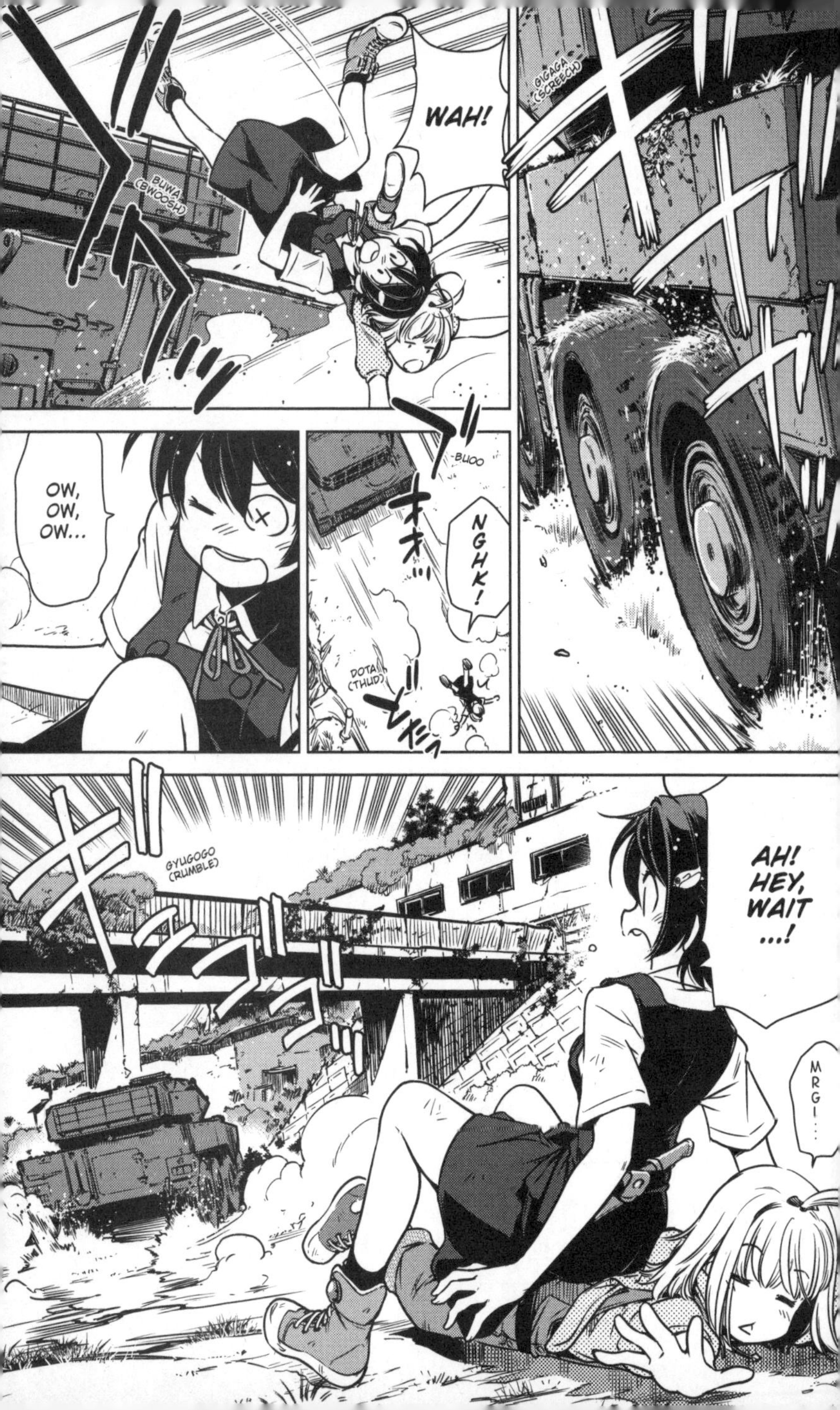
GIGAGA (SCREECH)
WAH!
BUWA (BWOOSH)
-BUOO
NGHK!
DOTA (THUD)
OW, OW, OW...
AH! HEY, WAIT...!
GYUGOGO (RUMBLE)
MRG!...

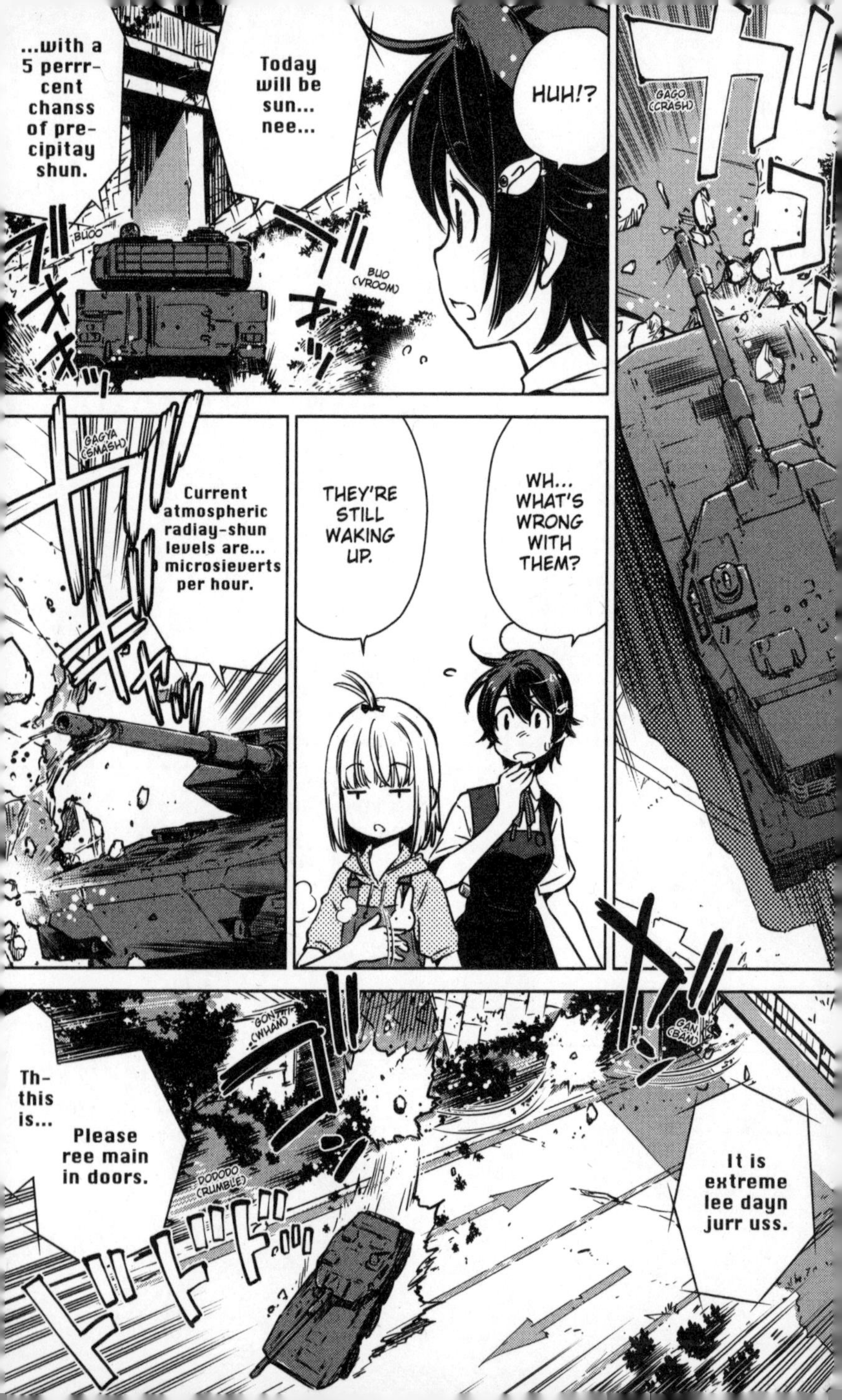

GAGO (CRASH)
HUH!?
Today will be sun... nee...
...with a 5 perrr-cent chanss of pre-cipitay shun.
BUO (VROOM)
BUOO
WH... WHAT'S WRONG WITH THEM?
THEY'RE STILL WAKING UP.
GAGYA (SMASH)
Current atmospheric radiay-shun levels are... microsieverts per hour.
GAN (BAM)
It is extreme lee dayn jurr uss.
GON (WHAM)
Th- this is...
Please ree main in doors.
DODODO (RUMBLE)

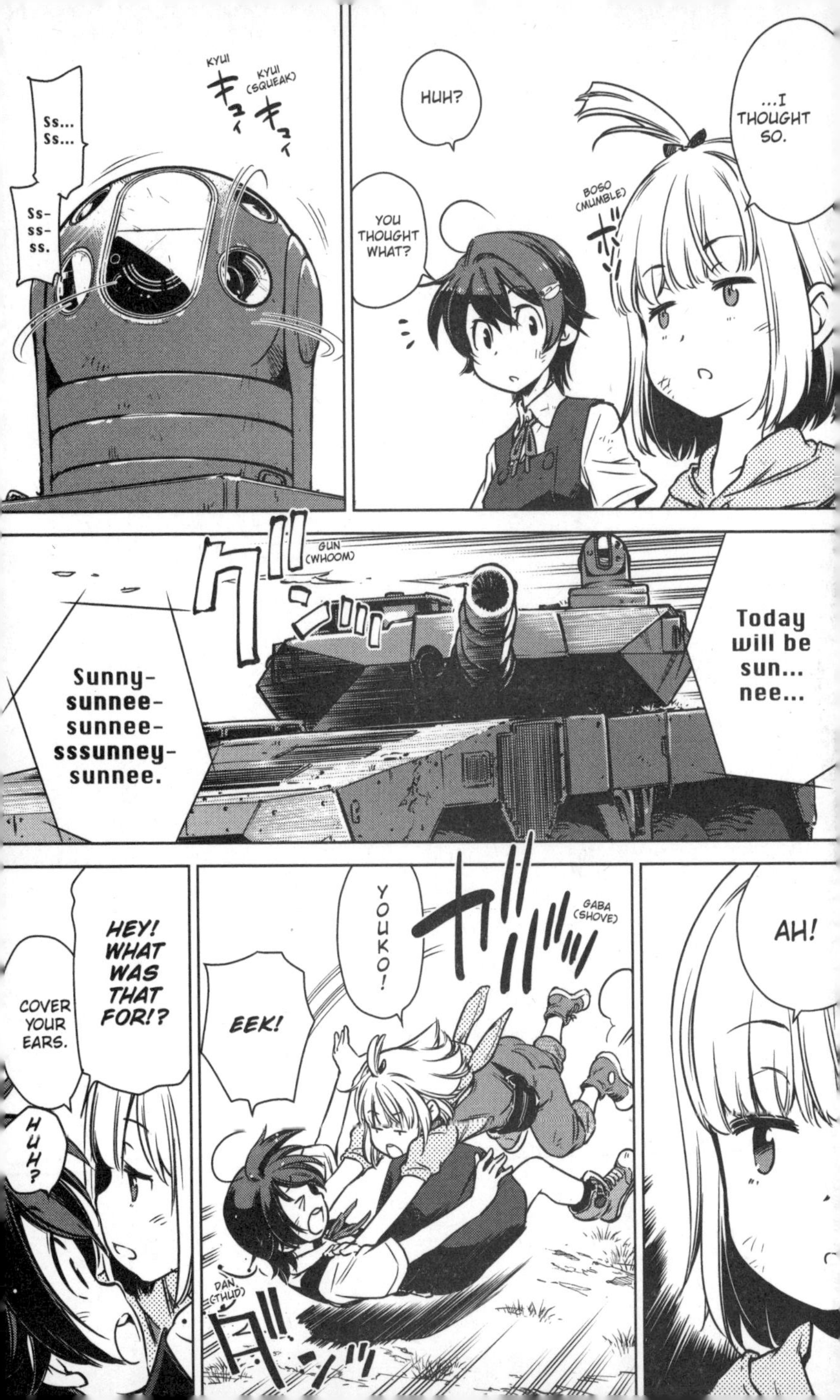
...I THOUGHT SO.
HUH?
BOSO (MUMBLE)
YOU THOUGHT WHAT?
KYUI
KYUI (SQUEAK)
Ss... Ss...
Ss-ss-ss.
GUN (WHOOM)
Today will be sun... nee...
Sunny-sunnee-sunnee-sssunney-sunnee.
AH!
YOUKO!
GABA (SHOVE)
EEK!
DAN (THUD)
HEY! WHAT WAS THAT FOR!?
COVER YOUR EARS.
HUH?

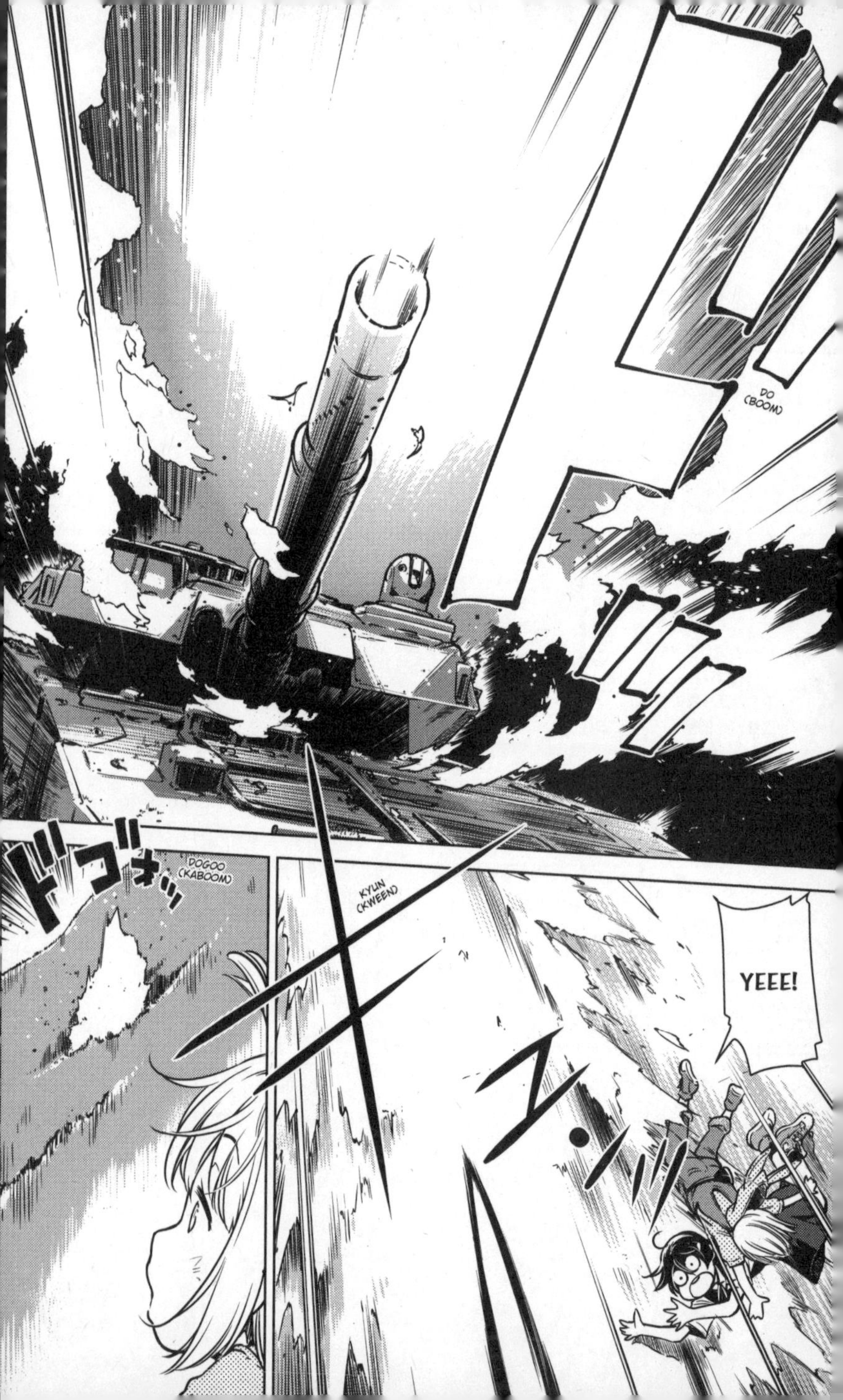
DO
(BOOM)
KYUN
(KWEEN)
YEEE!
DOGOO
(KABOOM)

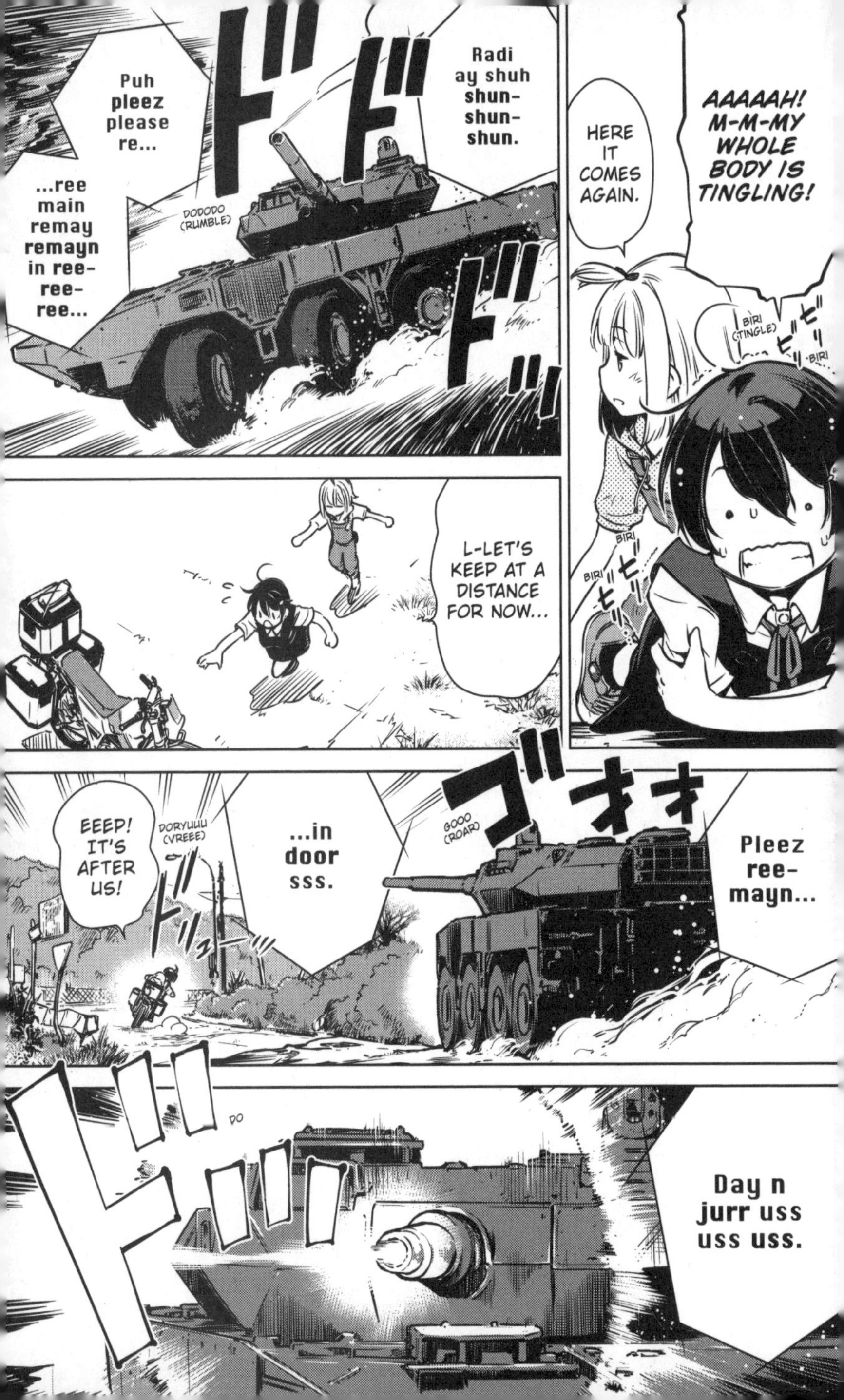
AAAAAH! M-M-MY WHOLE BODY IS TINGLING!
HERE IT COMES AGAIN.
BIRI (TINGLE)
BIRI
BIRI
BIRI
Radi ay shuh shun-shun-shun.
Puh pleez please re...
...ree main remay remayn in ree-ree-ree...
DODODO (RUMBLE)
L-LET'S KEEP AT A DISTANCE FOR NOW...
Pleez ree-mayn...
GOOO (ROAR)
...in door sss.
DORYUUU (VREEE)
EEEP! IT'S AFTER US!
Day n jurr uss uss uss.
DO

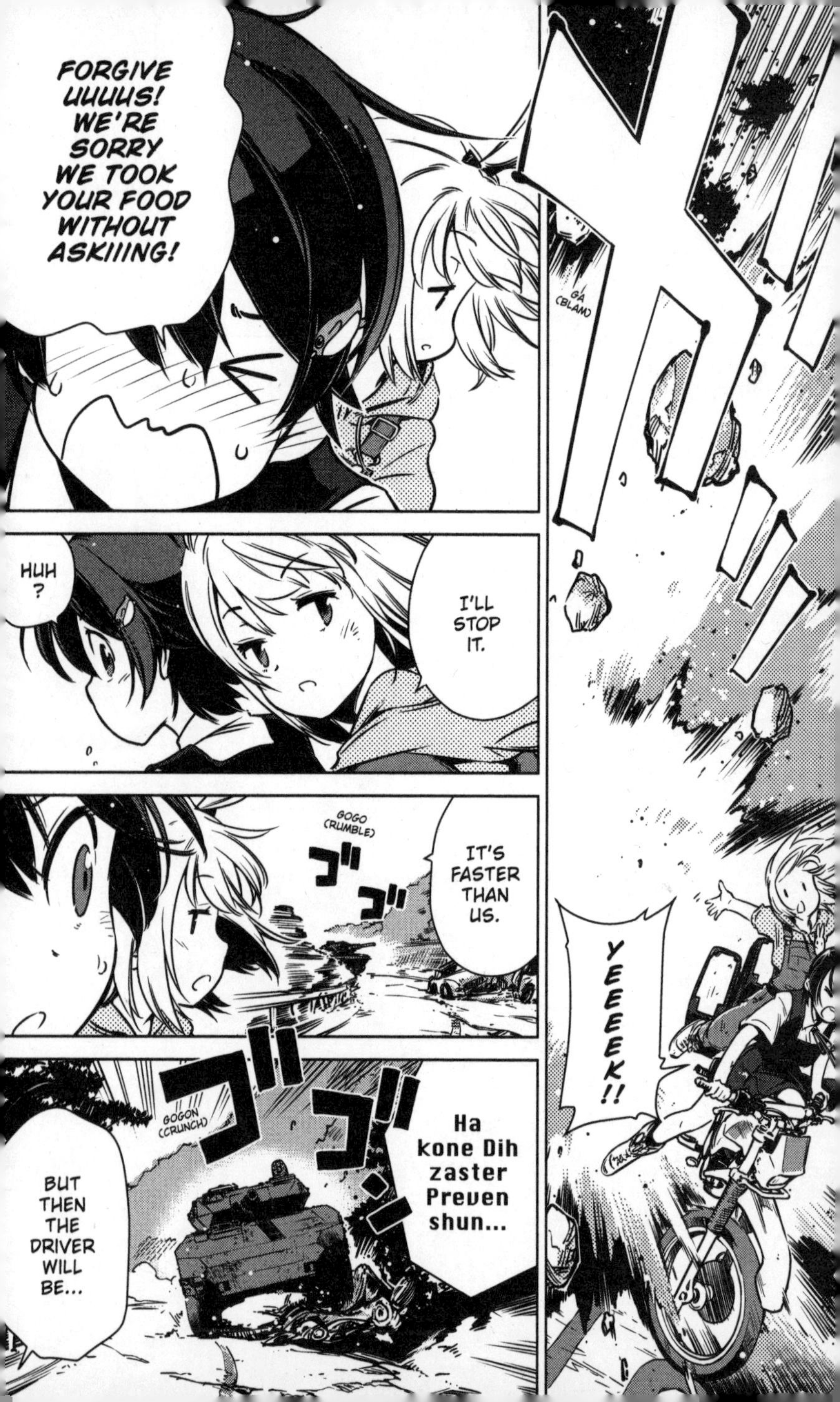
GA (BLAM)
YEEEEEK!!
FORGIVE UUUUS! WE'RE SORRY WE TOOK YOUR FOOD WITHOUT ASKIIING!
I'LL STOP IT.
HUH?
IT'S FASTER THAN US.
GOGO (RUMBLE)
Ha kone Dih zaster Preven shun...
GOGON (CRUNCH)
BUT THEN THE DRIVER WILL BE...

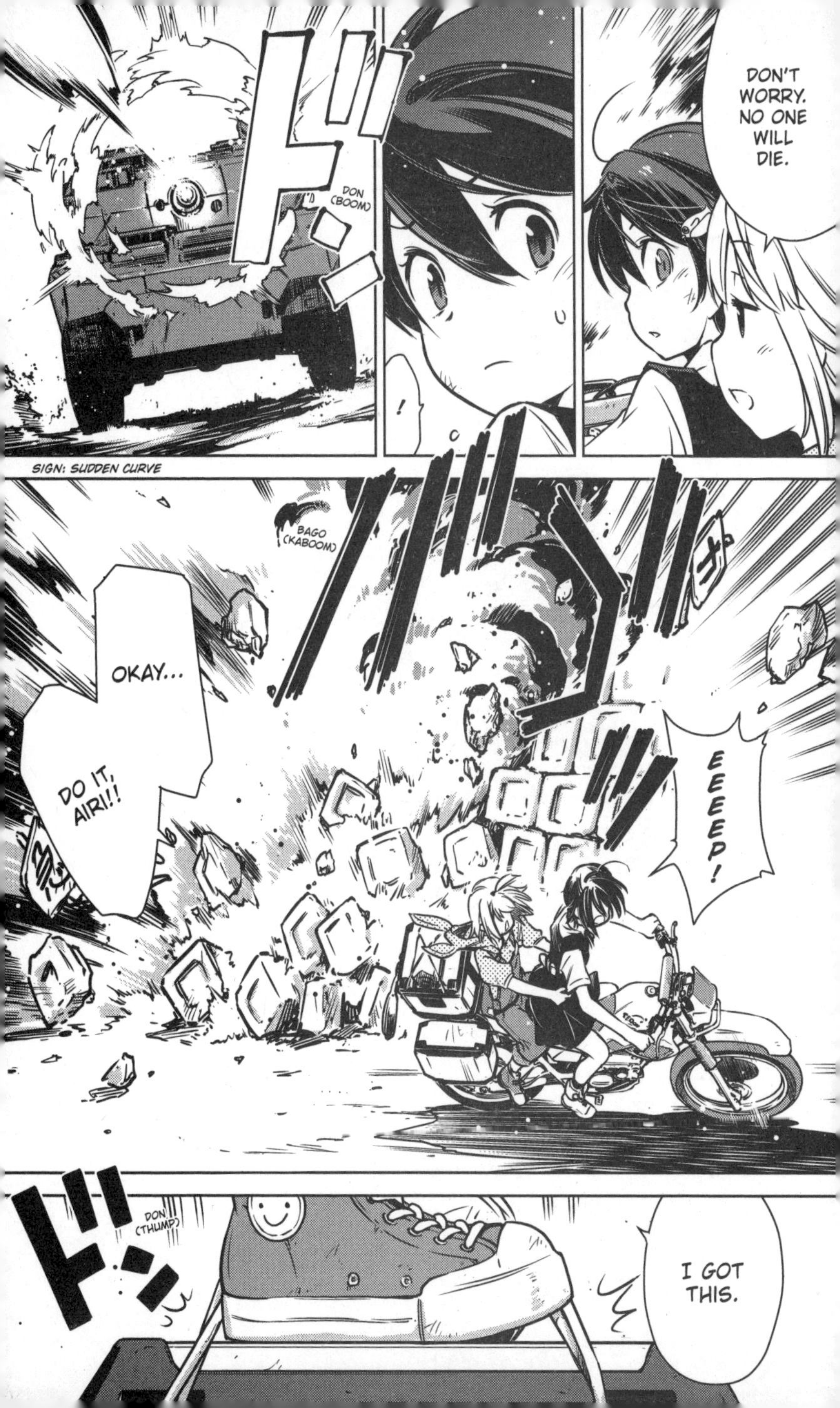
DON'T WORRY. NO ONE WILL DIE.
DON (BOOM)
SIGN: SUDDEN CURVE
BAGO (KABOOM)
EEEEEP!
OKAY...
DO IT, AIRI!!
I GOT THIS.
DON (THUMP)

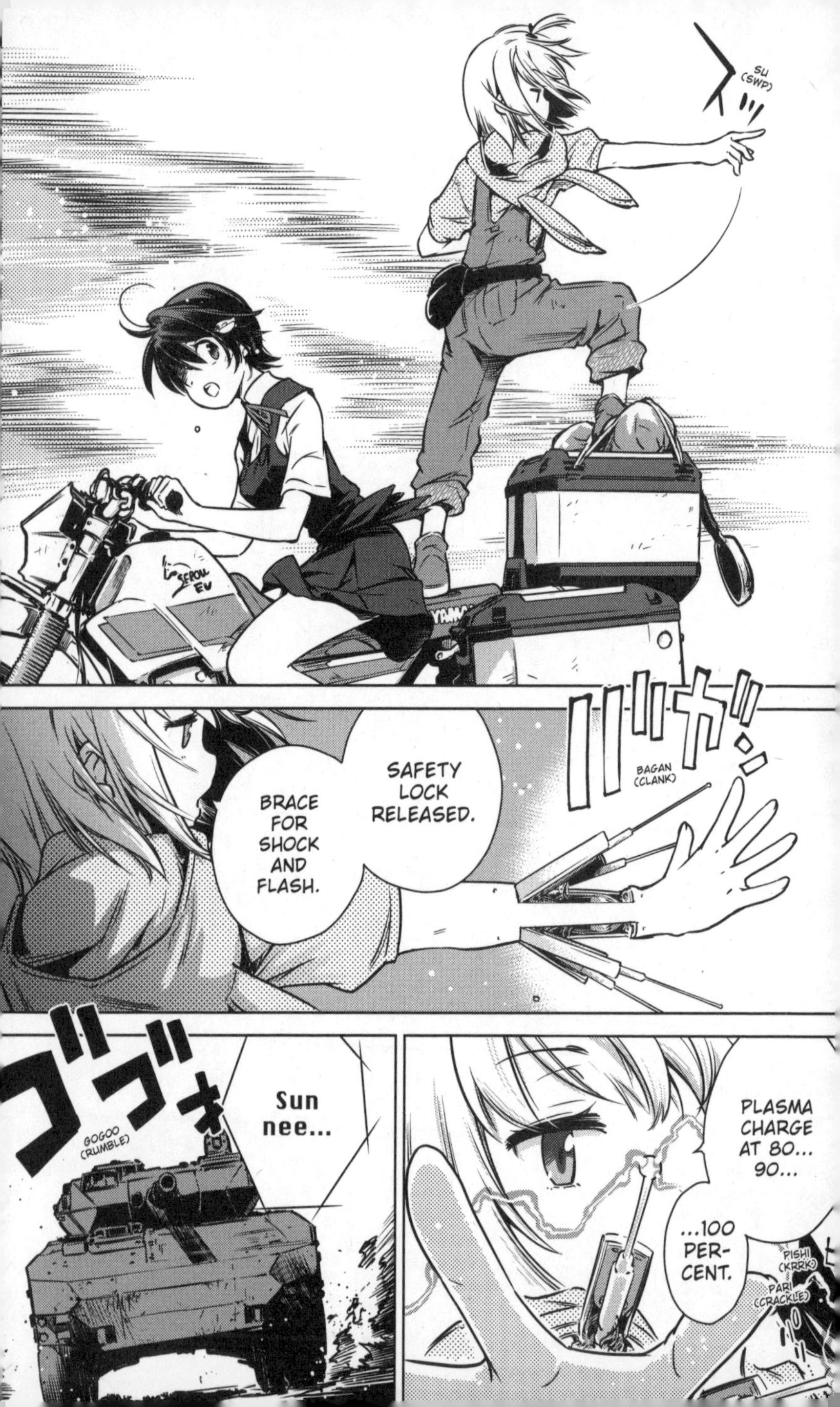
SU (SWP)
BAGAN (CLANK)
SAFETY LOCK RELEASED.
BRACE FOR SHOCK AND FLASH.
PLASMA CHARGE AT 80... 90...
...100 PER-CENT.
PISHI (KRRK)
PARI (CRACKLE)
Sun nee...
GOGOO (RUMBLE)

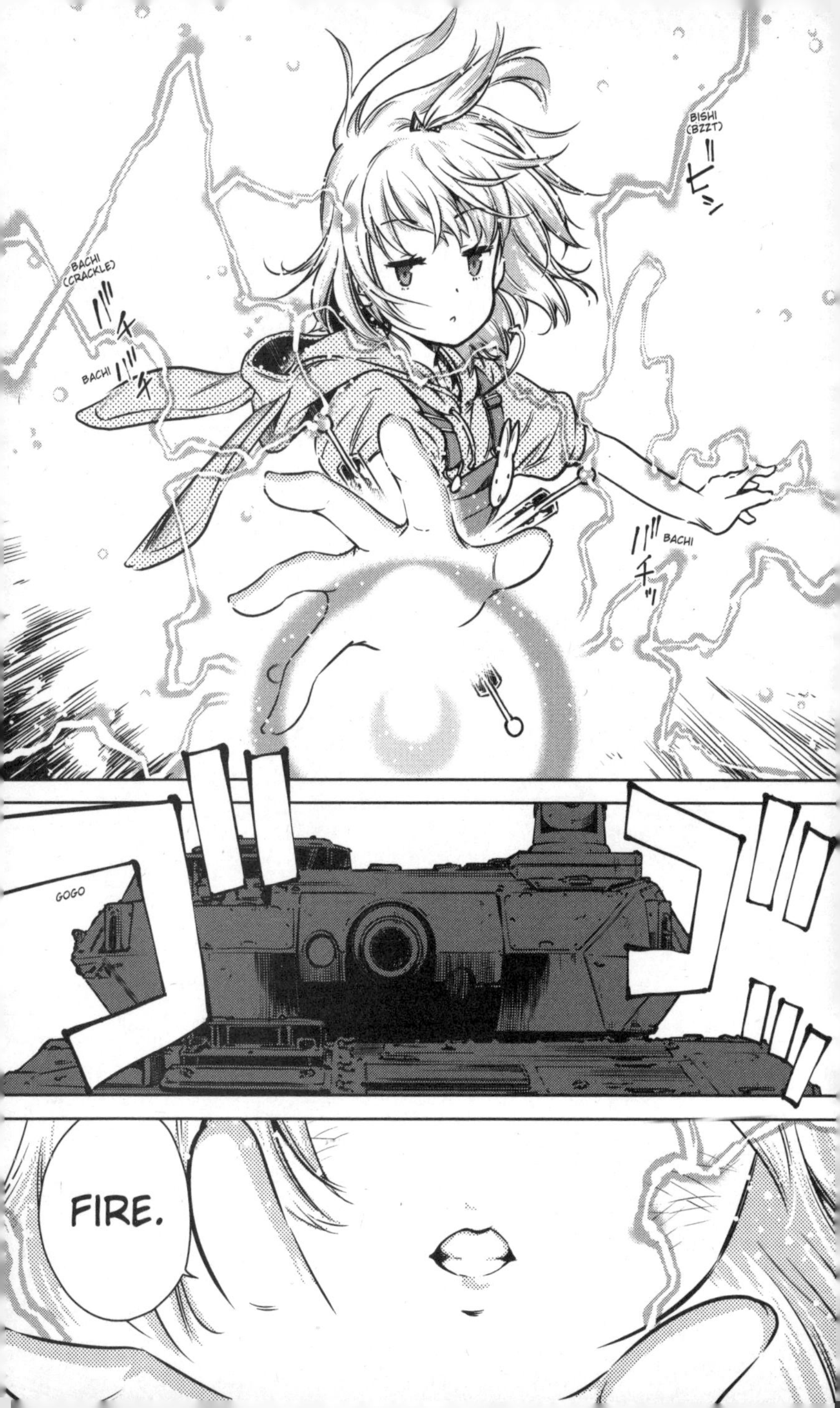
BISHI (BZZT)
BACHI (CRACKLE)
BACHI
BACHI
GOGO
FIRE.

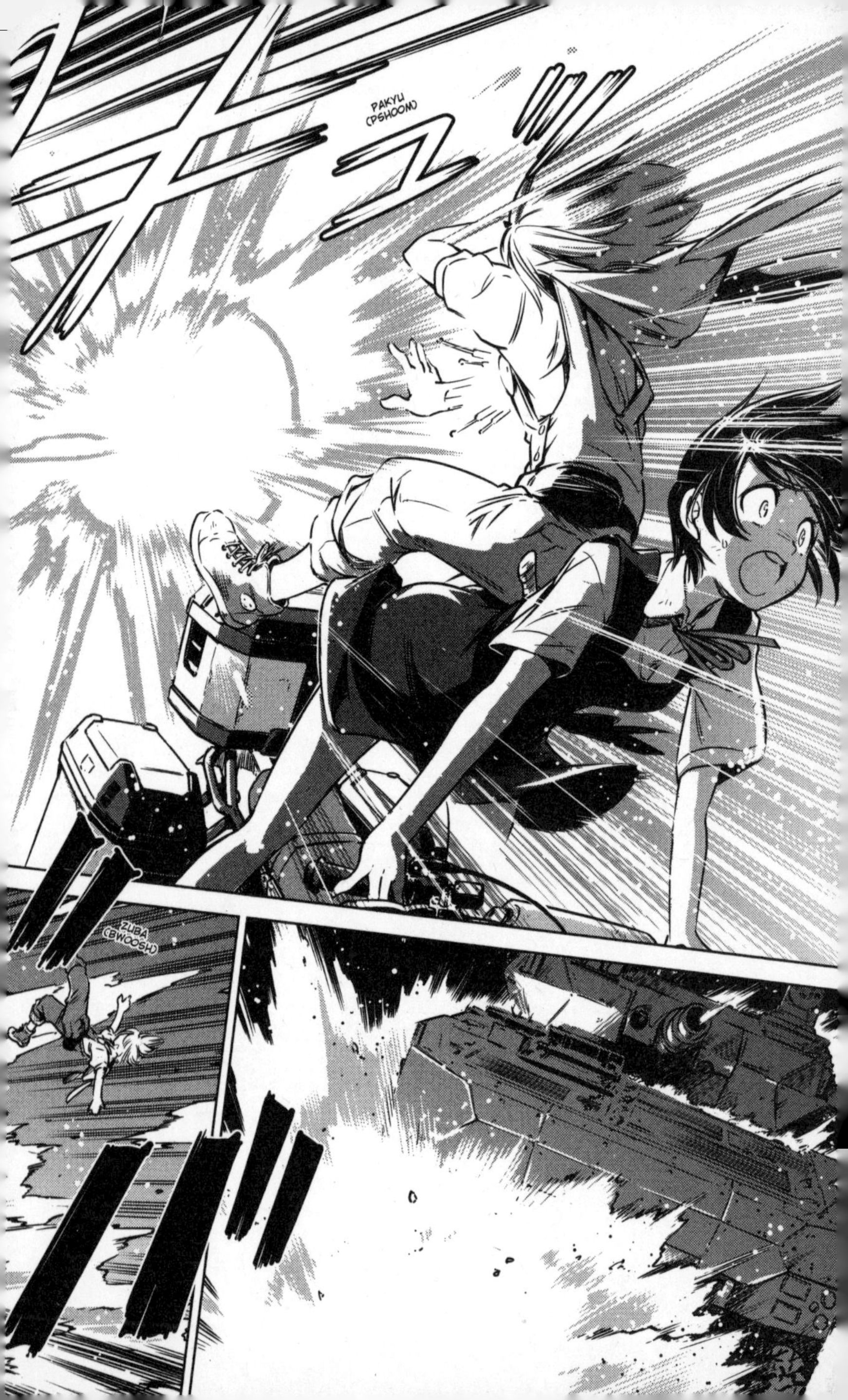
PAKYU (PSHOOM)
ZUBA (BWOOSH)

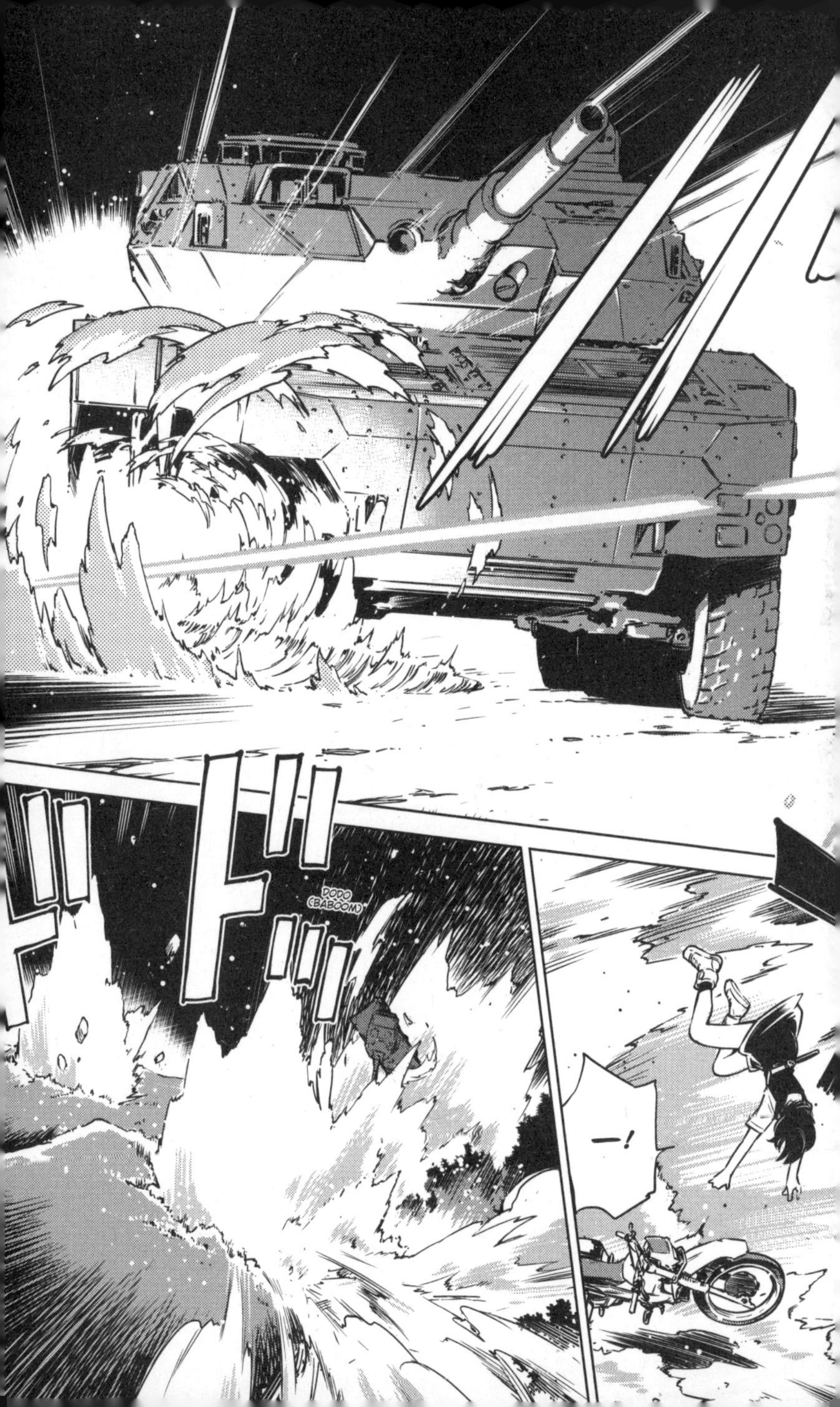
—!
DODO (BABOOM)

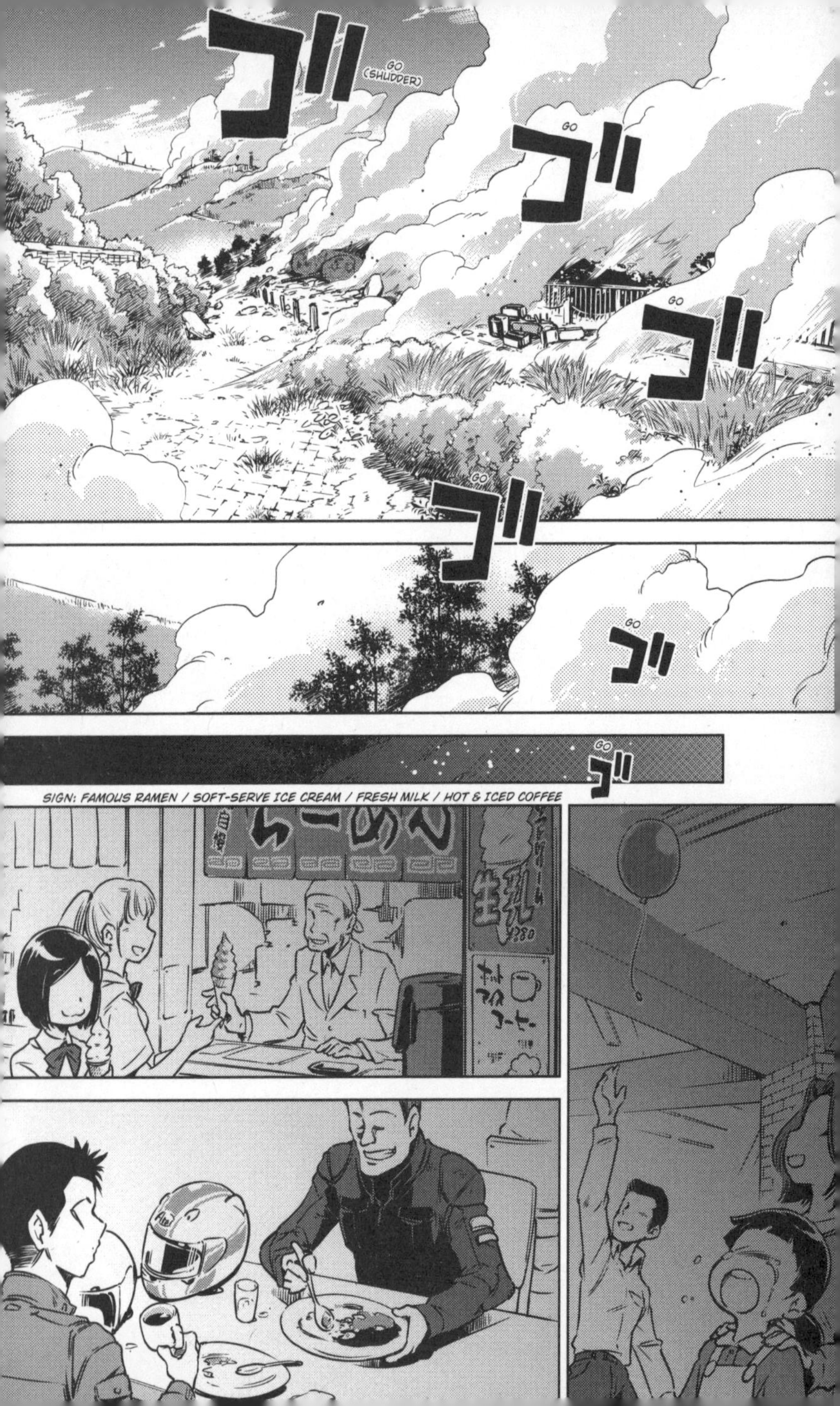
ゴ GO (SHUDDER)
ゴ GO
ゴ GO
ゴ GO
ゴ GO
ゴ GO
SIGN: FAMOUS RAMEN / SOFT-SERVE ICE CREAM / FRESH MILK / HOT & ICED COFFEE

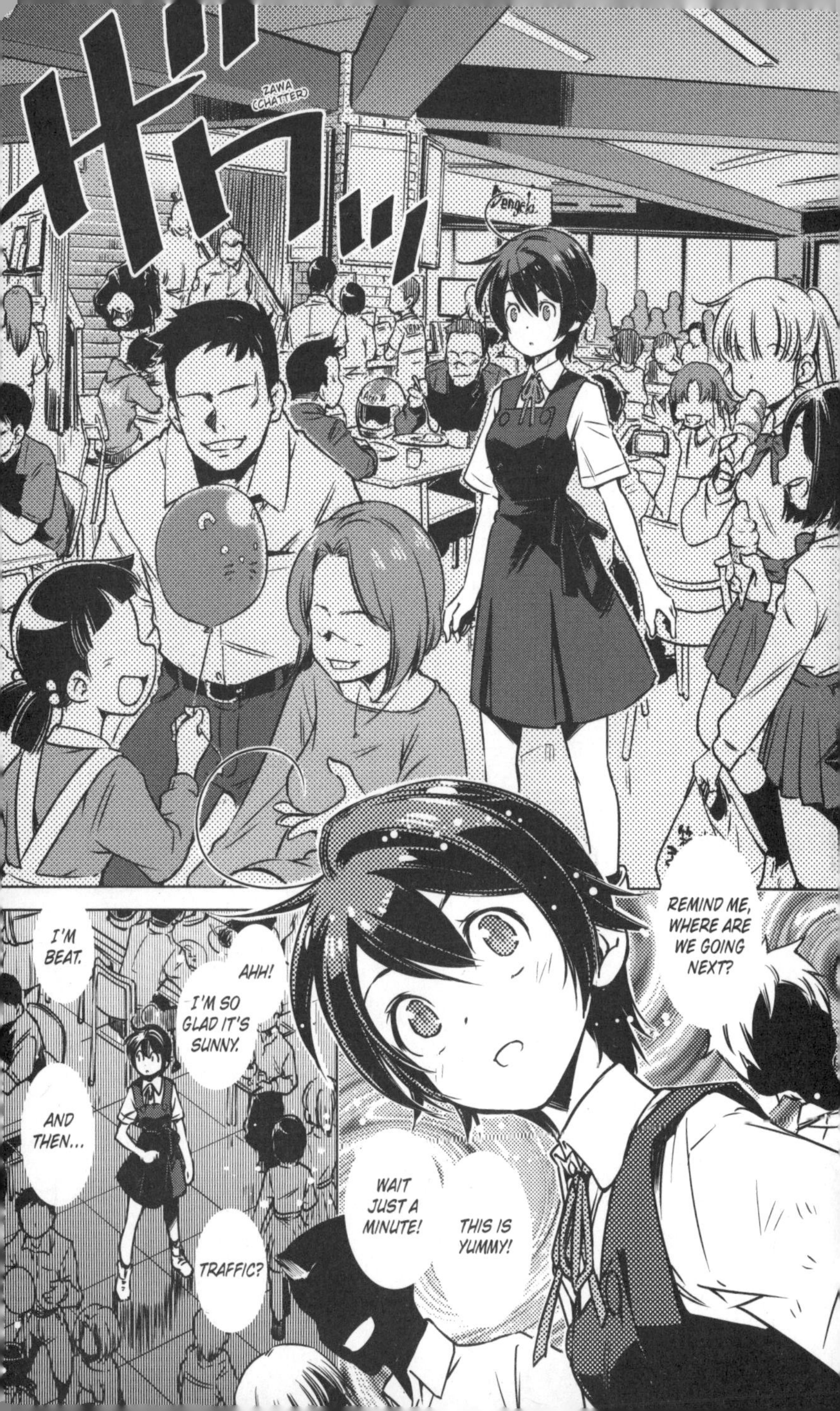
ザワッ
ZAWA (CHATTER)
REMIND ME, WHERE ARE WE GOING NEXT?
THIS IS YUMMY!
WAIT JUST A MINUTE!
AHH! I'M SO GLAD IT'S SUNNY.
I'M BEAT.
AND THEN...
TRAFFIC?

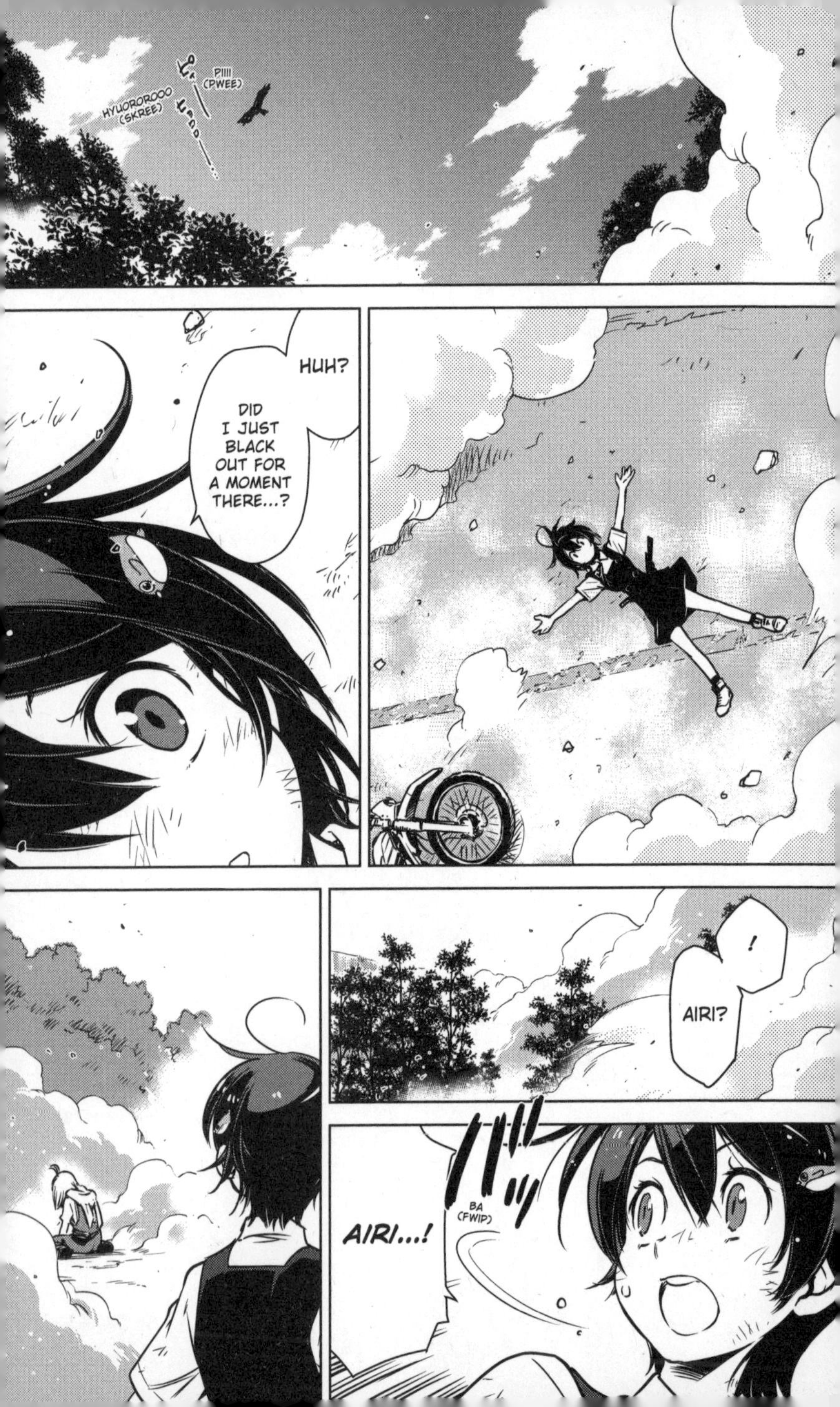
PIIII (PWEE)
HYUOROROOO (SKREE)
HUH?
DID I JUST BLACK OUT FOR A MOMENT THERE...?
!
AIRI?
BA (FWIP)
AIRI...!

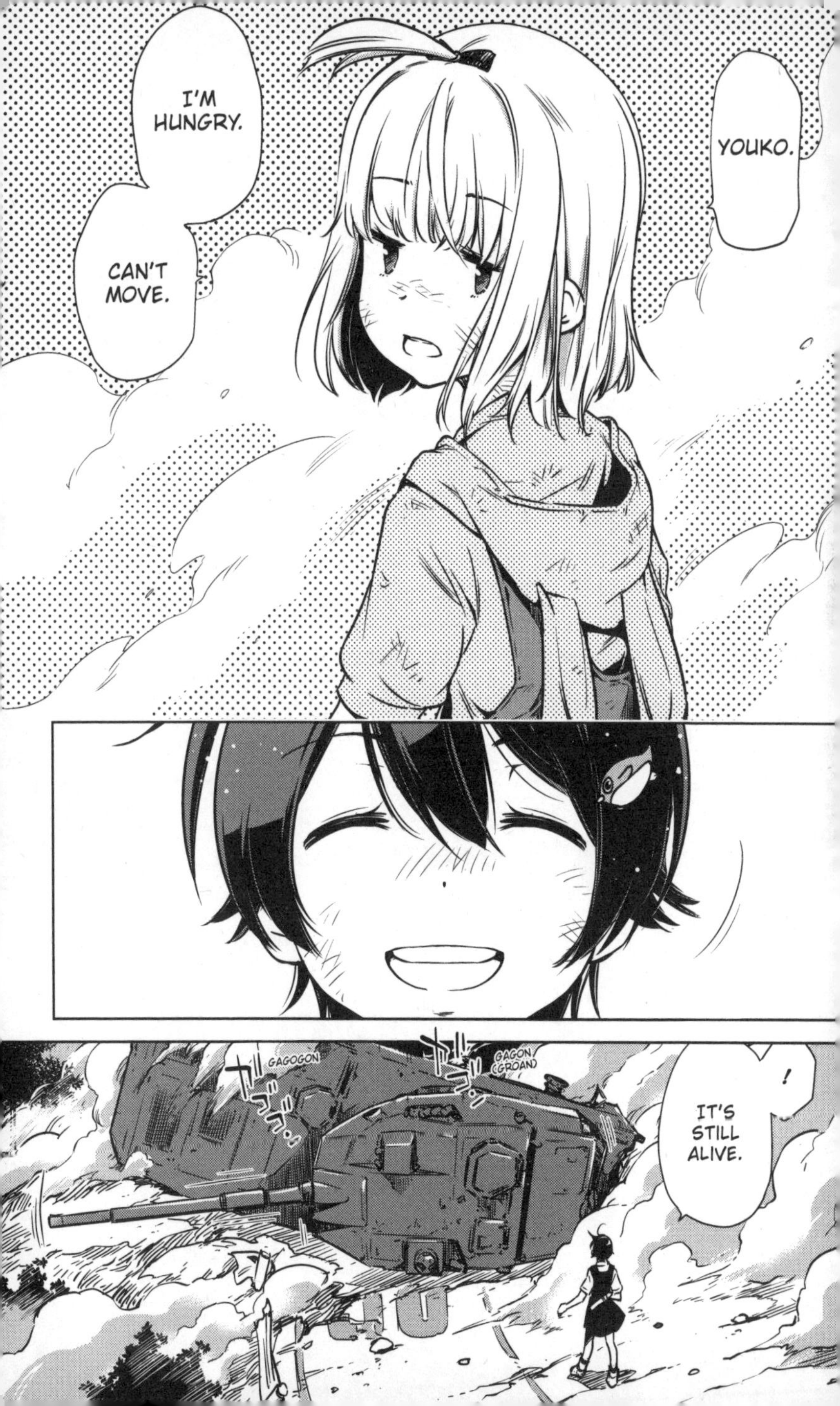
YOUKO.
I'M HUNGRY.
CAN'T MOVE.
!
IT'S STILL ALIVE.
GAGON (GROAN)
GAGOGON

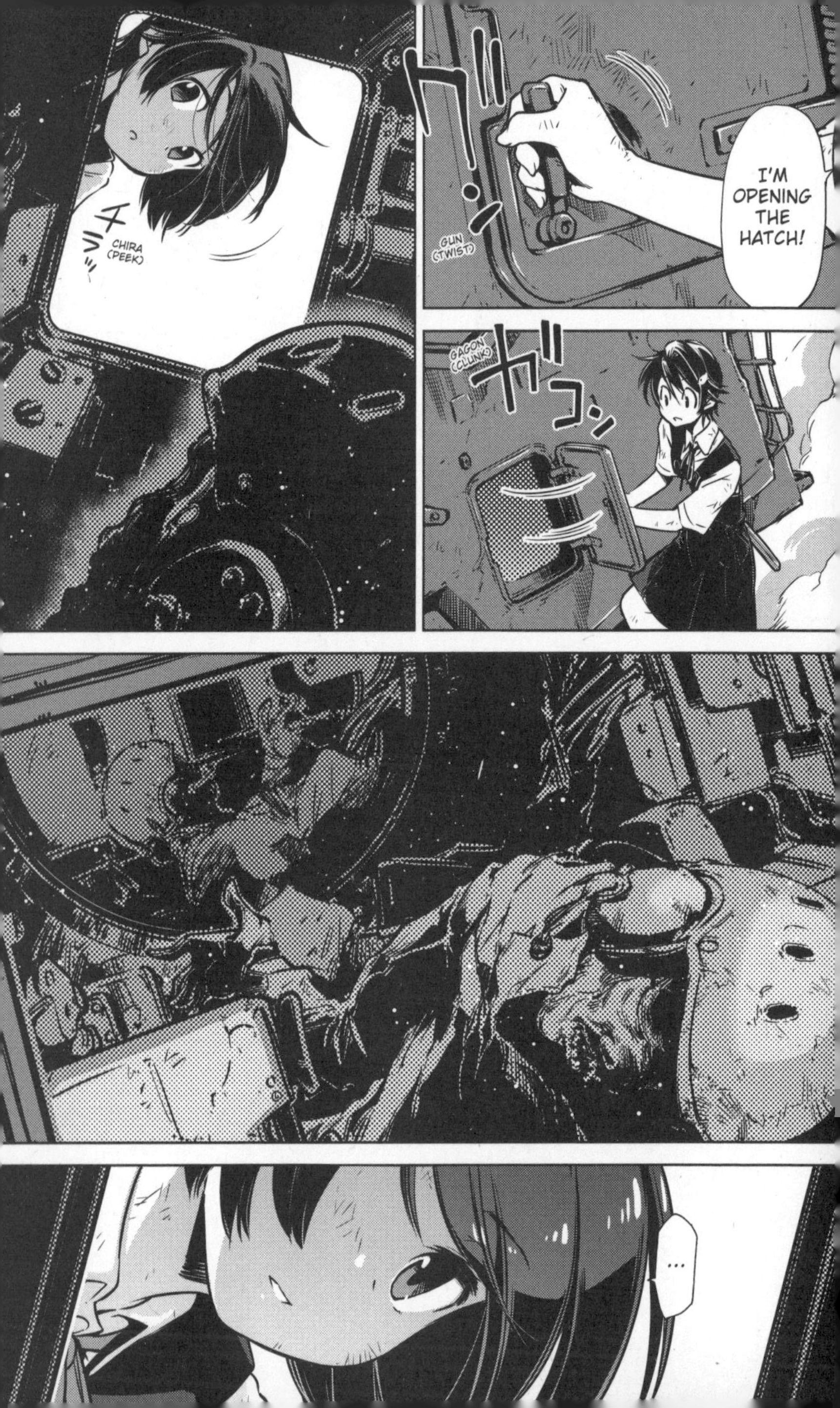
I'M OPENING THE HATCH!
GUN (TWIST)
GAGON (CLUNK)
CHIRA (PEEK)
...

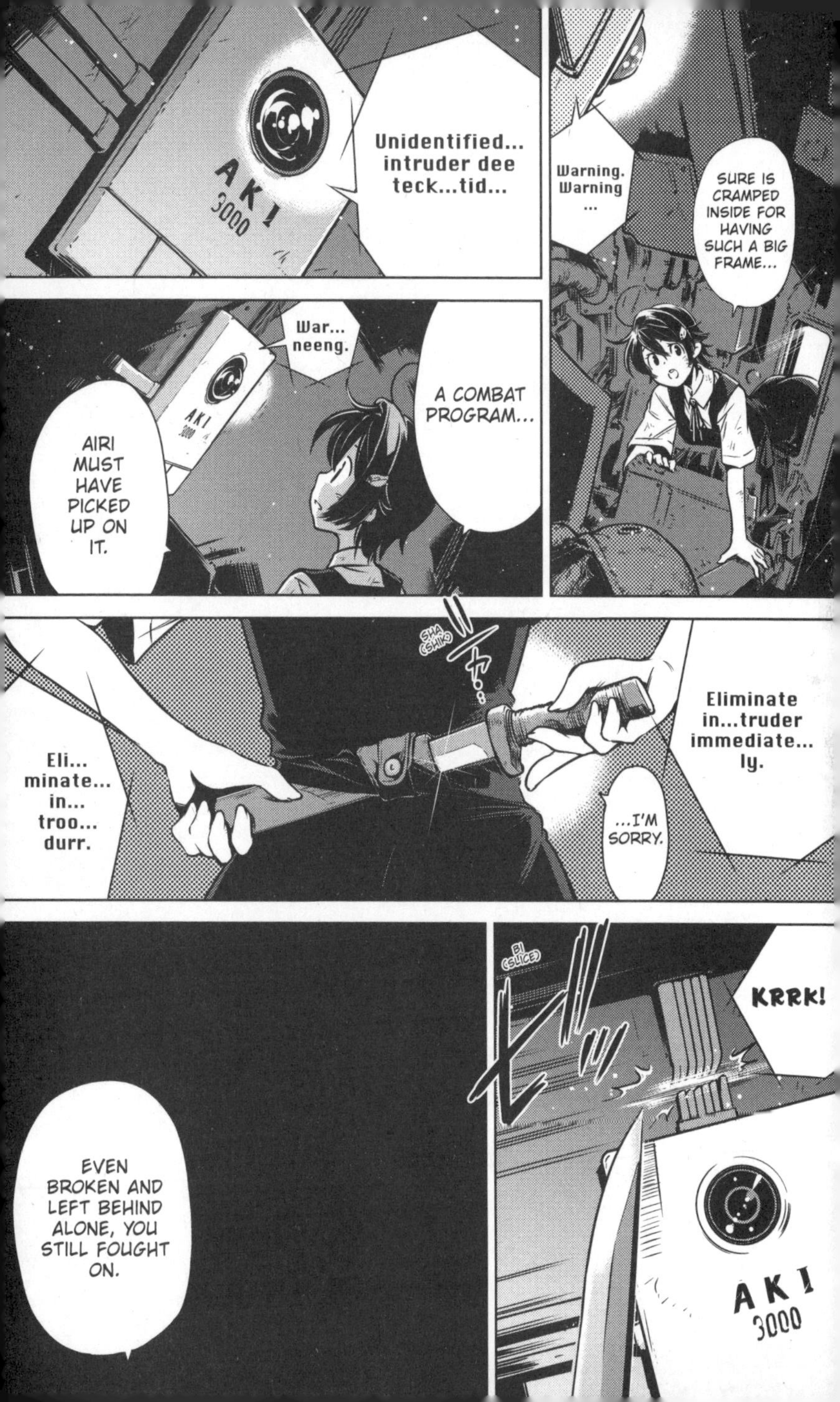
Warning. Warning ...
SURE IS CRAMPED INSIDE FOR HAVING SUCH A BIG FRAME...
Unidentified... intruder dee teck...tid...
AKI 3000
War... neeng.
A COMBAT PROGRAM...
AIRI MUST HAVE PICKED UP ON IT.
AKI 3000
SHA (SHIKI)
Eliminate in...truder immediate... ly.
...I'M SORRY.
Eli... minate... in... troo... durr.
BI (SLICE)
KRRK!
AKI 3000
EVEN BROKEN AND LEFT BEHIND ALONE, YOU STILL FOUGHT ON.

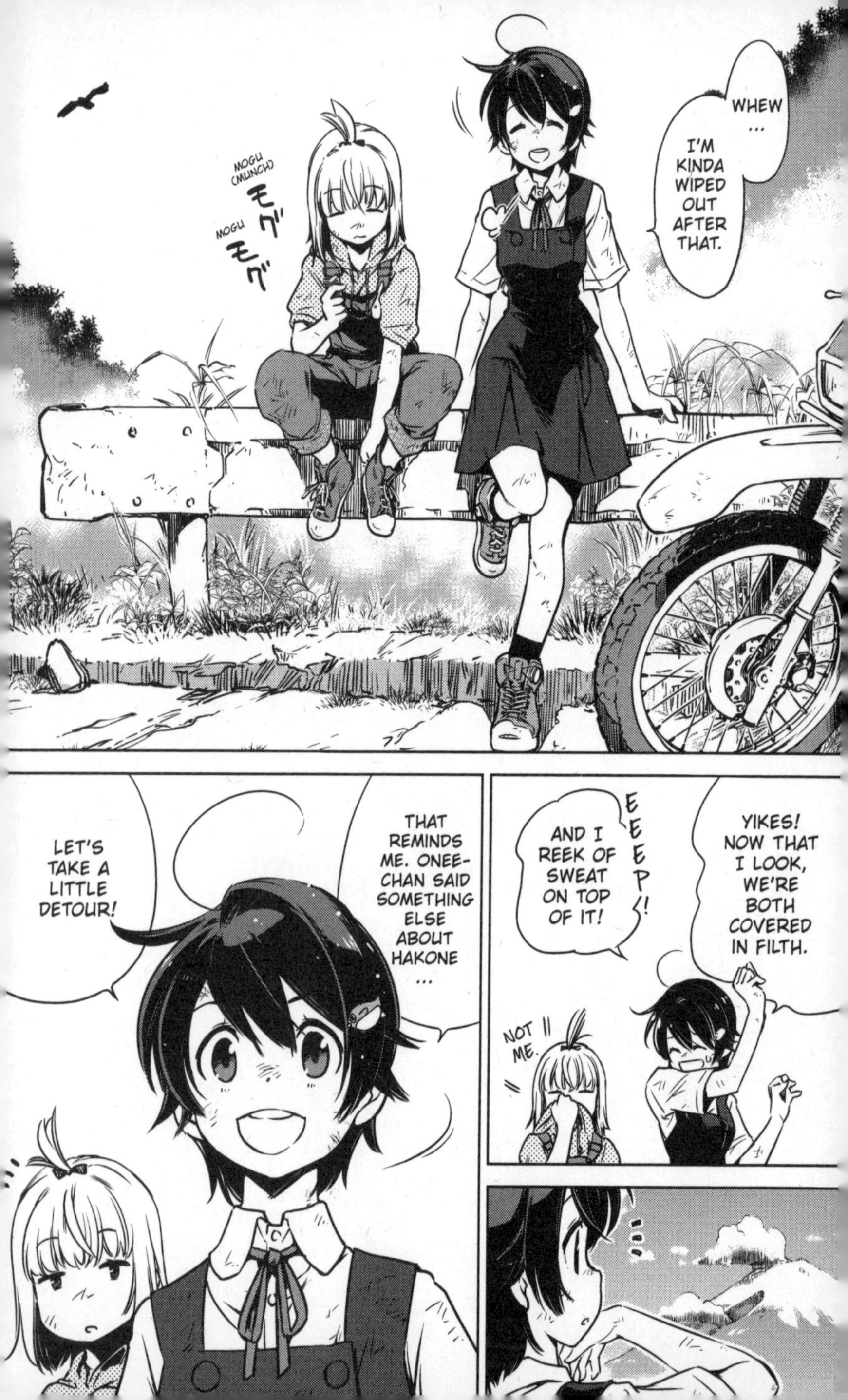

WHEW ... I'M KINDA WIPED OUT AFTER THAT.
MOGU (MUNCH) モグ
MOGU モグ
YIKES! NOW THAT I LOOK, WE'RE BOTH COVERED IN FILTH.
AND I REEK OF SWEAT ON TOP OF IT!
EEEP!!
NOT ME.
THAT REMINDS ME. ONEE-CHAN SAID SOMETHING ELSE ABOUT HAKONE ...
LET'S TAKE A LITTLE DETOUR!

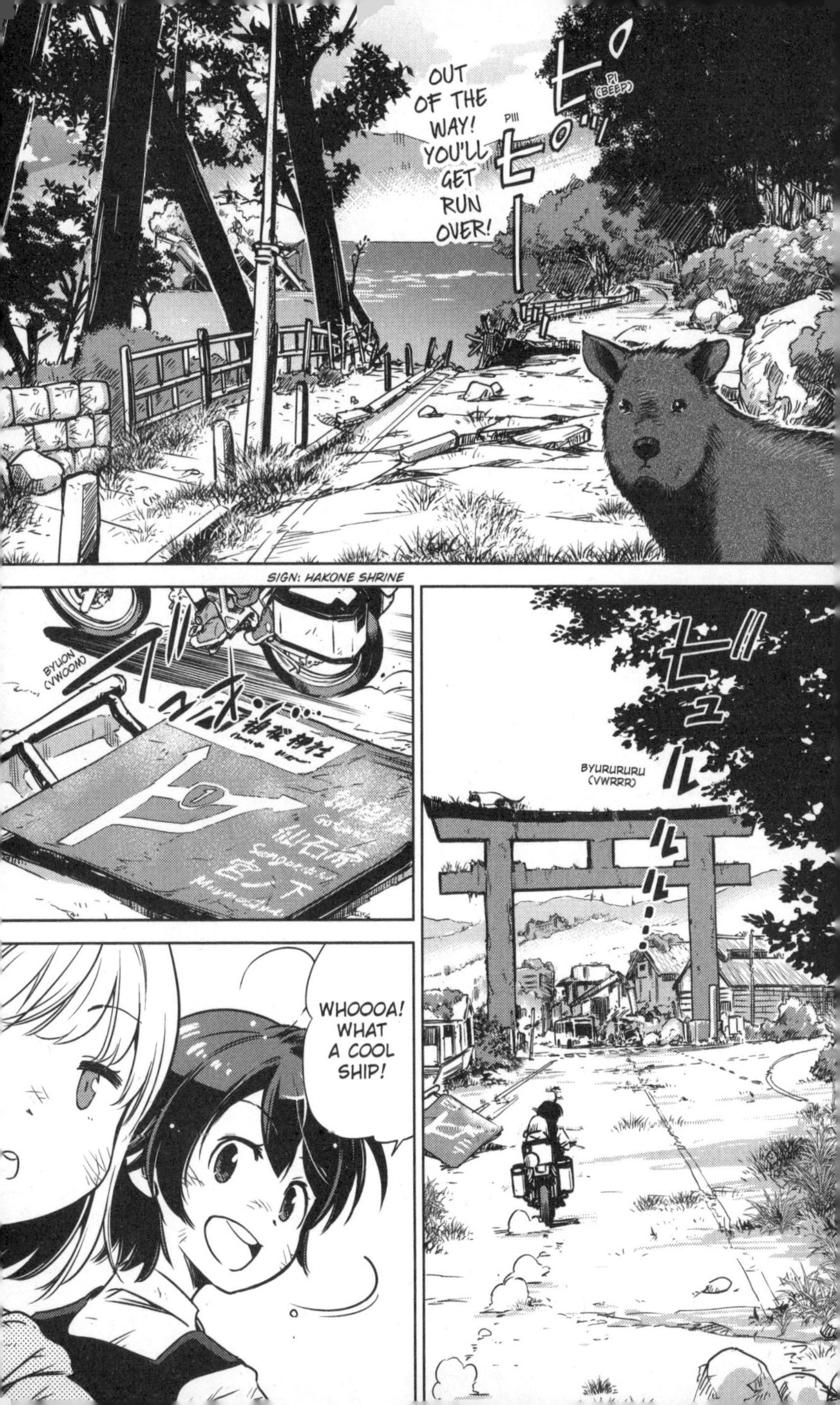

OUT OF THE WAY! YOU'LL GET RUN OVER!
PIII
PI (BEEP)
BYURURURU (VWRRR)
BYUON (VWOOM)
SIGN: HAKONE SHRINE
WHOOOA! WHAT A COOL SHIP!

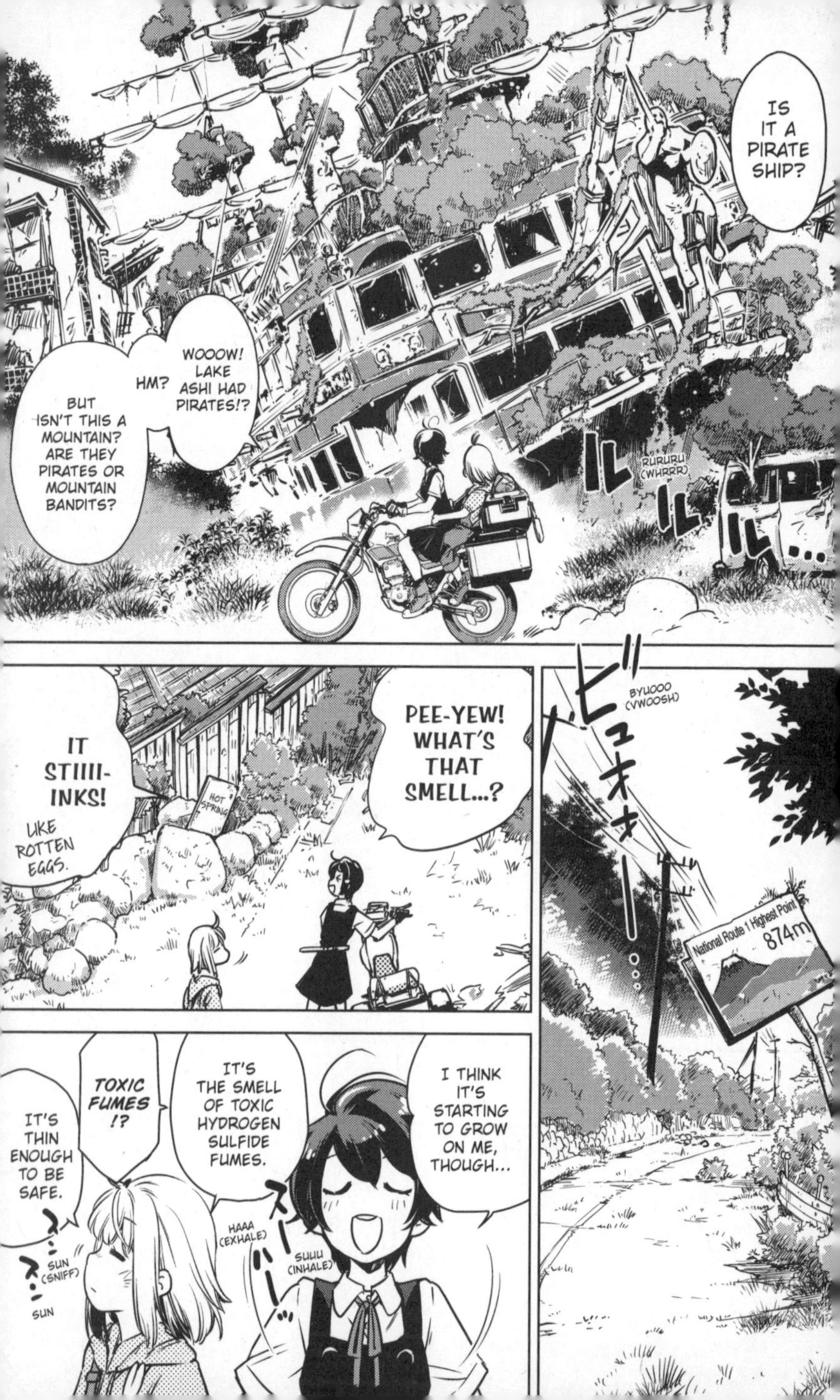

IS IT A PIRATE SHIP?
WOOOW! LAKE ASHI HAD PIRATES!?
HM?
BUT ISN'T THIS A MOUNTAIN? ARE THEY PIRATES OR MOUNTAIN BANDITS?
RURURU (WHRRR)
BYUOOO (VWOOSH)
National Route 1 Highest Point 874m
PEE-YEW! WHAT'S THAT SMELL...?
HOT SPRING
IT STIIII-INKS!
LIKE ROTTEN EGGS.
I THINK IT'S STARTING TO GROW ON ME, THOUGH...
SUUU (INHALE)
HAAA (EXHALE)
IT'S THE SMELL OF TOXIC HYDROGEN SULFIDE FUMES.
TOXIC FUMES!?
IT'S THIN ENOUGH TO BE SAFE.
SUN (SNIFF)
SUN

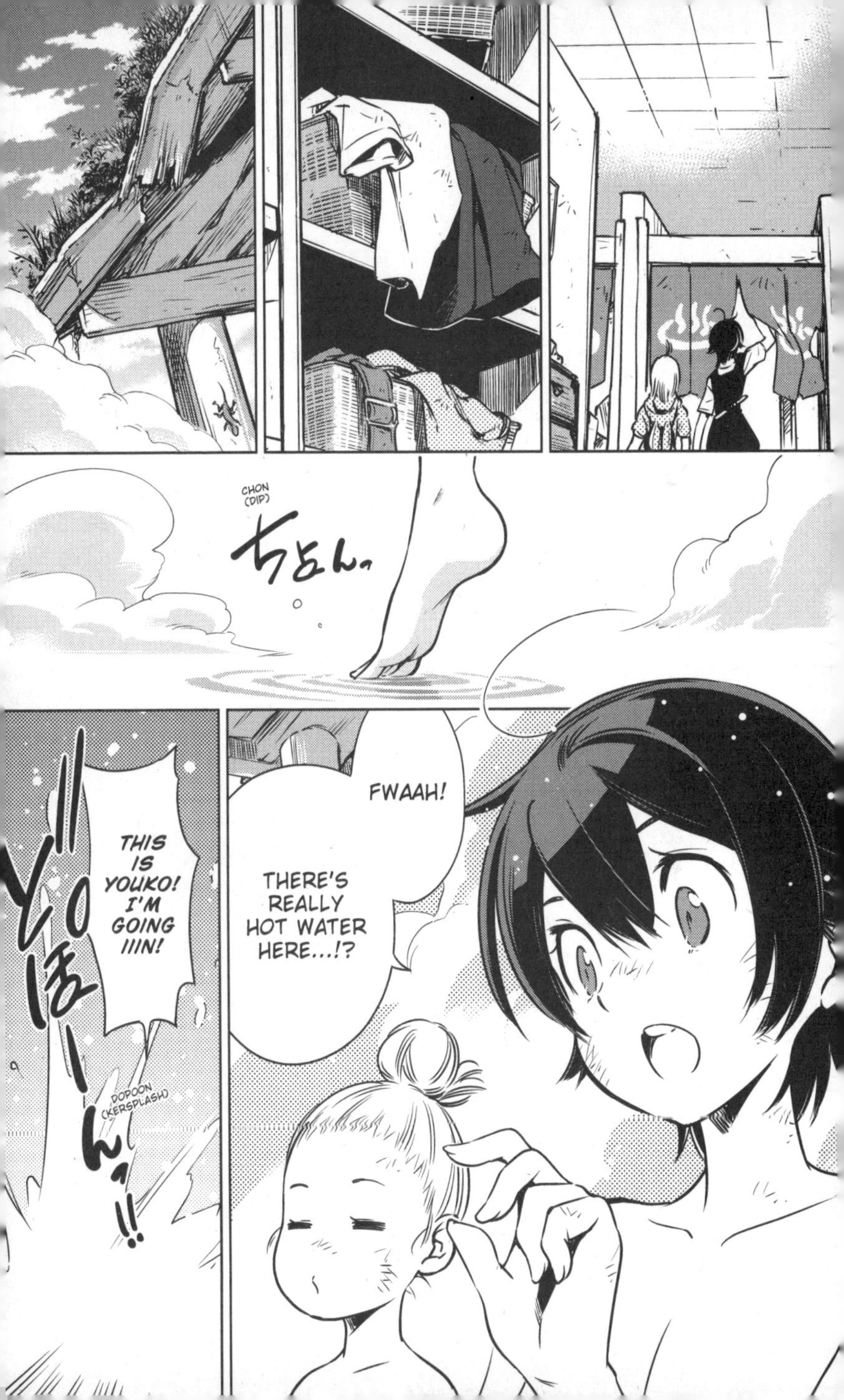
CHON (DIP)
ちょんっ
FWAAH!
THERE'S REALLY HOT WATER HERE...!?
THIS IS YOUKO! I'M GOING IIIN!
DOPOON (KERSPLASH)
どぼーんっ!!

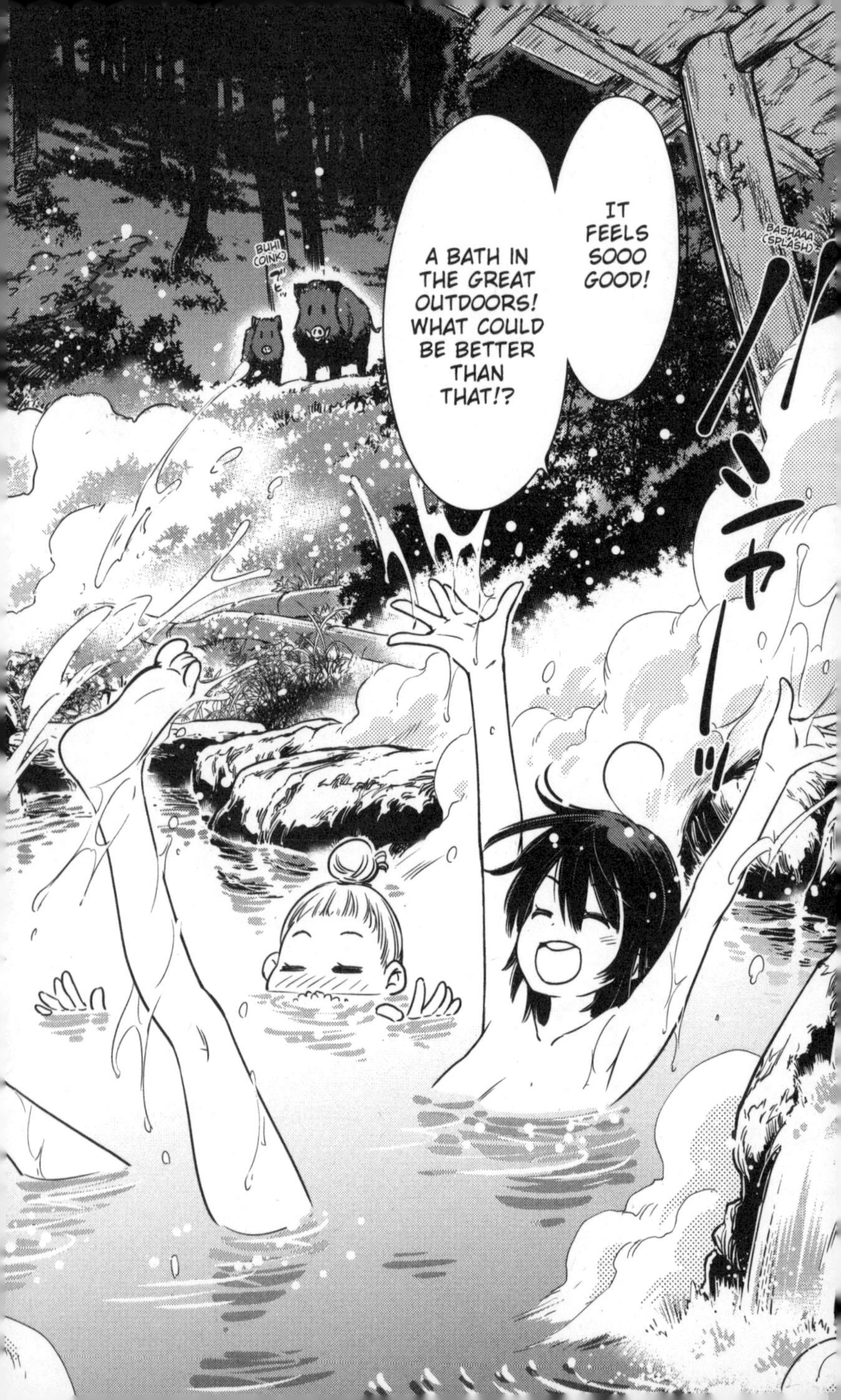
BASHAAA (SPLASH)
IT FEELS SOOO GOOD!
A BATH IN THE GREAT OUTDOORS! WHAT COULD BE BETTER THAN THAT!?
BUHI (OINK)

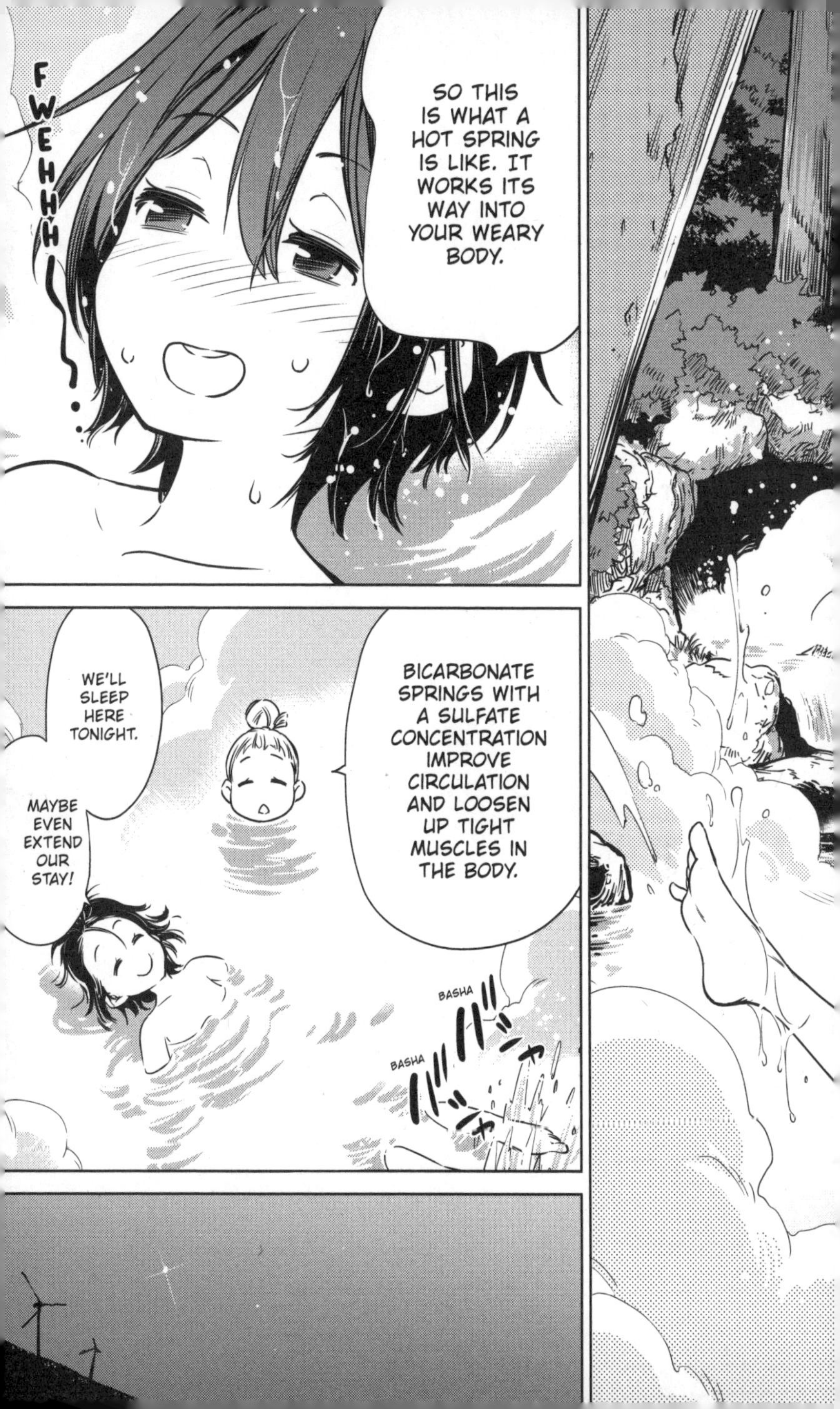

SO THIS IS WHAT A HOT SPRING IS LIKE. IT WORKS ITS WAY INTO YOUR WEARY BODY.
FWEHHHH
BICARBONATE SPRINGS WITH A SULFATE CONCENTRATION IMPROVE CIRCULATION AND LOOSEN UP TIGHT MUSCLES IN THE BODY.
WE'LL SLEEP HERE TONIGHT.
MAYBE EVEN EXTEND OUR STAY!
BASHA
BASHA

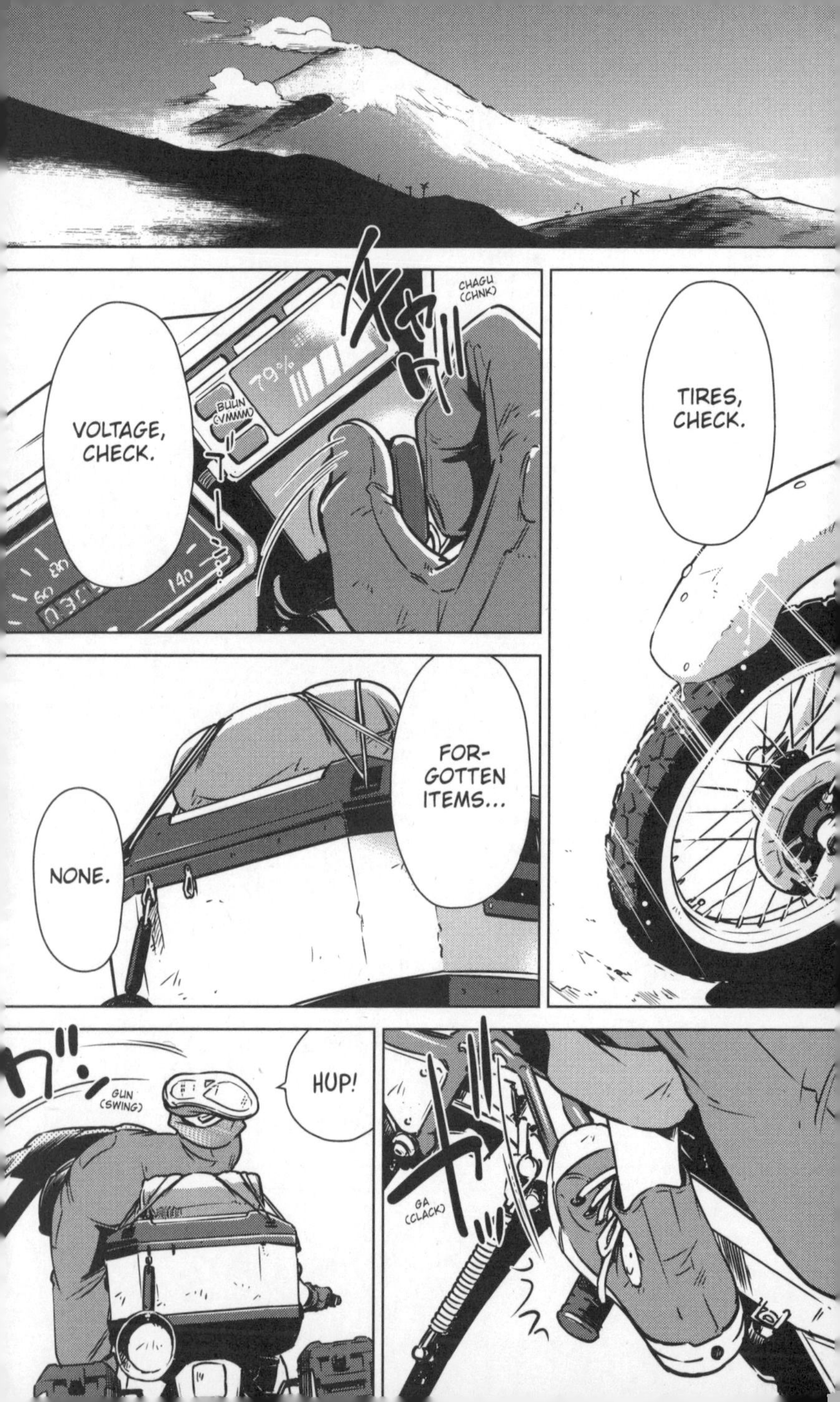
TIRES, CHECK.
CHAGU (CHNK)
BUUN (VMMM)
VOLTAGE, CHECK.
FOR-GOTTEN ITEMS...
NONE.
GA (CLACK)
HUP!
GUN (SWING)

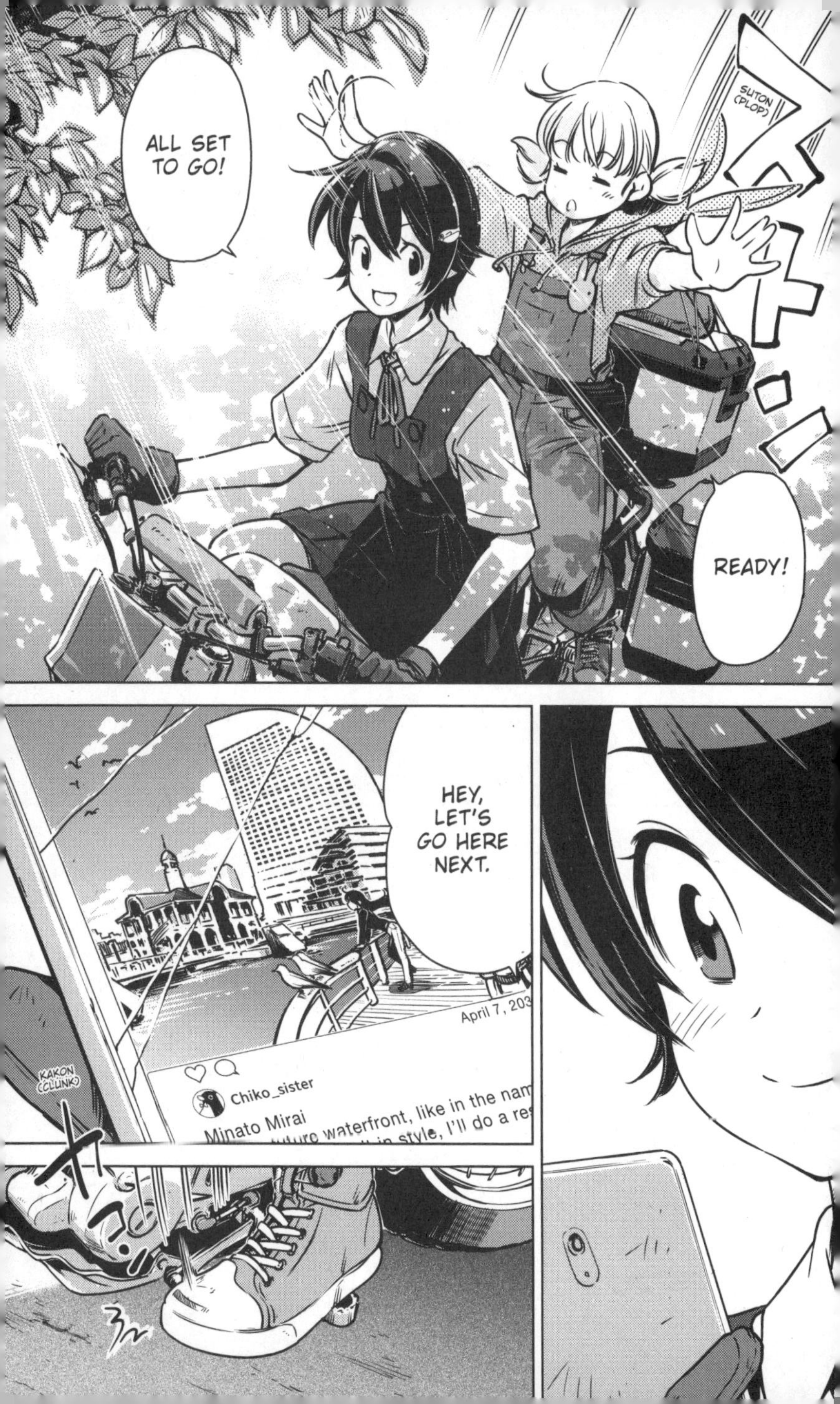
SUTON (PLOP)
READY!
ALL SET TO GO!
HEY, LET'S GO HERE NEXT.
April 7, 203
Chiko_sister
Minato Mirai
waterfront, like in the nam
in style, I'll do a res
KAKON (CLUNK)

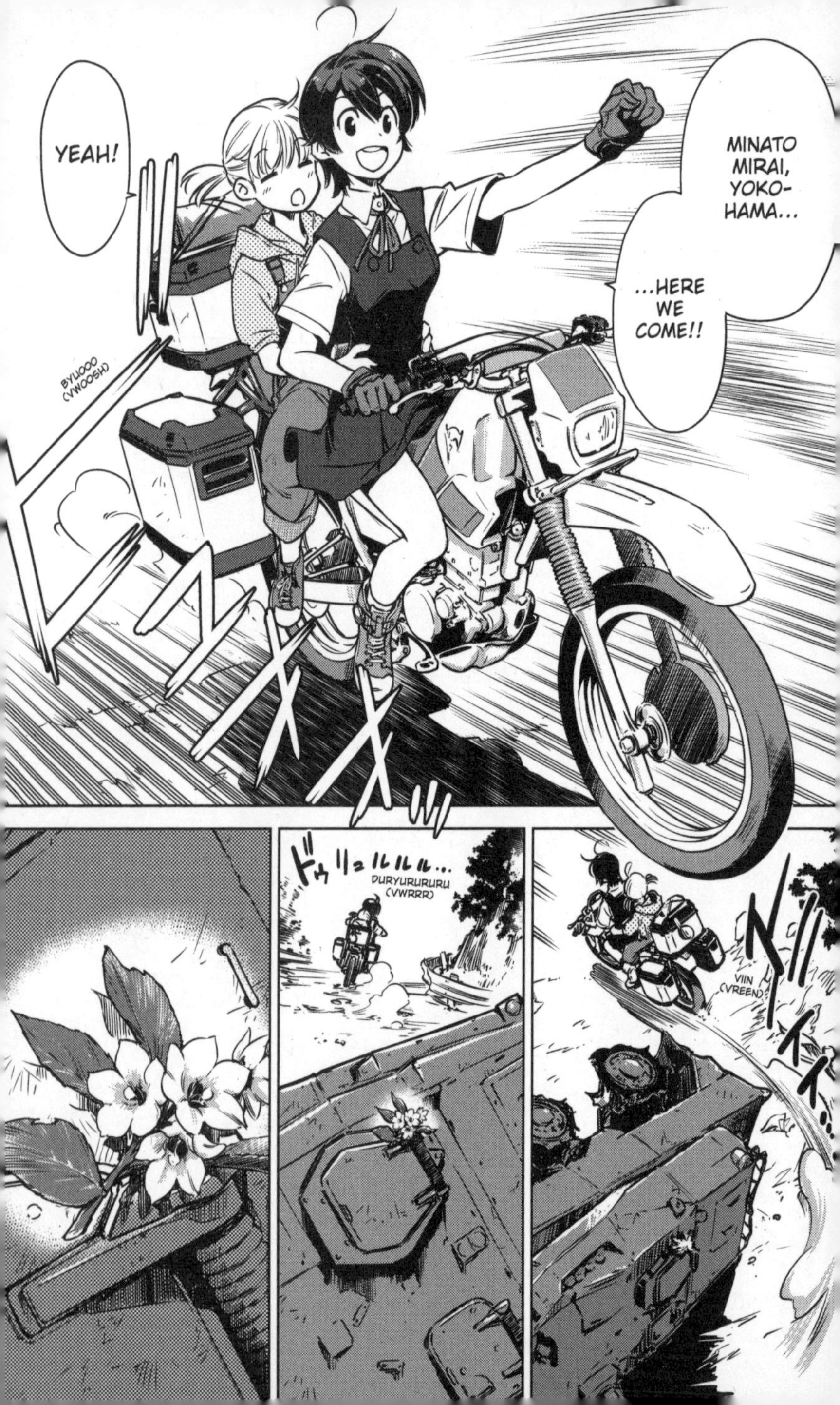
MINATO MIRAI, YOKO-HAMA...
...HERE WE COME!!
YEAH!
BYUOOO (VWOOSH)
VIIN (VREEN)
ドゥリュルルル…
DURYURURURU (VWRRR)

Touringram

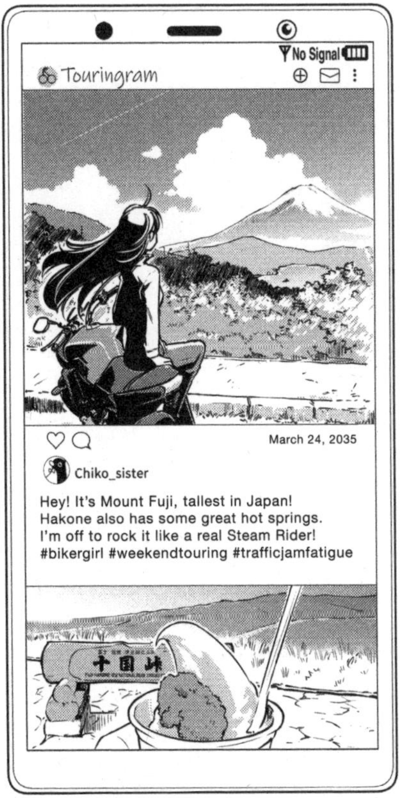
No Signal
Touringram
March 24, 2035
Chiko_sister
Hey! It's Mount Fuji, tallest in Japan!
Hakone also has some great hot springs.
I'm off to rock it like a real Steam Rider!
#bikergirl #weekendtouring #trafficjamfatigue
十国峠

SIGN: JUKKOKU PASS

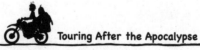
Touring After the Apocalypse

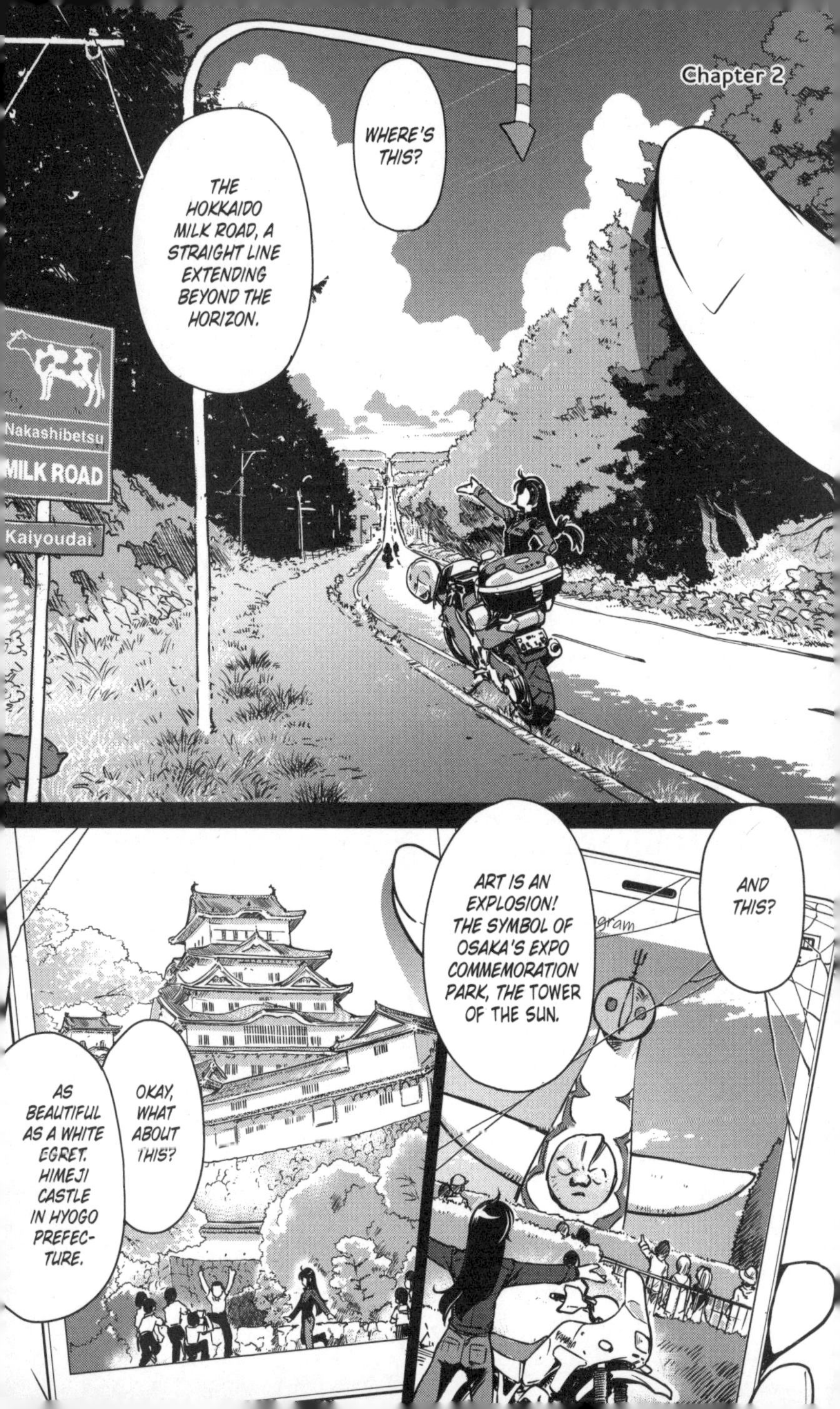
Chapter 2
WHERE'S THIS?
THE HOKKAIDO MILK ROAD, A STRAIGHT LINE EXTENDING BEYOND THE HORIZON.
Nakashibetsu
MILK ROAD
Kaiyoudai
AND THIS?
ART IS AN EXPLOSION! THE SYMBOL OF OSAKA'S EXPO COMMEMORATION PARK, THE TOWER OF THE SUN.
OKAY, WHAT ABOUT THIS?
AS BEAUTIFUL AS A WHITE EGRET. HIMEJI CASTLE IN HYOGO PREFECTURE.

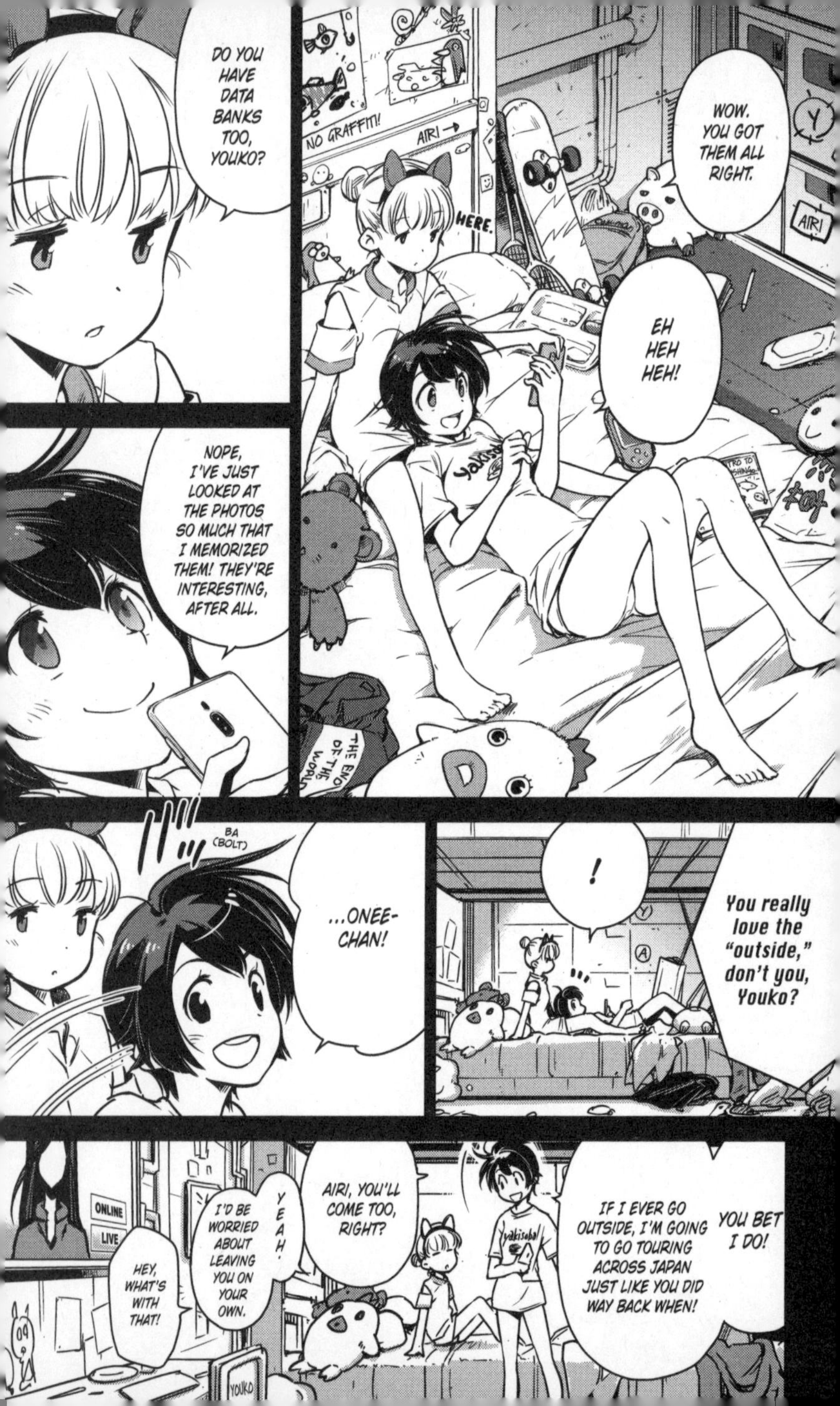
NO GRAFFITI!
AIRI →
AIRI!
WOW. YOU GOT THEM ALL RIGHT.
HERE.
EH HEH HEH!
yakisoba
THE END OF THE WORLD
DO YOU HAVE DATA BANKS TOO, YOUKO?
NOPE, I'VE JUST LOOKED AT THE PHOTOS SO MUCH THAT I MEMORIZED THEM! THEY'RE INTERESTING, AFTER ALL.
!
You really love the "outside," don't you, Youko?
BA (BOLT)
...ONEE-CHAN!
YOU BET I DO!
IF I EVER GO OUTSIDE, I'M GOING TO GO TOURING ACROSS JAPAN JUST LIKE YOU DID WAY BACK WHEN!
yakisoba!
AIRI, YOU'LL COME TOO, RIGHT?
YEAH!
I'D BE WORRIED ABOUT LEAVING YOU ON YOUR OWN.
HEY, WHAT'S WITH THAT!
ONLINE
LIVE
YOUKO

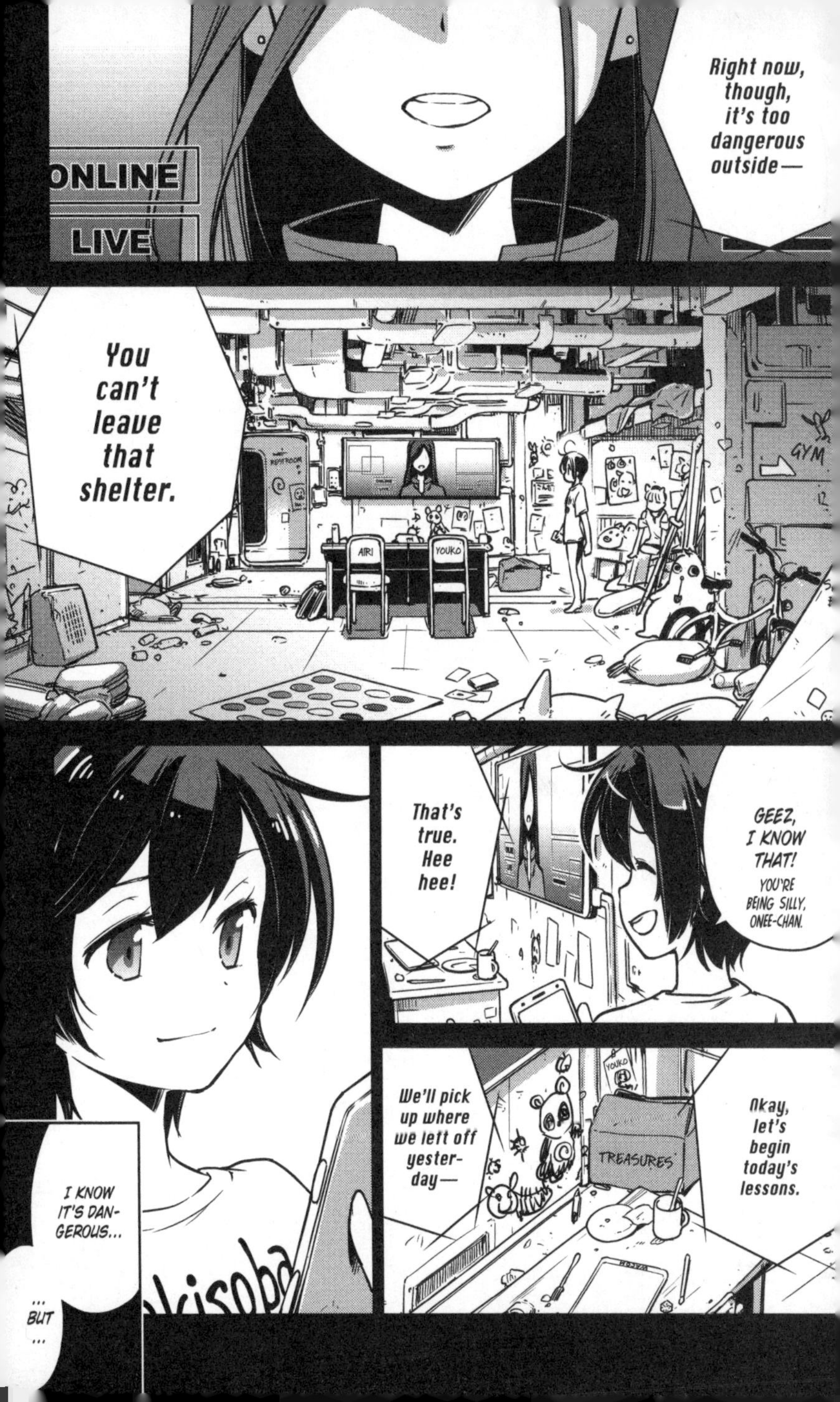
Right now, though, it's too dangerous outside—
ONLINE
LIVE
You can't leave that shelter.
RESTROOM
AIRI
YOUKO
GYM
GEEZ, I KNOW THAT! YOU'RE BEING SILLY, ONEE-CHAN.
That's true. Hee hee!
Okay, let's begin today's lessons.
We'll pick up where we left off yesterday—
YOUKO
TREASURES
I KNOW IT'S DANGEROUS...
...BUT...

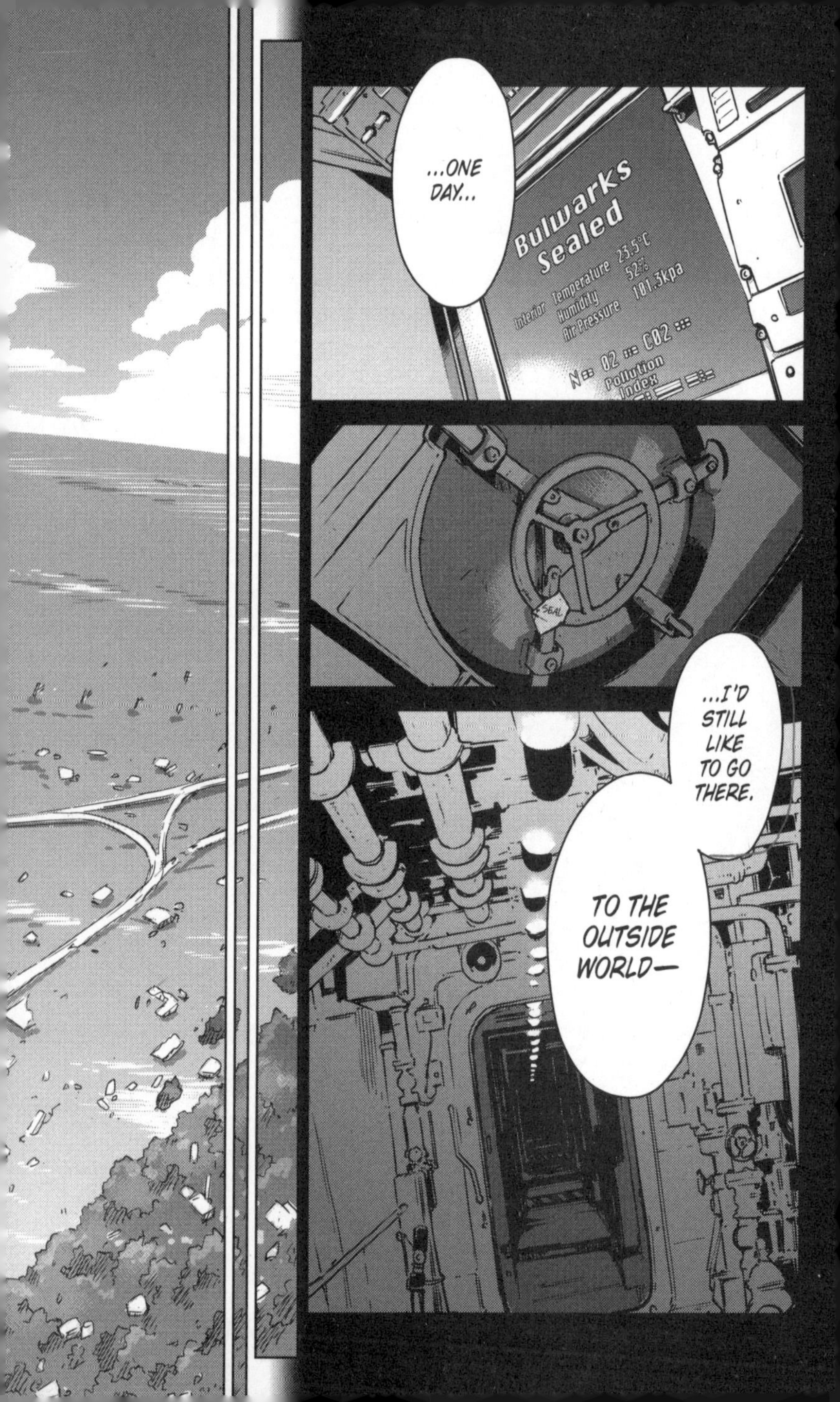
...ONE DAY...
Bulwarks Sealed
Interior Temperature 23.5°C
Humidity 52%
Air Pressure 101.3kpa
N 02 CO2
Pollution Index
SEAL
...I'D STILL LIKE TO GO THERE.
TO THE OUTSIDE WORLD—

| Chapter 2 | Yokohama and Yokosuka

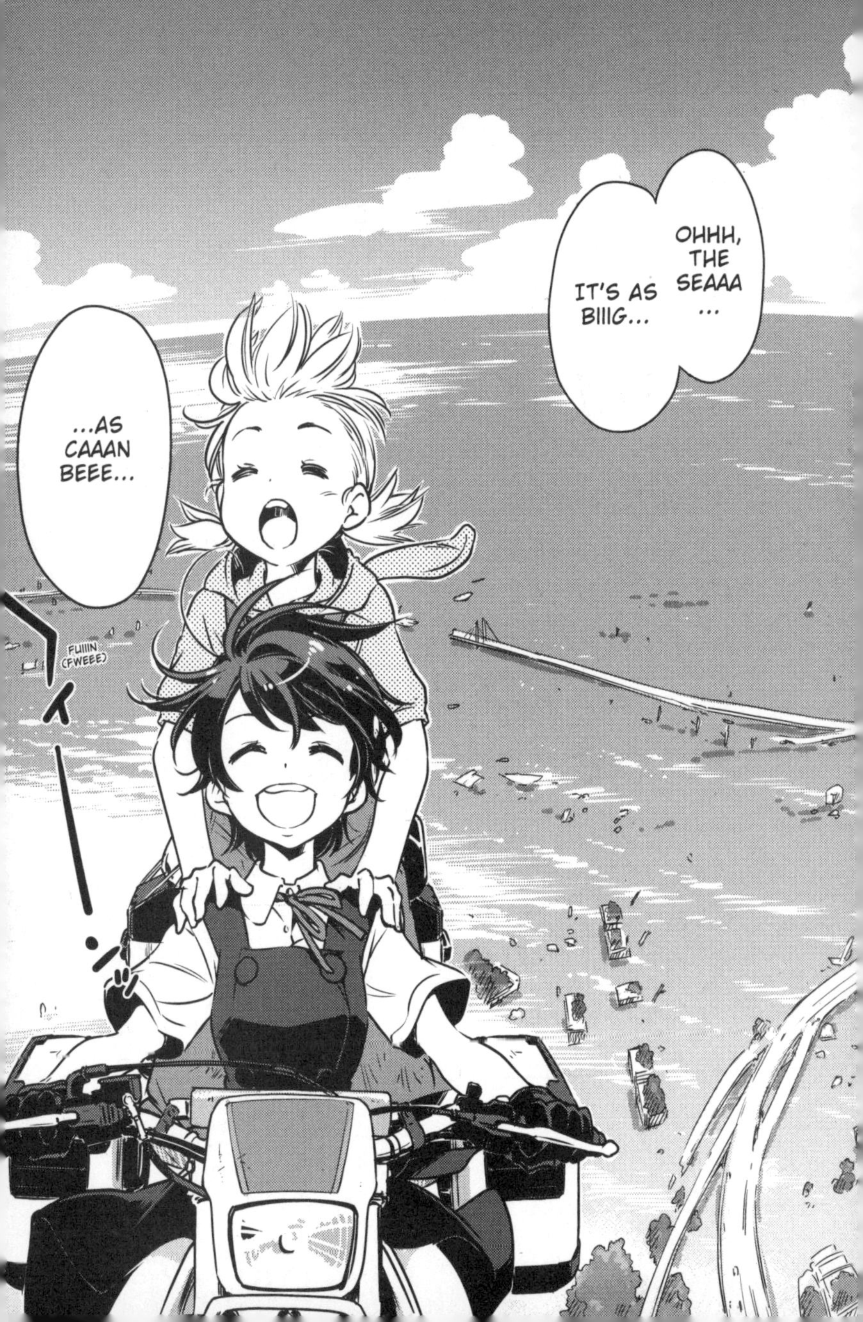
OHHH, THE SEAAA ...
IT'S AS BIIIG...
...AS CAAAN BEEE...
FUIIIN (FWEEE)

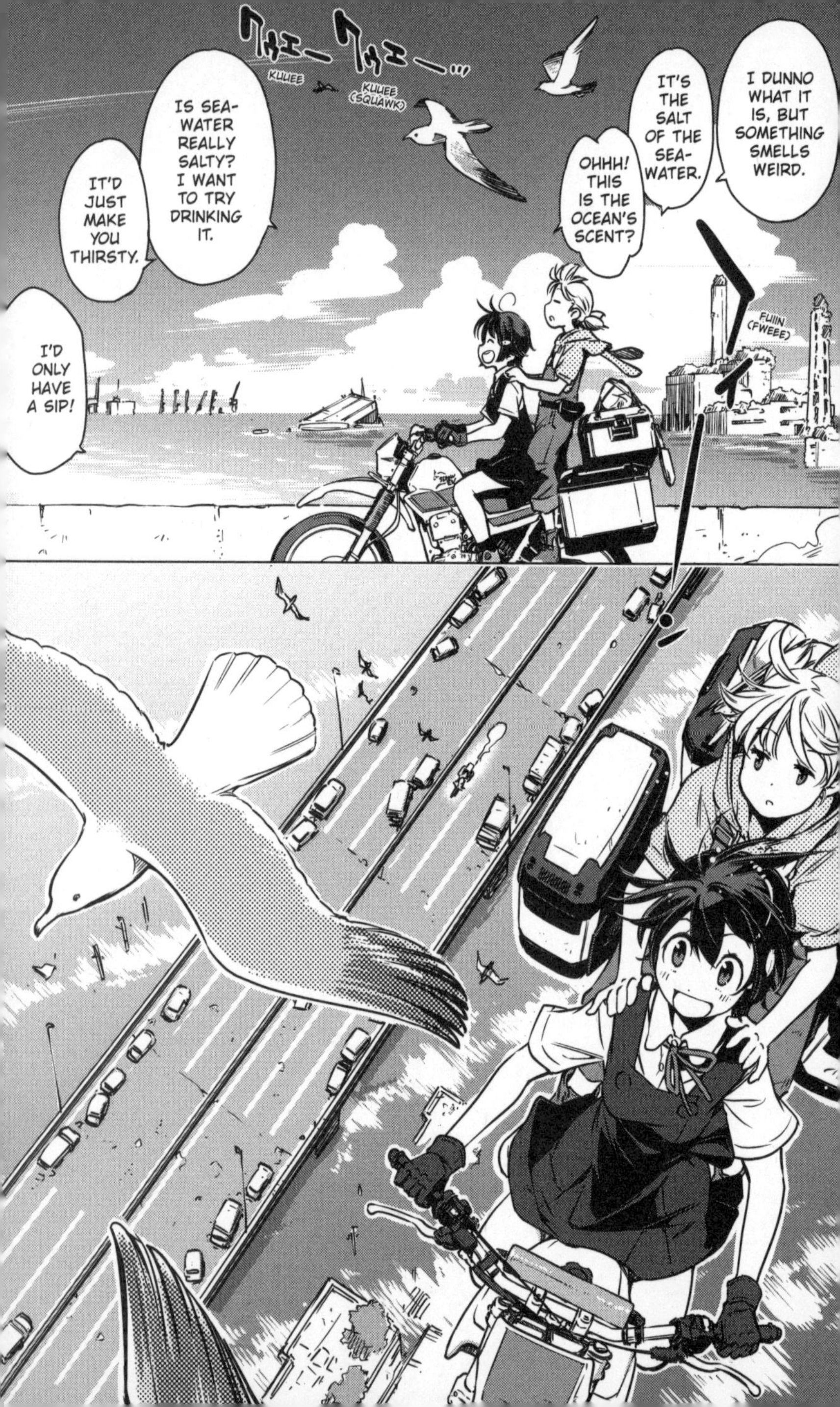
I DUNNO WHAT IT IS, BUT SOMETHING SMELLS WEIRD.
IT'S THE SALT OF THE SEA-WATER.
OHHH! THIS IS THE OCEAN'S SCENT?
FUIIN (FWEEE)
クウェー クウェー…
KUUEE (SQUAWK)
KUUEE
IS SEA-WATER REALLY SALTY? I WANT TO TRY DRINKING IT.
IT'D JUST MAKE YOU THIRSTY.
I'D ONLY HAVE A SIP!

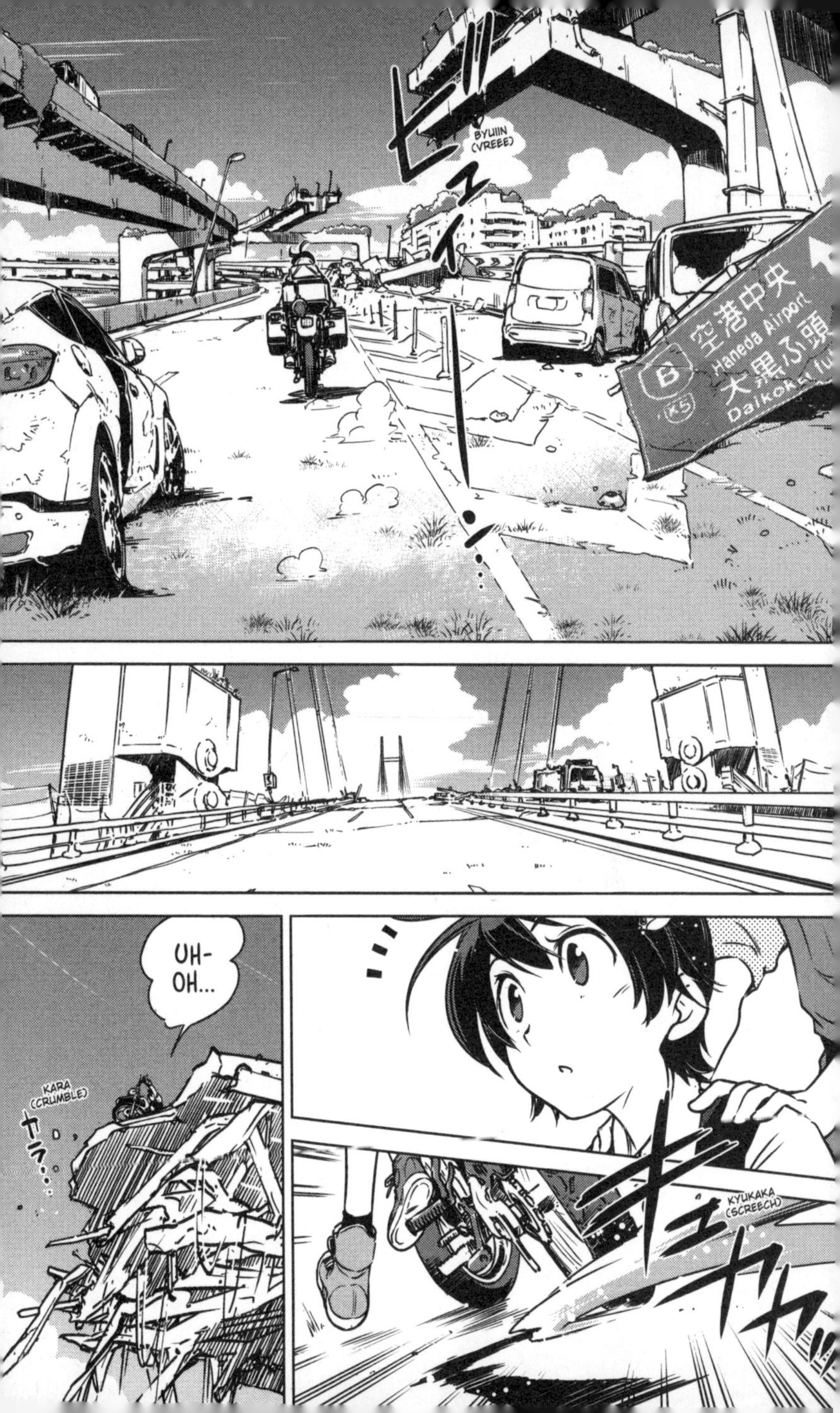
BYUIIN (VREEE)
空港中央
Haneda Airport
大黒ふ頭
KYUKAKA (SCREECH)
UH-OH...
KARA (CRUMBLE)

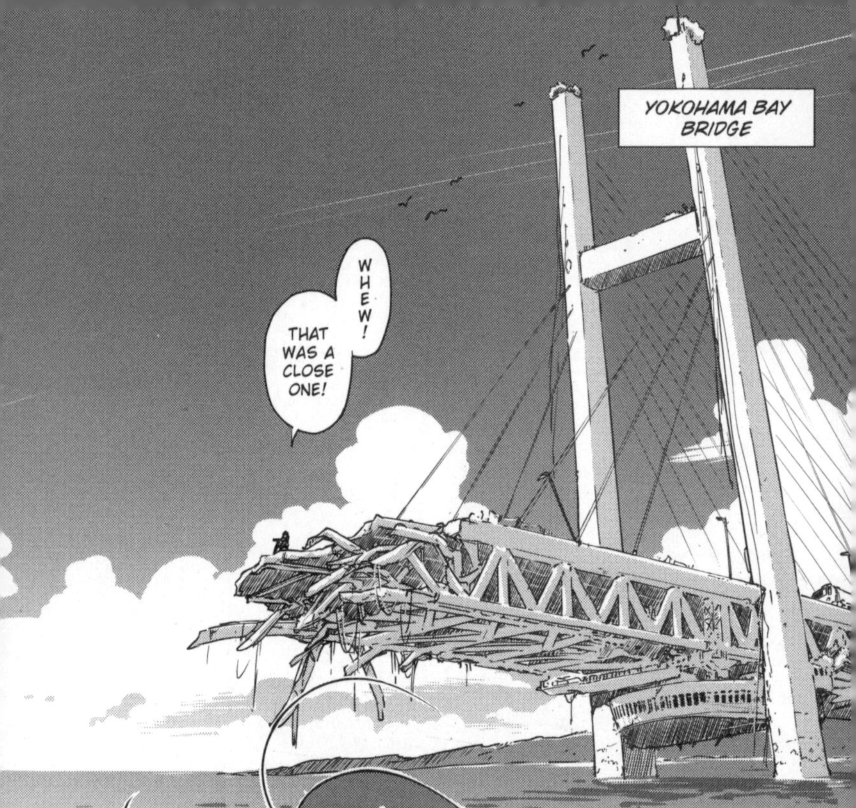

YOKOHAMA BAY BRIDGE
WHEW!
THAT WAS A CLOSE ONE!

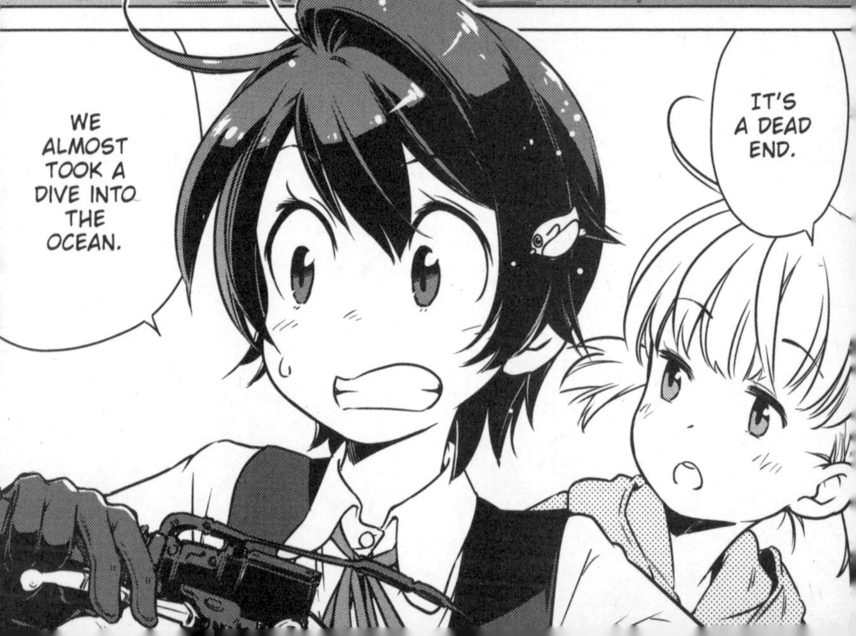

IT'S A DEAD END.
WE ALMOST TOOK A DIVE INTO THE OCEAN.

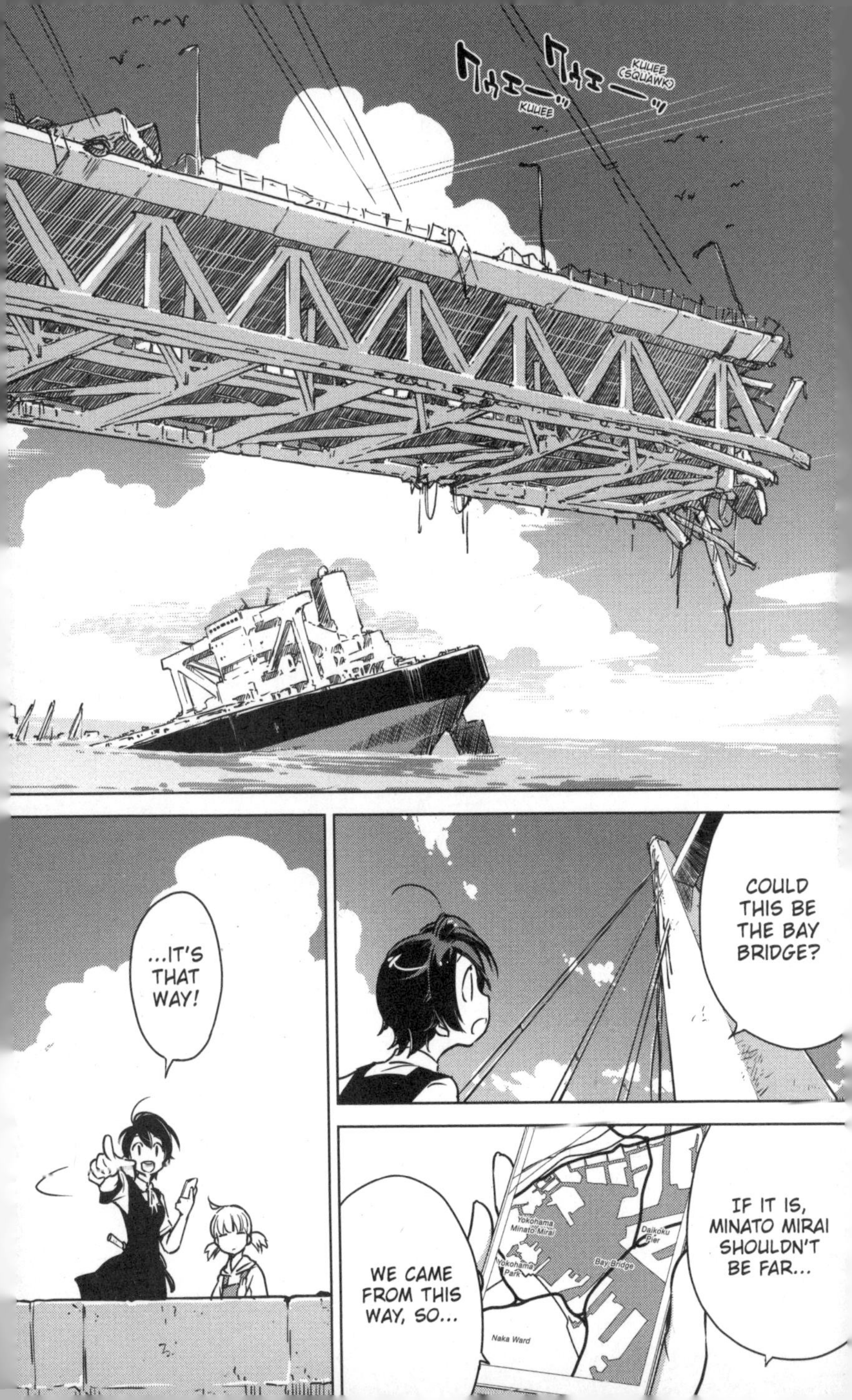
クゥエーーッ
KUUEE (SQUAWK)
クゥエーーッ
KUUEE
COULD THIS BE THE BAY BRIDGE?
IF IT IS, MINATO MIRAI SHOULDN'T BE FAR...
Yokohama Minato Mirai
Daikoku Pier
Yokohama Park
Bay Bridge
Naka Ward
WE CAME FROM THIS WAY, SO...
...IT'S THAT WAY!

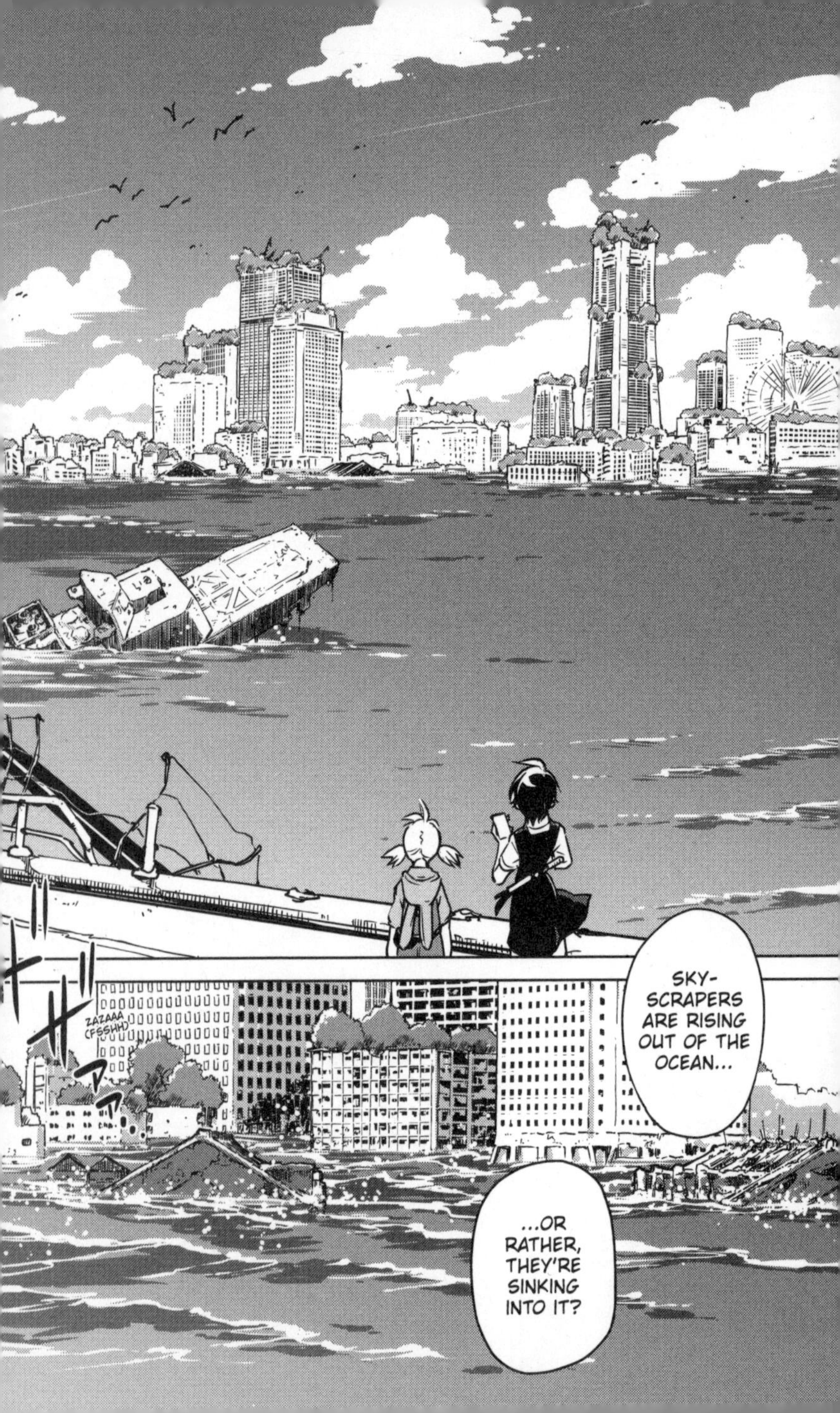
SKY-SCRAPERS ARE RISING OUT OF THE OCEAN...
ZAZAAA (FSSHH)
...OR RATHER, THEY'RE SINKING INTO IT?

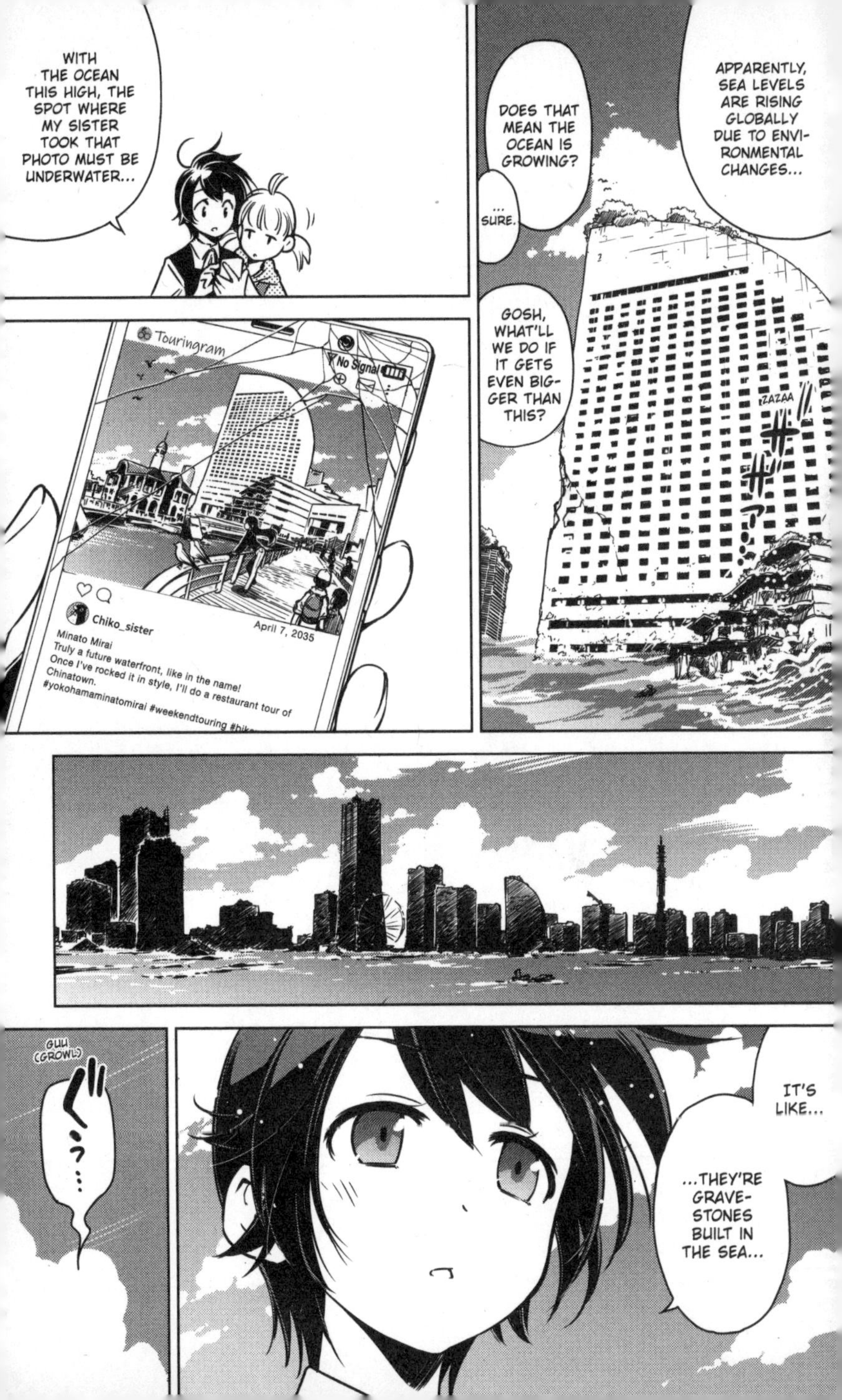
APPARENTLY, SEA LEVELS ARE RISING GLOBALLY DUE TO ENVIRONMENTAL CHANGES...
DOES THAT MEAN THE OCEAN IS GROWING?
...SURE.
GOSH, WHAT'LL WE DO IF IT GETS EVEN BIGGER THAN THIS?
ZAZAA
WITH THE OCEAN THIS HIGH, THE SPOT WHERE MY SISTER TOOK THAT PHOTO MUST BE UNDERWATER...
Touringram
No Signal
Chiko_sister
April 7, 2035
Minato Mirai
Truly a future waterfront, like in the name!
Once I've rocked it in style, I'll do a restaurant tour of Chinatown.
#yokohamaminatomirai #weekendtouring
IT'S LIKE...
...THEY'RE GRAVESTONES BUILT IN THE SEA...
GUU (GROWL)
ぐぅ…

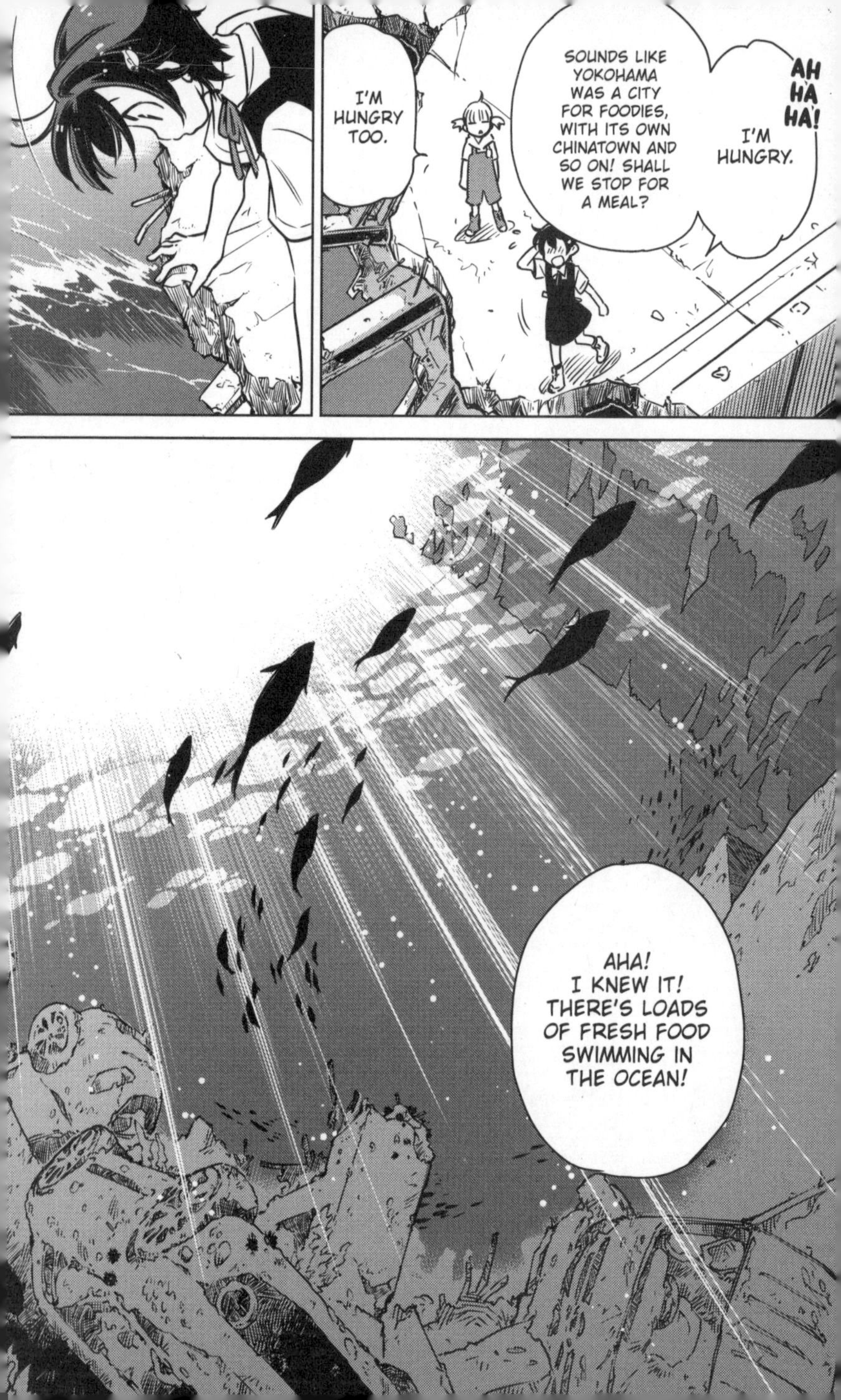
AH HA HA!
I'M HUNGRY.
SOUNDS LIKE YOKOHAMA WAS A CITY FOR FOODIES, WITH ITS OWN CHINATOWN AND SO ON! SHALL WE STOP FOR A MEAL?
I'M HUNGRY TOO.
AHA! I KNEW IT! THERE'S LOADS OF FRESH FOOD SWIMMING IN THE OCEAN!

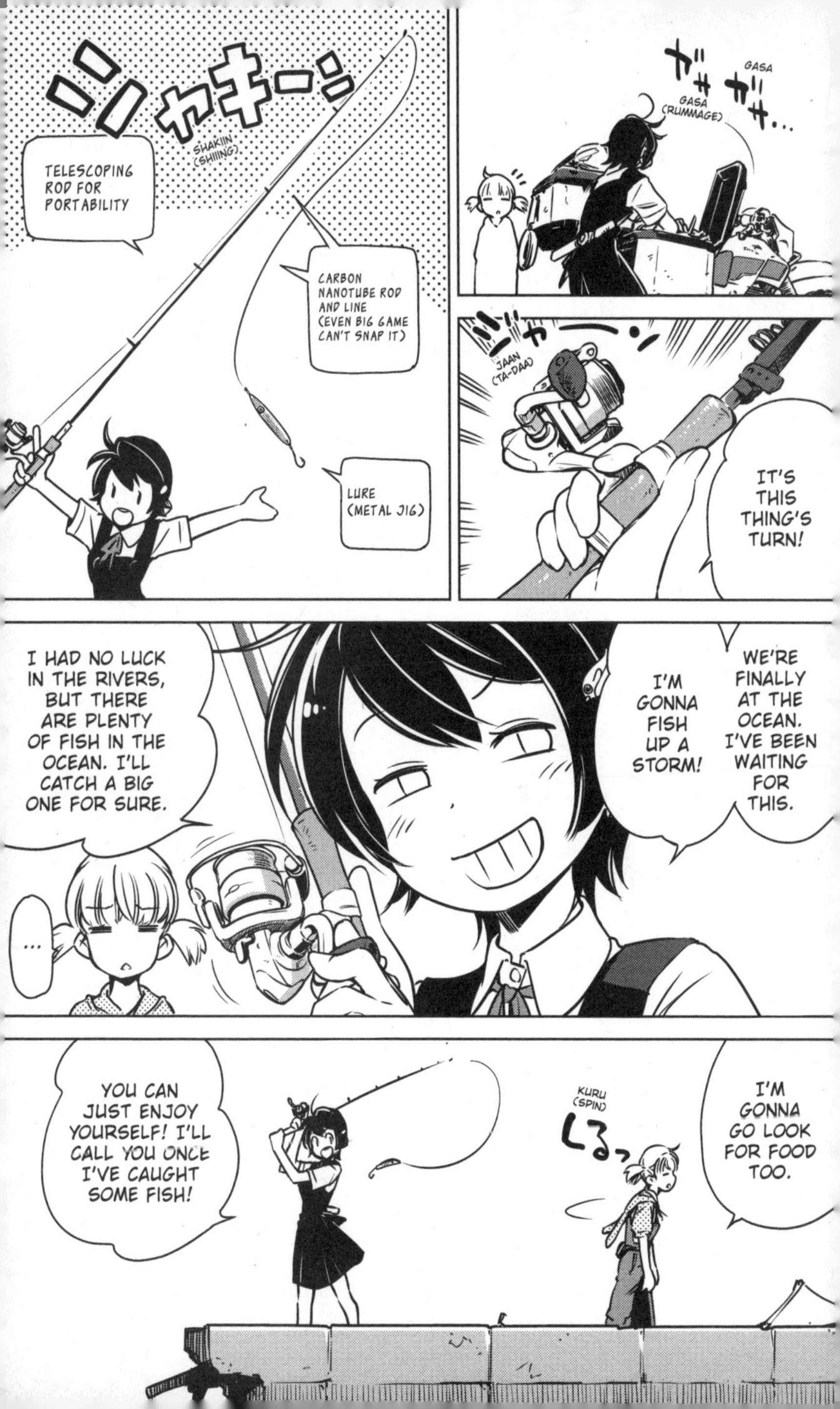
GASA
GASA (RUMMAGE)
JAAN (TA-DAA)
IT'S THIS THING'S TURN!
SHAKIIN (SHIIING)
TELESCOPING ROD FOR PORTABILITY
CARBON NANOTUBE ROD AND LINE (EVEN BIG GAME CAN'T SNAP IT)
LURE (METAL JIG)
WE'RE FINALLY AT THE OCEAN. I'VE BEEN WAITING FOR THIS.
I'M GONNA FISH UP A STORM!
I HAD NO LUCK IN THE RIVERS, BUT THERE ARE PLENTY OF FISH IN THE OCEAN. I'LL CATCH A BIG ONE FOR SURE.
...
I'M GONNA GO LOOK FOR FOOD TOO.
KURU (SPIN)
YOU CAN JUST ENJOY YOURSELF! I'LL CALL YOU ONCE I'VE CAUGHT SOME FISH!

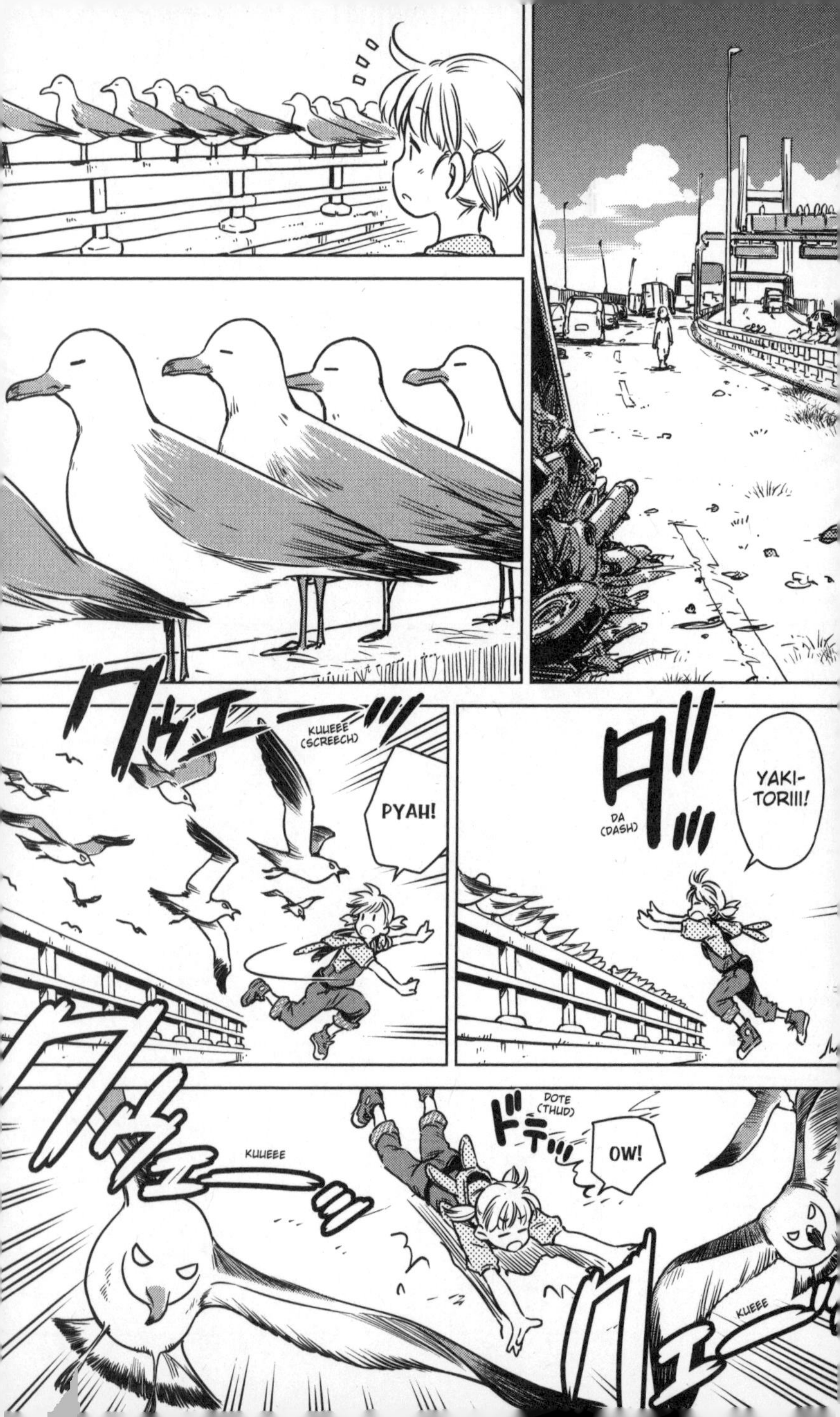
YAKI-TORIII!
DA (DASH)
KUWEEE (SCREECH)
PYAH!
DOTE (THUD)
OW!
KUWEEE
KUEEE

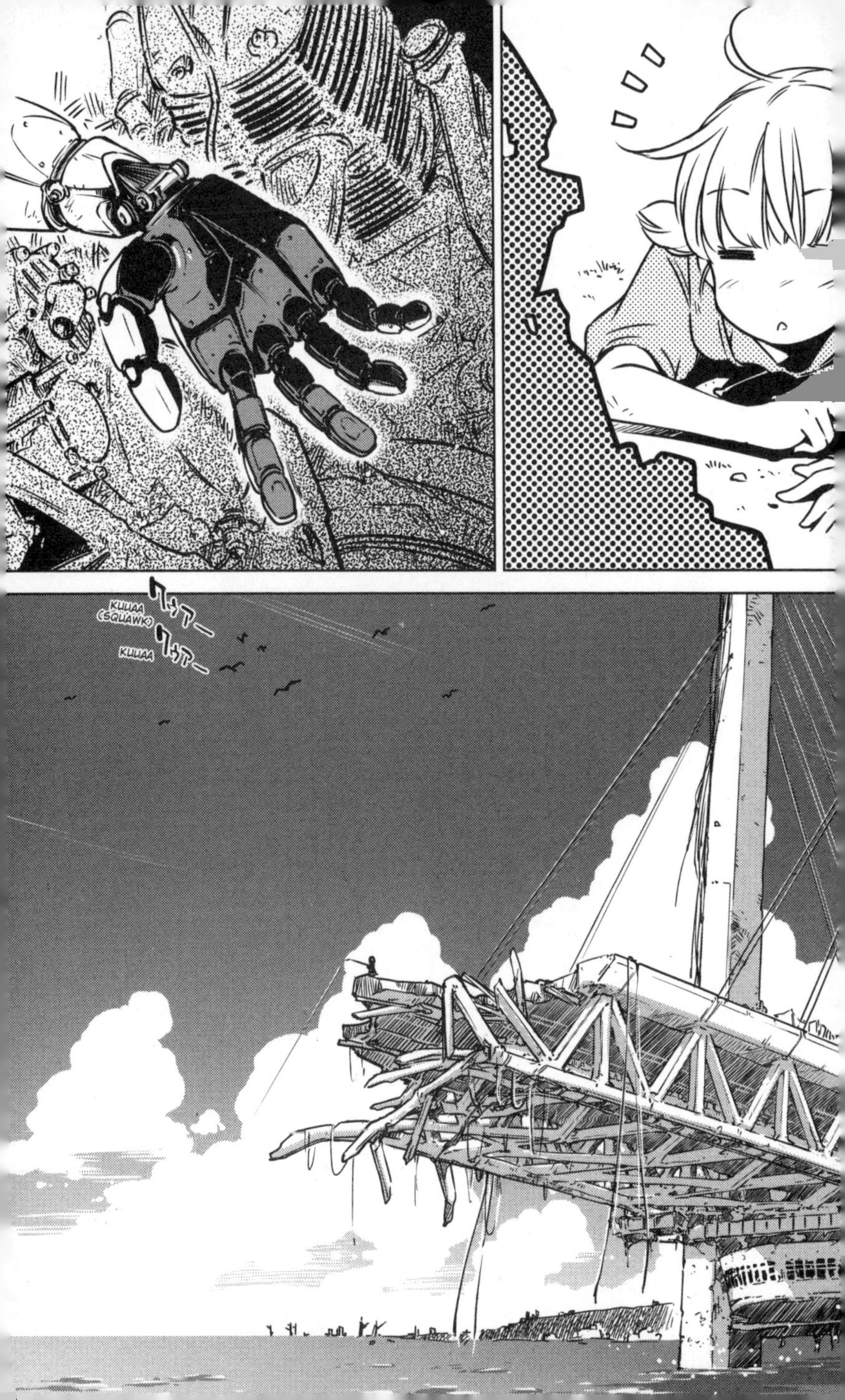
クゥアー
KUUAA (SQUAWK)
クゥアー
KUUAA

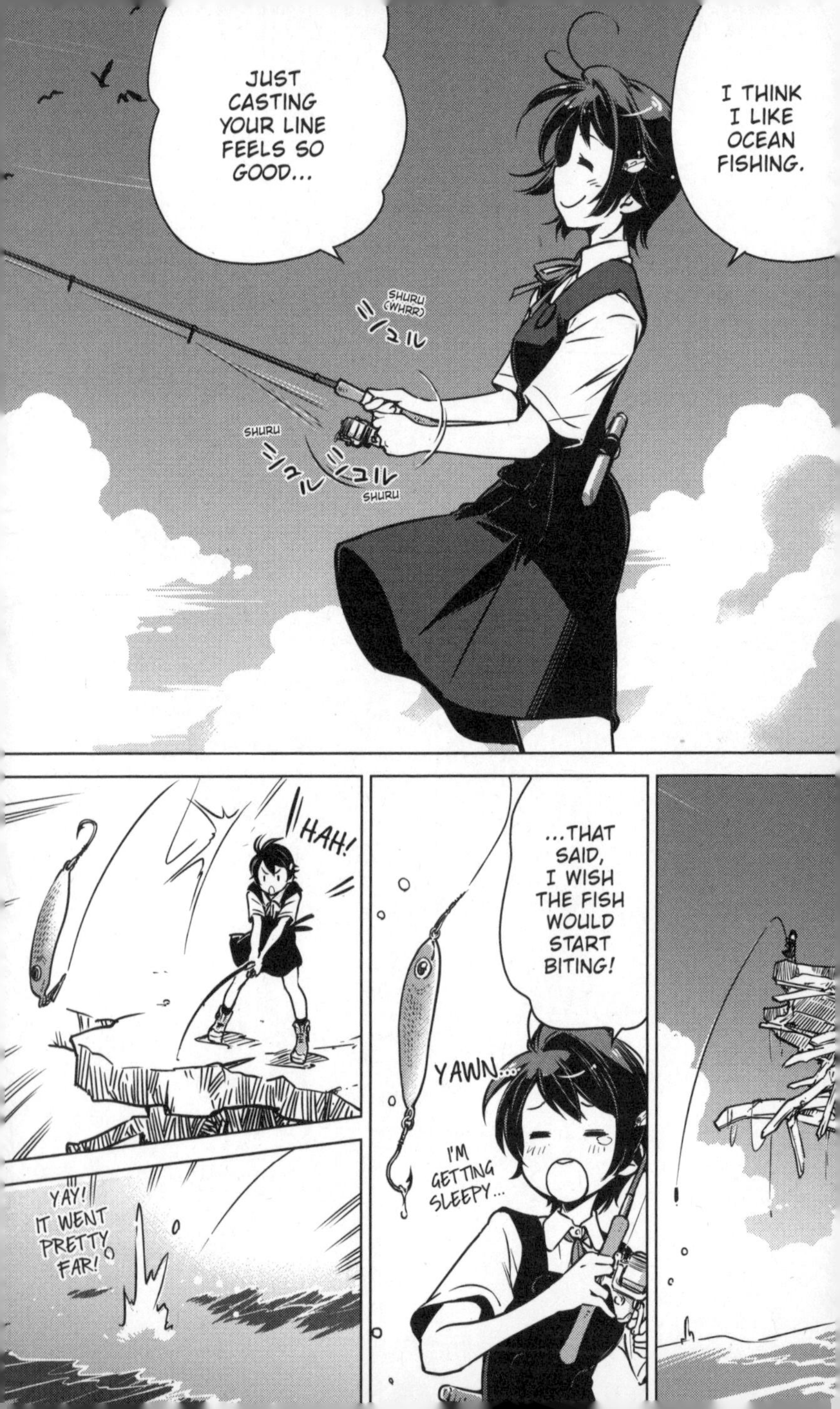
I THINK I LIKE OCEAN FISHING.
JUST CASTING YOUR LINE FEELS SO GOOD...
シュル
SHURU (WHRR)
シュル
SHURU
シュル
SHURU
...THAT SAID, I WISH THE FISH WOULD START BITING!
YAWN...
I'M GETTING SLEEPY...
HAH!
YAY! IT WENT PRETTY FAR!

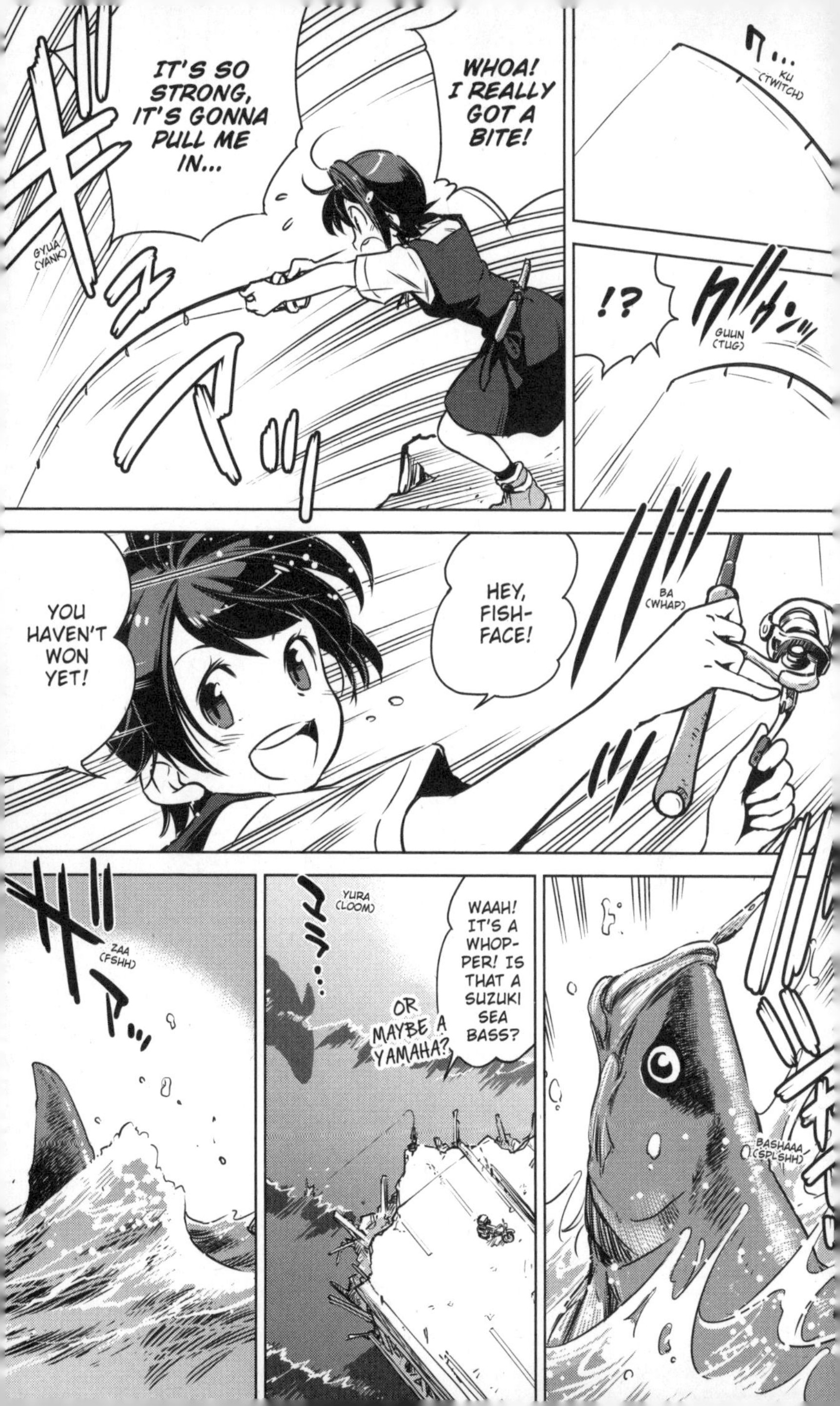
KU (TWITCH)
!?
GUUN (TUG)
WHOA! I REALLY GOT A BITE!
IT'S SO STRONG, IT'S GONNA PULL ME IN...
GYUA (YANK)
BA (WHAP)
HEY, FISH-FACE!
YOU HAVEN'T WON YET!
BASHAAA (SPLSHH)
YURA (LOOM)
WAAH! IT'S A WHOPPER! IS THAT A SUZUKI SEA BASS?
OR MAYBE A YAMAHA?
ZAA (FSHH)

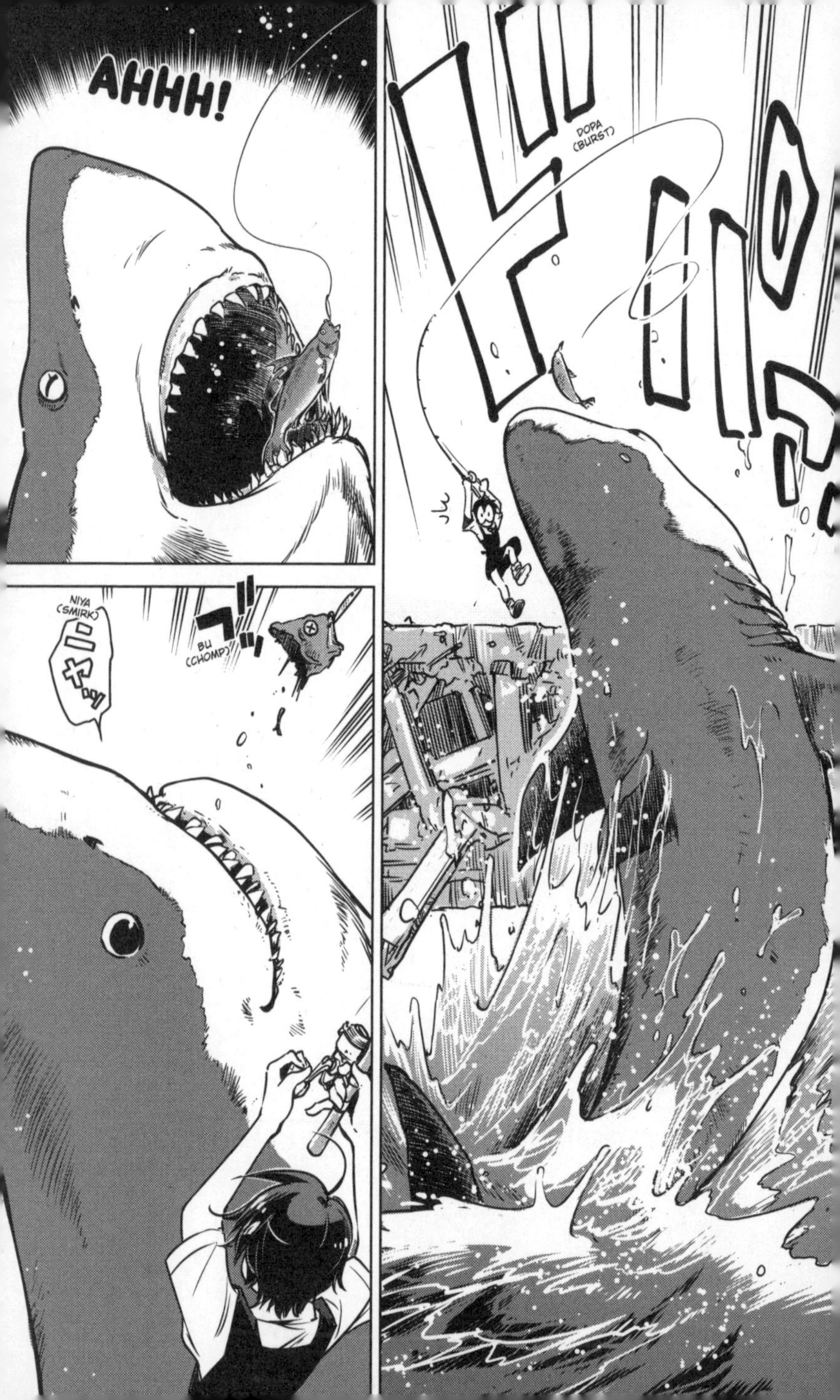
DOPA
(BURST)
AHHHH!
BU
(CHOMP)
NIYA
(SMIRK)

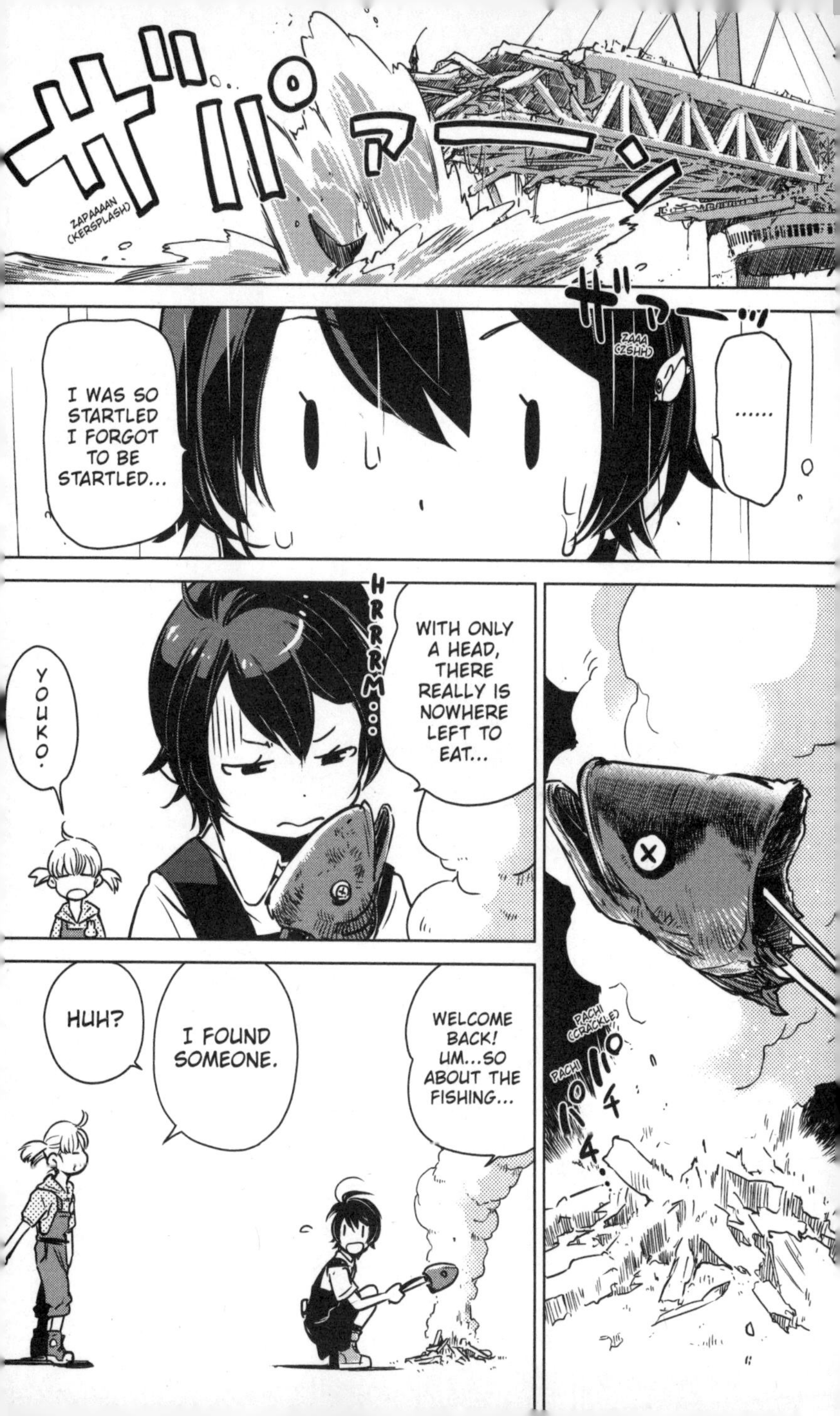
ザパァーン
ZAPAAAAN (KERSPLASH)
ザァーッ
ZAAA (ZSHH)
......
I WAS SO STARTLED I FORGOT TO BE STARTLED...
PACHI (CRACKLE)
PACHI
HRRRM...
WITH ONLY A HEAD, THERE REALLY IS NOWHERE LEFT TO EAT...
YOUKO.
WELCOME BACK! UM...SO ABOUT THE FISHING...
I FOUND SOMEONE.
HUH?

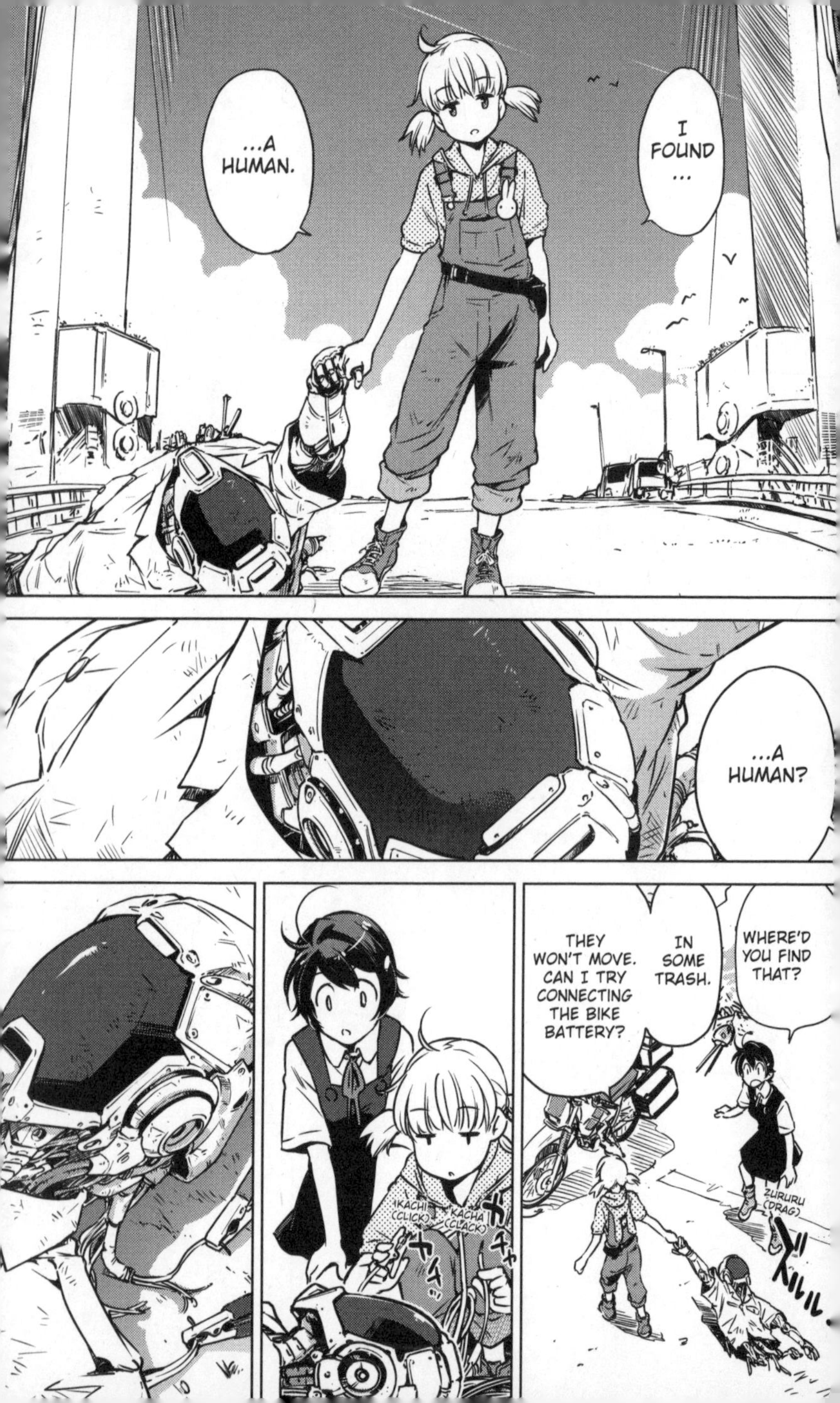
I FOUND ...
...A HUMAN.
...A HUMAN?
WHERE'D YOU FIND THAT?
IN SOME TRASH.
THEY WON'T MOVE. CAN I TRY CONNECTING THE BIKE BATTERY?
ZURURU (DRAG)
KACHA (CLACK)
KACHI (CLICK)

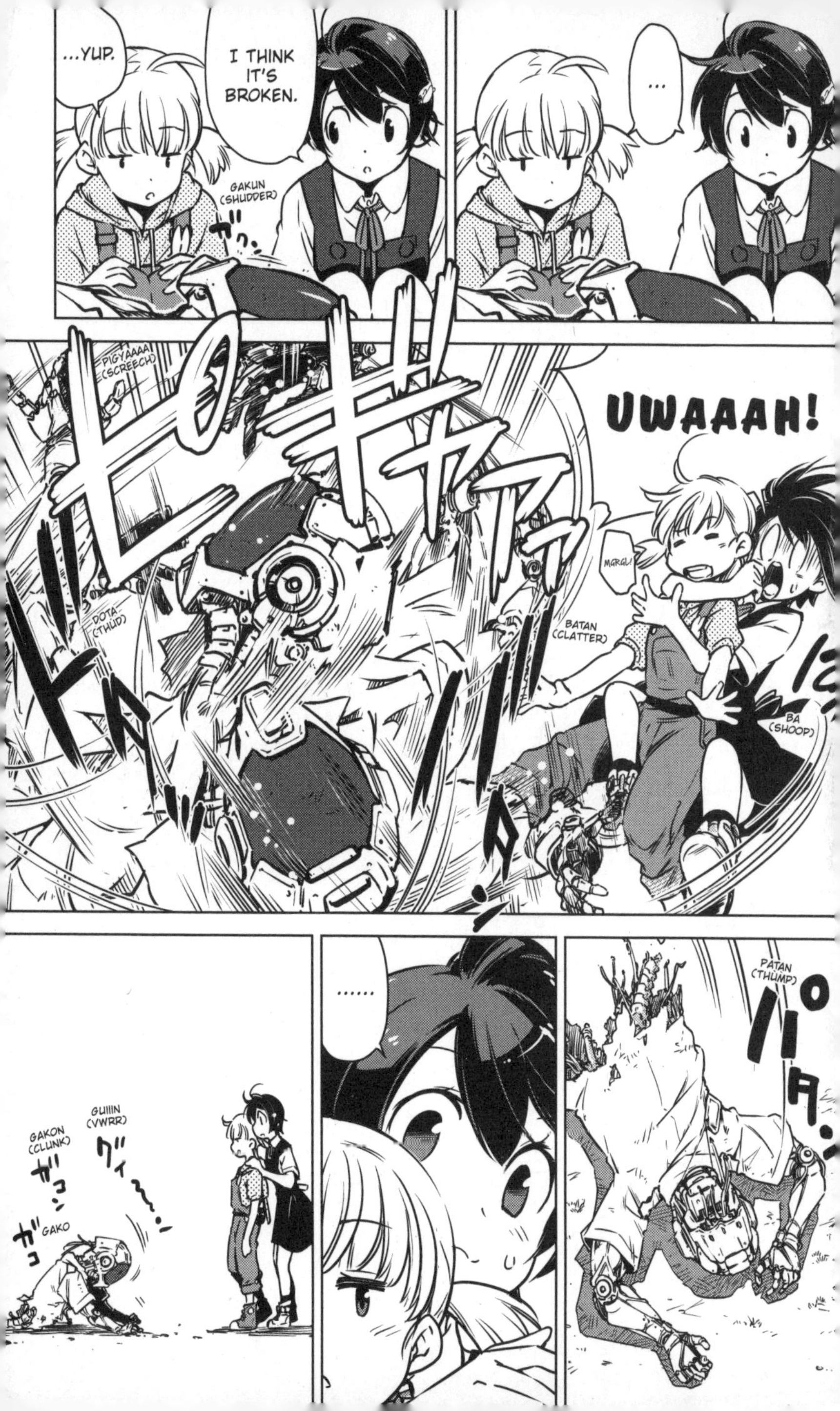
...
I THINK IT'S BROKEN.
...YUP.
GAKUN (SHUDDER)
UWAAAH!
MGRGL!
BATAN (CLATTER)
BA (SHOOP)
PIGYAAAA (SCREECH)
DOTA (THUD)
PATAN (THUMP)
......
GUIIIN (VWRR)
GAKON (CLUNK)
GAKO

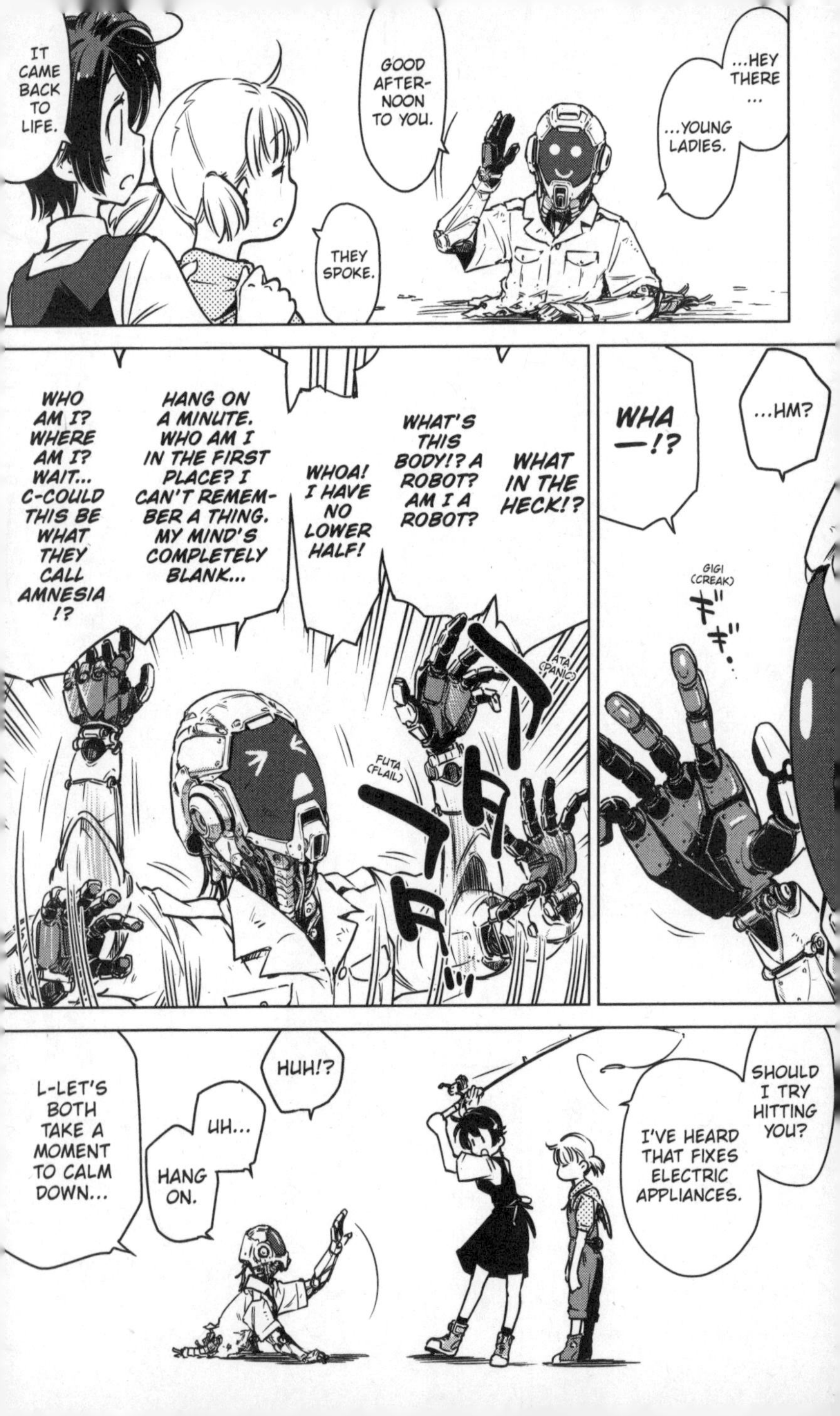
...HEY THERE... ...YOUNG LADIES.
GOOD AFTERNOON TO YOU.
THEY SPOKE.
IT CAME BACK TO LIFE.
...HM?
WHA—!?
GIGI (CREAK)
WHAT IN THE HECK!?
WHAT'S THIS BODY!? A ROBOT? AM I A ROBOT?
WHOA! I HAVE NO LOWER HALF!
HANG ON A MINUTE. WHO AM I IN THE FIRST PLACE? I CAN'T REMEMBER A THING. MY MIND'S COMPLETELY BLANK...
WHO AM I? WHERE AM I? WAIT... C-COULD THIS BE WHAT THEY CALL AMNESIA!?
ATA (PANIC)
FUTA (FLAIL)
SHOULD I TRY HITTING YOU?
I'VE HEARD THAT FIXES ELECTRIC APPLIANCES.
HUH!?
UH...
HANG ON.
L-LET'S BOTH TAKE A MOMENT TO CALM DOWN...

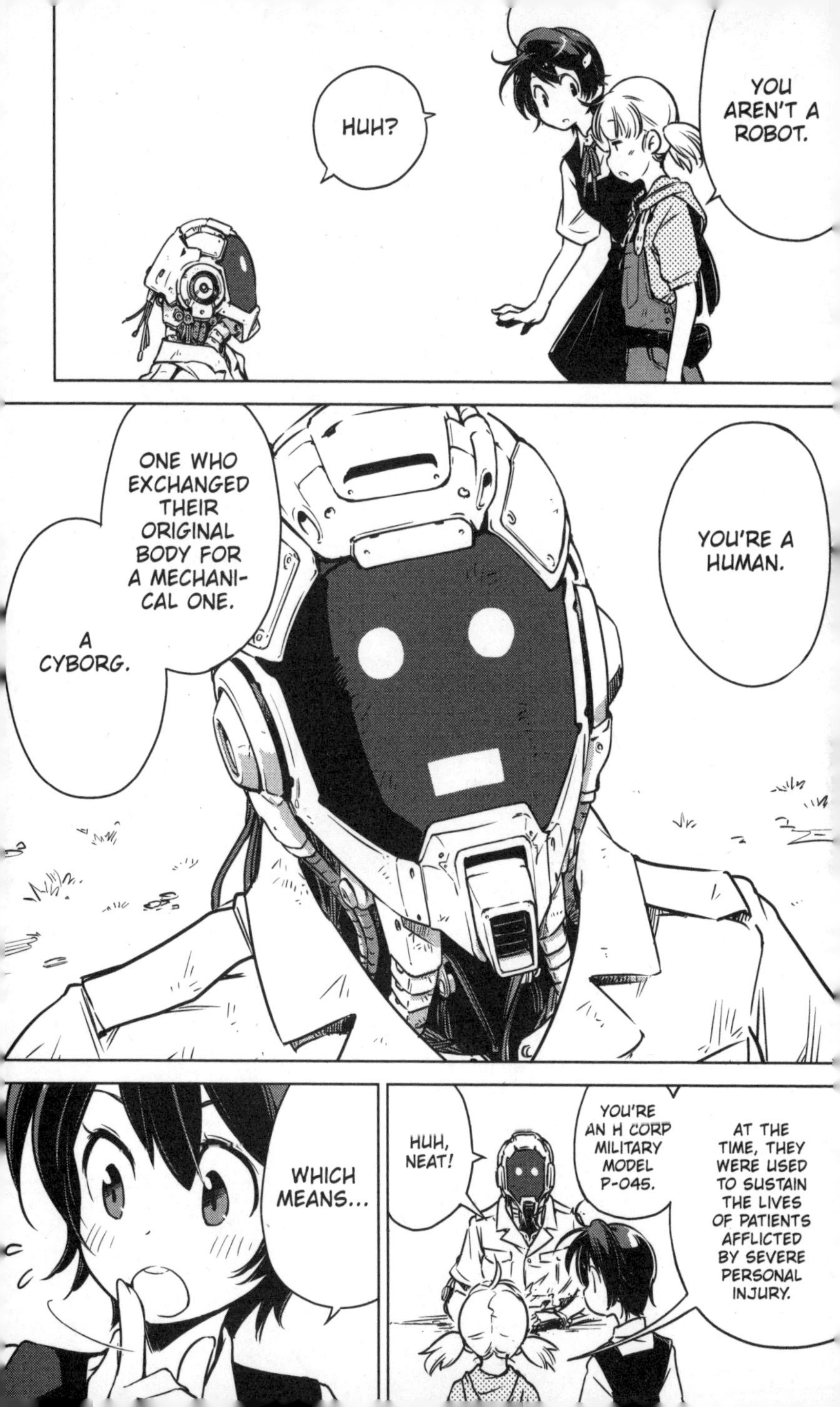
YOU AREN'T A ROBOT.
HUH?
YOU'RE A HUMAN.
ONE WHO EXCHANGED THEIR ORIGINAL BODY FOR A MECHANI-CAL ONE.
A CYBORG.
YOU'RE AN H CORP MILITARY MODEL P-045.
AT THE TIME, THEY WERE USED TO SUSTAIN THE LIVES OF PATIENTS AFFLICTED BY SEVERE PERSONAL INJURY.
HUH, NEAT!
WHICH MEANS...

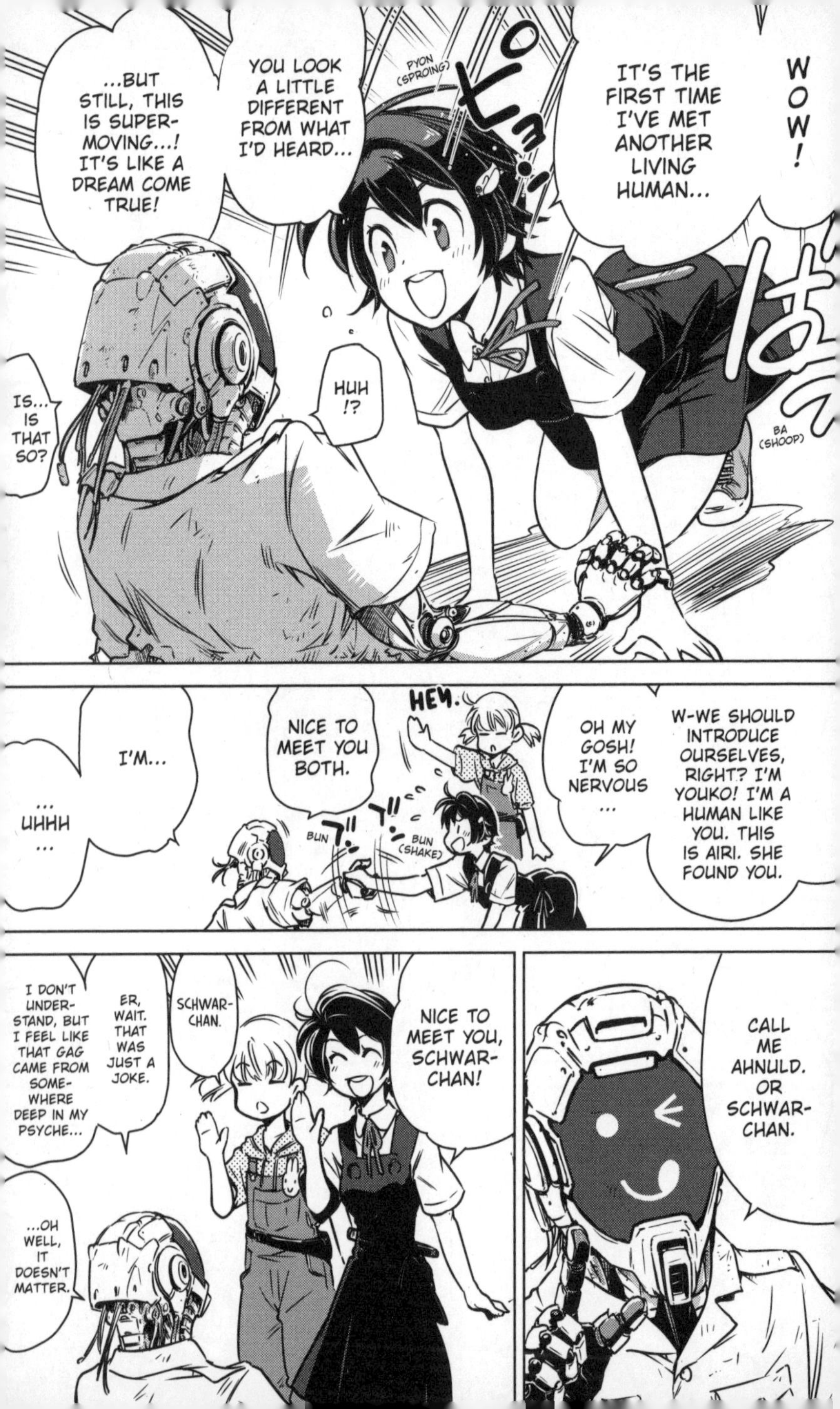
WOW!
IT'S THE FIRST TIME I'VE MET ANOTHER LIVING HUMAN...
PYON (SPROING)
YOU LOOK A LITTLE DIFFERENT FROM WHAT I'D HEARD...
...BUT STILL, THIS IS SUPER-MOVING...! IT'S LIKE A DREAM COME TRUE!
BA (SHOOP)
HUH!?
IS... IS THAT SO?
W-WE SHOULD INTRODUCE OURSELVES, RIGHT? I'M YOUKO! I'M A HUMAN LIKE YOU. THIS IS AIRI. SHE FOUND YOU.
OH MY GOSH! I'M SO NERVOUS...
HEY.
NICE TO MEET YOU BOTH.
BUN (SHAKE)
BUN
I'M...
... UHHH ...
CALL ME AHNULD. OR SCHWAR-CHAN.
NICE TO MEET YOU, SCHWAR-CHAN!
SCHWAR-CHAN.
ER, WAIT. THAT WAS JUST A JOKE.
I DON'T UNDER-STAND, BUT I FEEL LIKE THAT GAG CAME FROM SOME-WHERE DEEP IN MY PSYCHE...
...OH WELL, IT DOESN'T MATTER.

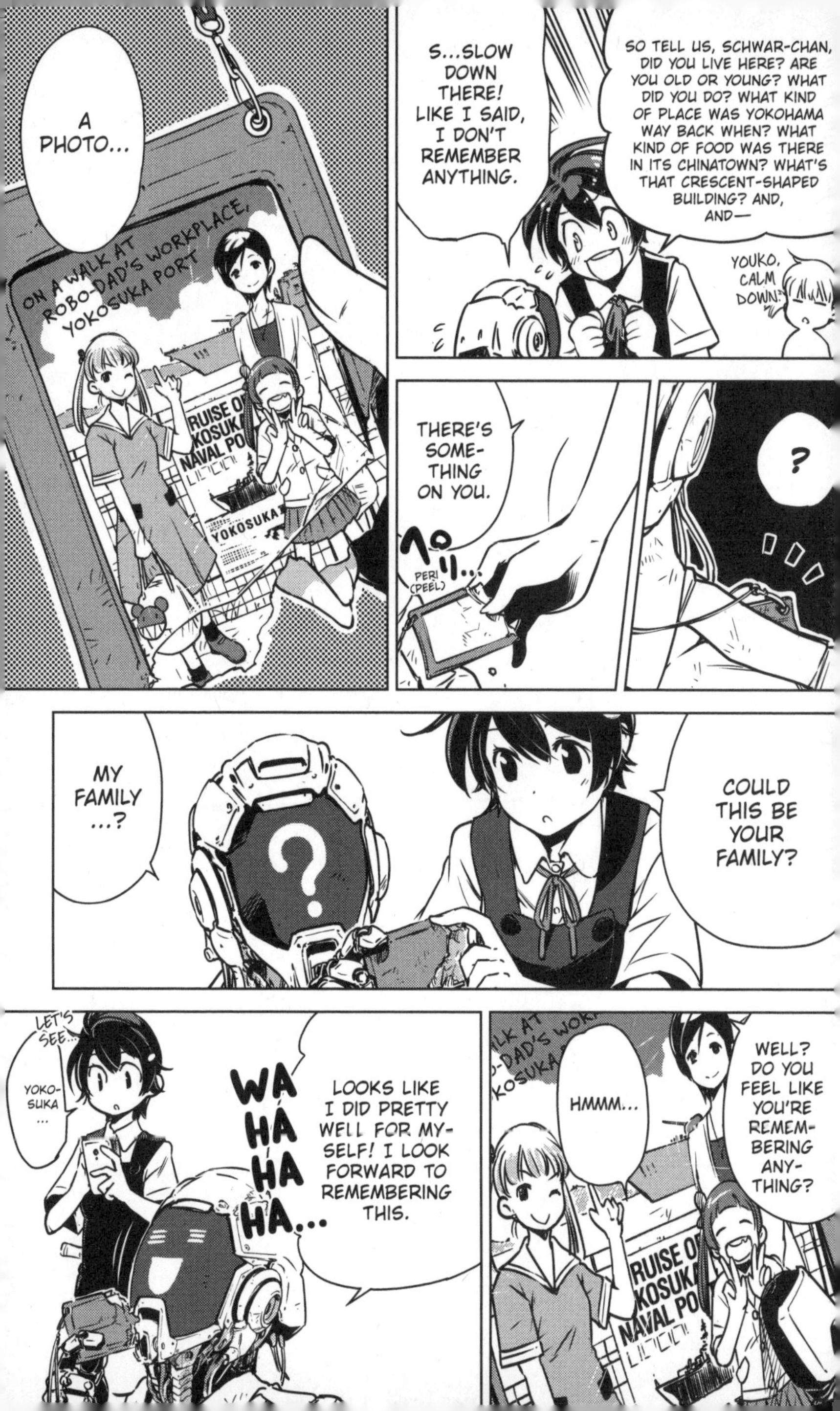
SO TELL US, SCHWAR-CHAN, DID YOU LIVE HERE? ARE YOU OLD OR YOUNG? WHAT DID YOU DO? WHAT KIND OF PLACE WAS YOKOHAMA WAY BACK WHEN? WHAT KIND OF FOOD WAS THERE IN ITS CHINATOWN? WHAT'S THAT CRESCENT-SHAPED BUILDING? AND, AND—
S...SLOW DOWN THERE! LIKE I SAID, I DON'T REMEMBER ANYTHING.
YOUKO, CALM DOWN.
?
THERE'S SOME-THING ON YOU.
PERI (PEEL)
A PHOTO...
ON A WALK AT ROBO-DAD'S WORKPLACE, YOKOSUKA PORT
RUISE OF KOSUKA NAVAL PO
YOKOSUKA
COULD THIS BE YOUR FAMILY?
MY FAMILY ...?
WELL? DO YOU FEEL LIKE YOU'RE REMEM-BERING ANY-THING?
HMMM...
LOOKS LIKE I DID PRETTY WELL FOR MY-SELF! I LOOK FORWARD TO REMEMBERING THIS.
WA HA HA HA...
LET'S SEE...
YOKO-SUKA ...

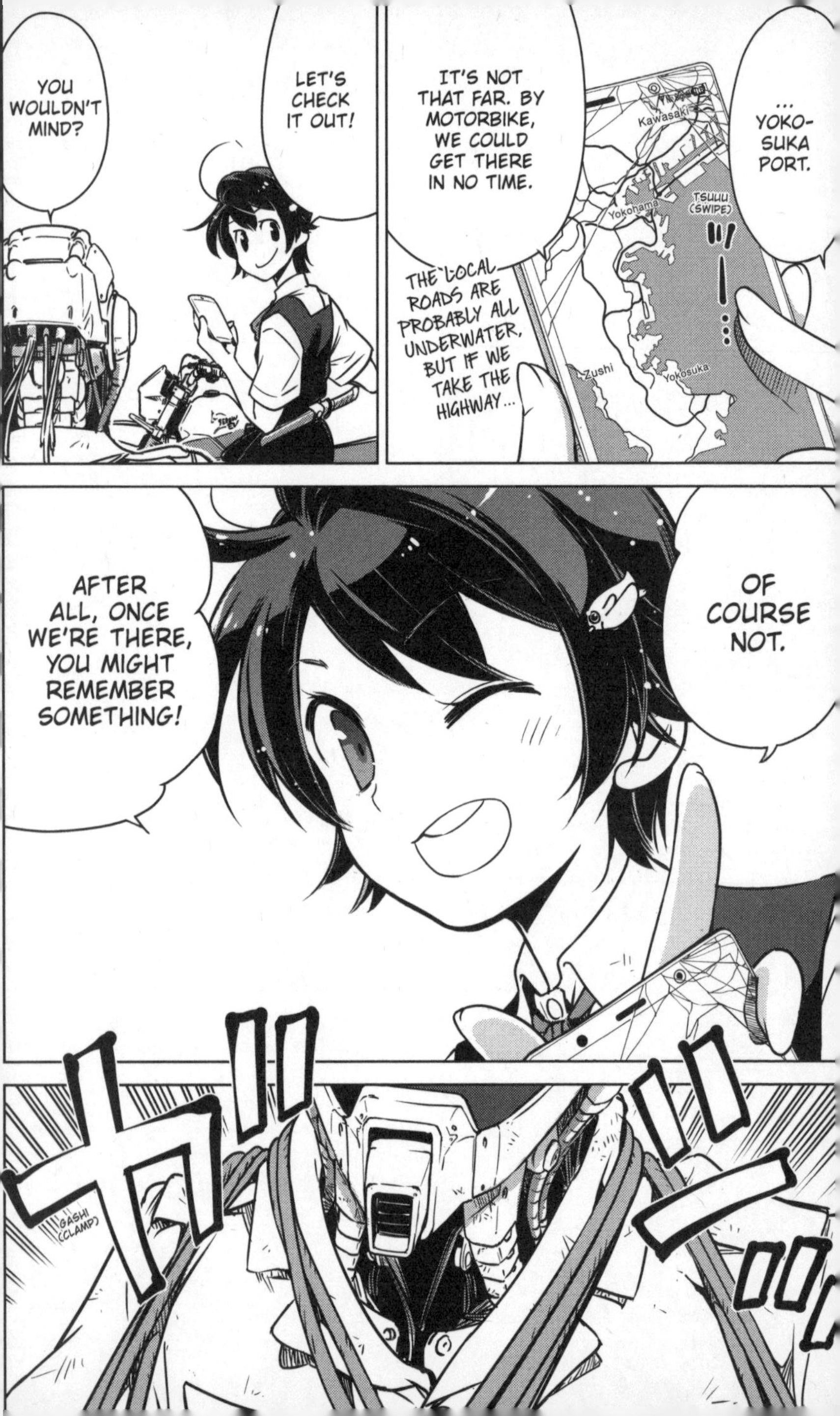
... YOKO-SUKA PORT.
TSUUU (SWIPE)
Kawasaki
Yokohama
Zushi
Yokosuka
IT'S NOT THAT FAR. BY MOTORBIKE, WE COULD GET THERE IN NO TIME.
THE LOCAL ROADS ARE PROBABLY ALL UNDERWATER, BUT IF WE TAKE THE HIGHWAY...
LET'S CHECK IT OUT!
YOU WOULDN'T MIND?
OF COURSE NOT.
AFTER ALL, ONCE WE'RE THERE, YOU MIGHT REMEMBER SOMETHING!
GASHI (CLAMP)

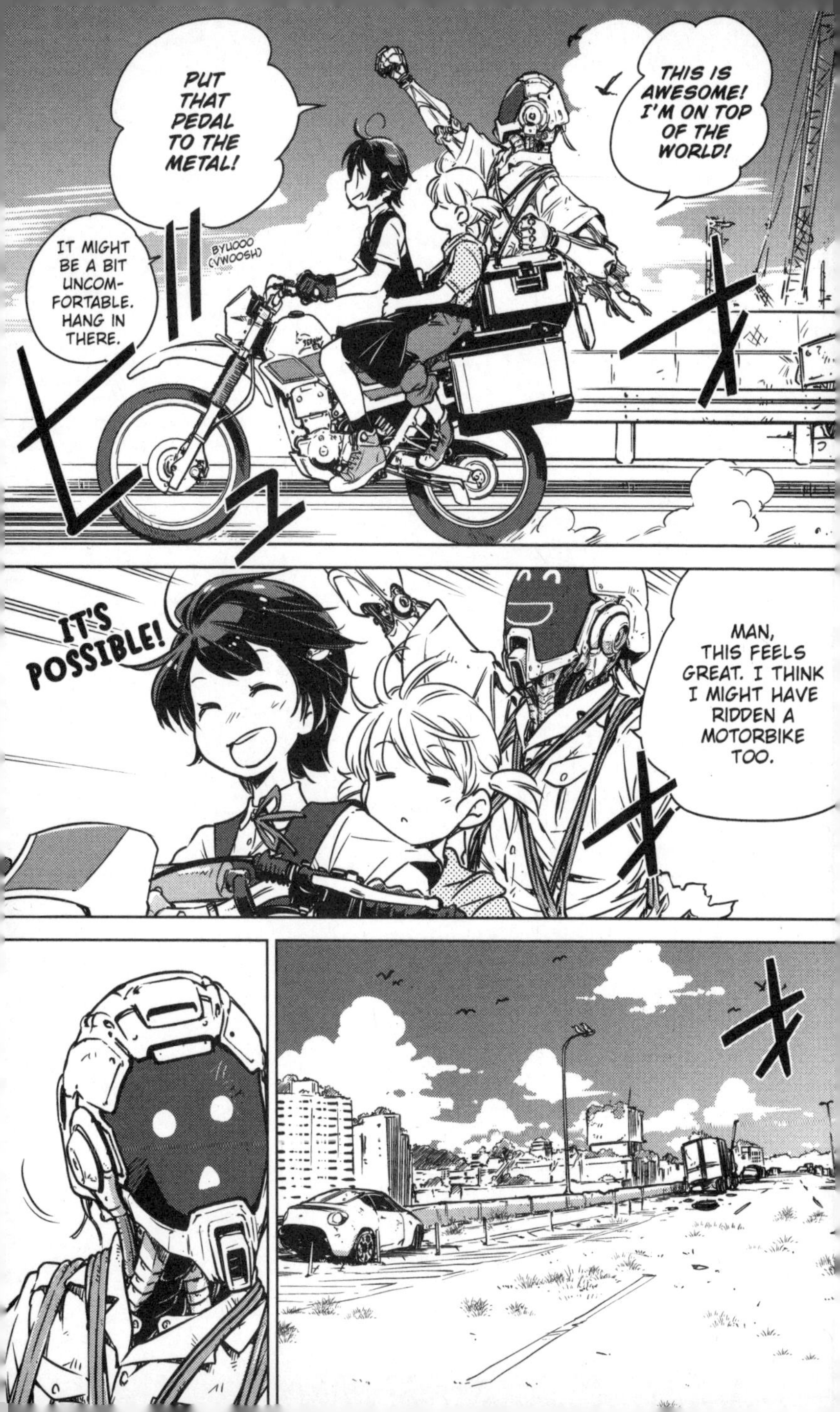
THIS IS AWESOME! I'M ON TOP OF THE WORLD!
PUT THAT PEDAL TO THE METAL!
BYUOOO (VWOOSH)
IT MIGHT BE A BIT UNCOM-FORTABLE. HANG IN THERE.
MAN, THIS FEELS GREAT. I THINK I MIGHT HAVE RIDDEN A MOTORBIKE TOO.
IT'S POSSIBLE!

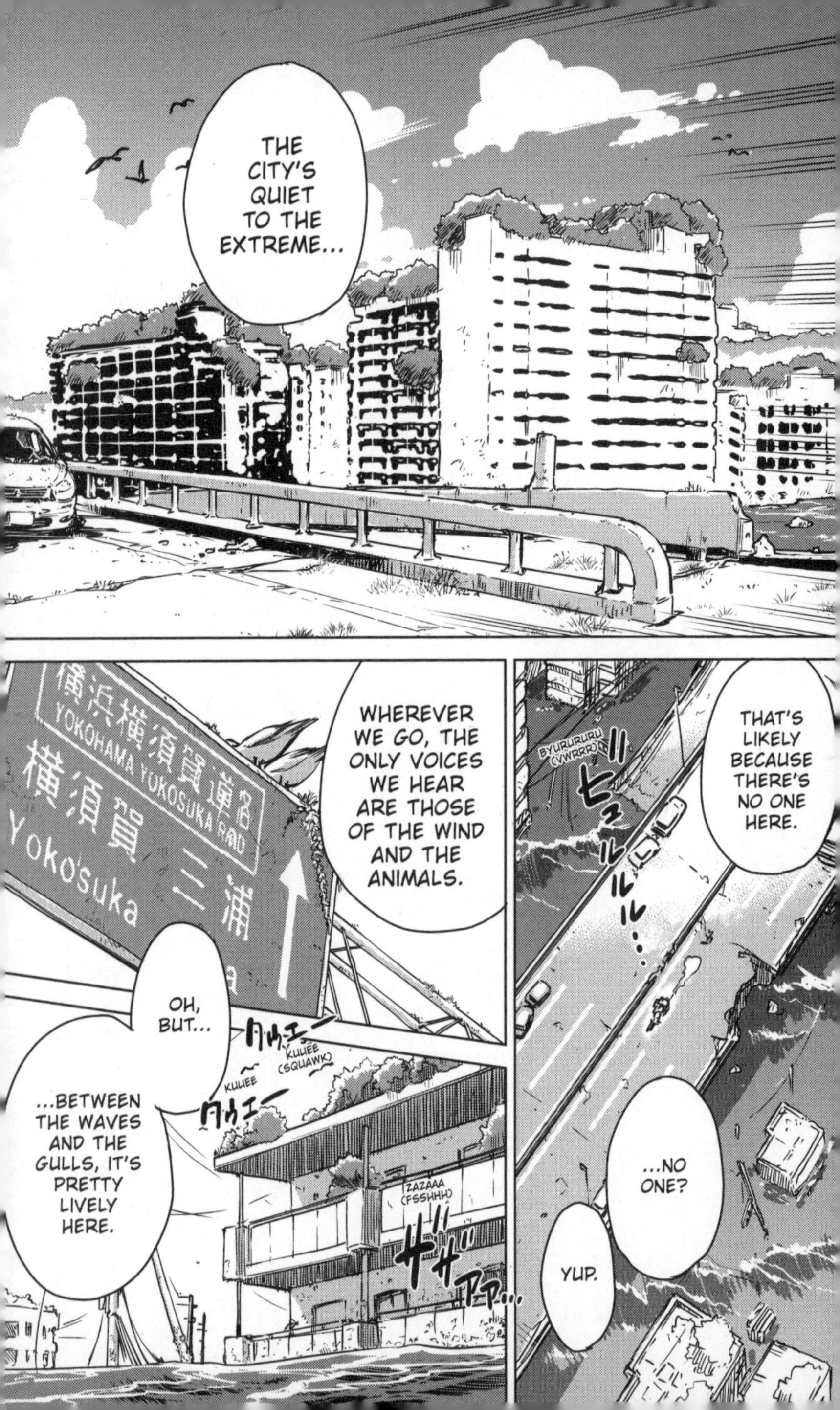
THE CITY'S QUIET TO THE EXTREME...
THAT'S LIKELY BECAUSE THERE'S NO ONE HERE.
BYURURURU (VWRRR)
...NO ONE?
YUP.
横浜横須賀道路
YOKOHAMA YOKOSUKA ROAD
横須賀
Yokosuka
三浦
WHEREVER WE GO, THE ONLY VOICES WE HEAR ARE THOSE OF THE WIND AND THE ANIMALS.
OH, BUT...
KUUEE (SQUAWK)
KUUEE
...BETWEEN THE WAVES AND THE GULLS, IT'S PRETTY LIVELY HERE.
ZAZAAA (FSSHHH)

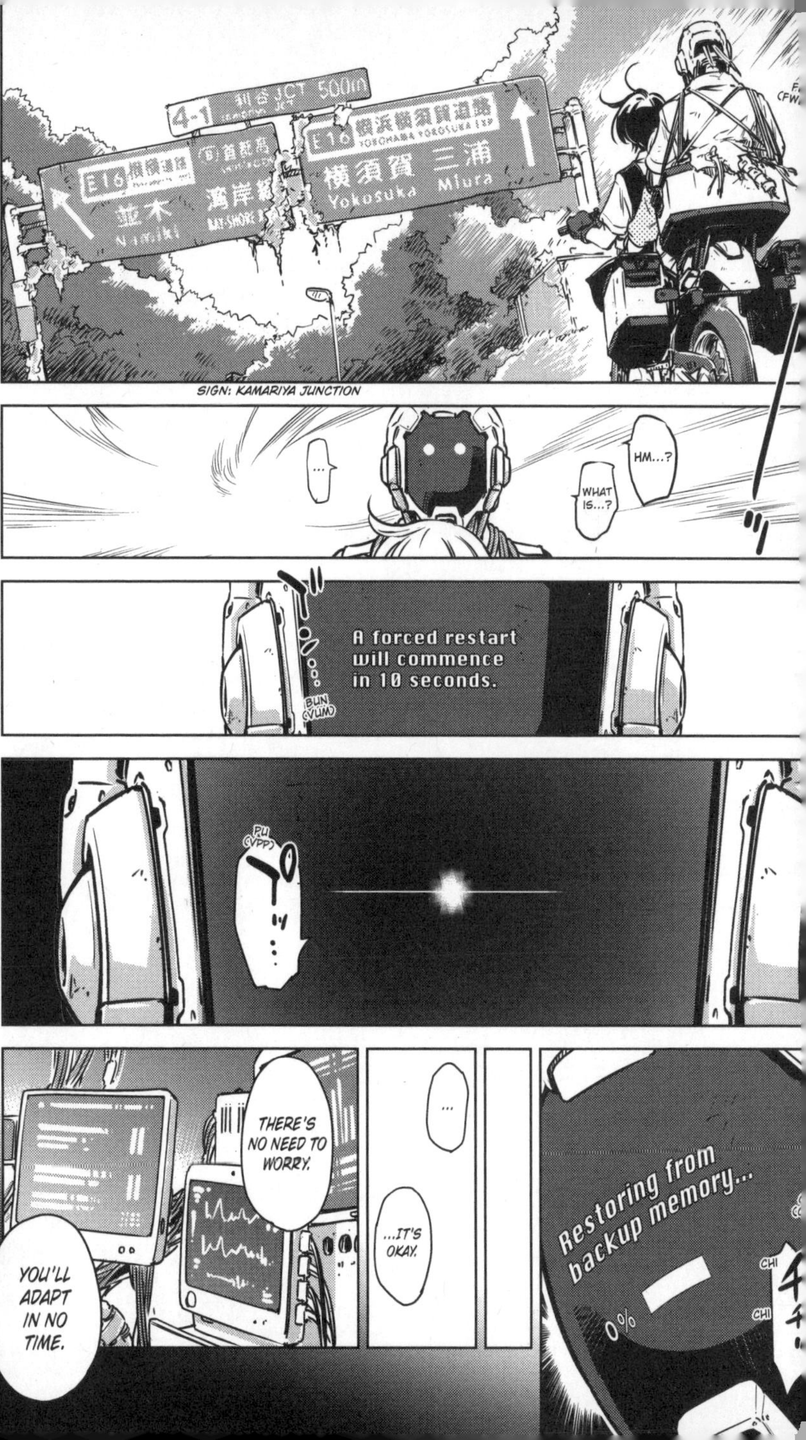
4-1
JCT 500m
E16 横浜横須賀道路
YOKOHAMA YOKOSUKA EXP
横須賀 三浦
Yokosuka Miura
E16
並木
Namiki
湾岸線
SIGN: KAMARIYA JUNCTION
HM...?
WHAT IS...?
...
A forced restart will commence in 10 seconds.
BUN (VUM)
PU (VPP)
Restoring from backup memory...
0%
CHI
CHI
...
...IT'S OKAY.
THERE'S NO NEED TO WORRY.
YOU'LL ADAPT IN NO TIME.

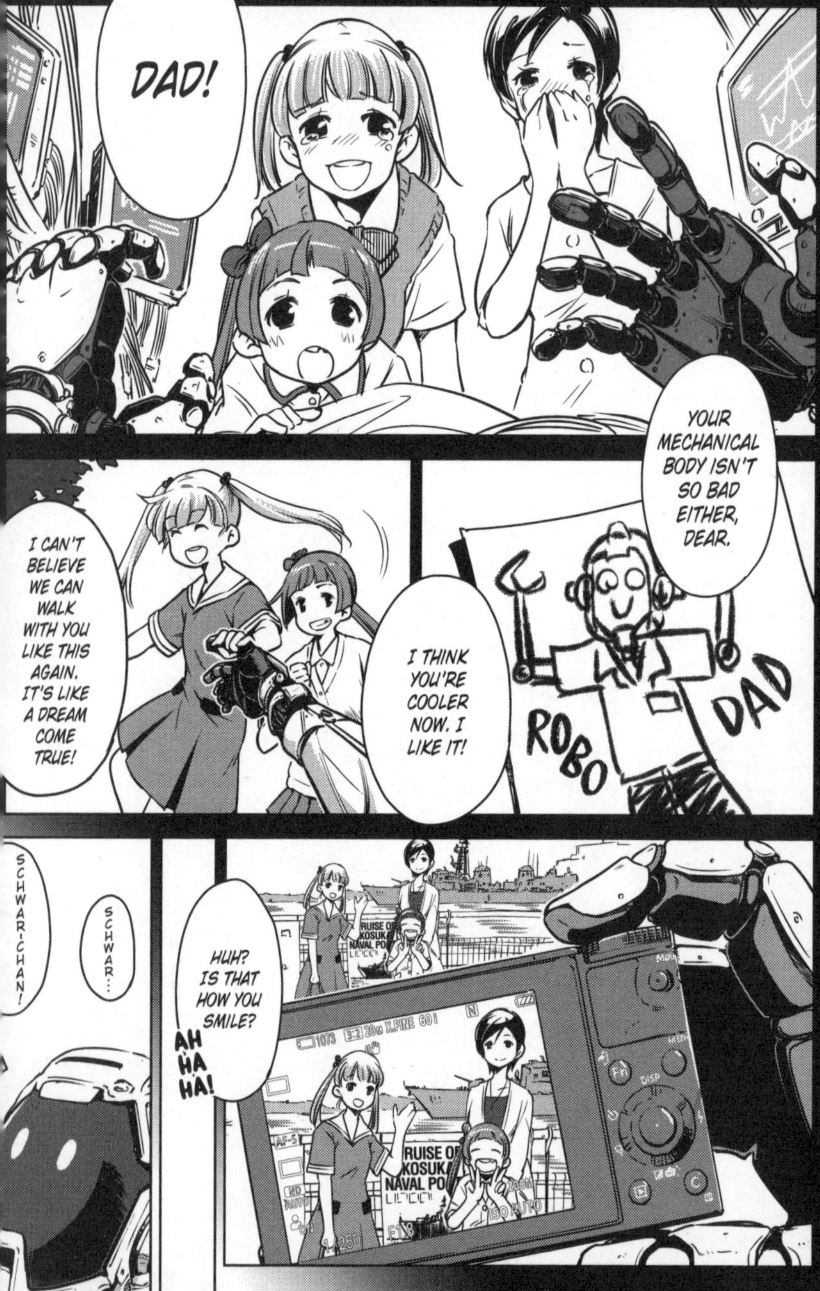
DAD!
YOUR MECHANICAL BODY ISN'T SO BAD EITHER, DEAR.
ROBO DAD
I THINK YOU'RE COOLER NOW. I LIKE IT!
I CAN'T BELIEVE WE CAN WALK WITH YOU LIKE THIS AGAIN. IT'S LIKE A DREAM COME TRUE!
HUH? IS THAT HOW YOU SMILE?
AH HA HA HA!
SCHWAR...
SCHWARI-CHAN!

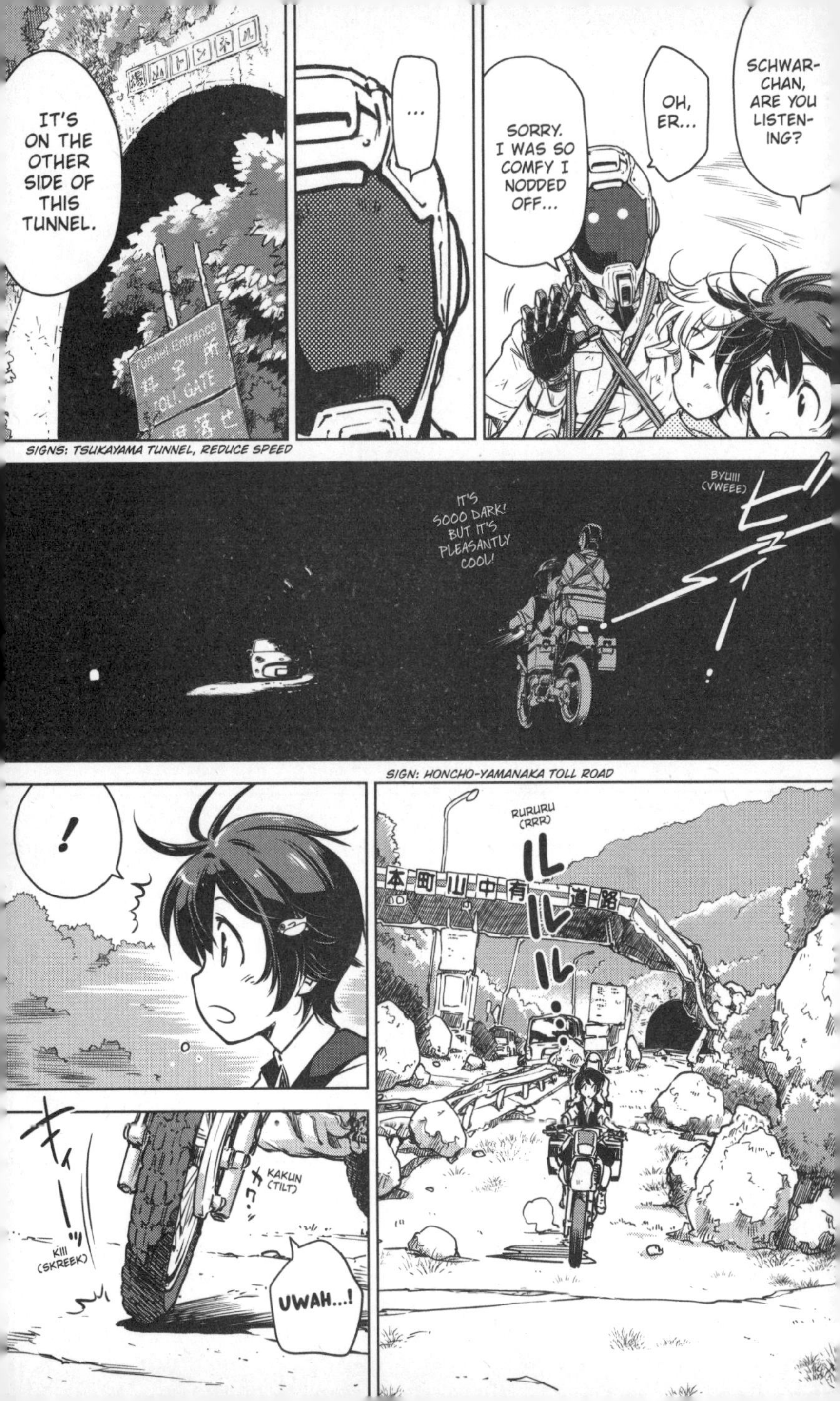
SCHWAR-CHAN, ARE YOU LISTENING?
OH, ER...
SORRY. I WAS SO COMFY I NODDED OFF...
...
IT'S ON THE OTHER SIDE OF THIS TUNNEL.
Tunnel Entrance
TOLL GATE
SIGNS: TSUKAYAMA TUNNEL, REDUCE SPEED
BYUIII (VWEEE)
IT'S SOOO DARK! BUT IT'S PLEASANTLY COOL!
SIGN: HONCHO-YAMANAKA TOLL ROAD
本町山中有
道路
RURURU (RRR)
!
KAKUN (TILT)
KIII (SKREEK)
UWAH...!

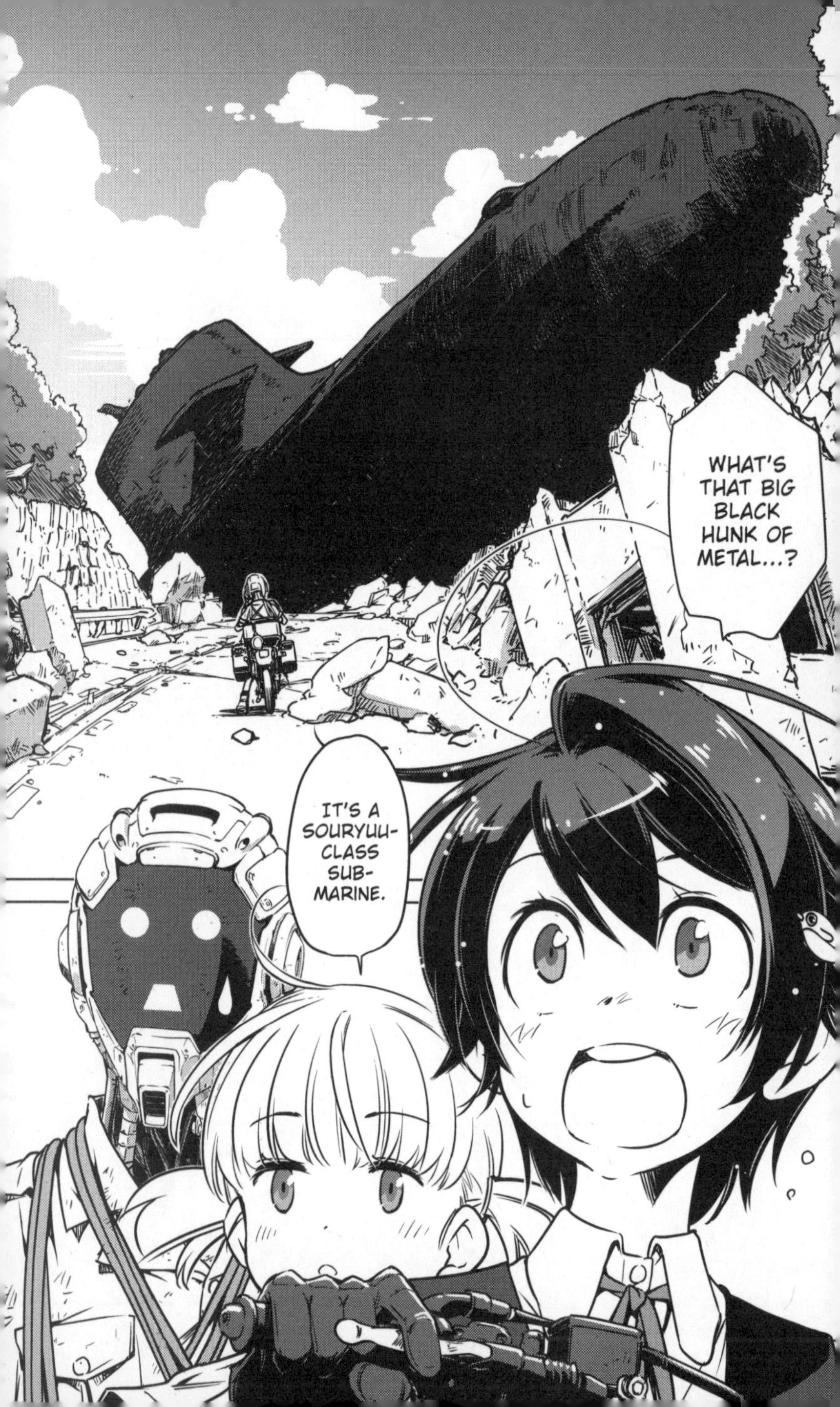
WHAT'S THAT BIG BLACK HUNK OF METAL...?
IT'S A SOURYUU-CLASS SUB-MARINE.

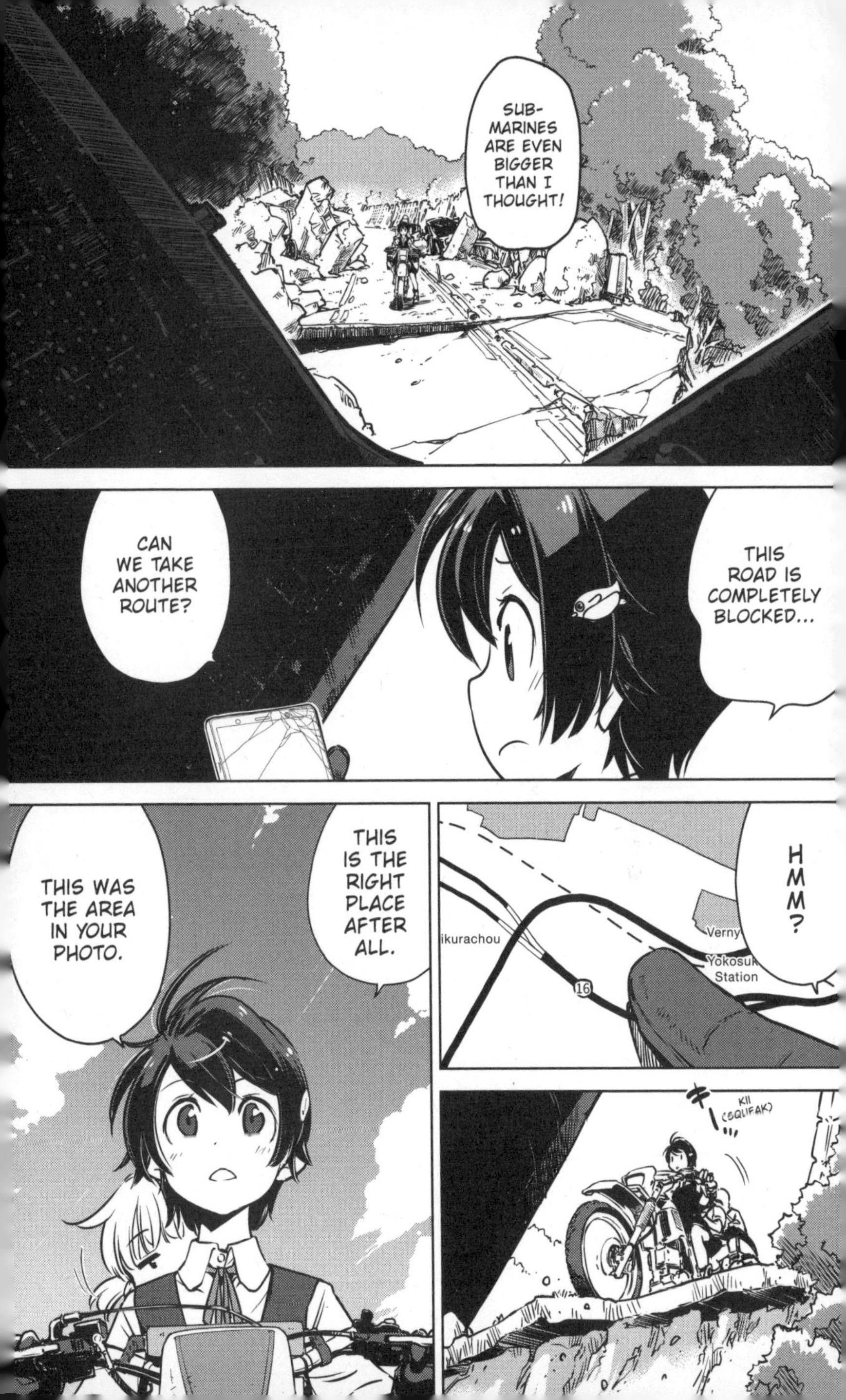
SUB-MARINES ARE EVEN BIGGER THAN I THOUGHT!
THIS ROAD IS COMPLETELY BLOCKED...
CAN WE TAKE ANOTHER ROUTE?
HMM?
Verny
Yokosuk
Station
16
ikurachou
キー
KII (SQUEAK)
THIS IS THE RIGHT PLACE AFTER ALL.
THIS WAS THE AREA IN YOUR PHOTO.

THIS IS
YOKOSUKA.

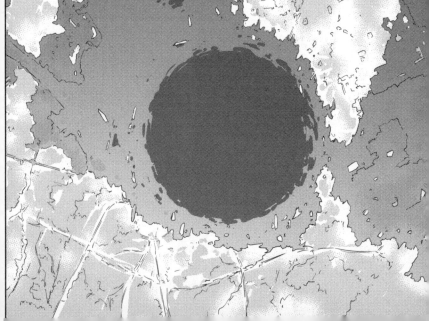

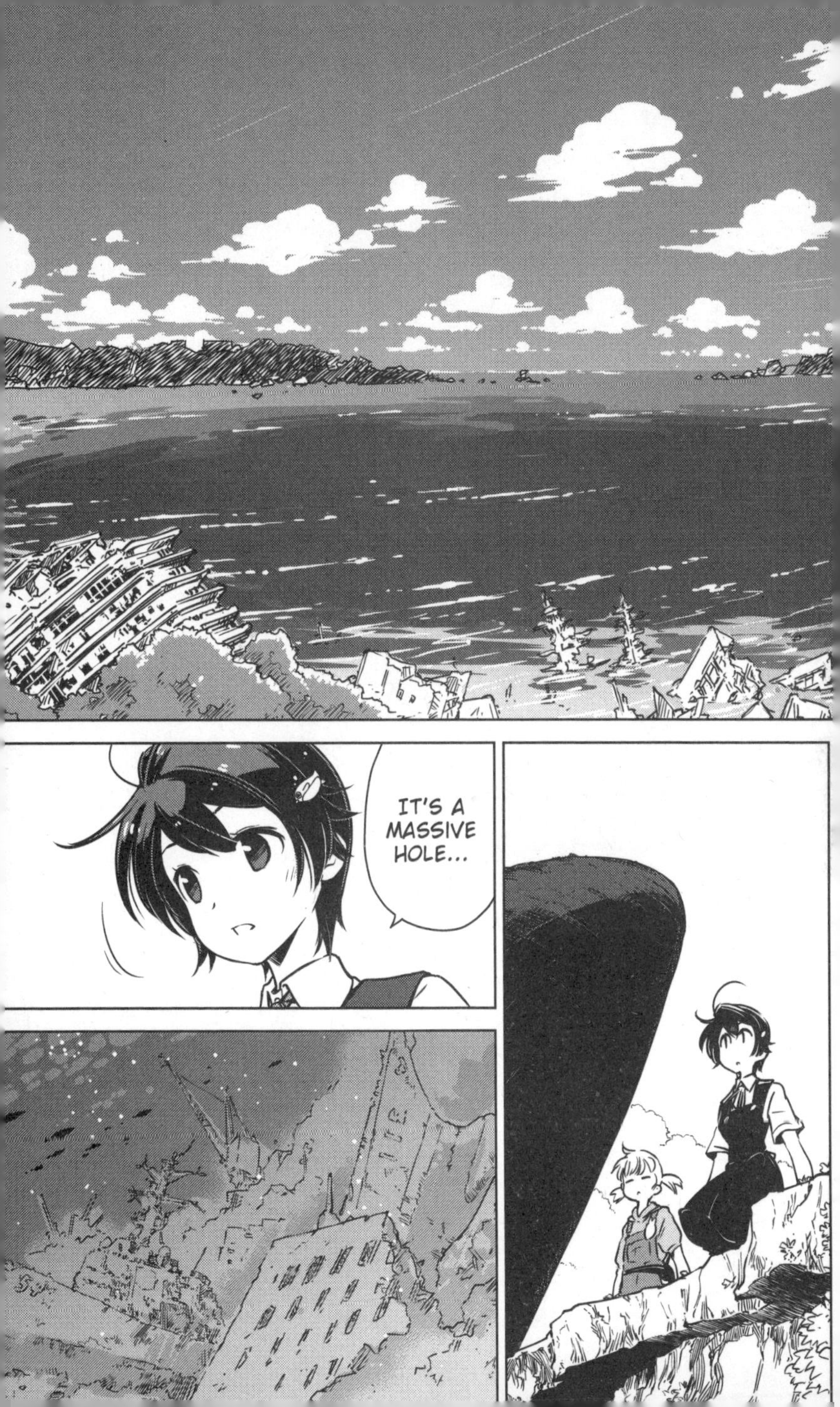
IT'S A MASSIVE HOLE...

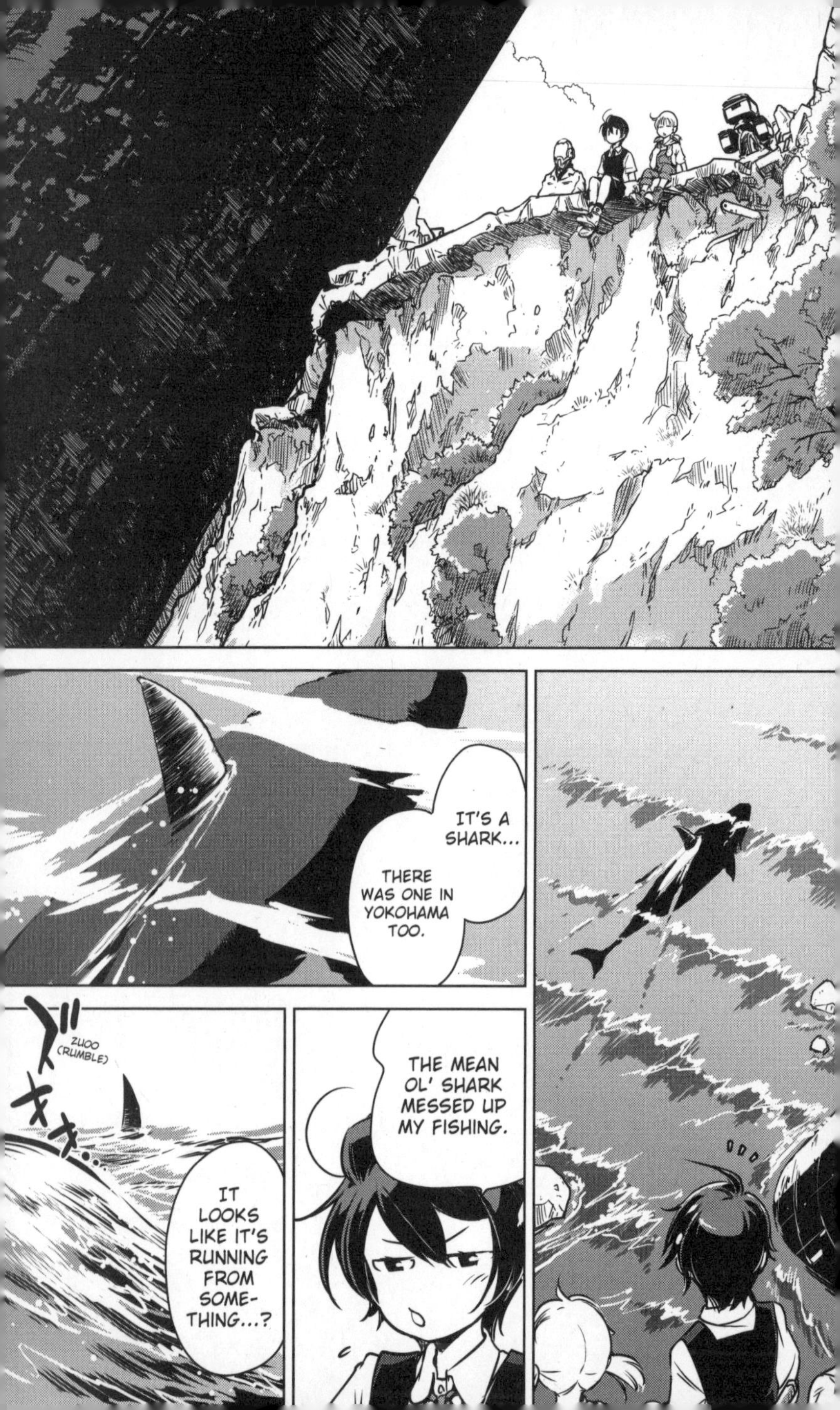
IT'S A SHARK...
THERE WAS ONE IN YOKOHAMA TOO.
THE MEAN OL' SHARK MESSED UP MY FISHING.
ZUOO (RUMBLE)
IT LOOKS LIKE IT'S RUNNING FROM SOMETHING...?

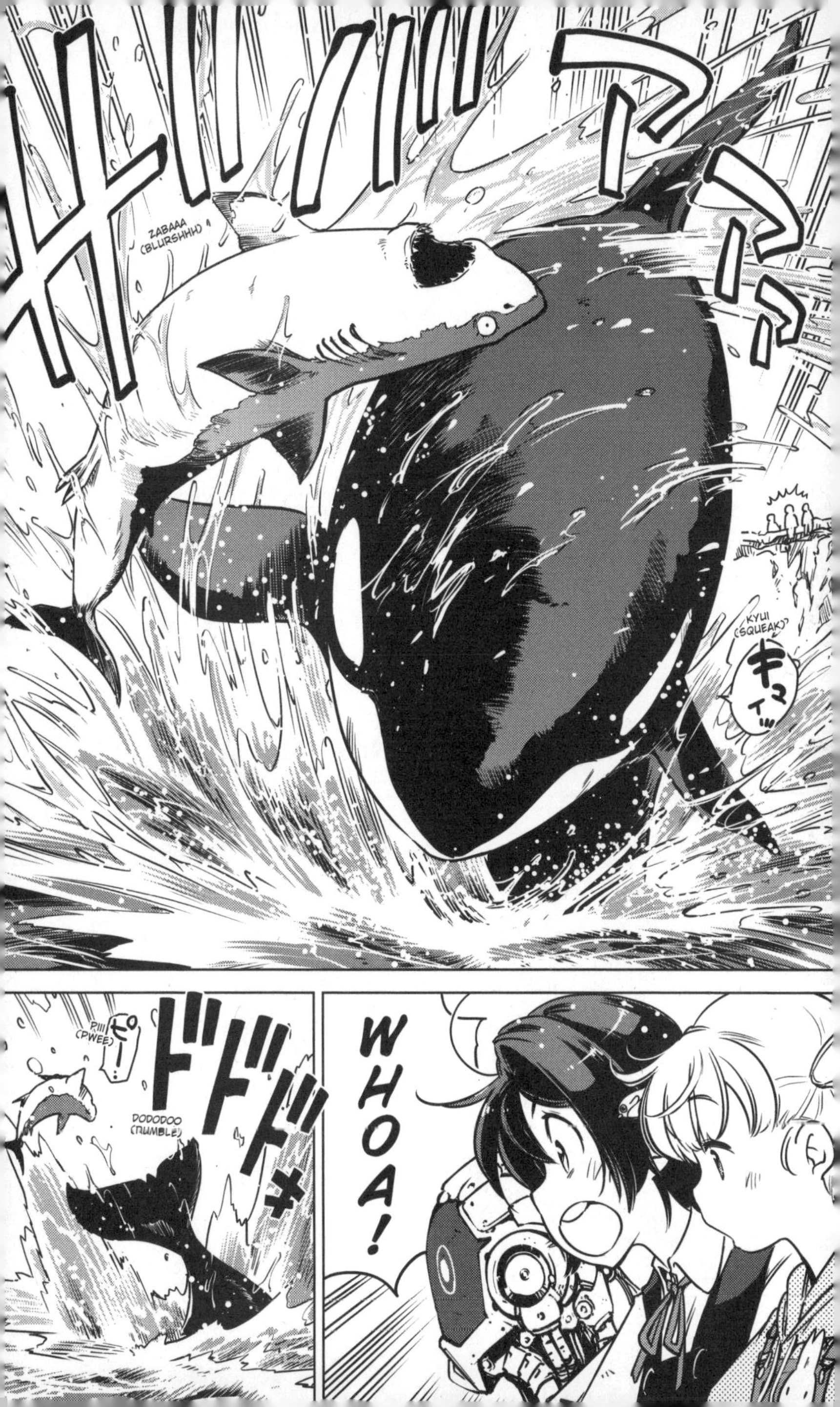
ZABAAA
(BLURSHHH)
KYUI
(SQUEAK)
WHOA!
PIII
(PWEE)
DODODOO
(RUMBLE)

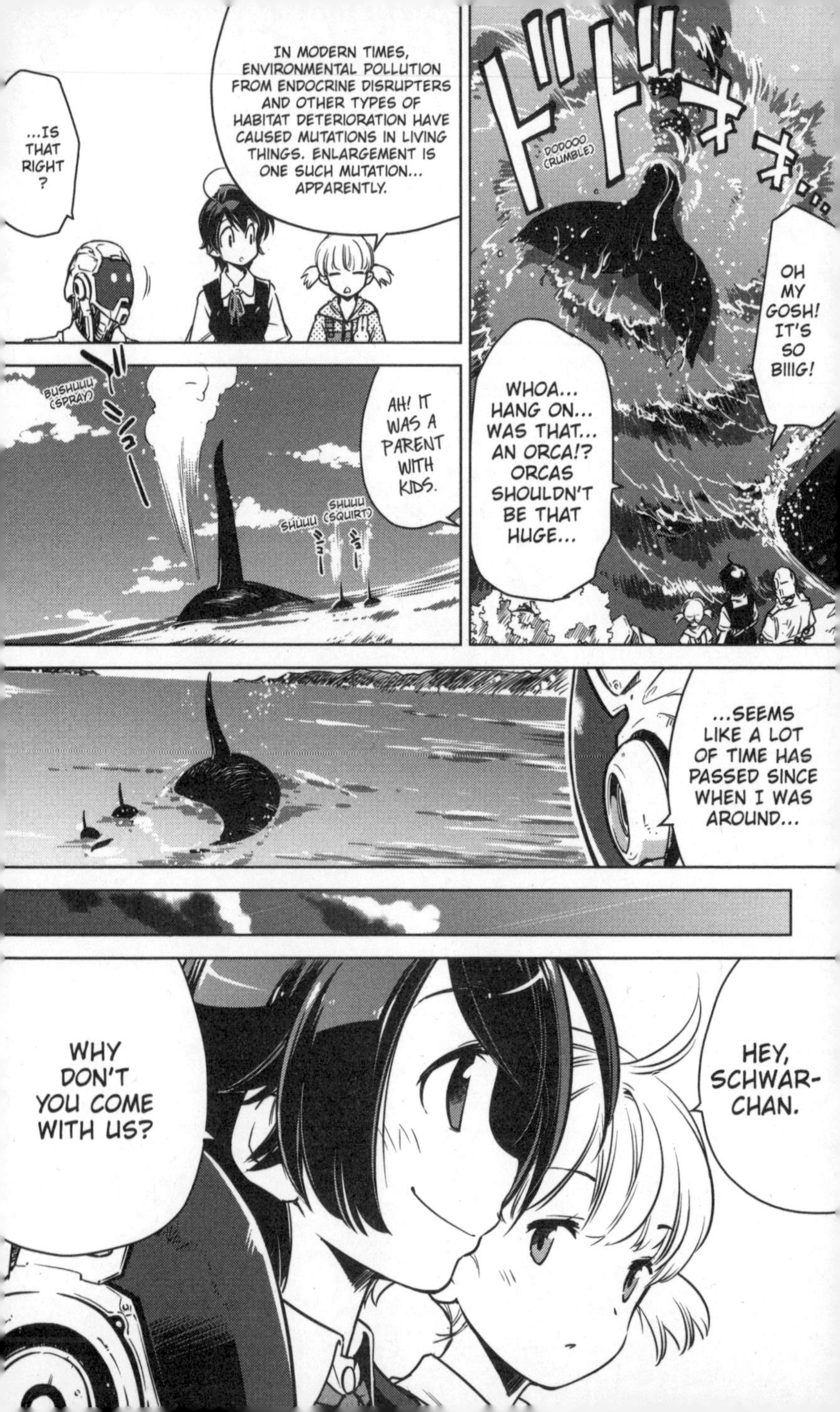
DODOOO (RUMBLE)
OH MY GOSH! IT'S SO BIIIG!
WHOA... HANG ON... WAS THAT... AN ORCA!? ORCAS SHOULDN'T BE THAT HUGE...
IN MODERN TIMES, ENVIRONMENTAL POLLUTION FROM ENDOCRINE DISRUPTERS AND OTHER TYPES OF HABITAT DETERIORATION HAVE CAUSED MUTATIONS IN LIVING THINGS. ENLARGEMENT IS ONE SUCH MUTATION... APPARENTLY.
...IS THAT RIGHT?
AH! IT WAS A PARENT WITH KIDS.
BUSHUUU (SPRAY)
SHUUU (SQUIRT)
SHUUU
...SEEMS LIKE A LOT OF TIME HAS PASSED SINCE WHEN I WAS AROUND...
HEY, SCHWAR-CHAN.
WHY DON'T YOU COME WITH US?

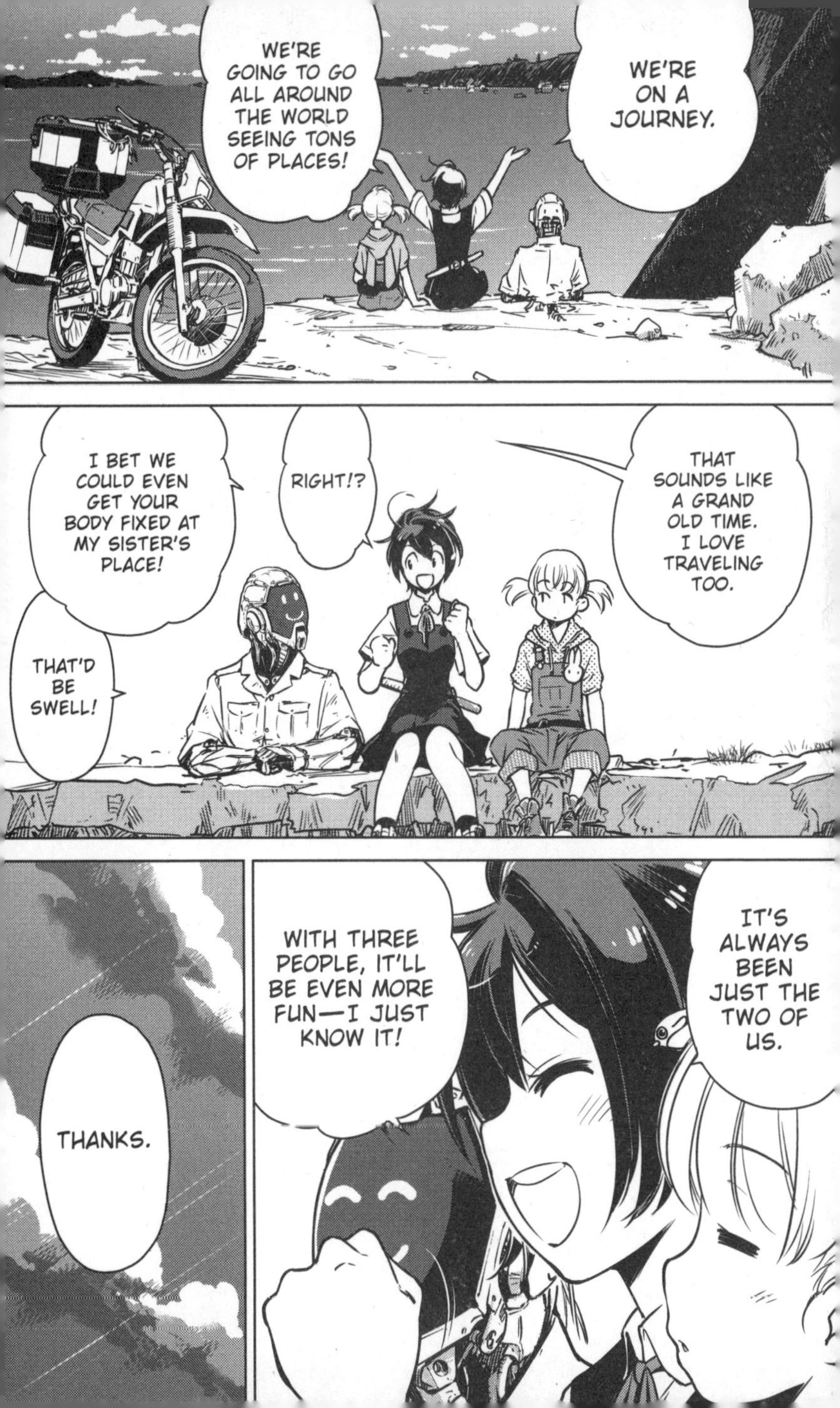
WE'RE ON A JOURNEY.
WE'RE GOING TO GO ALL AROUND THE WORLD SEEING TONS OF PLACES!
THAT SOUNDS LIKE A GRAND OLD TIME. I LOVE TRAVELING TOO.
RIGHT!?
I BET WE COULD EVEN GET YOUR BODY FIXED AT MY SISTER'S PLACE!
THAT'D BE SWELL!
IT'S ALWAYS BEEN JUST THE TWO OF US.
WITH THREE PEOPLE, IT'LL BE EVEN MORE FUN—I JUST KNOW IT!
THANKS.

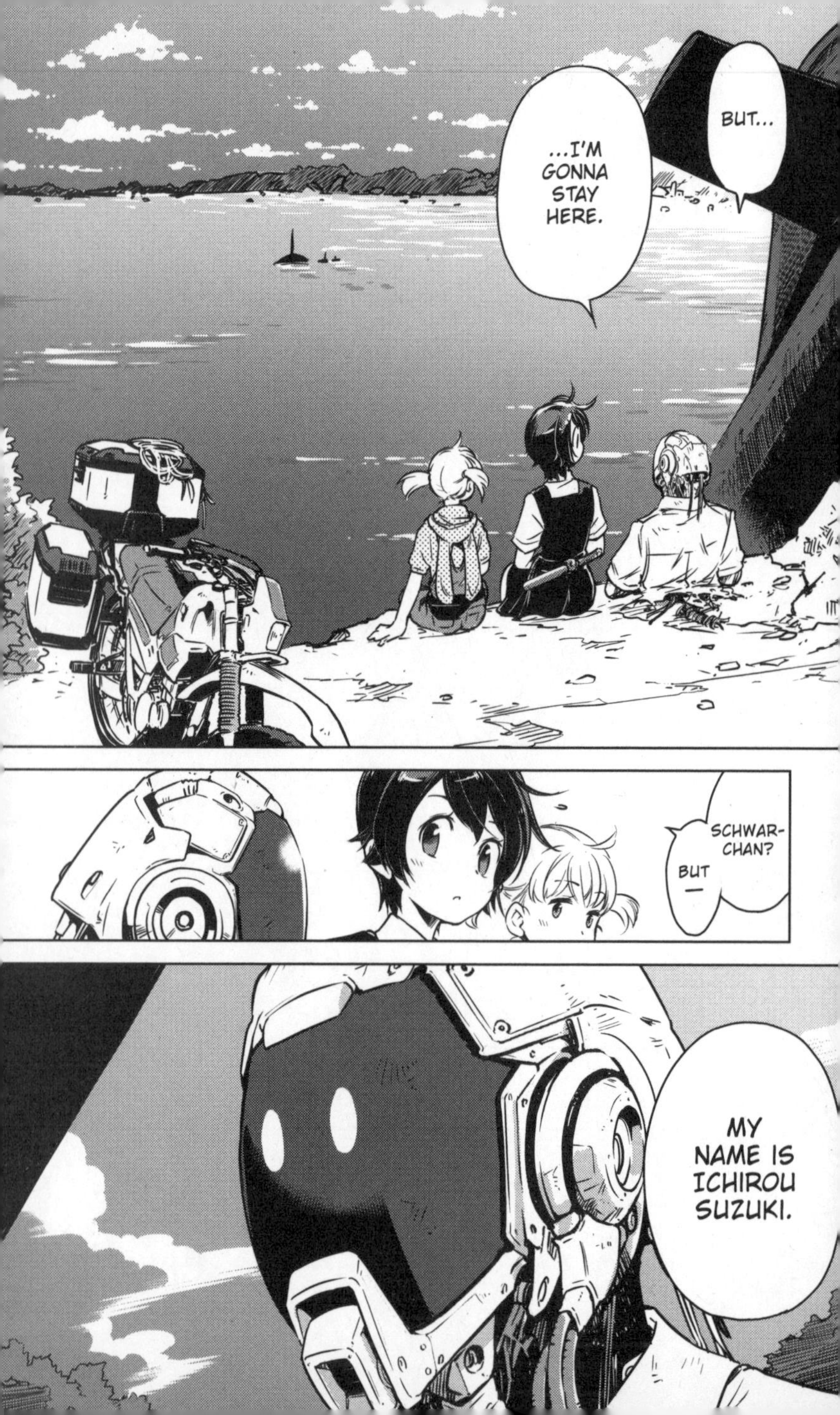
BUT...
...I'M GONNA STAY HERE.
SCHWAR-CHAN? BUT —
MY NAME IS ICHIROU SUZUKI.

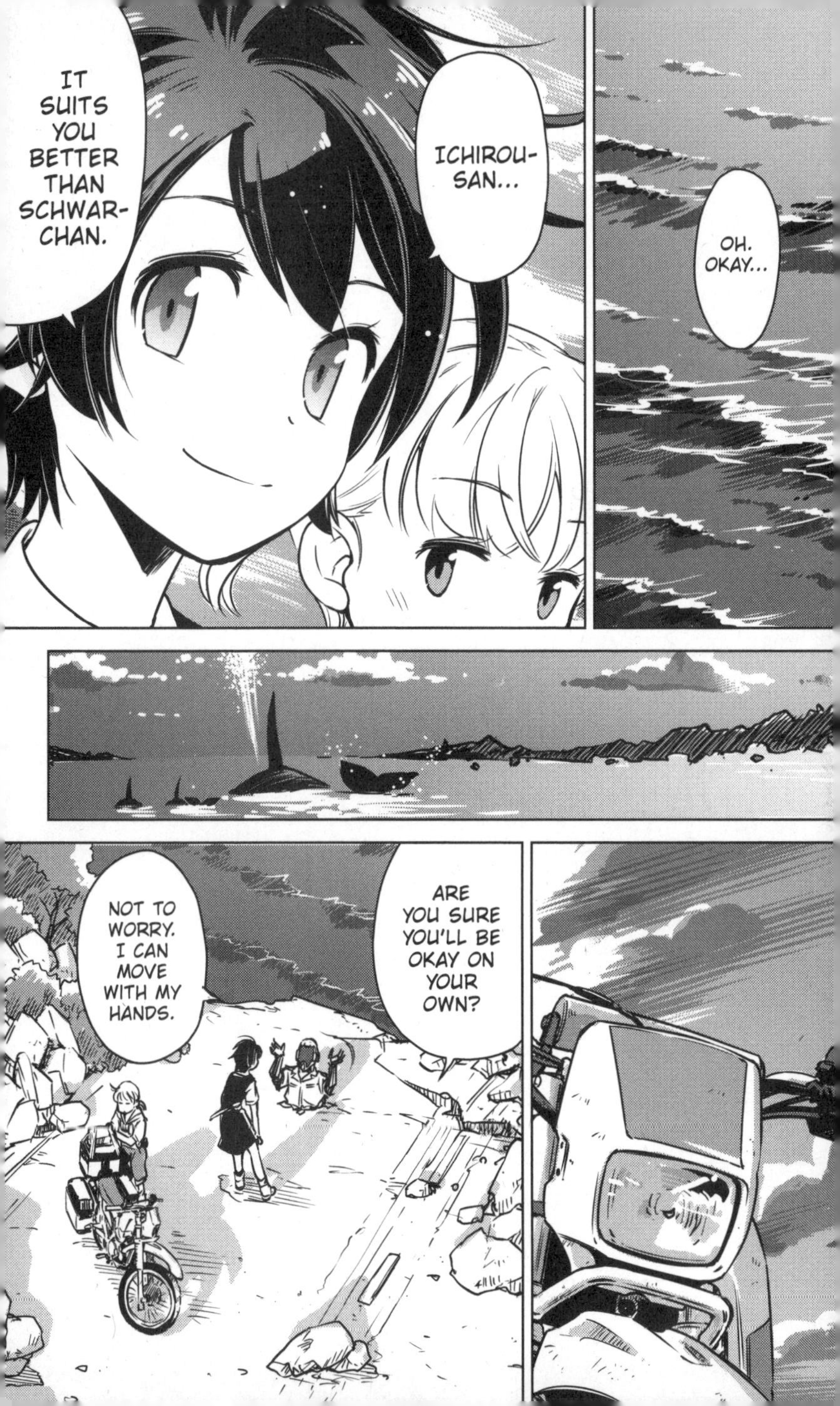
OH. OKAY...
ICHIROU-SAN...
IT SUITS YOU BETTER THAN SCHWAR-CHAN.
ARE YOU SURE YOU'LL BE OKAY ON YOUR OWN?
NOT TO WORRY. I CAN MOVE WITH MY HANDS.

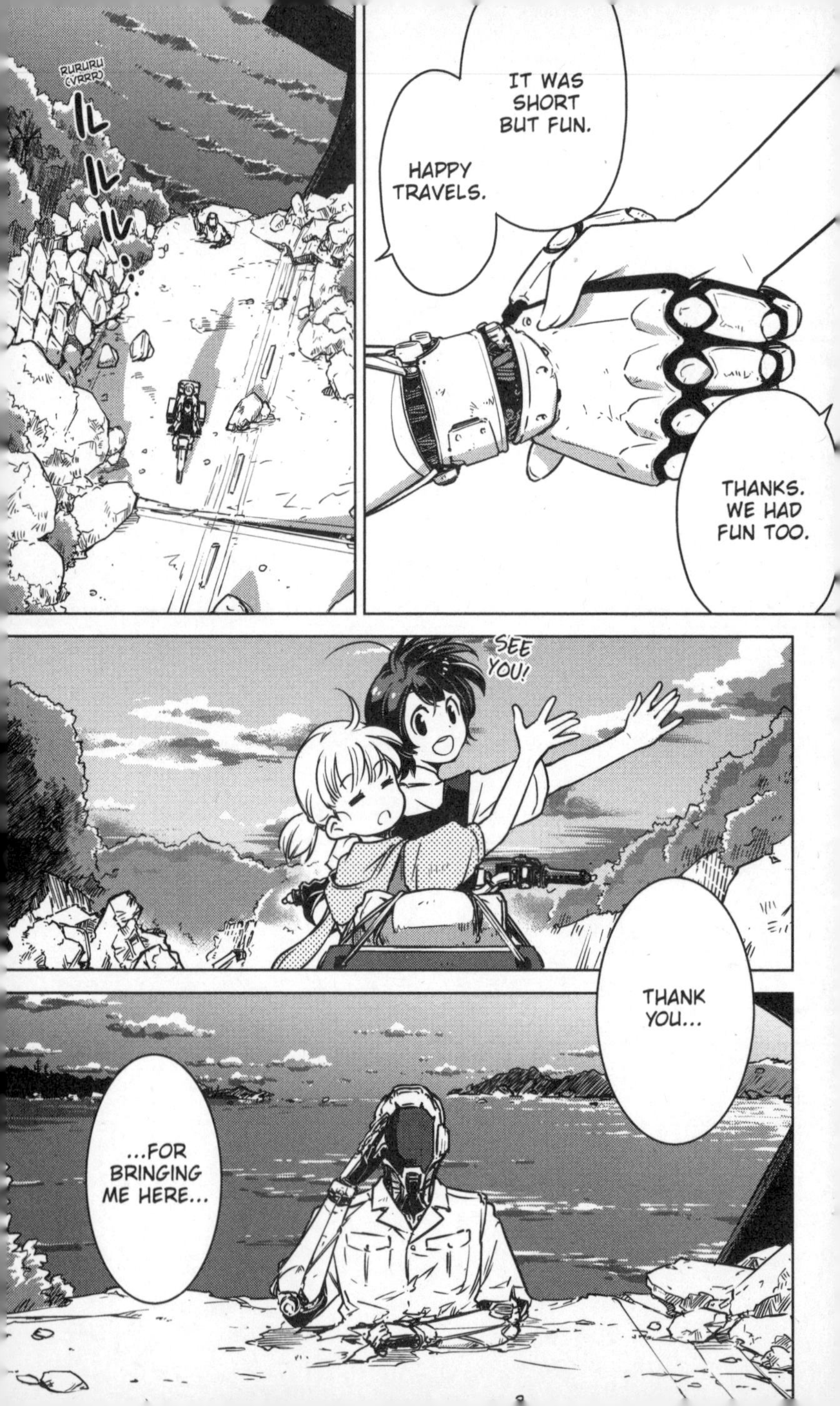

IT WAS SHORT BUT FUN.
HAPPY TRAVELS.
THANKS. WE HAD FUN TOO.
RURURU (VRRR)
ルルル…
SEE YOU!
THANK YOU...
...FOR BRINGING ME HERE...

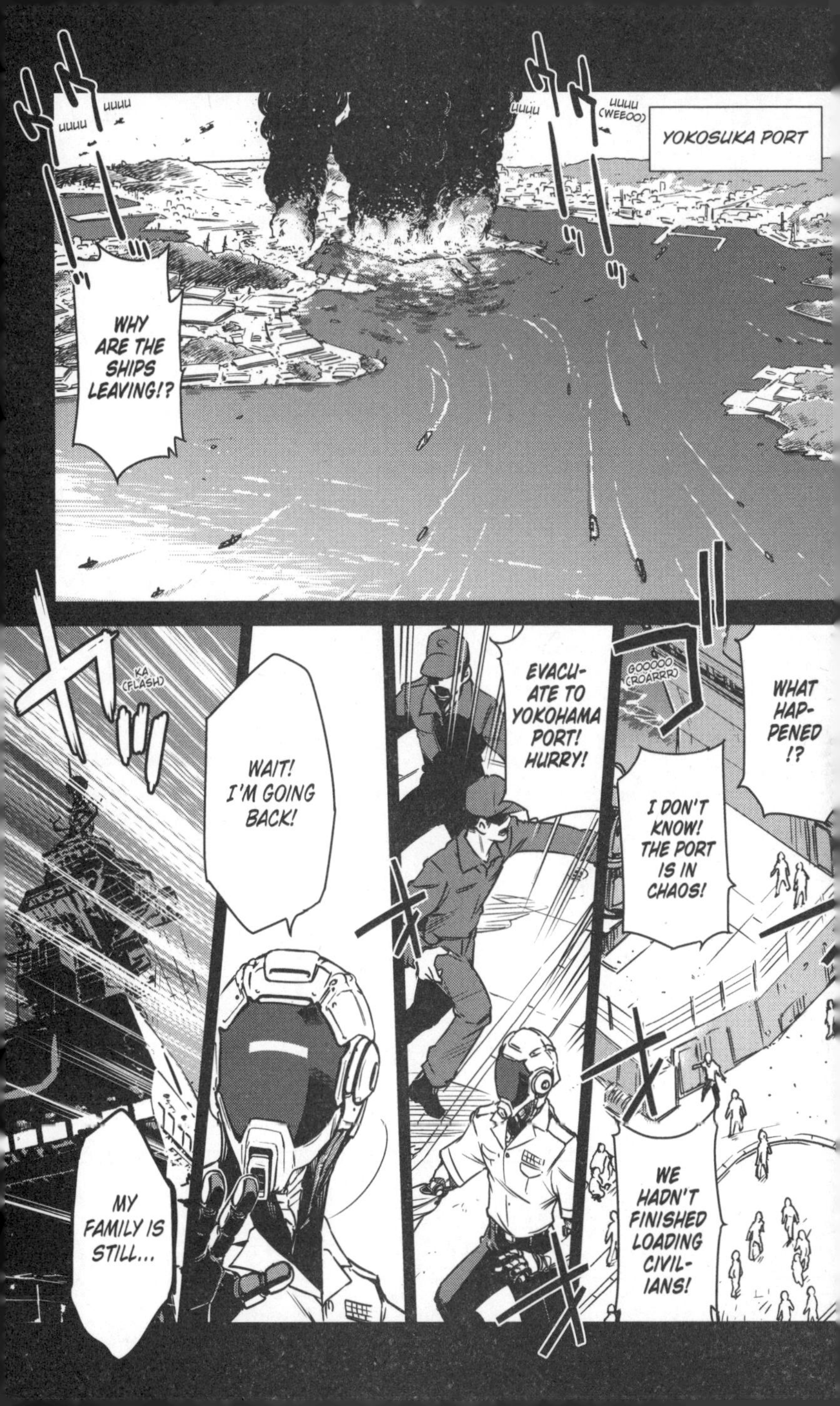
YOKOSUKA PORT
UUUU (WEEOO)
UUUU
UUUU
UUUU
WHY ARE THE SHIPS LEAVING!?
GOOOOO (ROARRR)
WHAT HAPPENED!?
I DON'T KNOW! THE PORT IS IN CHAOS!
WE HADN'T FINISHED LOADING CIVILIANS!
EVACUATE TO YOKOHAMA PORT! HURRY!
WAIT! I'M GOING BACK!
MY FAMILY IS STILL...
KA (FLASH)

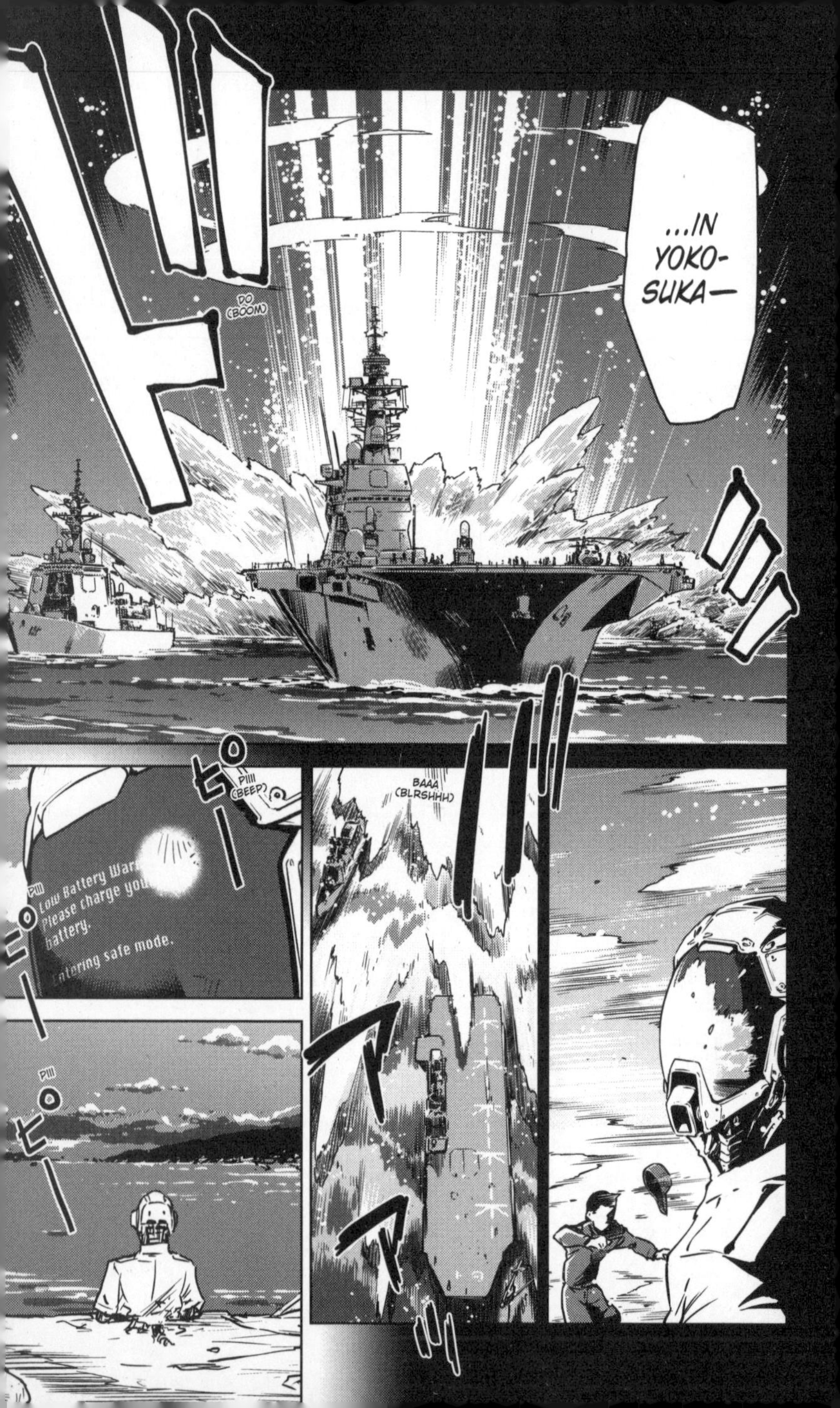
...IN YOKOSUKA—
DO (BOOM)
BAAA (BLRSHHH)
PIIII (BEEP)
PIII
Low Battery War
Please charge you
battery.
ntering safe mode.
PIII

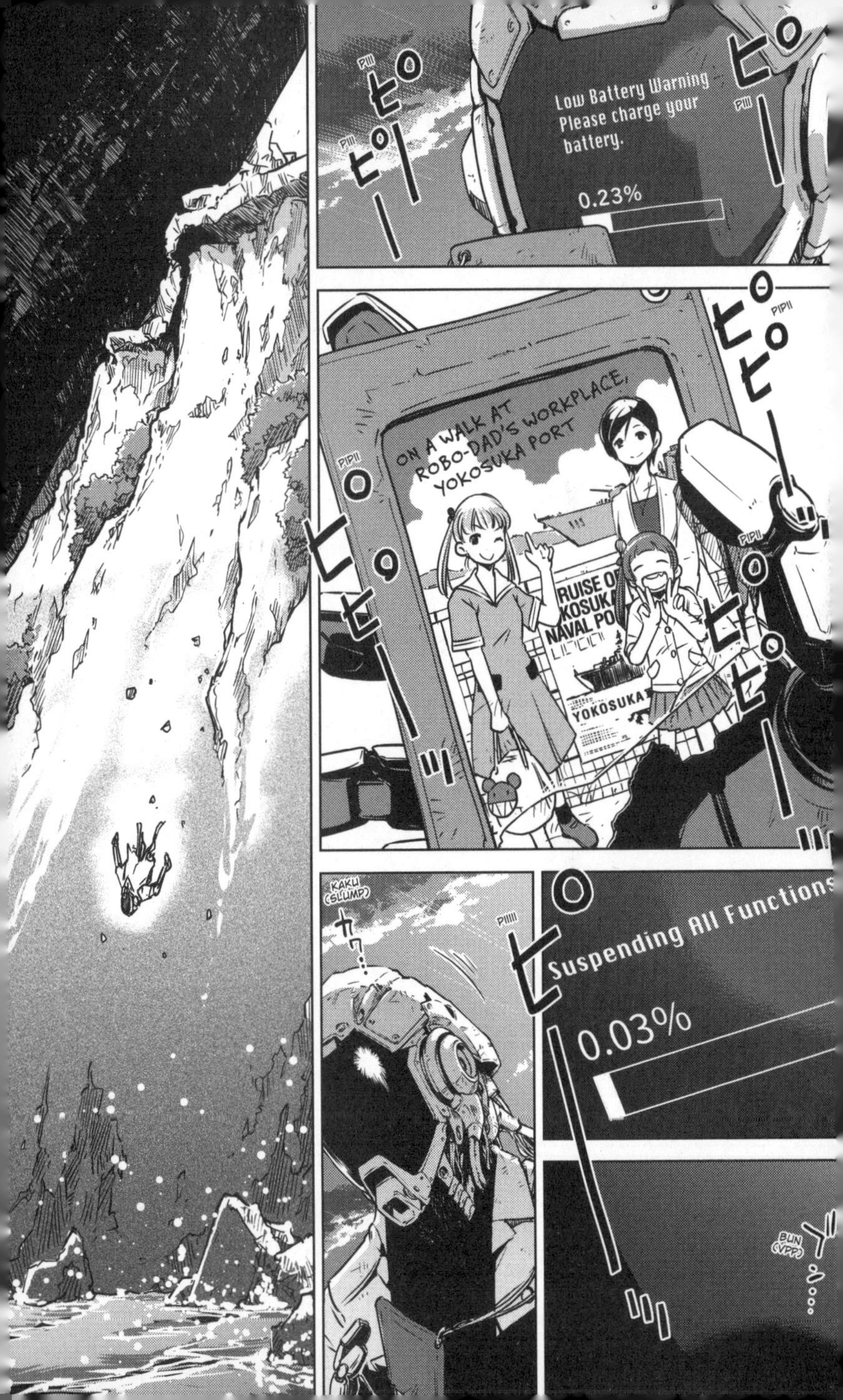
PIII
PIII
Low Battery Warning
Please charge your battery.
0.23%
PIII
PIPII
ON A WALK AT ROBO-DAD'S WORKPLACE, YOKOSUKA PORT
YOKOSUKA
PIPII
PIPII
Suspending All Functions
0.03%
PIIII
BUN (VPP)
KAKU (SLUMP)

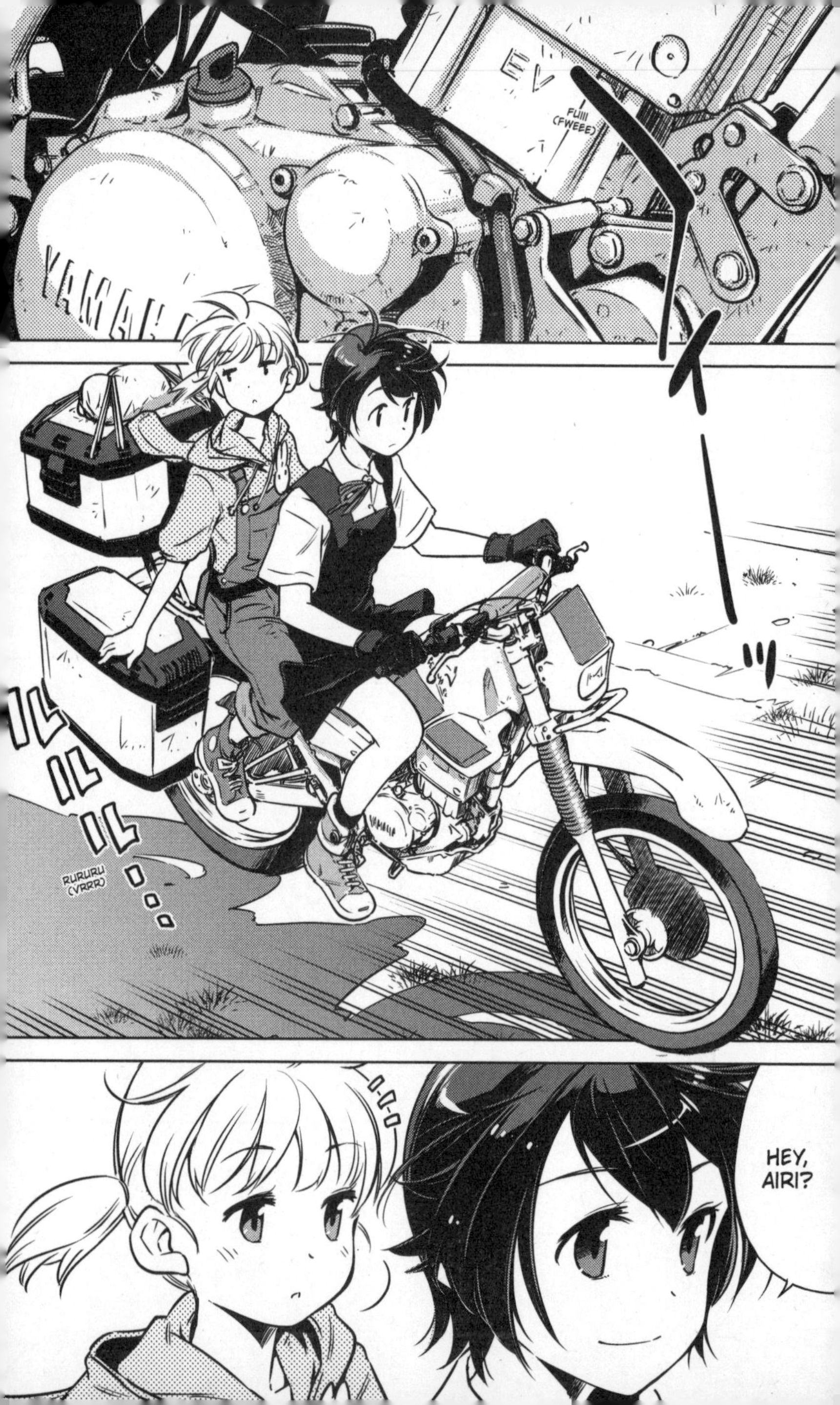
FUIII
(FWEEE)
RURURU
(VRRR)
HEY,
AIRI?

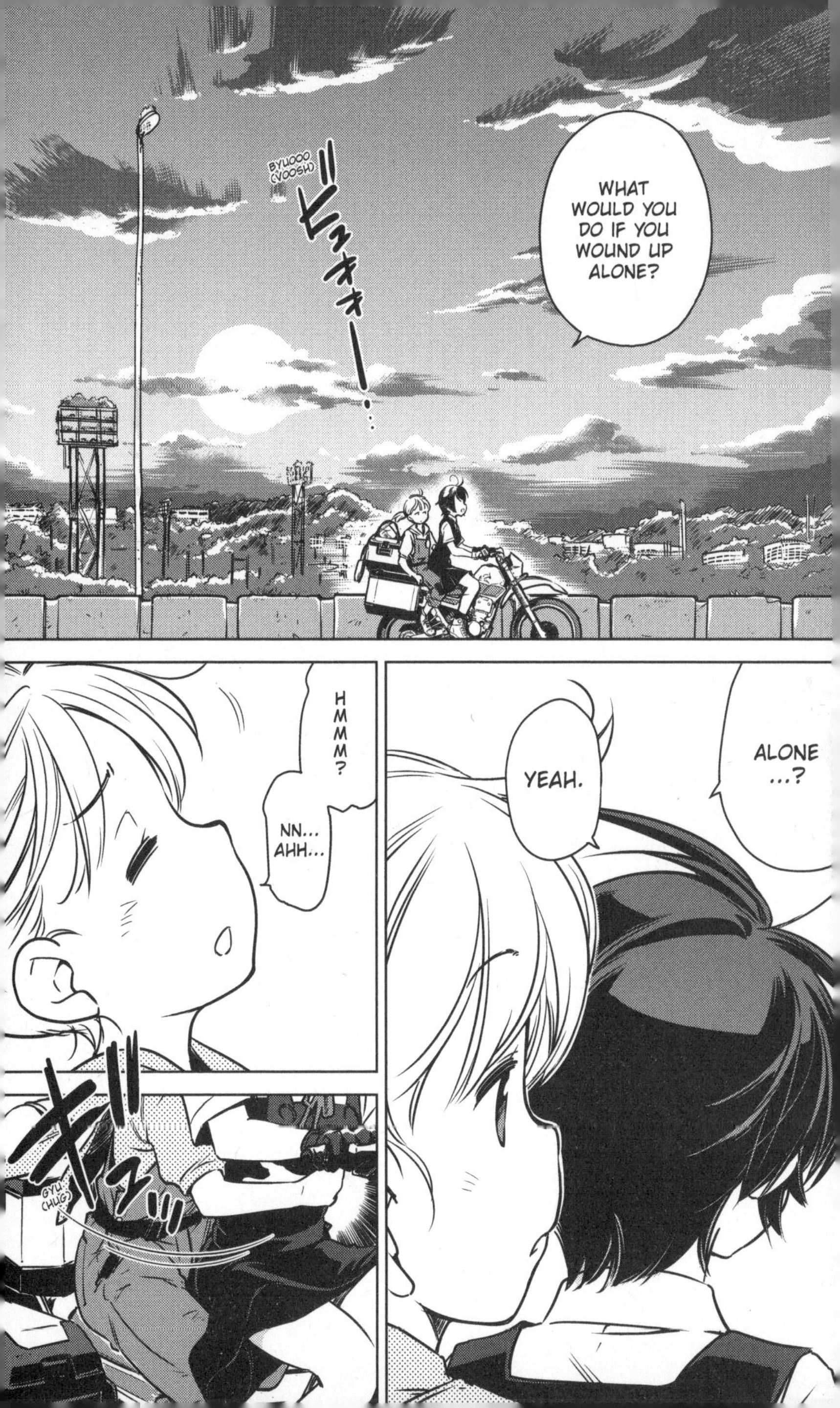
BYUOOO (VOOSH)
WHAT WOULD YOU DO IF YOU WOUND UP ALONE?
ALONE ...?
YEAH.
HMMMM?
NN... AHH...
GYU (HUG)

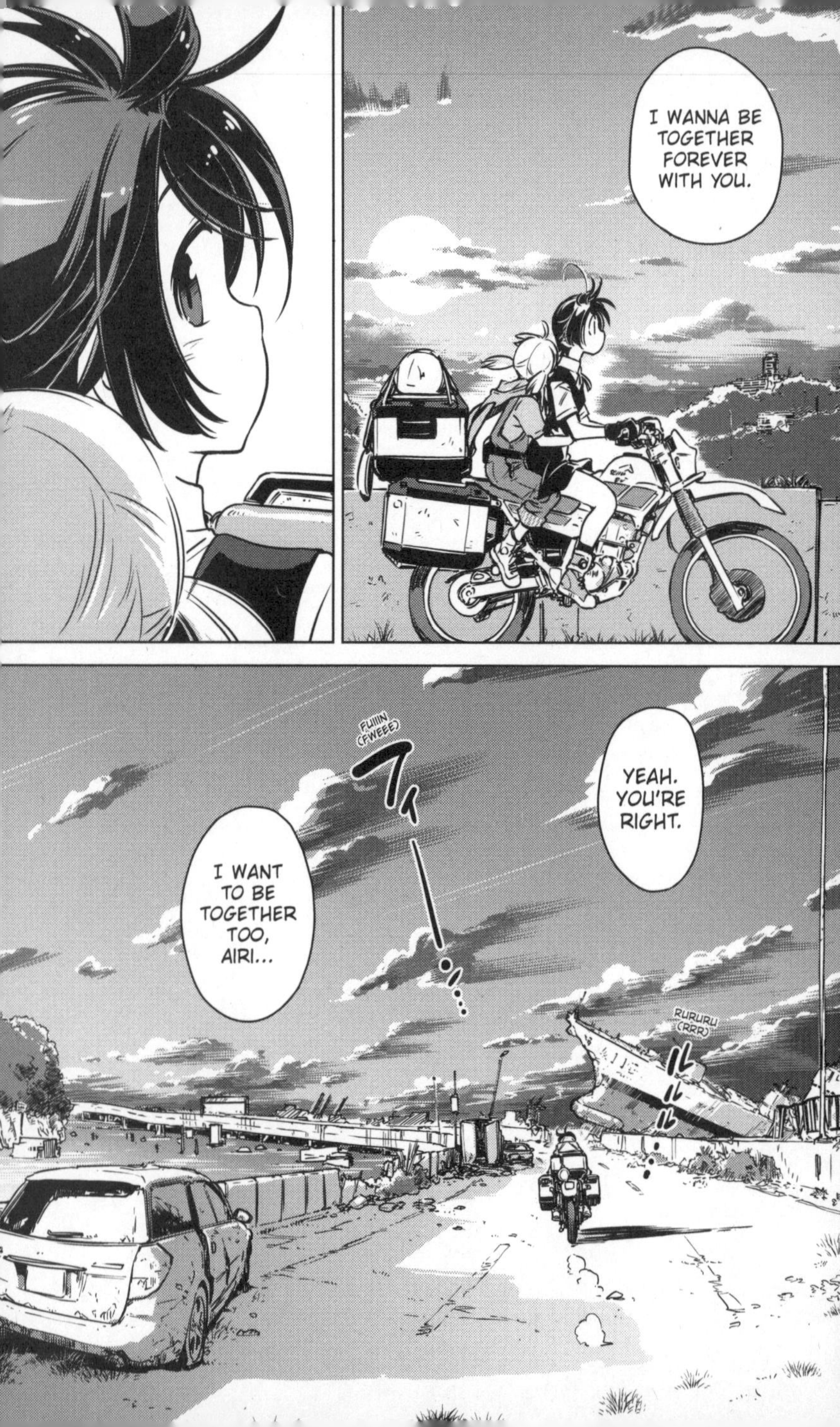
I WANNA BE TOGETHER FOREVER WITH YOU.
YEAH. YOU'RE RIGHT.
FUIIIN (FWEEE)
I WANT TO BE TOGETHER TOO, AIRI...
RURURU (RRR)

Touringram

▼ No Signal 🔋

🚲 Touringram ⊕ ✉ ⋮

April 7, 2035

Chiko_sister

Minato Mirai
Truly a future waterfront, like in the name!
Once I've rocked it in style, I'll do a restaurant tour of
Chinatown.
#yokohamaminatomirai #weekendtouring #bikergirl

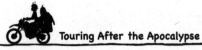
Touring After the Apocalypse

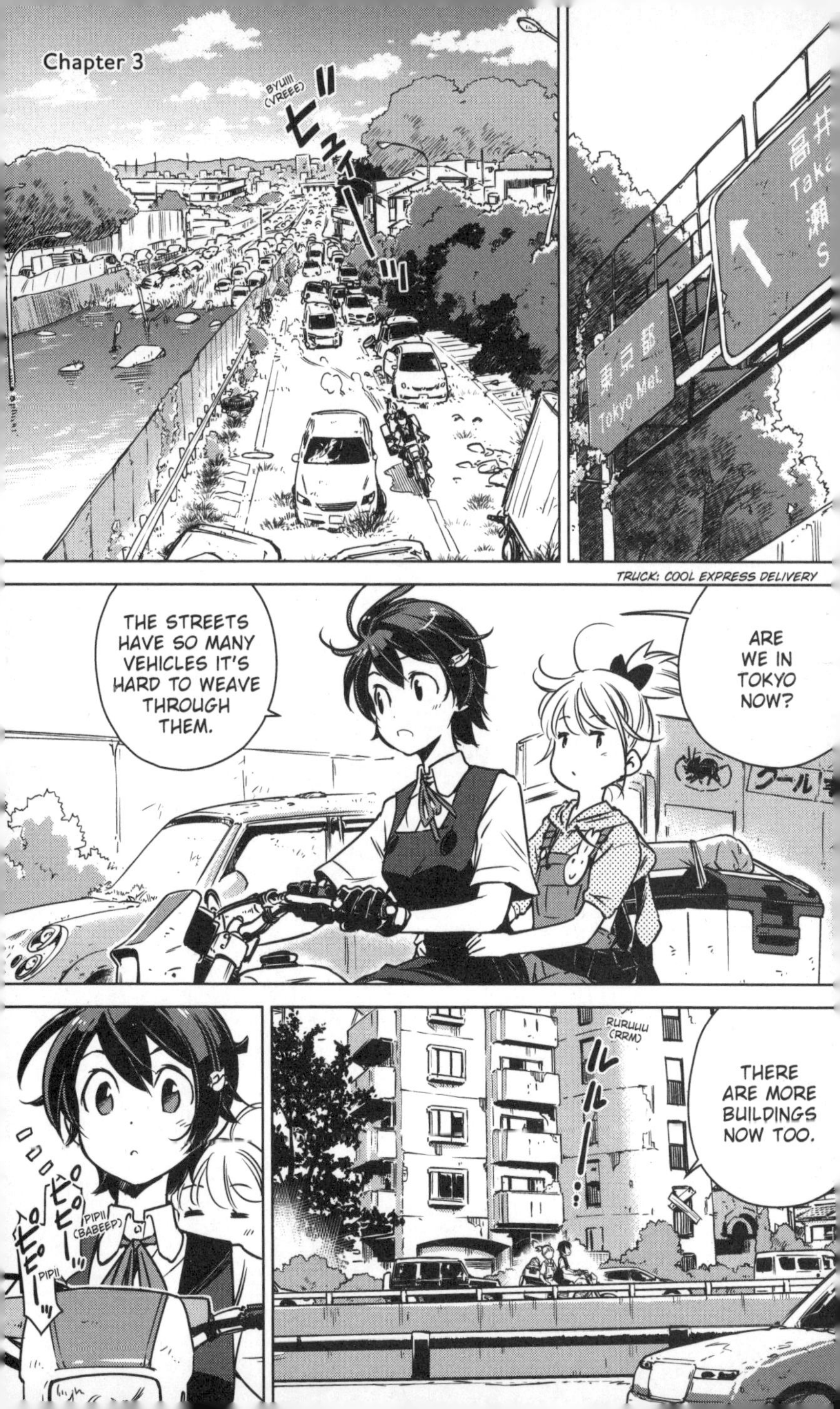
東京都
Tokyo Met
高井
Taka
瀬
Chapter 3
BYUIII (VREEE)
TRUCK: COOL EXPRESS DELIVERY
ARE WE IN TOKYO NOW?
THE STREETS HAVE SO MANY VEHICLES IT'S HARD TO WEAVE THROUGH THEM.
クール
RURUUU (RRM)
THERE ARE MORE BUILDINGS NOW TOO.
PIPI! (BABEEP)
PIPI!

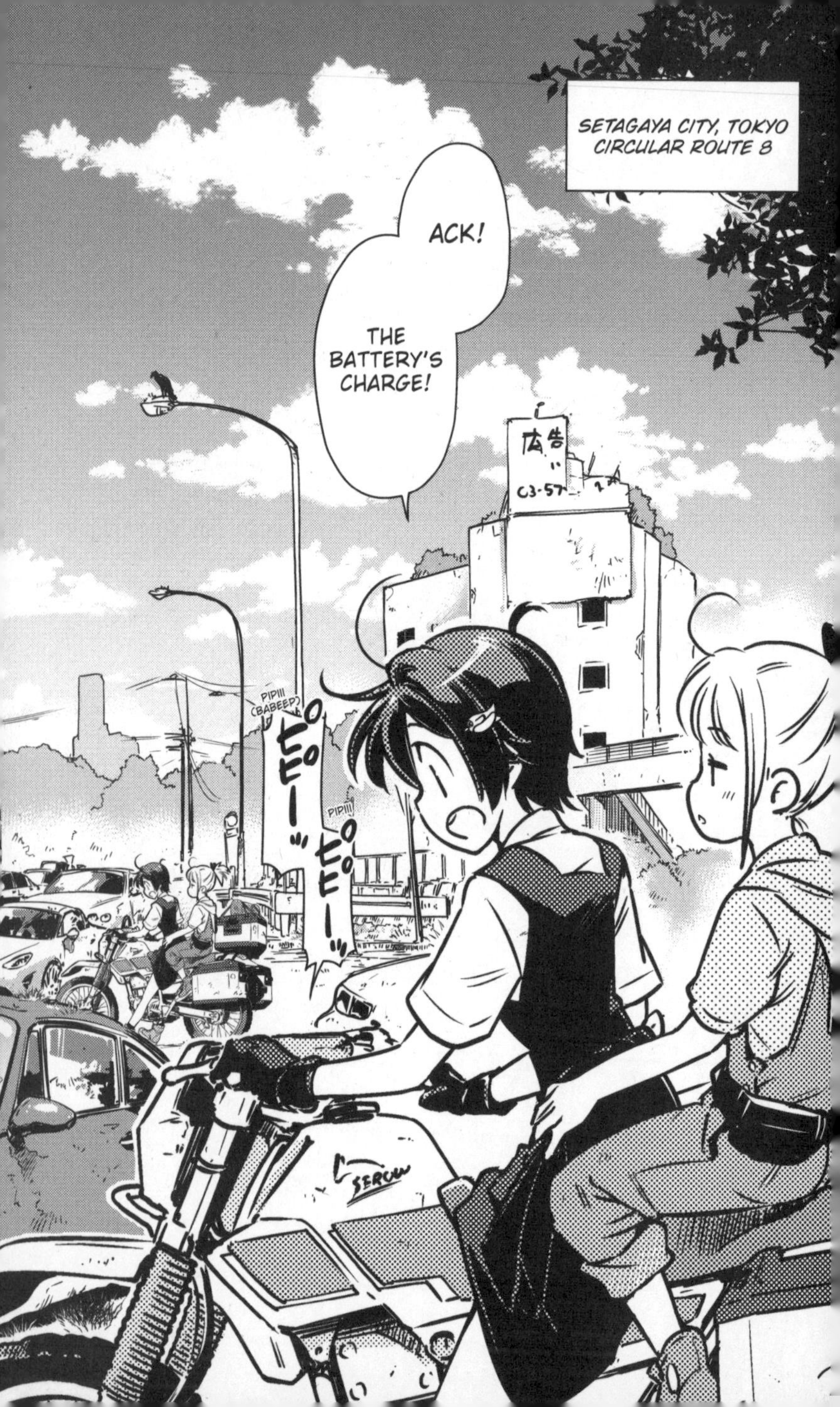
SETAGAYA CITY, TOKYO
CIRCULAR ROUTE 8
ACK!
THE BATTERY'S CHARGE!
PIPIII (BABEEP)
PIPIII

Chapter 3 | Setagaya

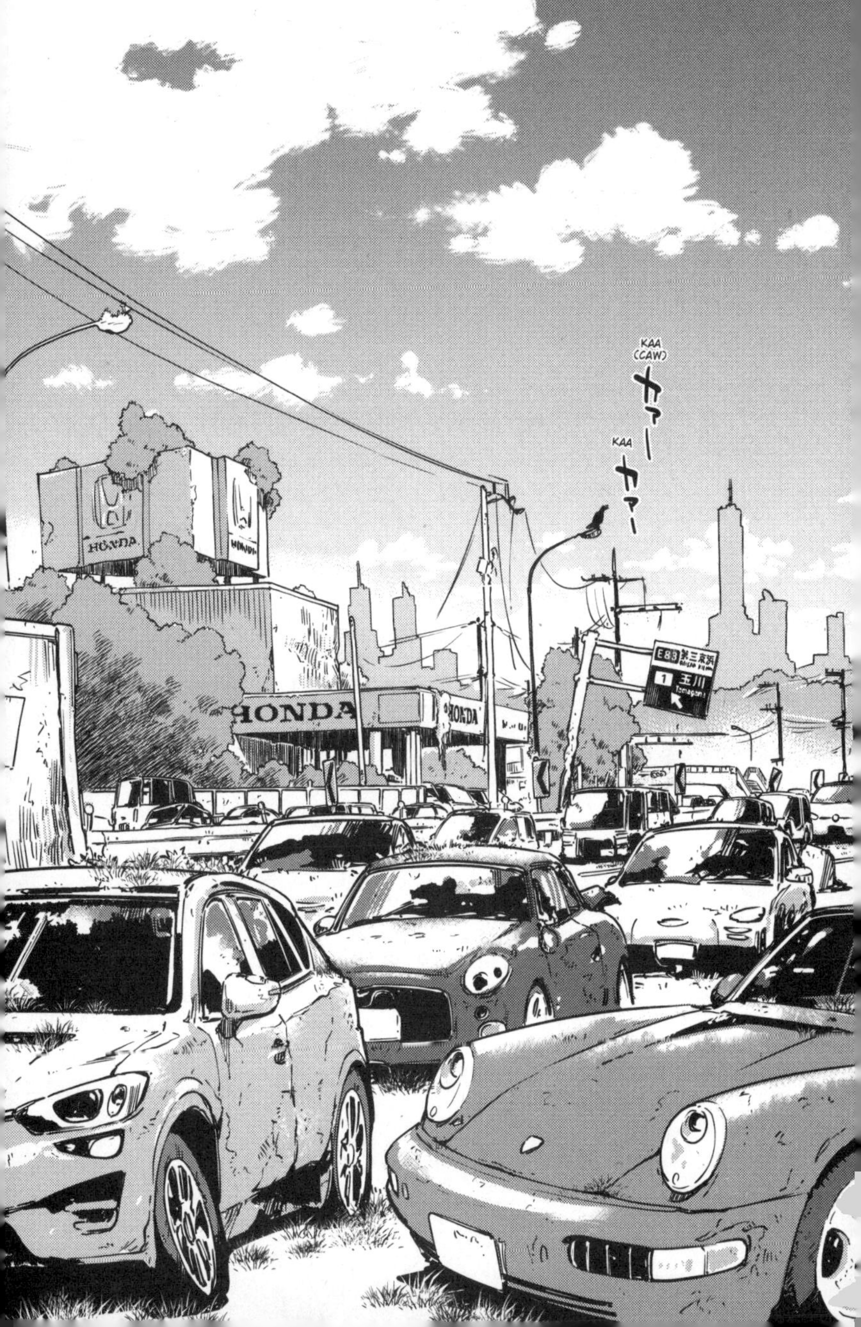
KAA
(CAW)
カァー
KAA
カァー
HONDA
HONDA
HONDA

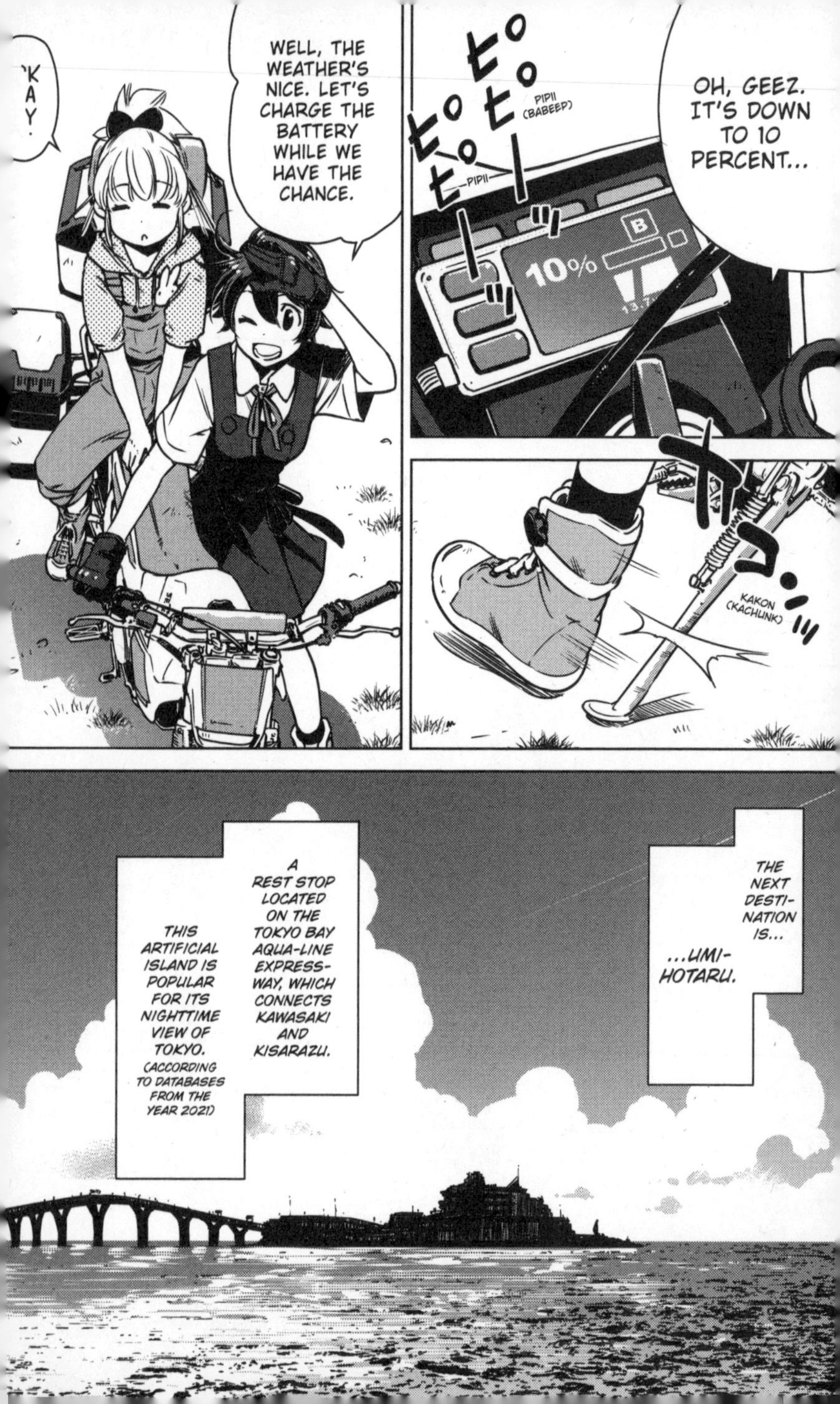
OH, GEEZ. IT'S DOWN TO 10 PERCENT...
PIPII (BABEEP)
PIPII
10%
B
KAKON (KACHUNK)
WELL, THE WEATHER'S NICE. LET'S CHARGE THE BATTERY WHILE WE HAVE THE CHANCE.
'KAY.
THE NEXT DESTINATION IS...
...UMI-HOTARU.
A REST STOP LOCATED ON THE TOKYO BAY AQUA-LINE EXPRESSWAY, WHICH CONNECTS KAWASAKI AND KISARAZU.
THIS ARTIFICIAL ISLAND IS POPULAR FOR ITS NIGHTTIME VIEW OF TOKYO.
(ACCORDING TO DATABASES FROM THE YEAR 2021)

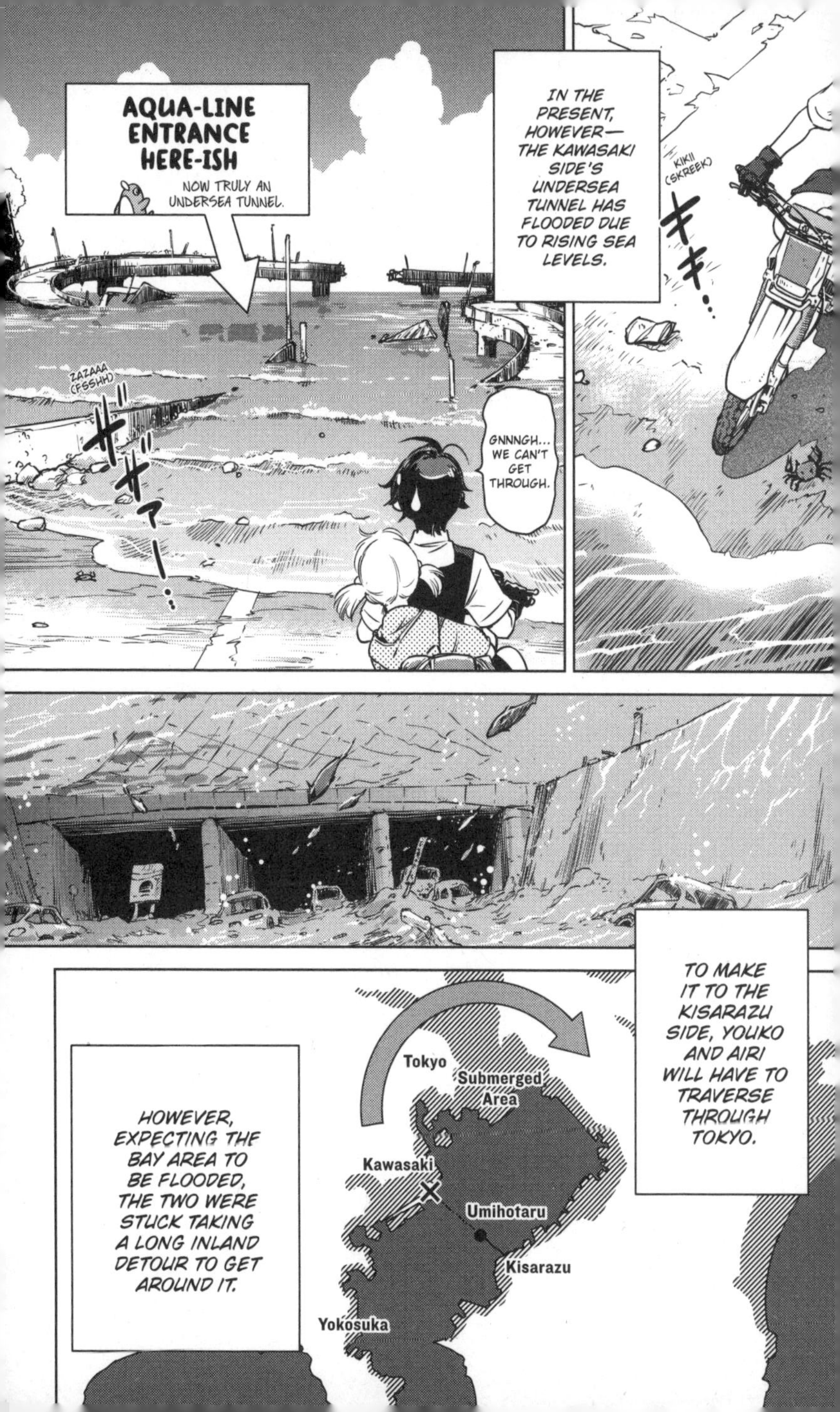
KIKII (SKREEK)
キキ…
IN THE PRESENT, HOWEVER— THE KAWASAKI SIDE'S UNDERSEA TUNNEL HAS FLOODED DUE TO RISING SEA LEVELS.
AQUA-LINE ENTRANCE HERE-ISH
NOW TRULY AN UNDERSEA TUNNEL.
ZAZAAA (FSSHH)
ザザァー…
GNNNGH... WE CAN'T GET THROUGH.
TO MAKE IT TO THE KISARAZU SIDE, YOUKO AND AIRI WILL HAVE TO TRAVERSE THROUGH TOKYO.
Tokyo
Submerged Area
Kawasaki
Umihotaru
Kisarazu
Yokosuka
HOWEVER, EXPECTING THE BAY AREA TO BE FLOODED, THE TWO WERE STUCK TAKING A LONG INLAND DETOUR TO GET AROUND IT.

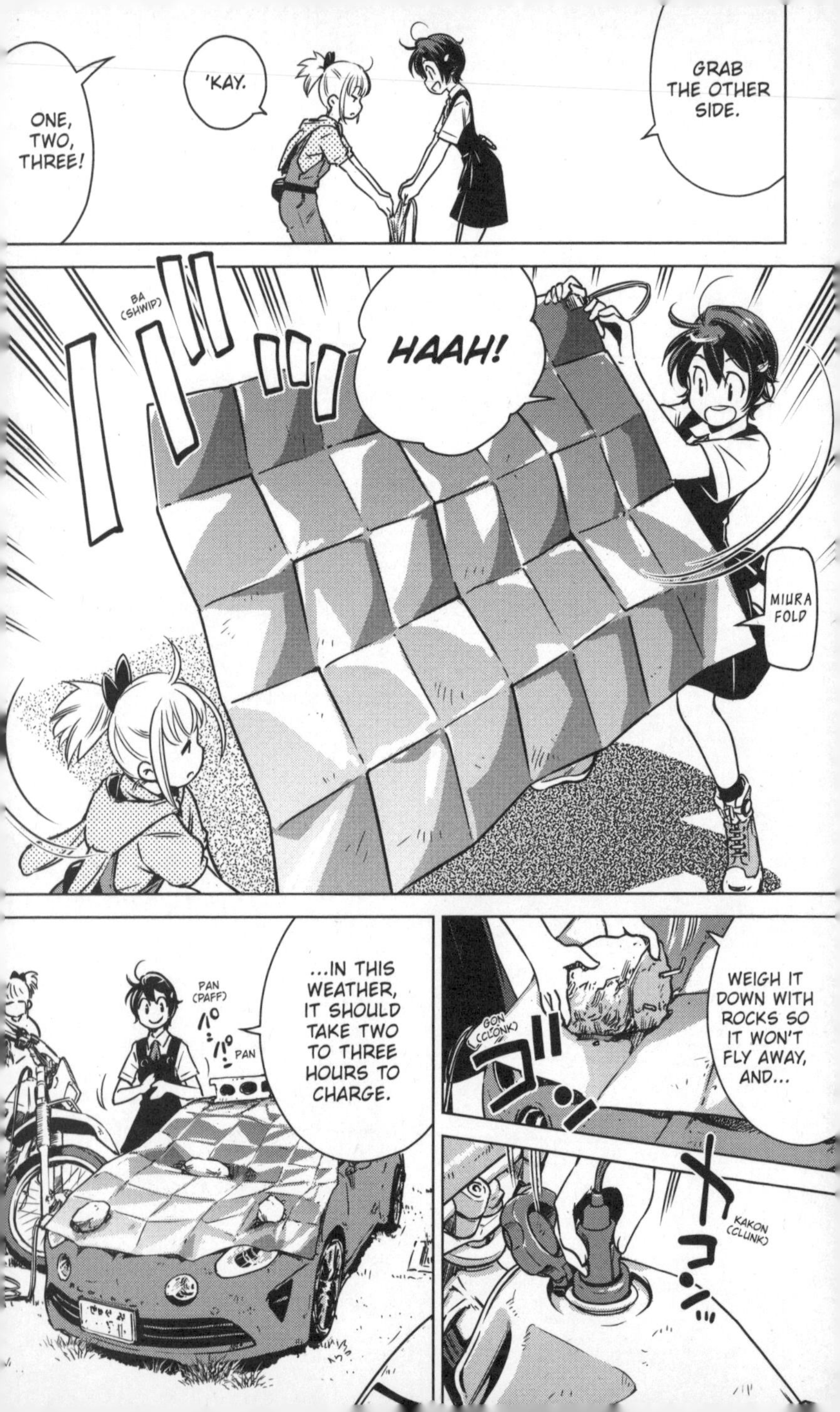
GRAB THE OTHER SIDE.
'KAY.
ONE, TWO, THREE!
HAAH!
BA (SHWIP)
MIURA FOLD
WEIGH IT DOWN WITH ROCKS SO IT WON'T FLY AWAY, AND...
GON (CLONK)
KAKON (CLUNK)
...IN THIS WEATHER, IT SHOULD TAKE TWO TO THREE HOURS TO CHARGE.
PAN (PAFF)
PAN

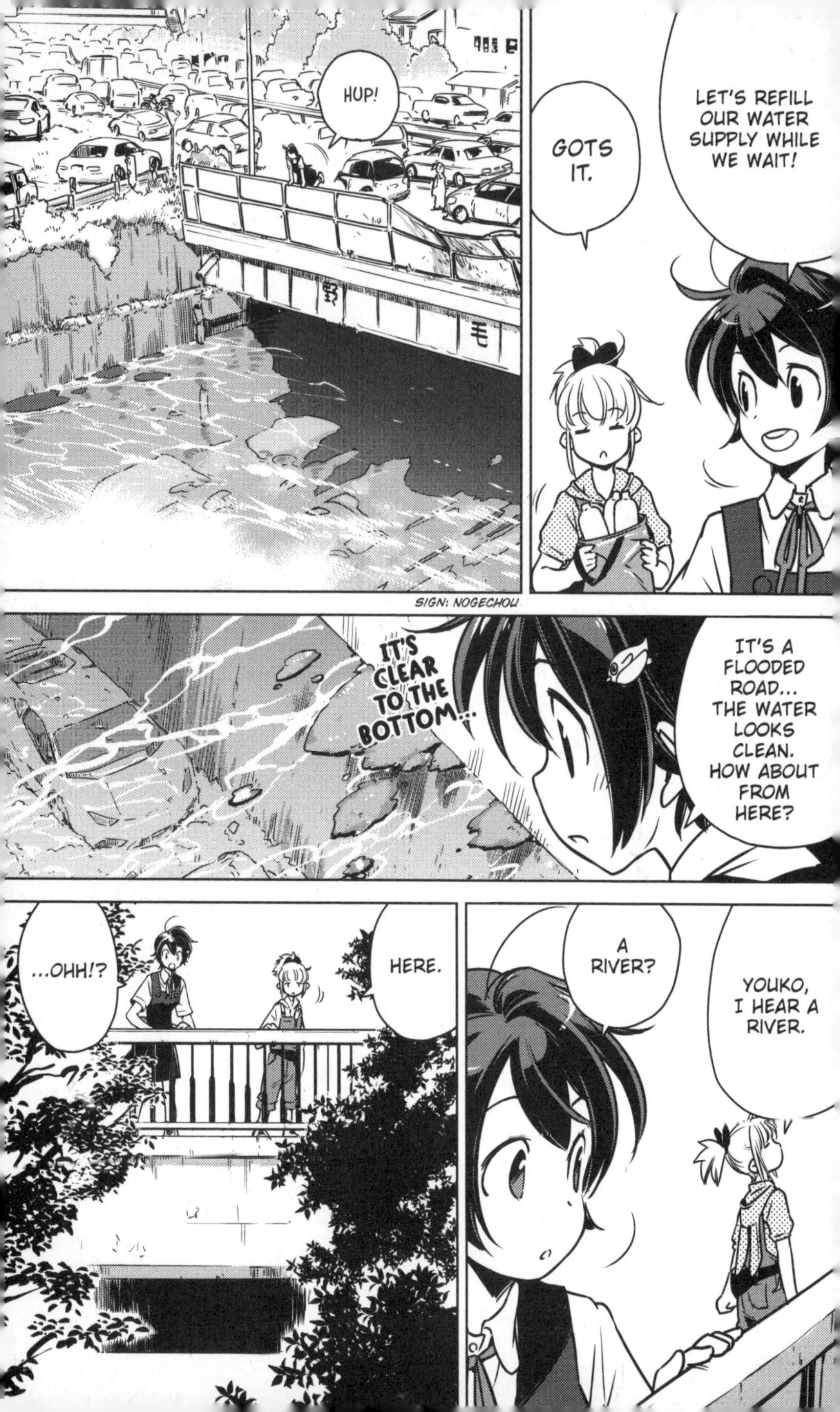
LET'S REFILL OUR WATER SUPPLY WHILE WE WAIT!
GOTS IT.
HUP!
SIGN: NOGECHOU
IT'S A FLOODED ROAD... THE WATER LOOKS CLEAN. HOW ABOUT FROM HERE?
IT'S CLEAR TO THE BOTTOM...
YOUKO, I HEAR A RIVER.
A RIVER?
HERE.
...OHH!?

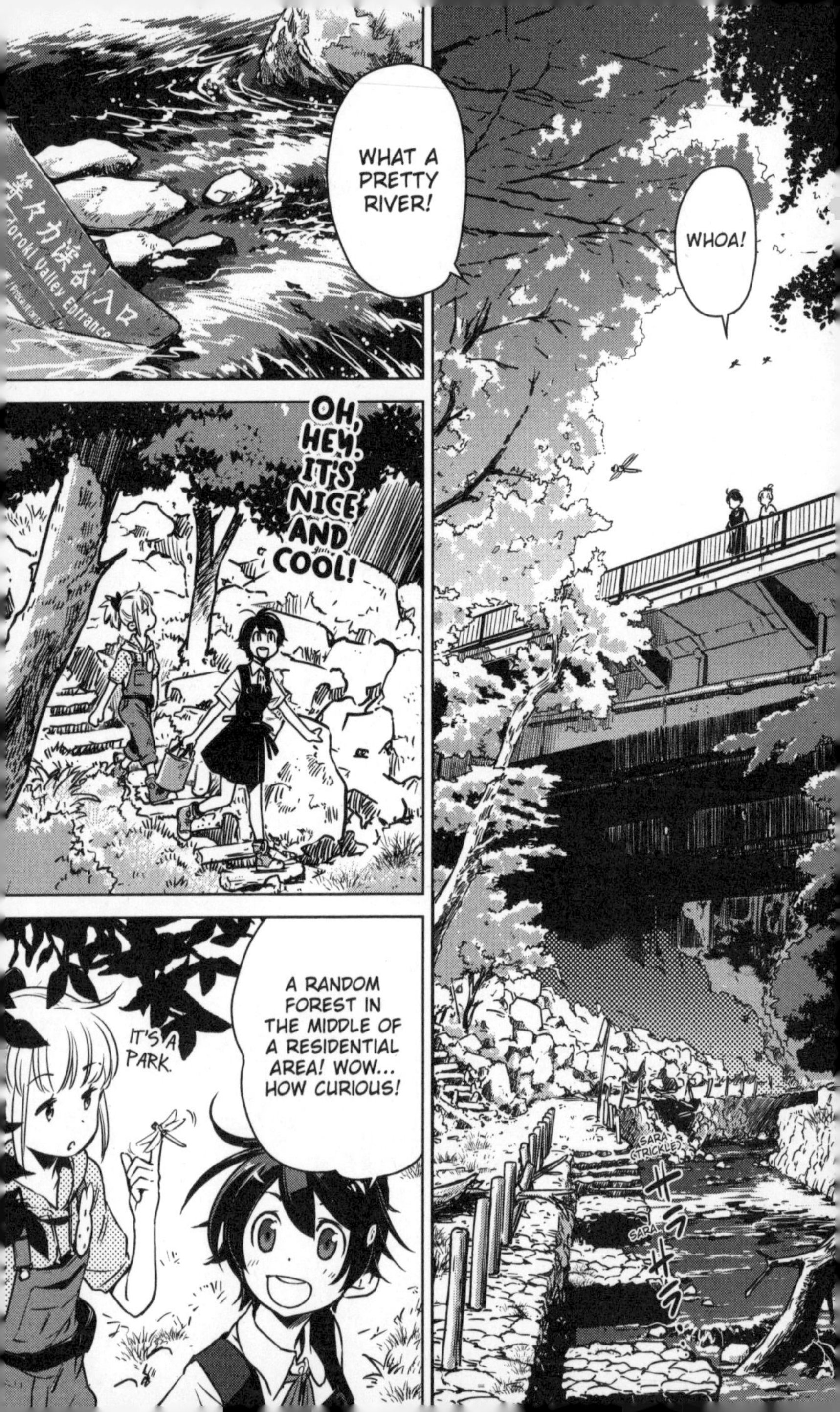
WHOA!
SARA (TRICKLE)
SARA
WHAT A PRETTY RIVER!
等々力渓谷入口
OH, HEY. IT'S NICE AND COOL!
A RANDOM FOREST IN THE MIDDLE OF A RESIDENTIAL AREA! WOW... HOW CURIOUS!
IT'S A PARK.

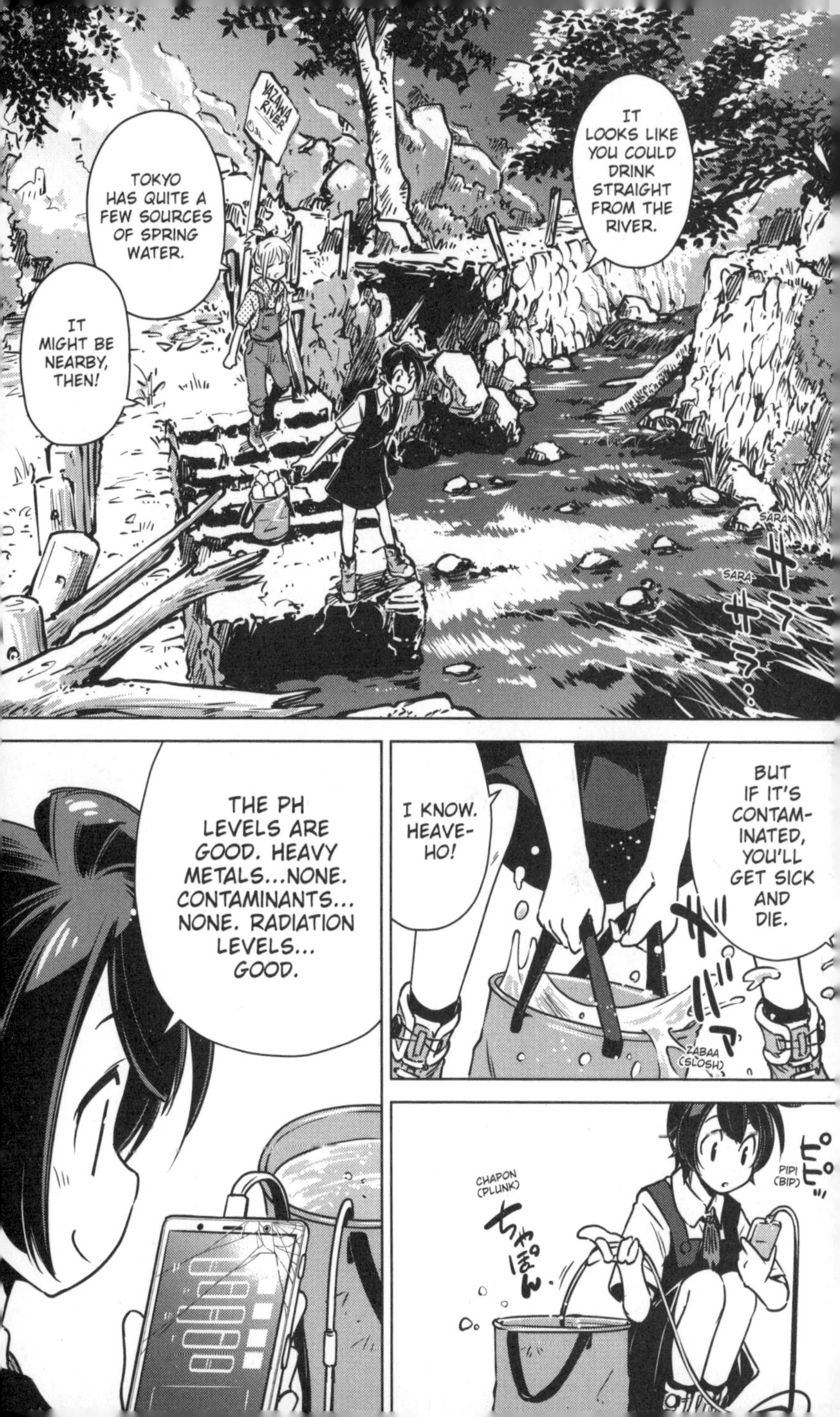
YAZAWA RIVER
IT LOOKS LIKE YOU COULD DRINK STRAIGHT FROM THE RIVER.
TOKYO HAS QUITE A FEW SOURCES OF SPRING WATER.
IT MIGHT BE NEARBY, THEN!
SARA SARA
BUT IF IT'S CONTAM-INATED, YOU'LL GET SICK AND DIE.
I KNOW. HEAVE-HO!
ZABAA (SLOSH)
PIPI (BIP)
CHAPON (PLUNK)
THE PH LEVELS ARE GOOD. HEAVY METALS...NONE. CONTAMINANTS... NONE. RADIATION LEVELS... GOOD.

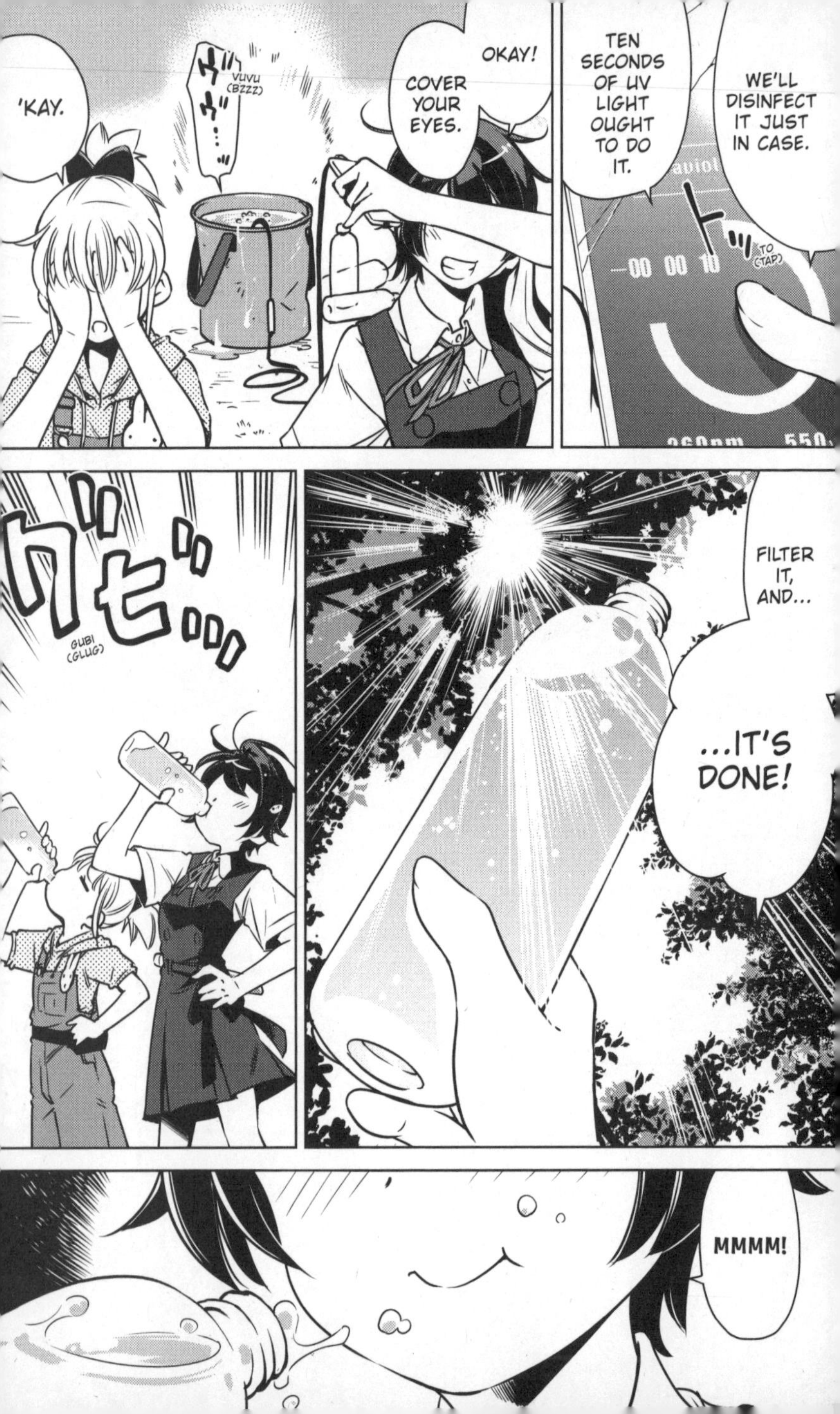
WE'LL DISINFECT IT JUST IN CASE.
TEN SECONDS OF UV LIGHT OUGHT TO DO IT.
00 00 10
TO (TAP)
OKAY!
COVER YOUR EYES.
VUVU (BZZZ)
'KAY.
FILTER IT, AND...
...IT'S DONE!
GUBI (GLUG)
MMMM!

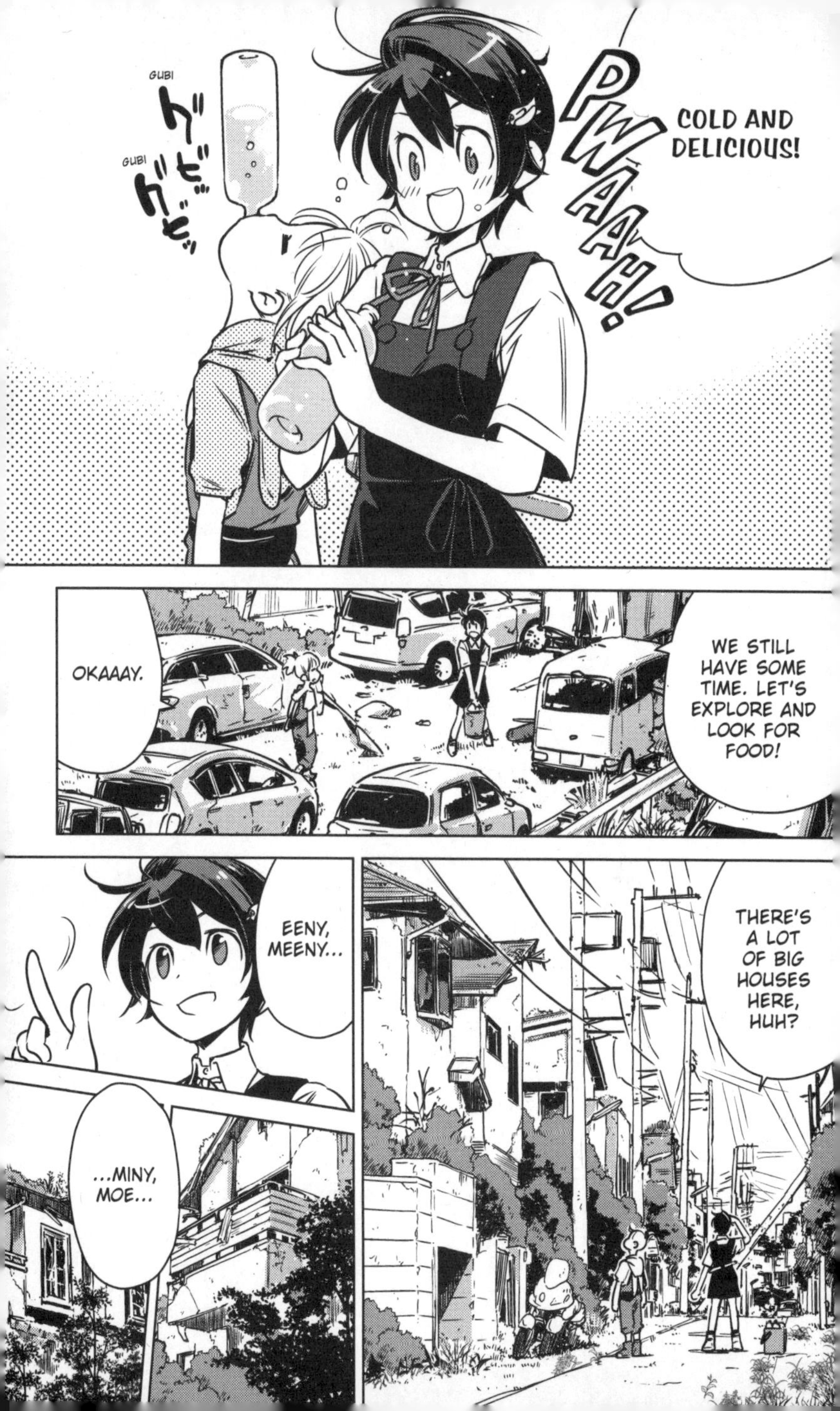
PWAAH!
COLD AND DELICIOUS!
GUBI
GUBI
WE STILL HAVE SOME TIME. LET'S EXPLORE AND LOOK FOR FOOD!
OKAAAY.
THERE'S A LOT OF BIG HOUSES HERE, HUH?
EENY, MEENY...
...MINY, MOE...

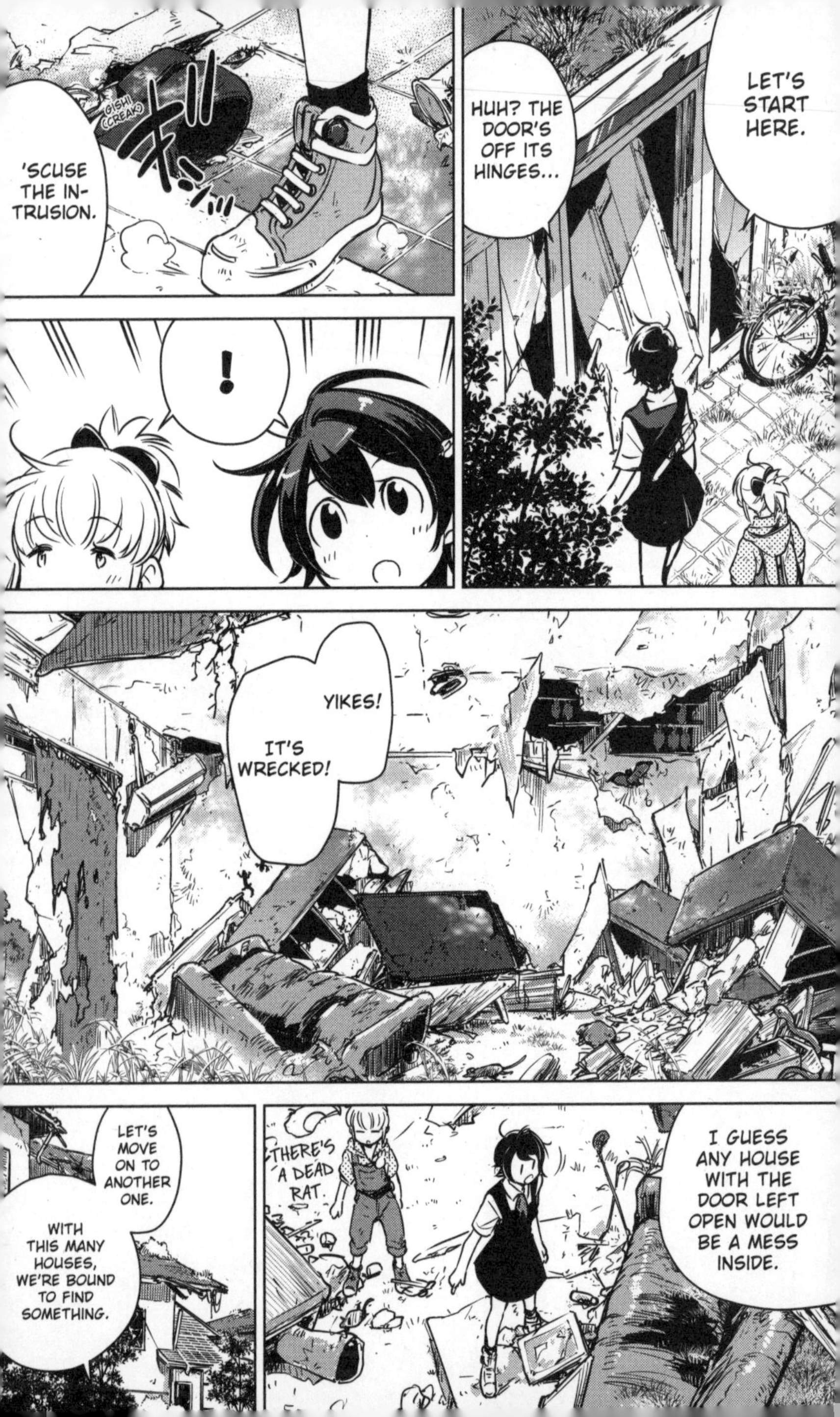
LET'S START HERE.
HUH? THE DOOR'S OFF ITS HINGES...
GISHI (CREAK)
'SCUSE THE IN-TRUSION.
!
YIKES!
IT'S WRECKED!
I GUESS ANY HOUSE WITH THE DOOR LEFT OPEN WOULD BE A MESS INSIDE.
THERE'S A DEAD RAT.
LET'S MOVE ON TO ANOTHER ONE.
WITH THIS MANY HOUSES, WE'RE BOUND TO FIND SOMETHING.

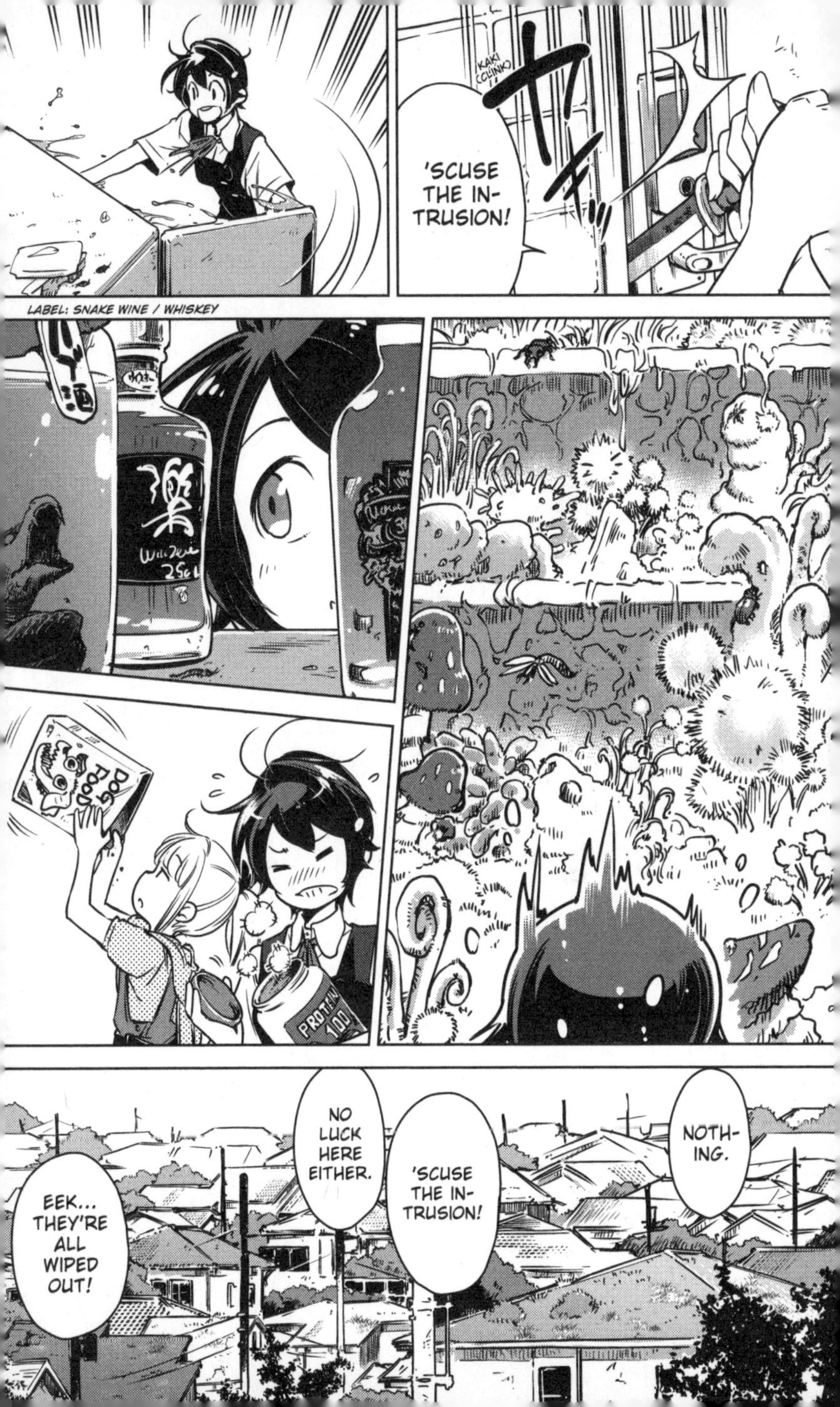
KAKI (CLINK)
'SCUSE THE IN-TRUSION!
LABEL: SNAKE WINE / WHISKEY
DOG FOOD
PROTEIN 100
NOTH-ING.
'SCUSE THE IN-TRUSION!
NO LUCK HERE EITHER.
EEK... THEY'RE ALL WIPED OUT!

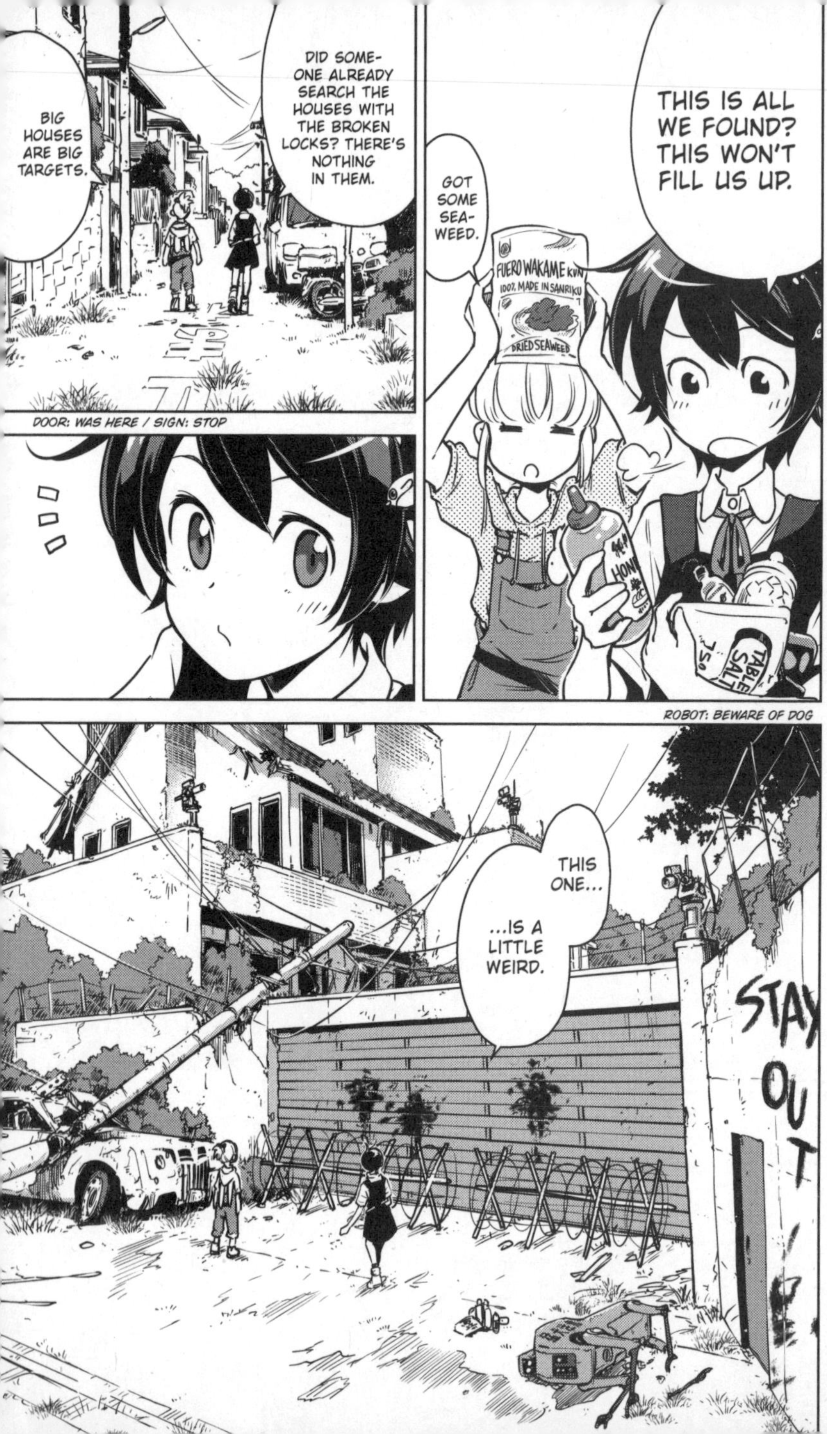
THIS IS ALL WE FOUND? THIS WON'T FILL US UP.
GOT SOME SEA-WEED.
FUERO WAKAME KUN
100% MADE IN SANRIKU
DRIED SEAWEED
TABLE SALT
DID SOME-ONE ALREADY SEARCH THE HOUSES WITH THE BROKEN LOCKS? THERE'S NOTHING IN THEM.
BIG HOUSES ARE BIG TARGETS.
DOOR: WAS HERE / SIGN: STOP
ROBOT: BEWARE OF DOG
THIS ONE...
...IS A LITTLE WEIRD.
STAY OUT

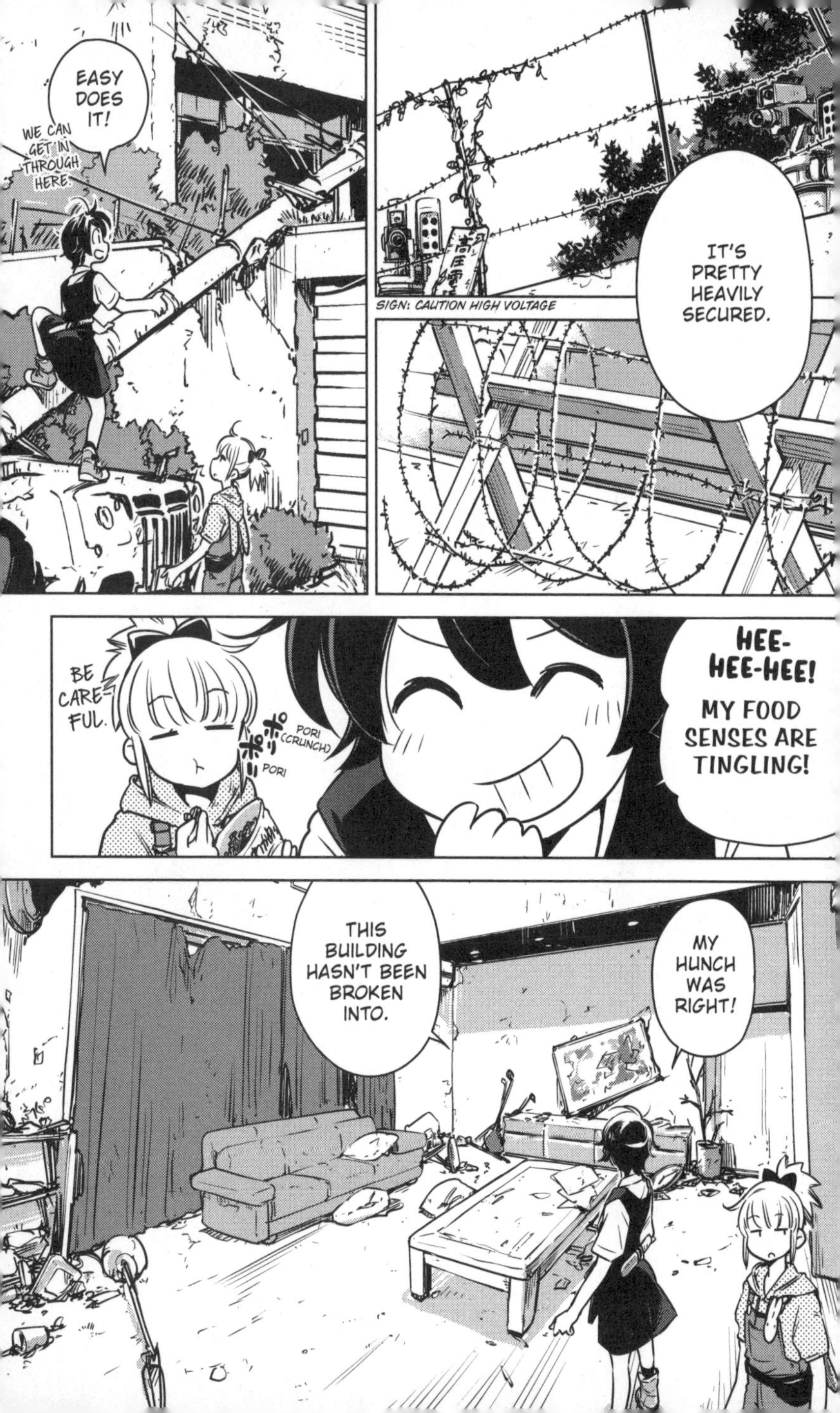
SIGN: CAUTION HIGH VOLTAGE
IT'S PRETTY HEAVILY SECURED.
EASY DOES IT!
WE CAN GET IN THROUGH HERE.
HEE-HEE-HEE! MY FOOD SENSES ARE TINGLING!
ポリ PORI (CRUNCH)
ポリ PORI
BE CAREFUL.
MY HUNCH WAS RIGHT!
THIS BUILDING HASN'T BEEN BROKEN INTO.

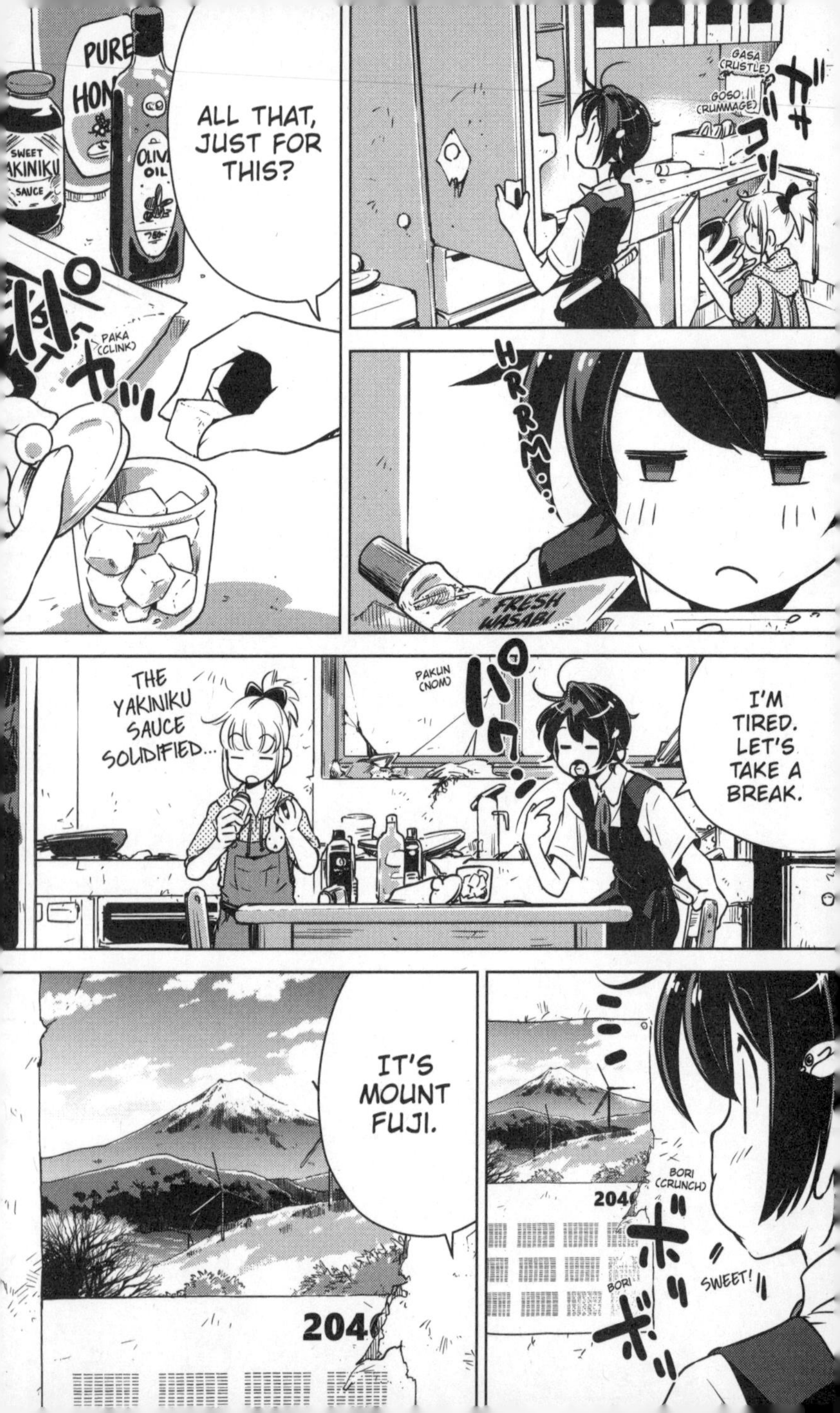
GASA (RUSTLE)
GOSO (RUMMAGE)
HRRM...
FRESH WASABI
ALL THAT, JUST FOR THIS?
PURE
SWEET YAKINIKU SAUCE
OIL
PAKA (CLINK)
I'M TIRED. LET'S TAKE A BREAK.
PAKUN (NOM)
THE YAKINIKU SAUCE SOLIDIFIED...
BORI (CRUNCH)
BORI
SWEET!
IT'S MOUNT FUJI.

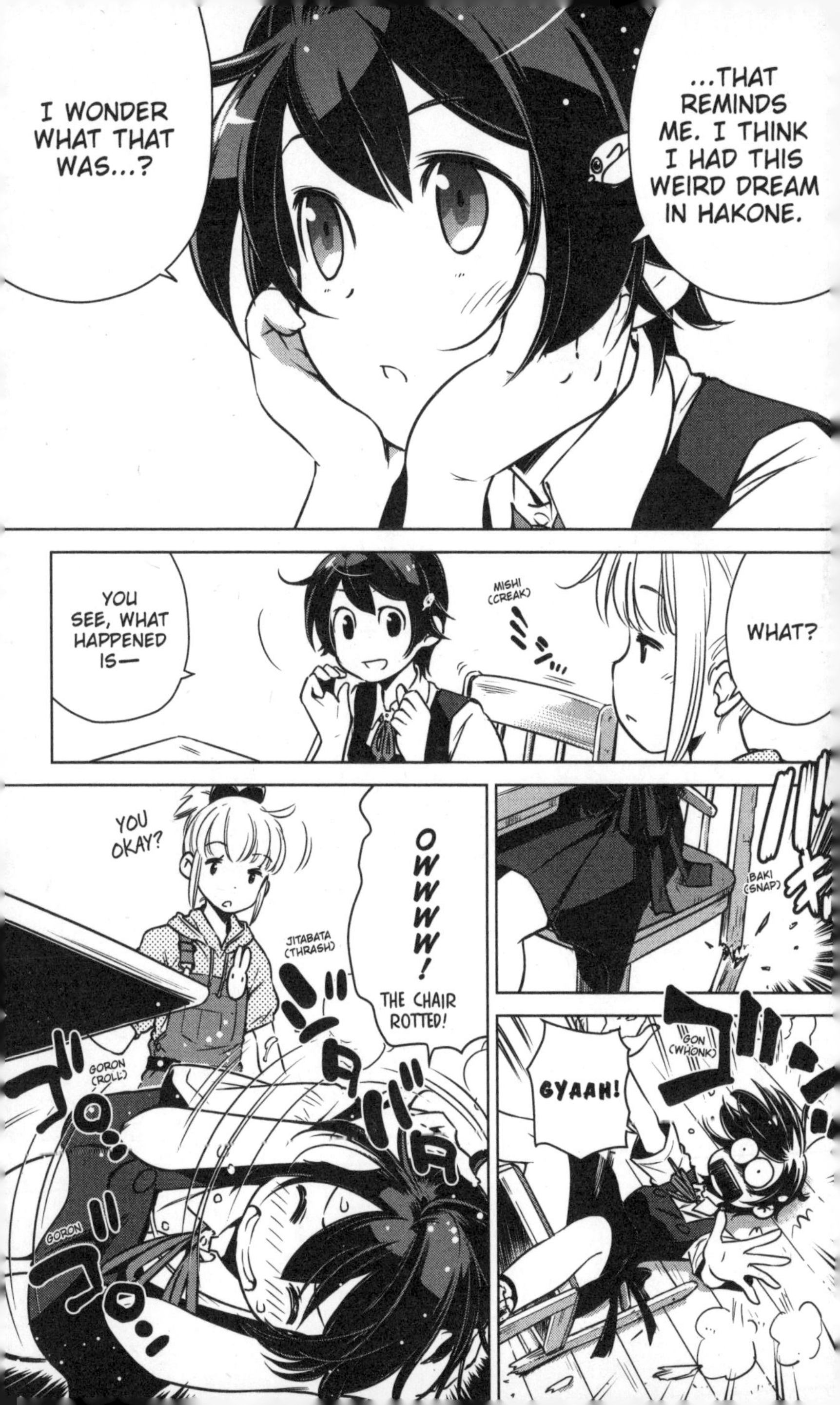
...THAT REMINDS ME. I THINK I HAD THIS WEIRD DREAM IN HAKONE.
I WONDER WHAT THAT WAS...?
WHAT?
MISHI (CREAK)
YOU SEE, WHAT HAPPENED IS—
BAKI (SNAP)
GON (WHONK)
GYAAH!
OWWWWW!
THE CHAIR ROTTED!
YOU OKAY?
JITABATA (THRASH)
GORON (ROLL)
GORON

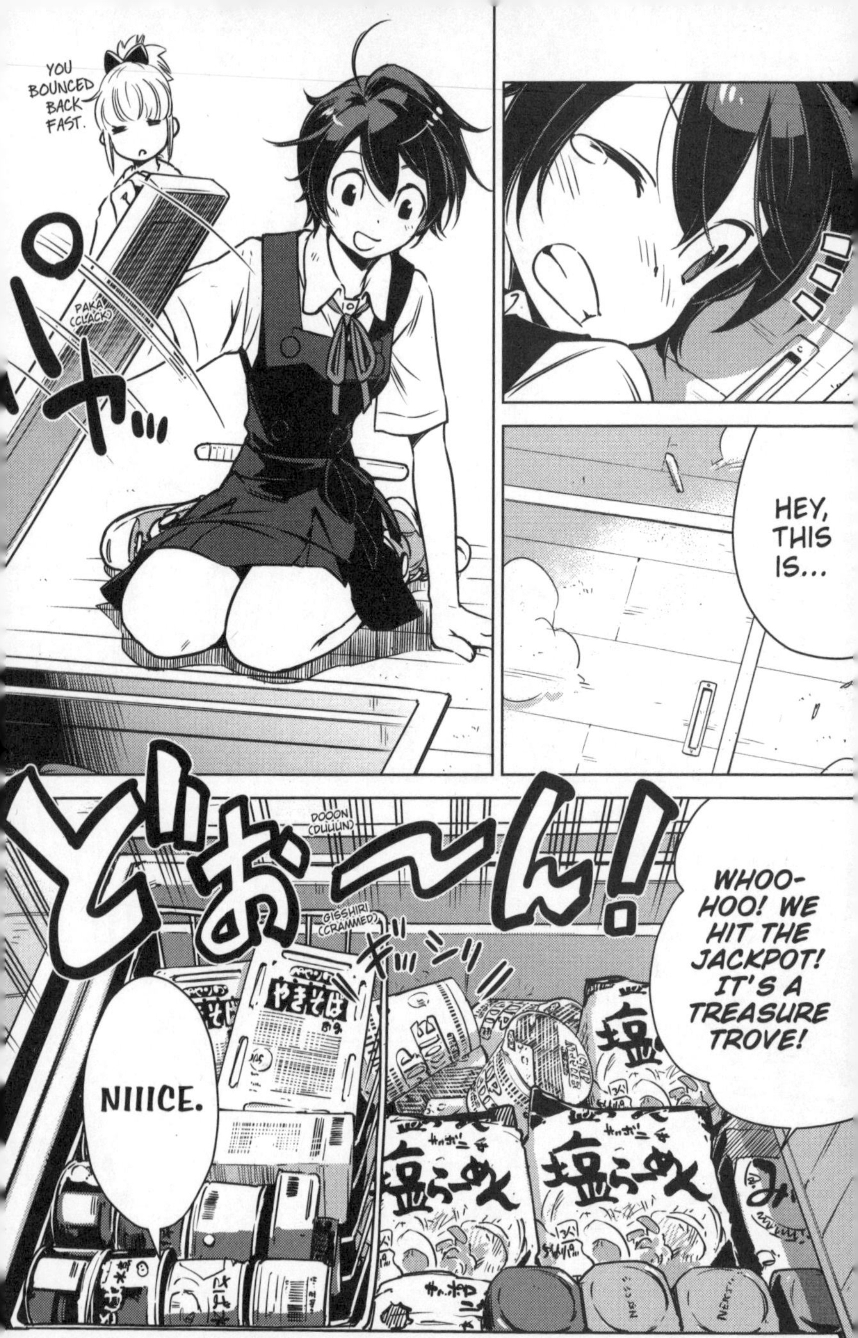
HEY, THIS IS...
YOU BOUNCED BACK FAST.
PAKA (CLACK)
WHOO-HOO! WE HIT THE JACKPOT! IT'S A TREASURE TROVE!
DOOON (DUUUN)
GISSHIRI (CRAMMED)
やきそば
塩らーめん
NIIICE.

PACKAGES: PEYOUNG YAKISOBA / MACKEREL / SAPPORO NIBAN SALT RAMEN

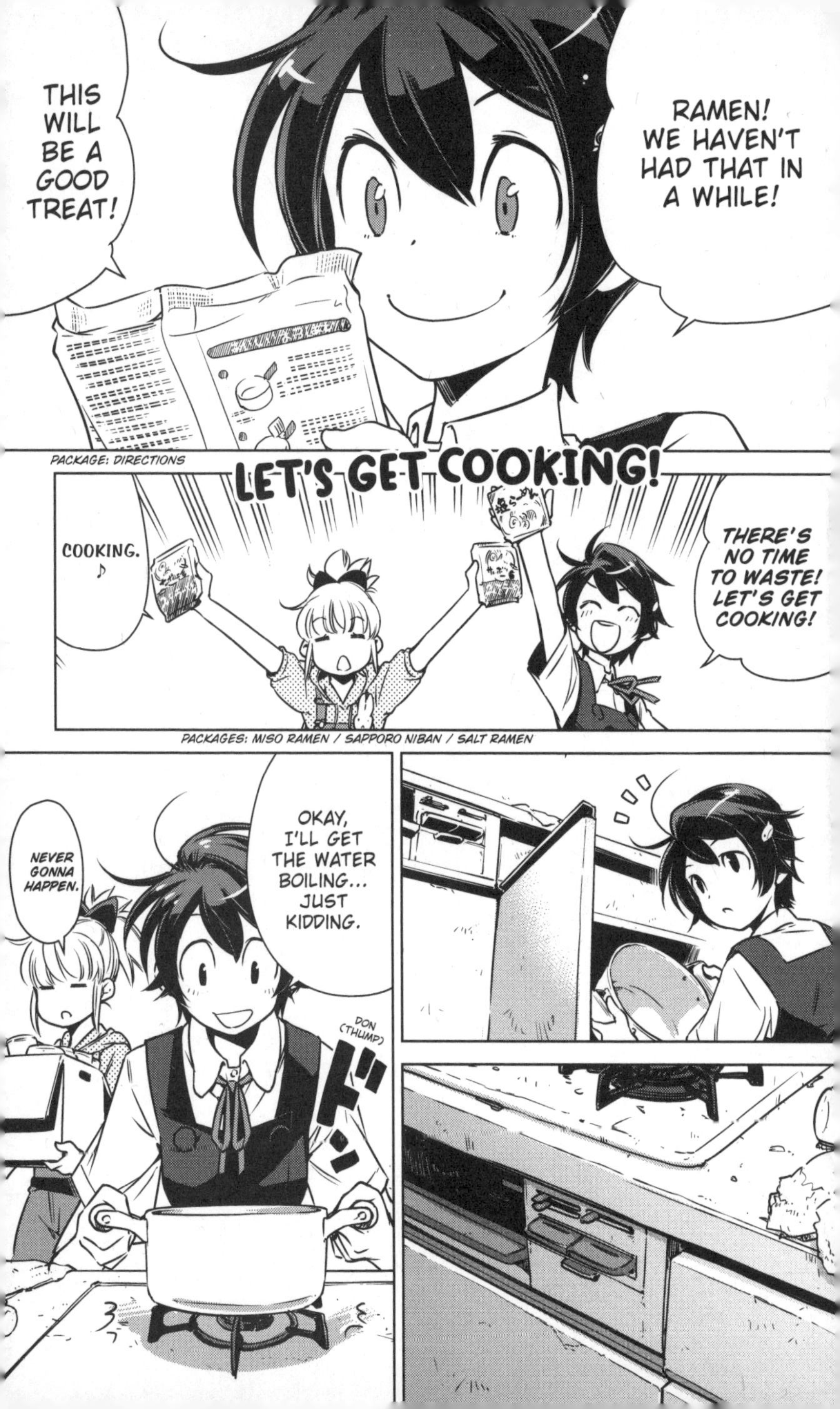
RAMEN! WE HAVEN'T HAD THAT IN A WHILE!
THIS WILL BE A GOOD TREAT!
PACKAGE: DIRECTIONS
LET'S GET COOKING!
THERE'S NO TIME TO WASTE! LET'S GET COOKING!
COOKING. ♪
PACKAGES: MISO RAMEN / SAPPORO NIBAN / SALT RAMEN
OKAY, I'LL GET THE WATER BOILING... JUST KIDDING.
NEVER GONNA HAPPEN.
DON (THUMP)

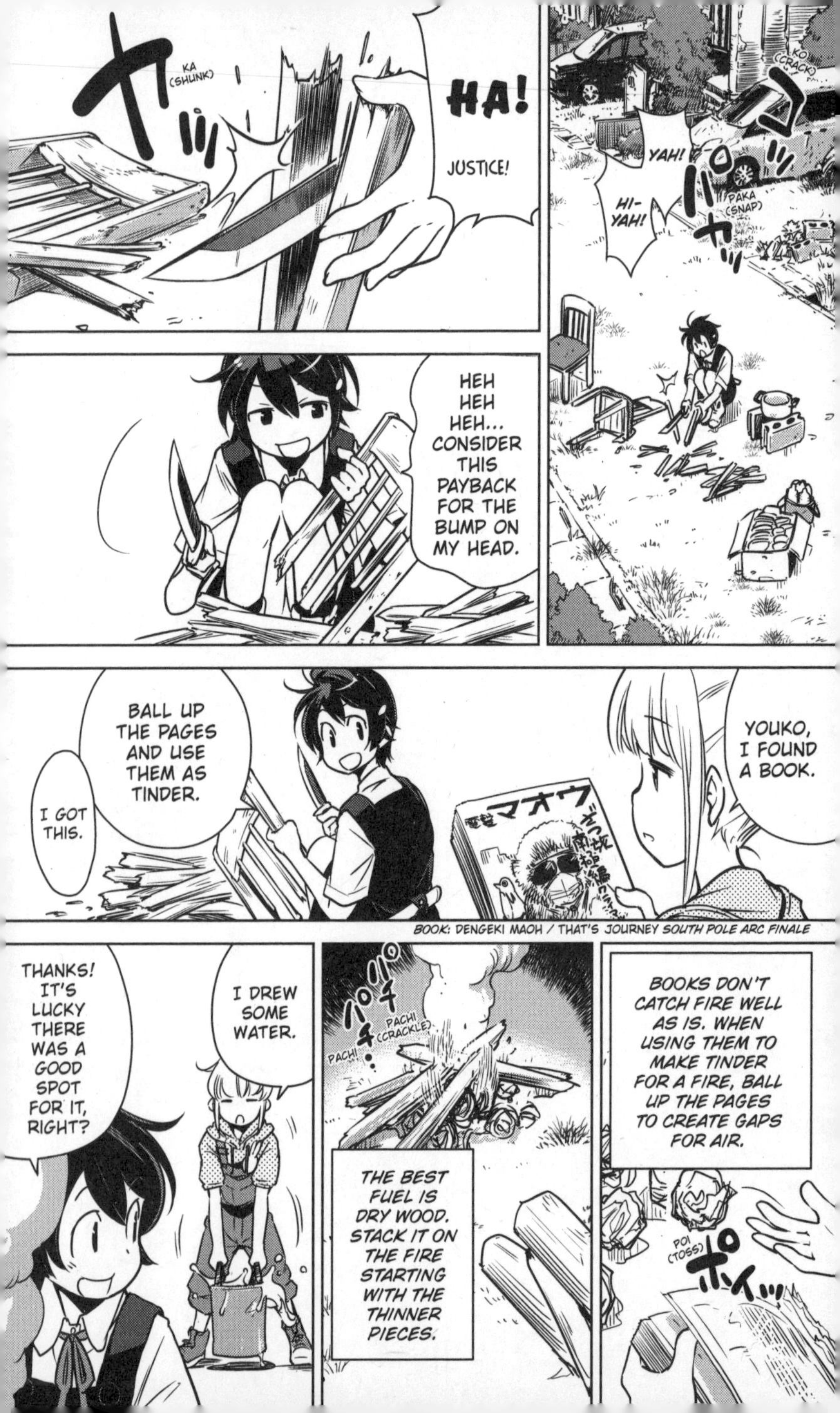
KO (CRACK)
YAH!
HI-YAH!
PAKA (SNAP)
KA (SHUNK)
HA!
JUSTICE!
HEH HEH HEH... CONSIDER THIS PAYBACK FOR THE BUMP ON MY HEAD.
YOUKO, I FOUND A BOOK.
BALL UP THE PAGES AND USE THEM AS TINDER.
I GOT THIS.
BOOK: DENGEKI MAOH / THAT'S JOURNEY SOUTH POLE ARC FINALE
BOOKS DON'T CATCH FIRE WELL AS IS. WHEN USING THEM TO MAKE TINDER FOR A FIRE, BALL UP THE PAGES TO CREATE GAPS FOR AIR.
POI (TOSS)
PACHI (CRACKLE)
PACHI
THE BEST FUEL IS DRY WOOD. STACK IT ON THE FIRE STARTING WITH THE THINNER PIECES.
I DREW SOME WATER.
THANKS! IT'S LUCKY THERE WAS A GOOD SPOT FOR IT, RIGHT?

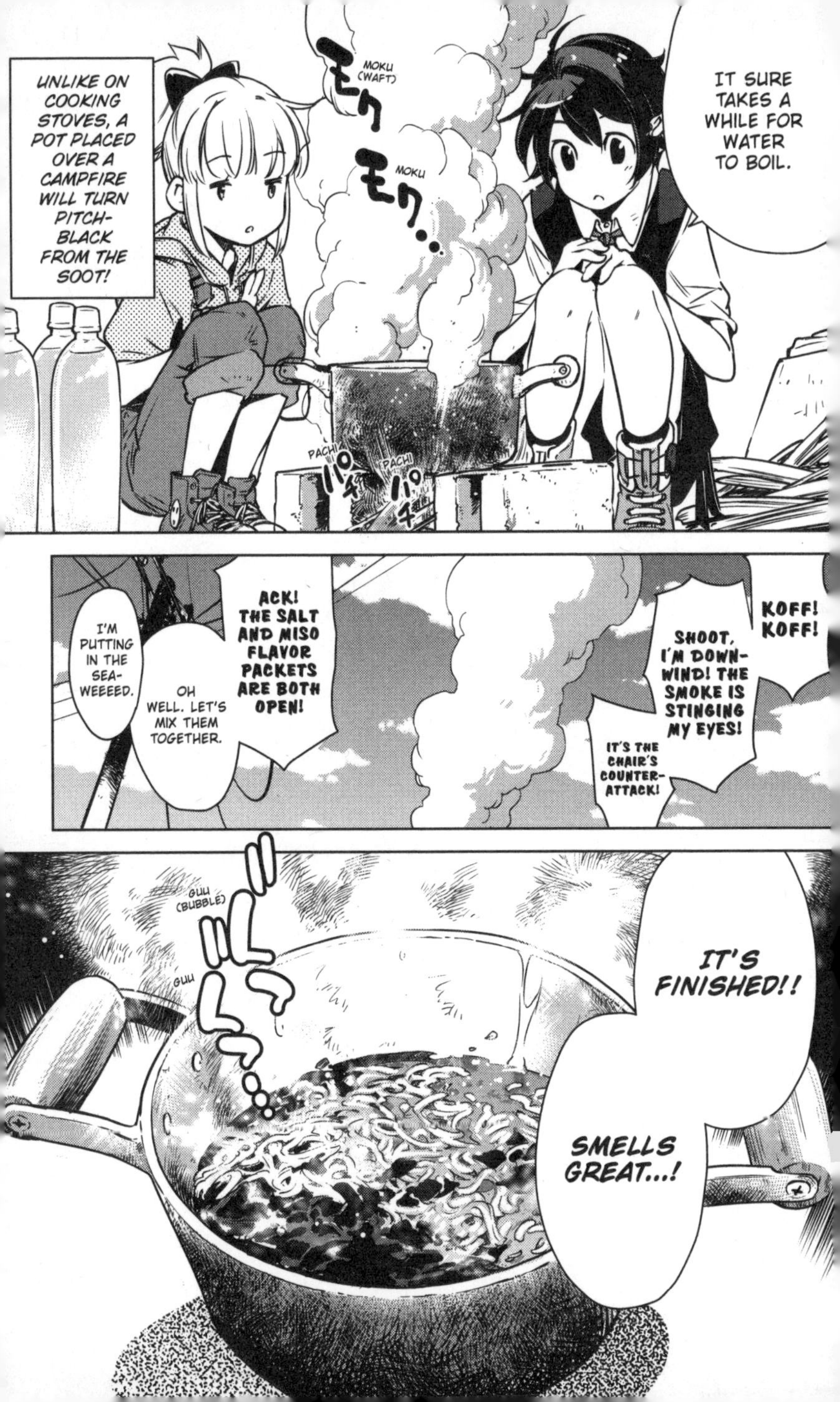
IT SURE TAKES A WHILE FOR WATER TO BOIL.
MOKU (WAFT)
MOKU
PACHI
PACHI
UNLIKE ON COOKING STOVES, A POT PLACED OVER A CAMPFIRE WILL TURN PITCH-BLACK FROM THE SOOT!
KOFF! KOFF!
SHOOT, I'M DOWN-WIND! THE SMOKE IS STINGING MY EYES!
IT'S THE CHAIR'S COUNTER-ATTACK!
ACK! THE SALT AND MISO FLAVOR PACKETS ARE BOTH OPEN!
I'M PUTTING IN THE SEA-WEEEED.
OH WELL. LET'S MIX THEM TOGETHER.
IT'S FINISHED!!
SMELLS GREAT...!
GUU (BUBBLE)
GUU

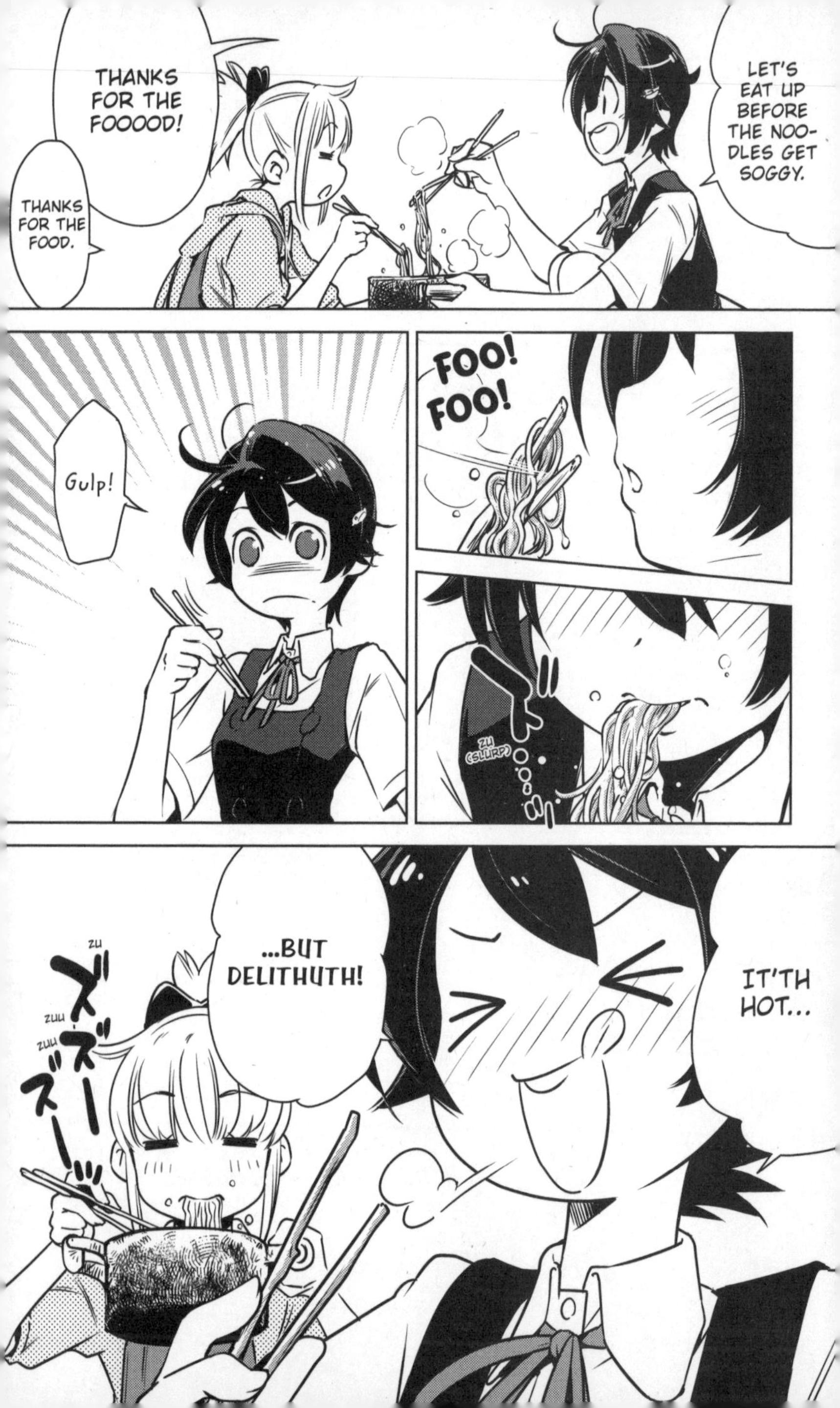
LET'S EAT UP BEFORE THE NOO-DLES GET SOGGY.
THANKS FOR THE FOOOOD!
THANKS FOR THE FOOD.
FOO! FOO!
ZU (SLURP)
Gulp!
IT'TH HOT...
...BUT DELITHUTH!
ZU ZUU ZUU

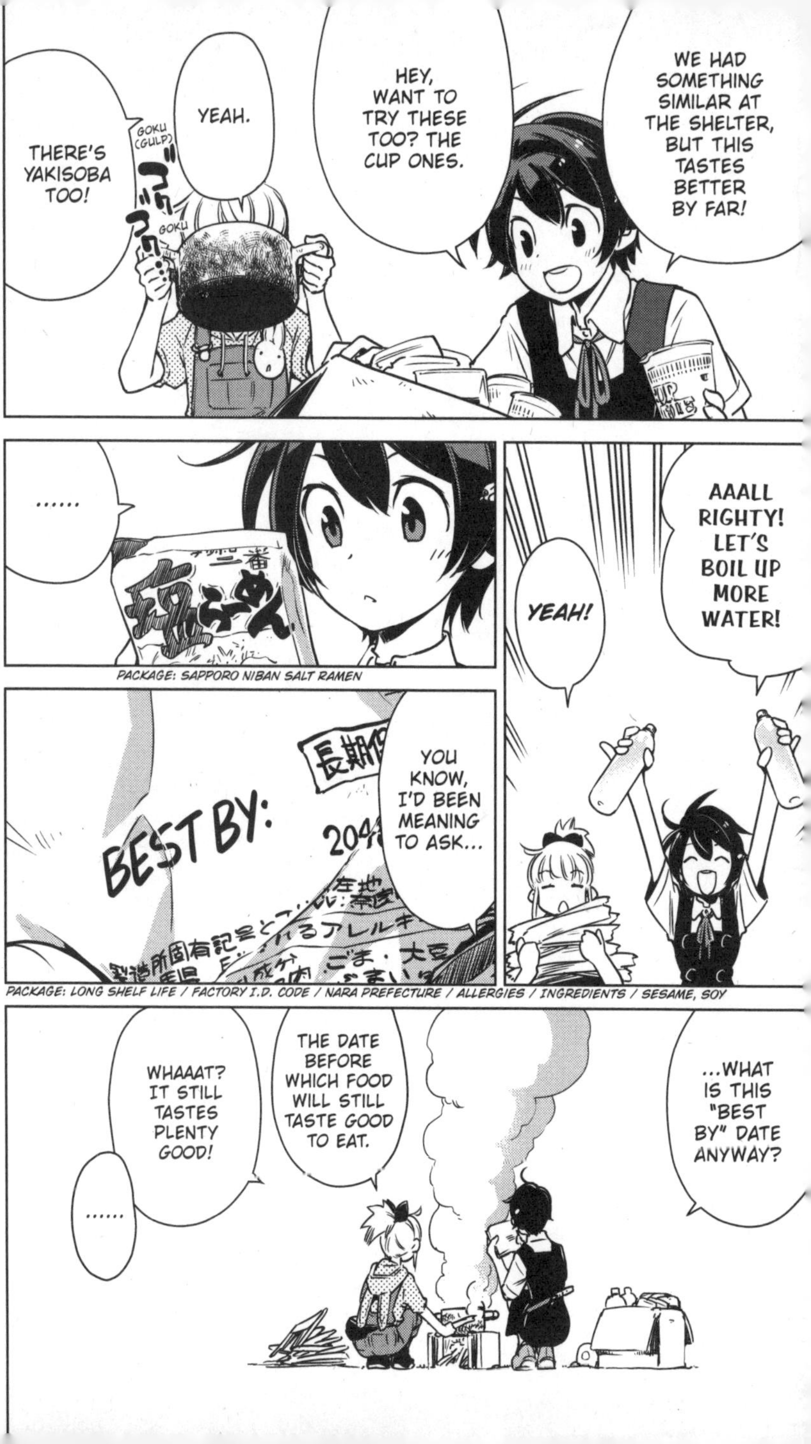
WE HAD SOMETHING SIMILAR AT THE SHELTER, BUT THIS TASTES BETTER BY FAR!
HEY, WANT TO TRY THESE TOO? THE CUP ONES.
YEAH.
GOKU (GULP)
GOKU
THERE'S YAKISOBA TOO!
AAALL RIGHTY! LET'S BOIL UP MORE WATER!
YEAH!
......
PACKAGE: SAPPORO NIBAN SALT RAMEN
YOU KNOW, I'D BEEN MEANING TO ASK...
BEST BY:
PACKAGE: LONG SHELF LIFE / FACTORY I.D. CODE / NARA PREFECTURE / ALLERGIES / INGREDIENTS / SESAME, SOY
...WHAT IS THIS "BEST BY" DATE ANYWAY?
THE DATE BEFORE WHICH FOOD WILL STILL TASTE GOOD TO EAT.
WHAAAT? IT STILL TASTES PLENTY GOOD!
......

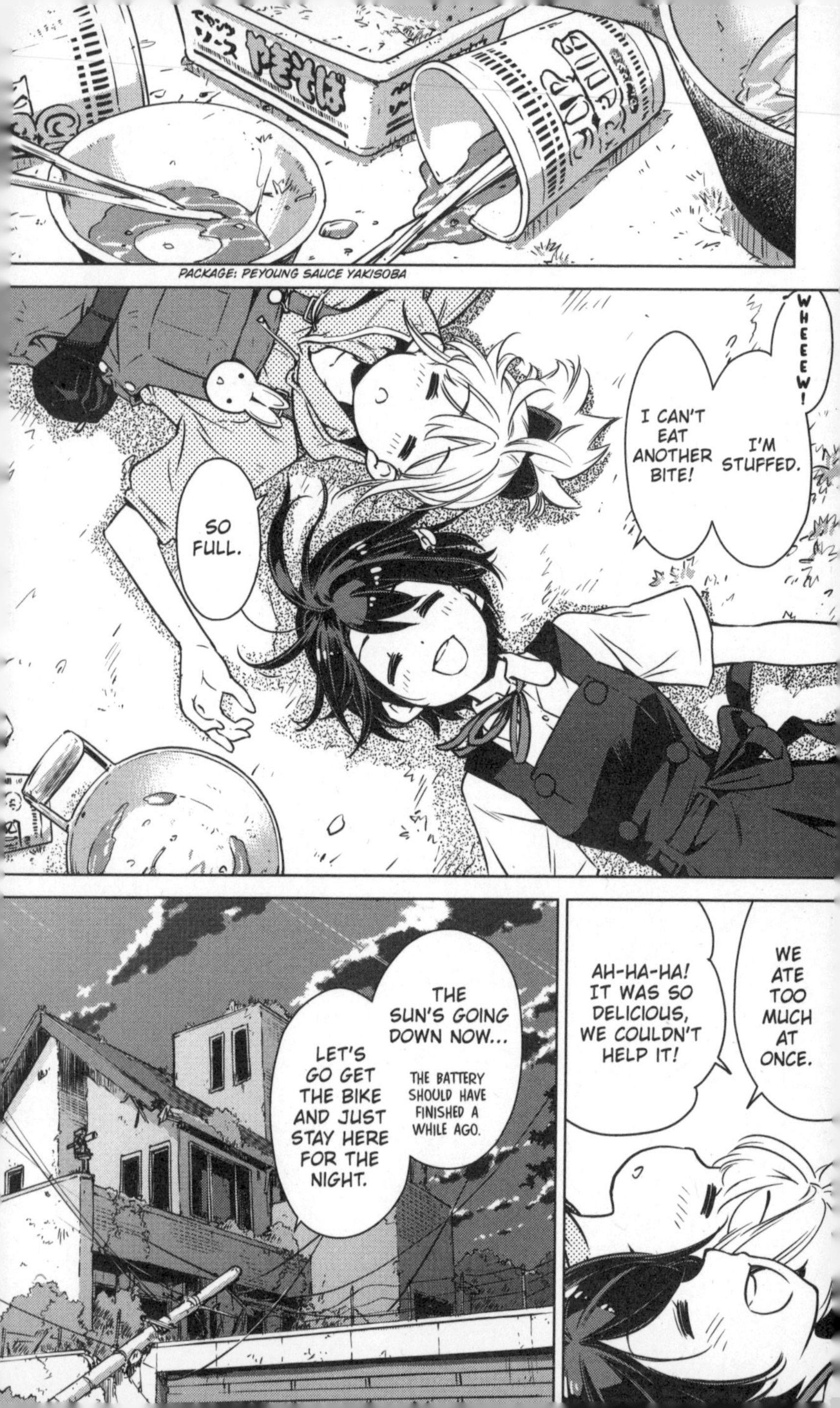
やきそば
PACKAGE: PEYOUNG SAUCE YAKISOBA
WHEEEW!
I'M STUFFED.
I CAN'T EAT ANOTHER BITE!
SO FULL.
WE ATE TOO MUCH AT ONCE.
AH-HA-HA! IT WAS SO DELICIOUS, WE COULDN'T HELP IT!
THE SUN'S GOING DOWN NOW...
THE BATTERY SHOULD HAVE FINISHED A WHILE AGO.
LET'S GO GET THE BIKE AND JUST STAY HERE FOR THE NIGHT.

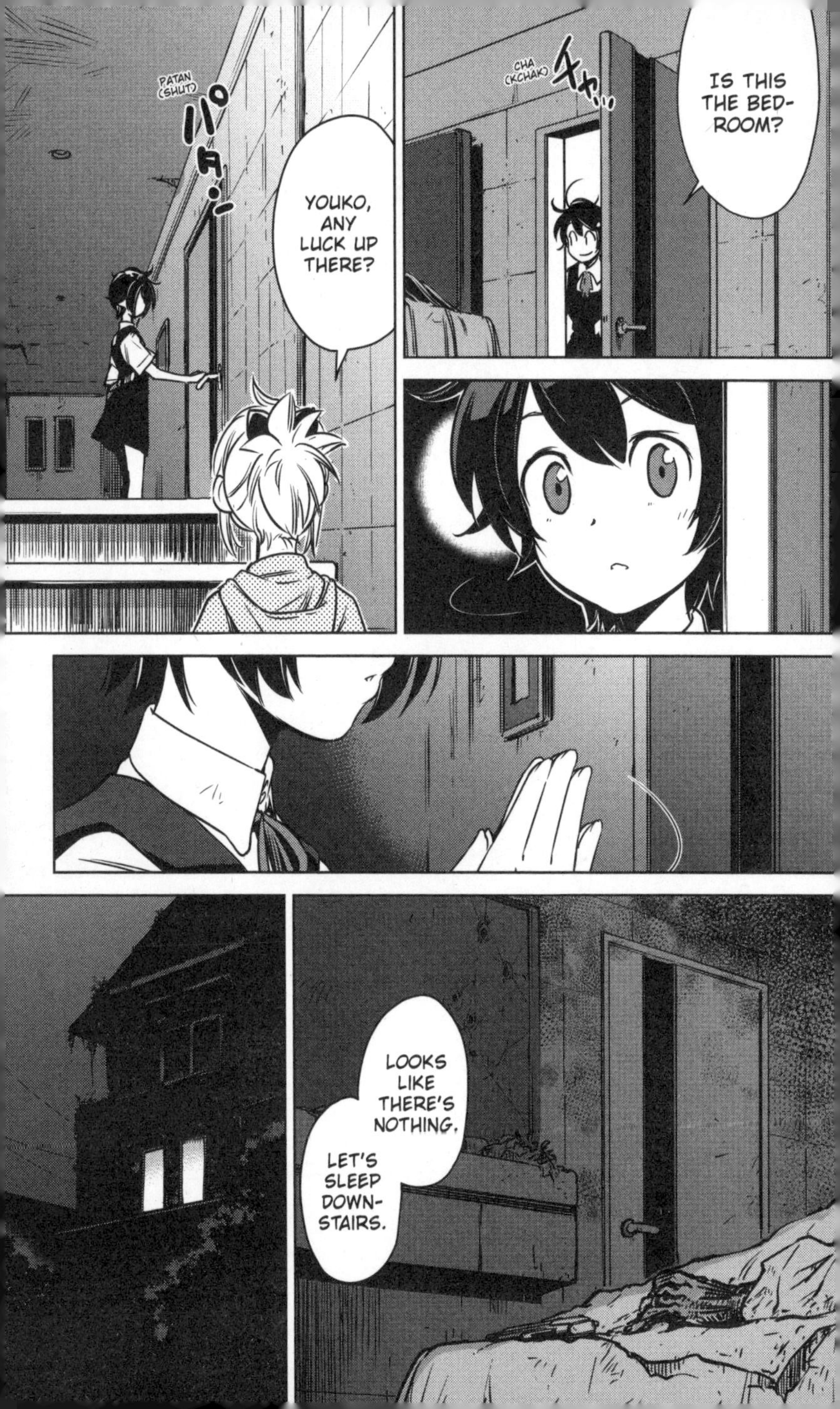
CHA (KCHAK)
IS THIS THE BED-ROOM?
PATAN (SHUT)
YOUKO, ANY LUCK UP THERE?
LOOKS LIKE THERE'S NOTHING.
LET'S SLEEP DOWN-STAIRS.

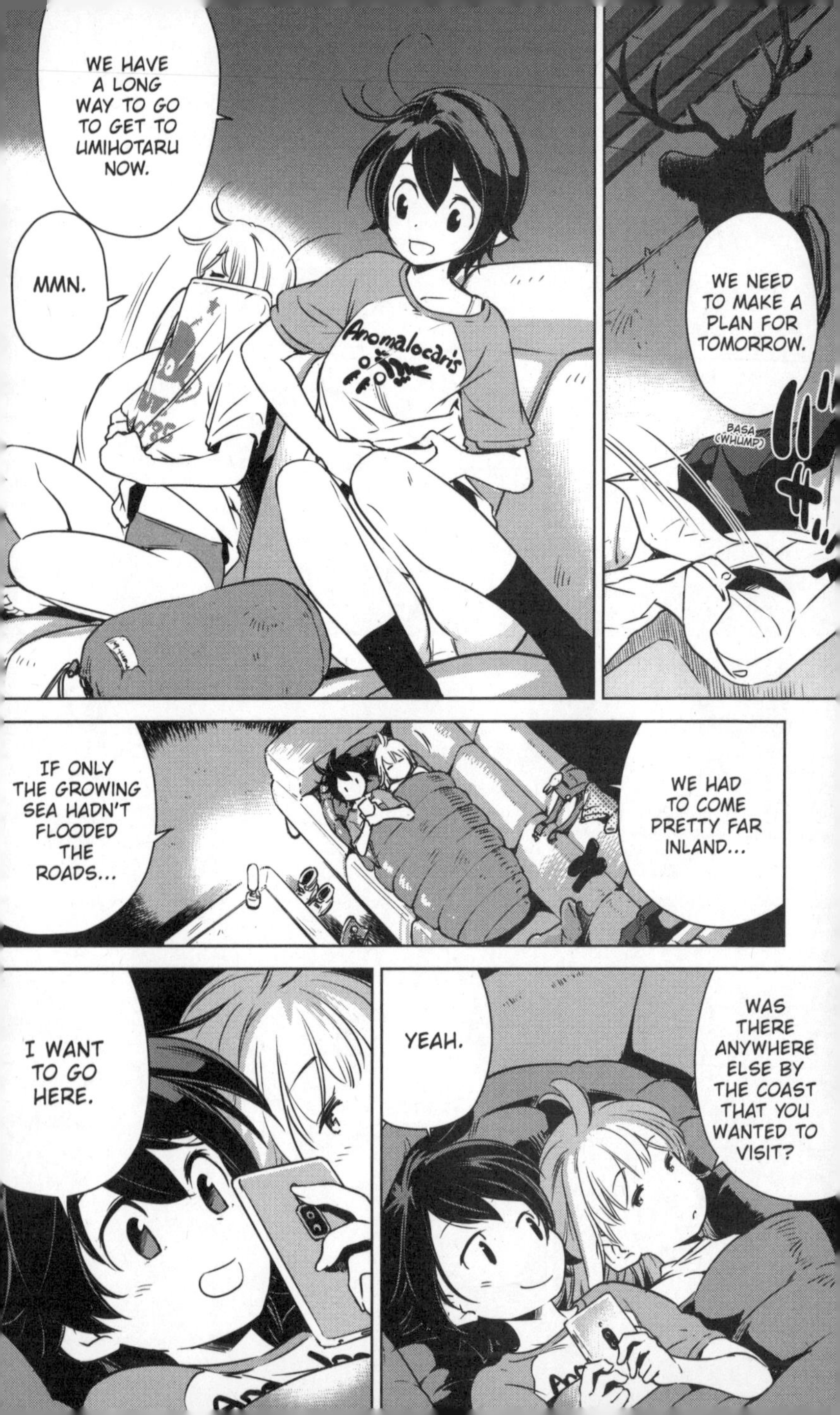
WE NEED TO MAKE A PLAN FOR TOMORROW.
BASA (WHUMP)
WE HAVE A LONG WAY TO GO TO GET TO UMIHOTARU NOW.
MMN.
Anomalocaris
WE HAD TO COME PRETTY FAR INLAND...
IF ONLY THE GROWING SEA HADN'T FLOODED THE ROADS...
WAS THERE ANYWHERE ELSE BY THE COAST THAT YOU WANTED TO VISIT?
YEAH.
I WANT TO GO HERE.

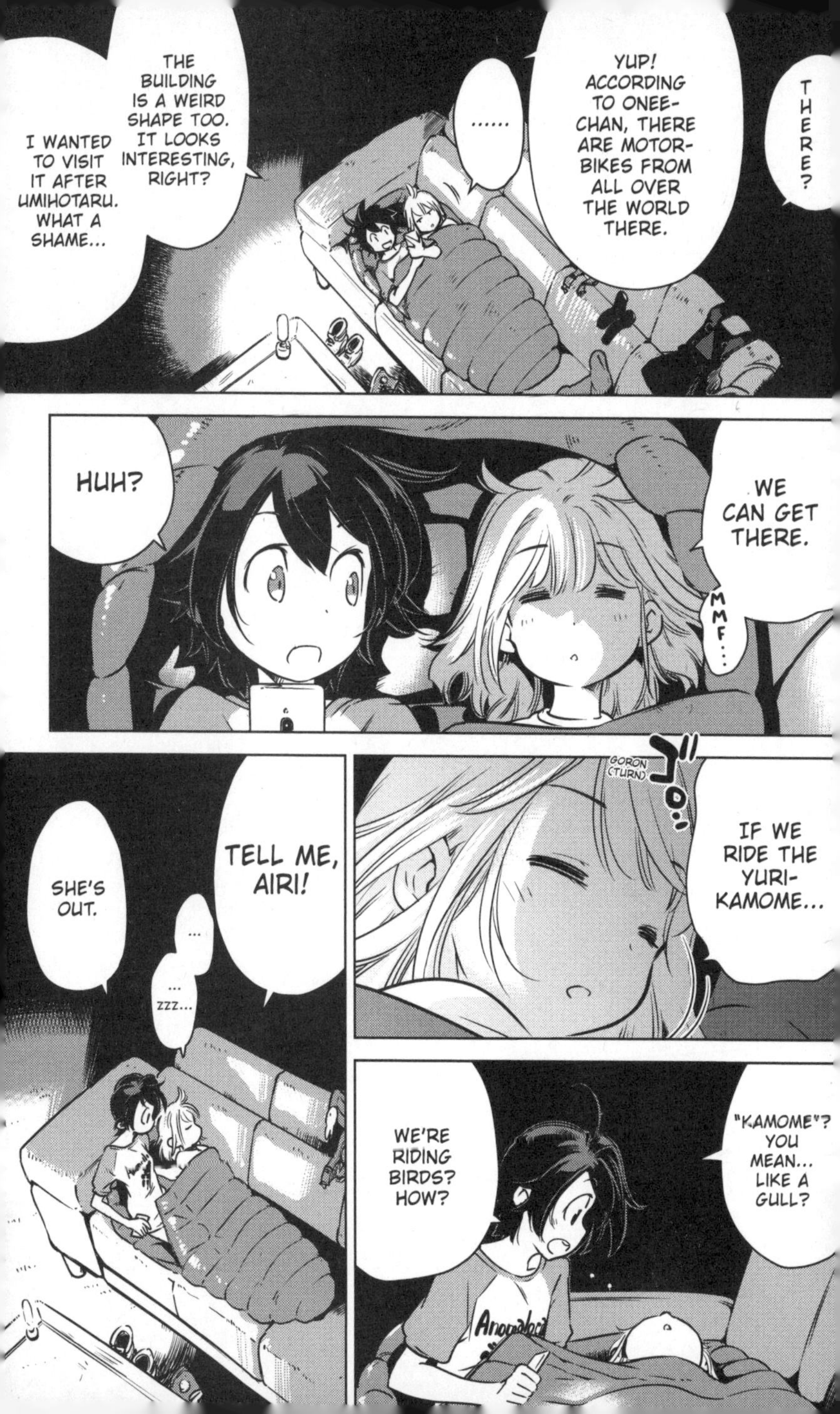
THERE?
YUP! ACCORDING TO ONEE-CHAN, THERE ARE MOTOR-BIKES FROM ALL OVER THE WORLD THERE.
......
THE BUILDING IS A WEIRD SHAPE TOO. IT LOOKS INTERESTING, RIGHT?
I WANTED TO VISIT IT AFTER UMIHOTARU. WHAT A SHAME...
WE CAN GET THERE.
MMF...
HUH?
GORON (TURN)
IF WE RIDE THE YURI-KAMOME...
"KAMOME"? YOU MEAN... LIKE A GULL?
WE'RE RIDING BIRDS? HOW?
TELL ME, AIRI!
...
... zzz...
SHE'S OUT.

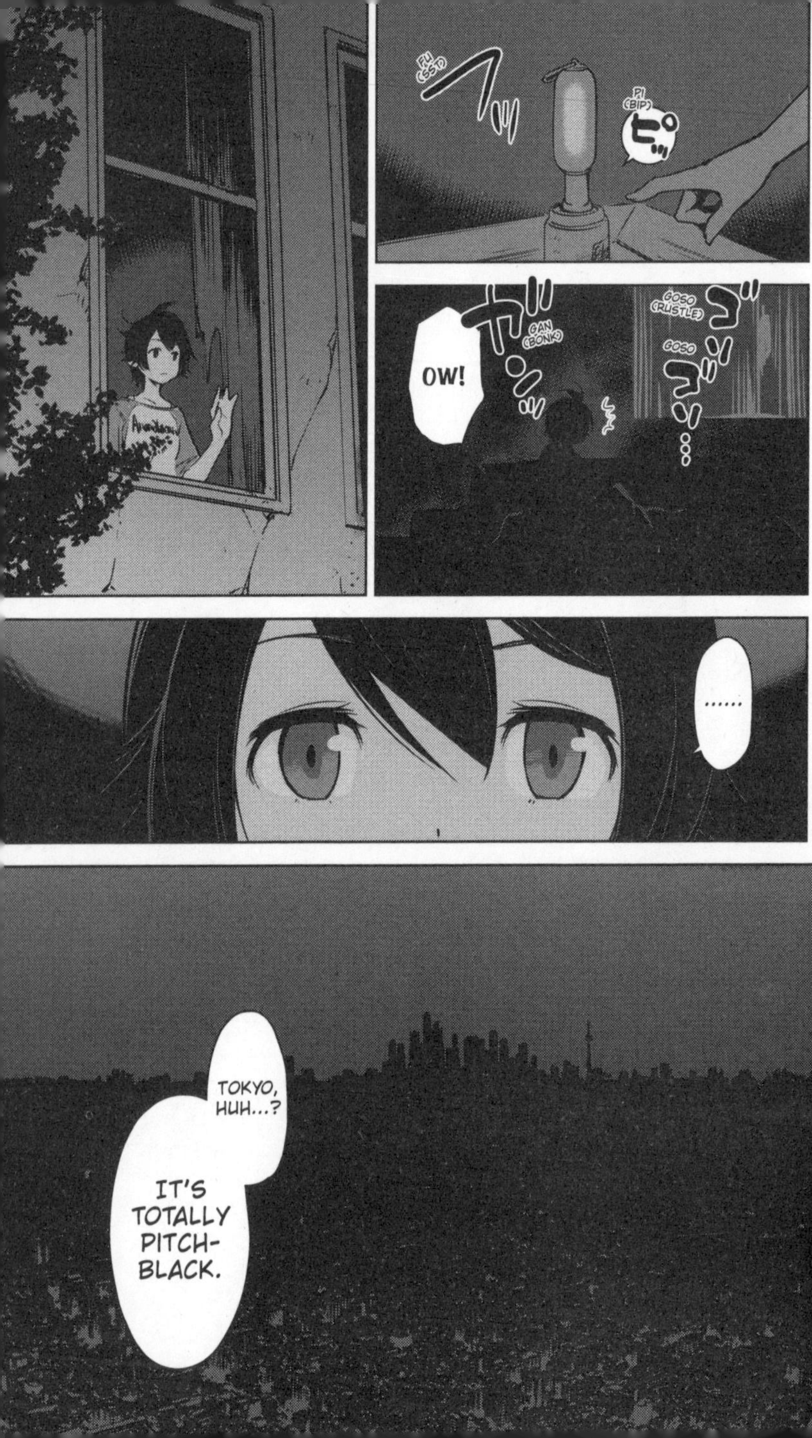
PI (BIP)
FU (SST)
GOSO (RUSTLE)
GOSO
GAN (BONK)
OW!
......
TOKYO, HUH...?
IT'S TOTALLY PITCH-BLACK.

YOUKO'S!

YAMAHA Serow 225 (Electric Conversion)

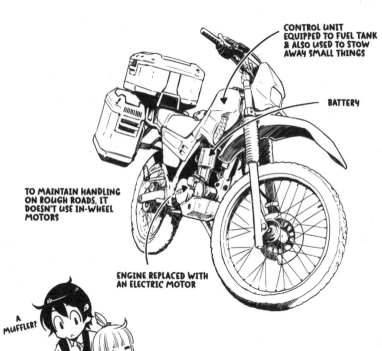

CONTROL UNIT
EQUIPPED TO FUEL TANK
& ALSO USED TO STOW
AWAY SMALL THINGS

BATTERY

TO MAINTAIN HANDLING
ON ROUGH ROADS, IT
DOESN'T USE IN-WHEEL
MOTORS

ENGINE REPLACED WITH
AN ELECTRIC MOTOR

A
MUFFLER?

What is the Serow 225?

A motorcycle released by Yamaha Motor
Company in 1985. Easy to handle, its
popularity has endured over many years with
everyone from beginners to veterans, and
because it's easy to walk (due to a low seat),
it has many female riders as well. An off-road
bike suitable for mountain paths, but also good
for riding around town, casual touring, and
short trips, it's an excellent motorcycle.

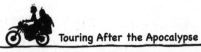
Touring After the Apocalypse

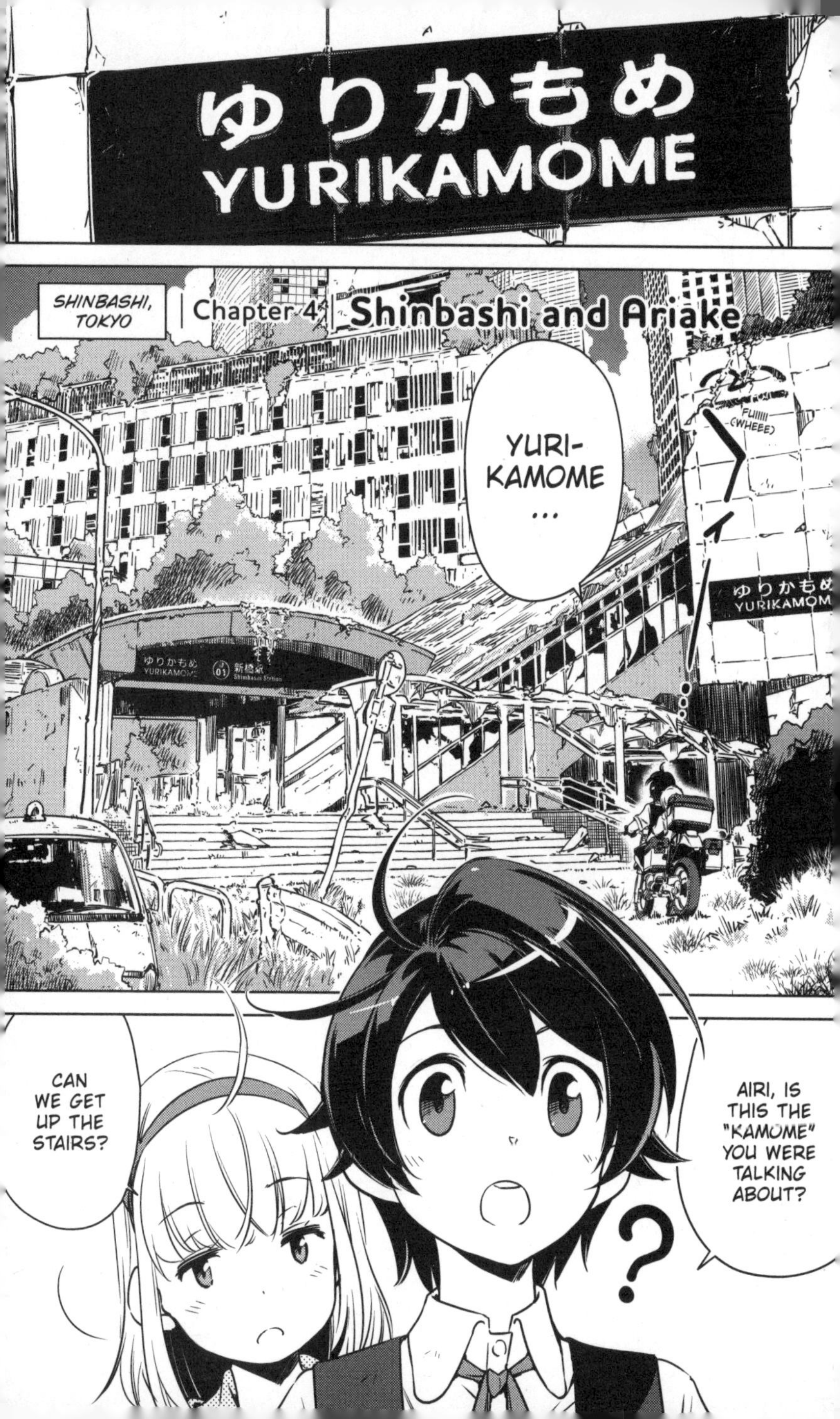
ゆりかもめ
YURIKAMOME
FUIIIII
(WHEEE)
ゆりかもめ
YURIKAMOM
YURI-KAMOME ...
Chapter 4 Shinbashi and Ariake
SHINBASHI, TOKYO
ゆりかもめ YURIKAMOME
新橋駅 Shinbashi Station
AIRI, IS THIS THE "KAMOME" YOU WERE TALKING ABOUT?
?
CAN WE GET UP THE STAIRS?

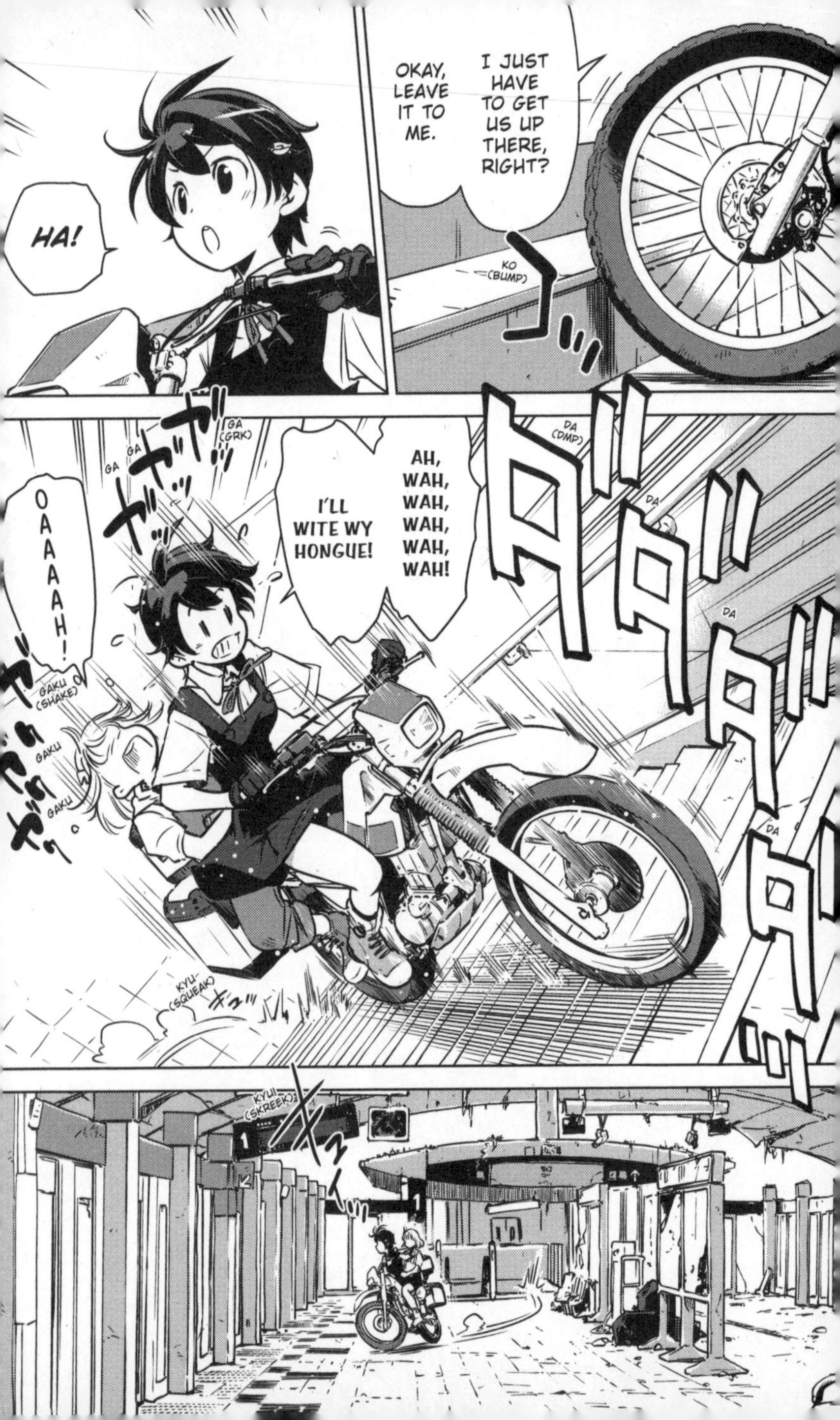
I JUST HAVE TO GET US UP THERE, RIGHT?
OKAY, LEAVE IT TO ME.
KO (BUMP)
HA!
DA (DMP)
DA
DA
DA
AH, WAH, WAH, WAH, WAH, WAH!
I'LL WITE WY HONGUE!
GA (GRK)
GA
GA
OAAAAAAH!
GAKU (SHAKE)
GAKU
GAKU
KYU (SQUEAK)
KYUI (SKREEK)

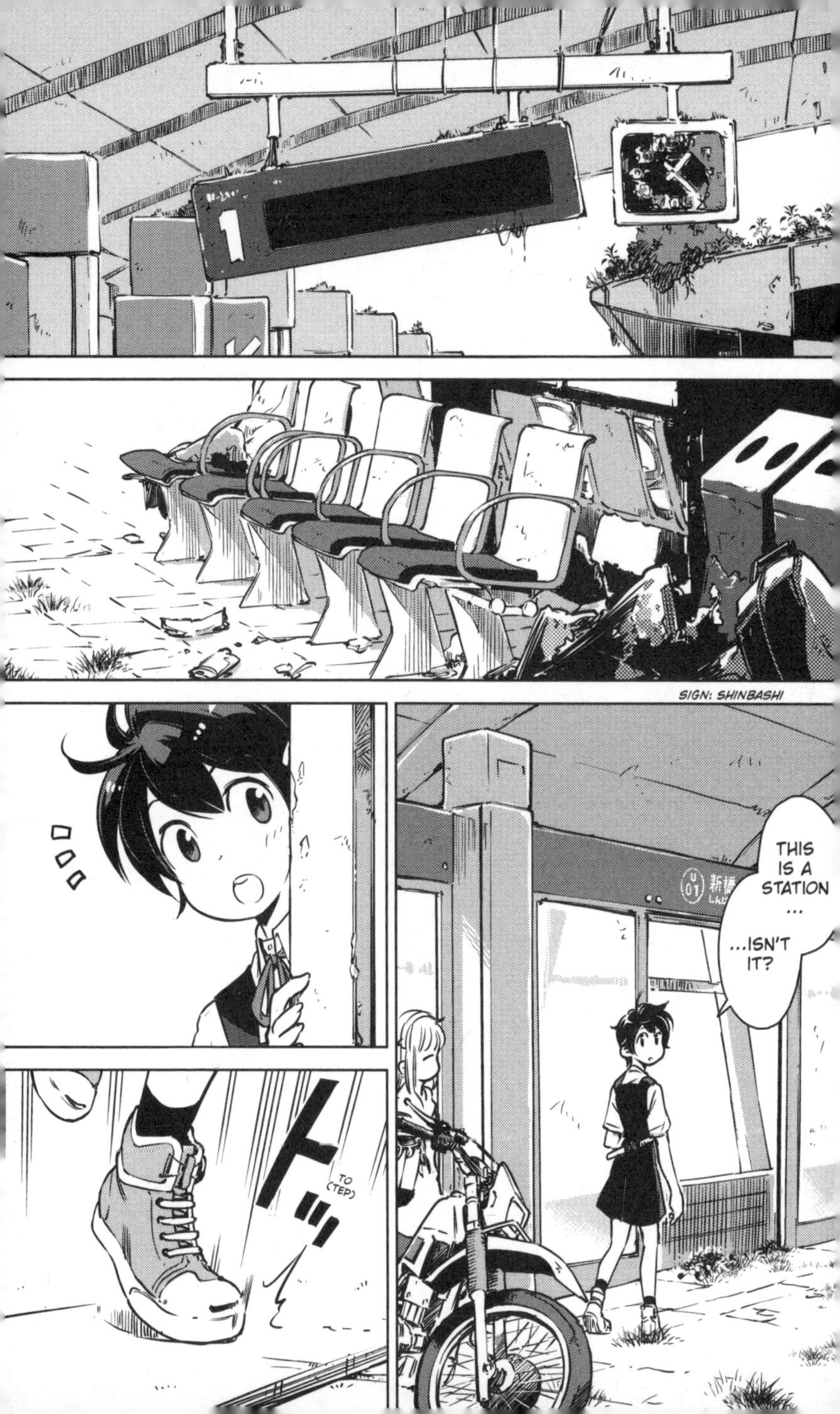
SIGN: SHINBASHI
新橋
THIS IS A STATION ...
...ISN'T IT?
TO (TEP)

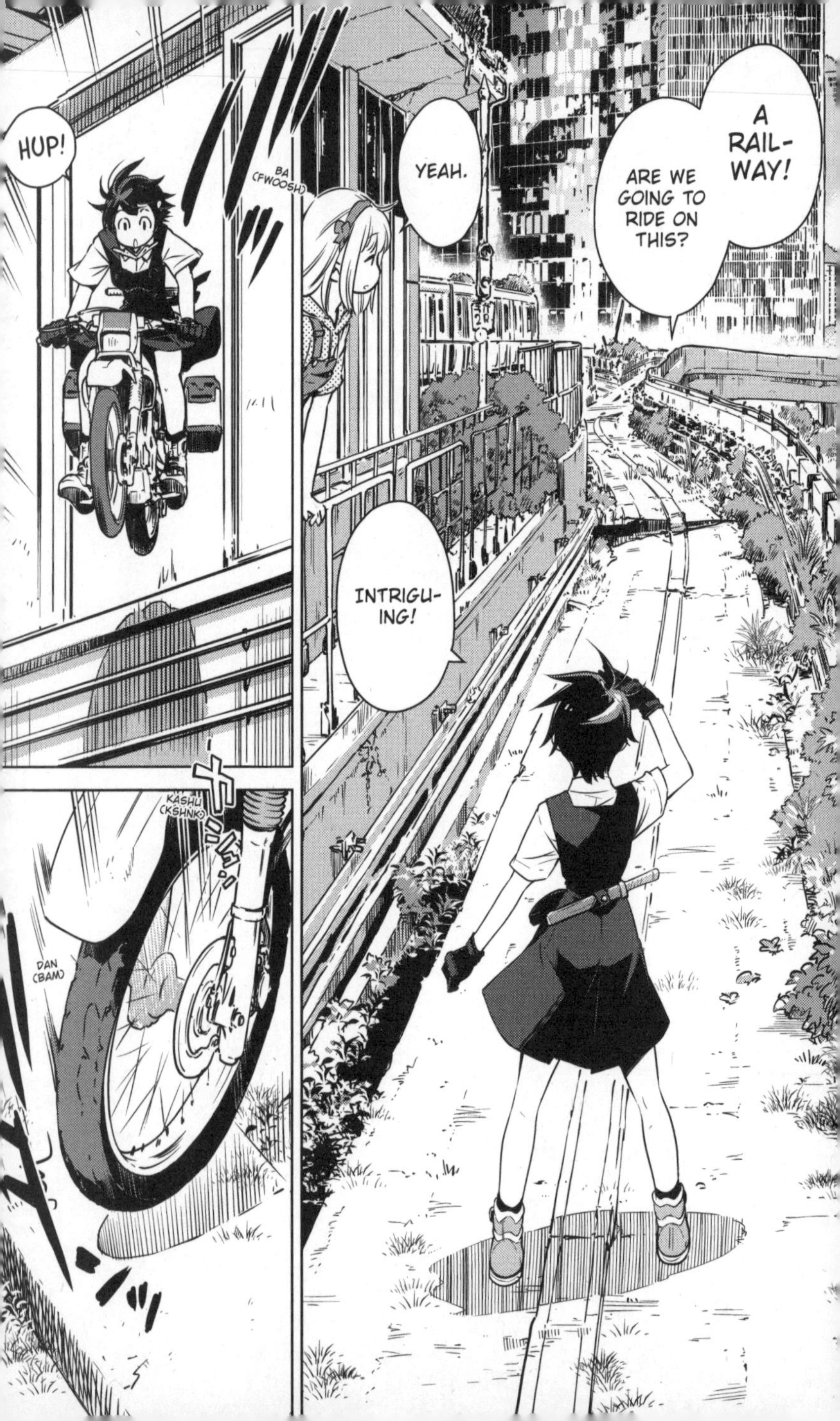
A RAIL-WAY!
ARE WE GOING TO RIDE ON THIS?
YEAH.
INTRIGU-ING!
HUP!
BA (FWOOSH)
KASHU (KSHNK)
DAN (BAM)

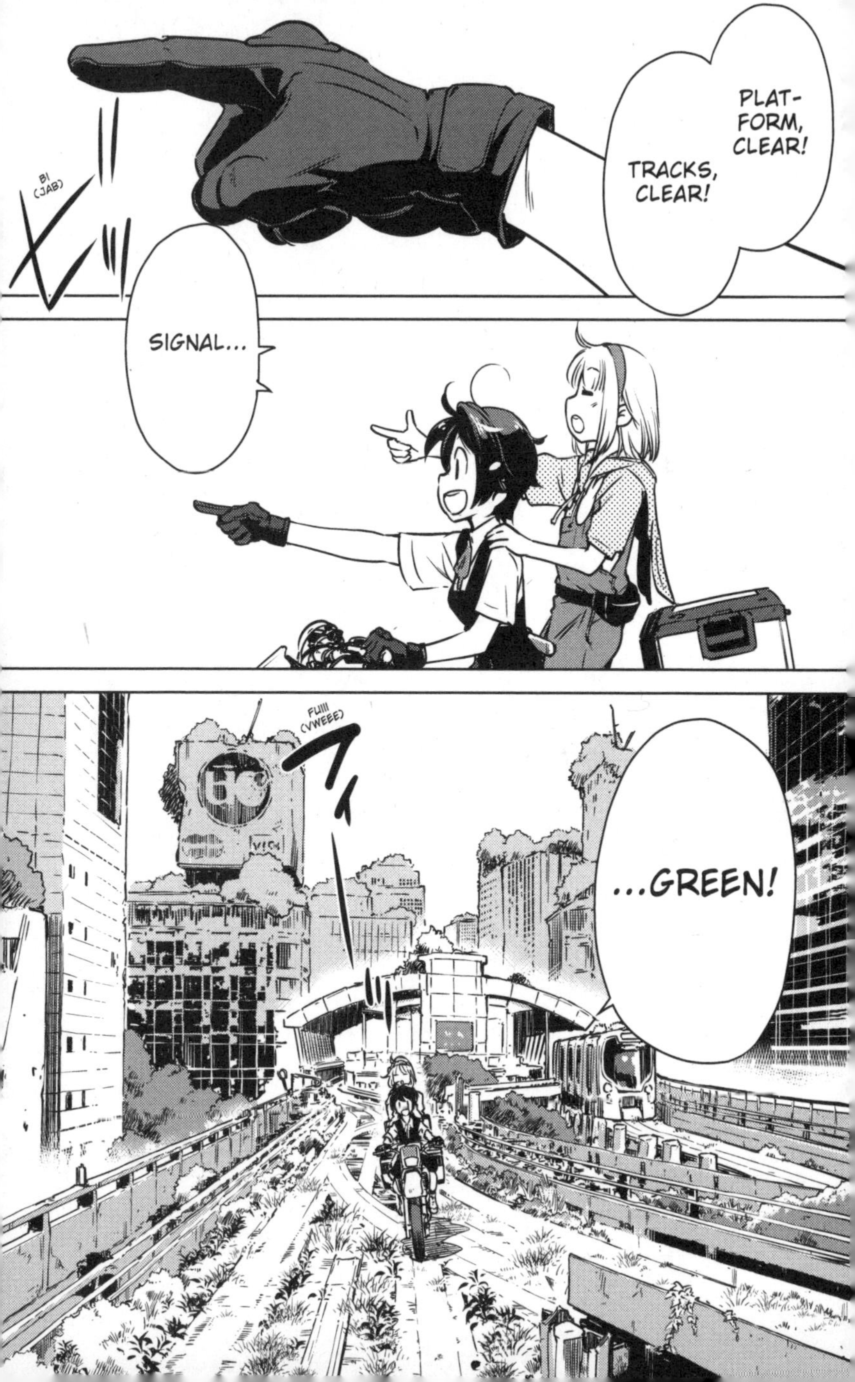
PLAT-FORM, CLEAR!
TRACKS, CLEAR!
BI (JAB)
SIGNAL...
...GREEN!
FUIII (VWEEE)

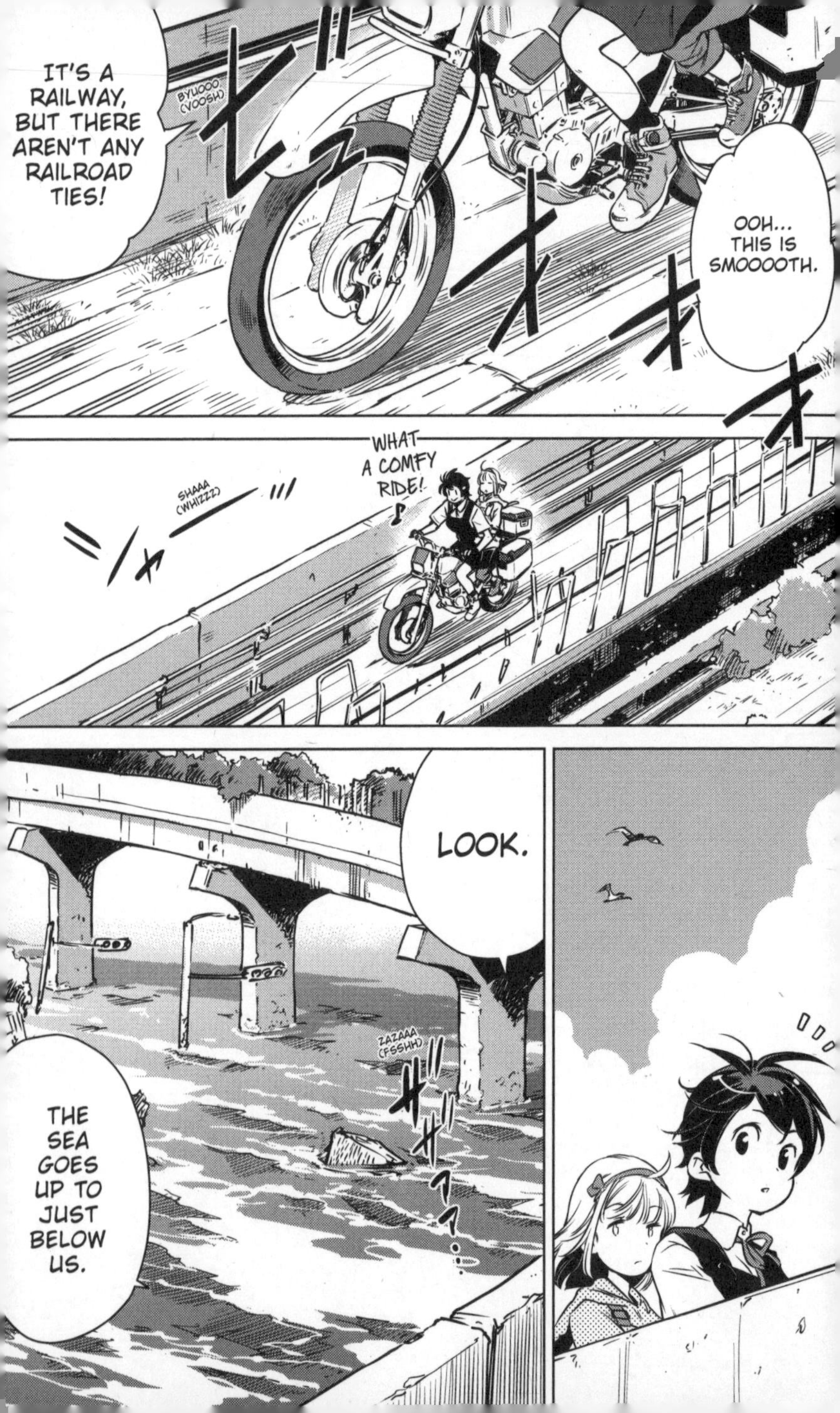
OOH... THIS IS SMOOOOTH.
BYUOOO (VOOSH)
IT'S A RAILWAY, BUT THERE AREN'T ANY RAILROAD TIES!
WHAT A COMFY RIDE!
SHAAA (WHIZZZ)
LOOK.
ZAZAAA (FSSHH)
THE SEA GOES UP TO JUST BELOW US.

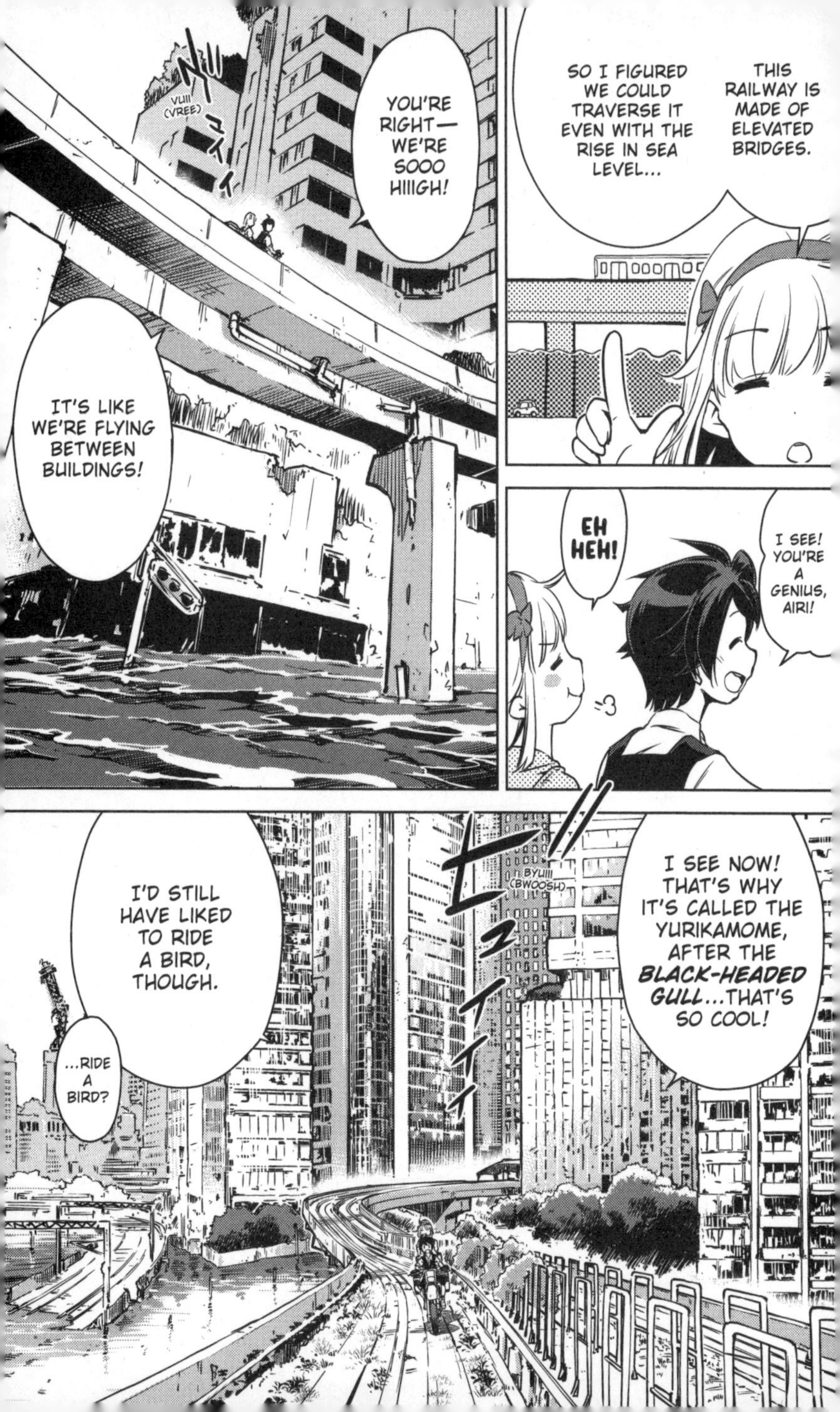
THIS RAILWAY IS MADE OF ELEVATED BRIDGES.
SO I FIGURED WE COULD TRAVERSE IT EVEN WITH THE RISE IN SEA LEVEL...
I SEE! YOU'RE A GENIUS, AIRI!
EH HEH!
VUIII (VREE)
YOU'RE RIGHT—WE'RE SOOO HIIIGH!
IT'S LIKE WE'RE FLYING BETWEEN BUILDINGS!
BYUIII (BWOOSH)
I SEE NOW! THAT'S WHY IT'S CALLED THE YURIKAMOME, AFTER THE ***BLACK-HEADED GULL***...THAT'S SO COOL!
I'D STILL HAVE LIKED TO RIDE A BIRD, THOUGH.
...RIDE A BIRD?

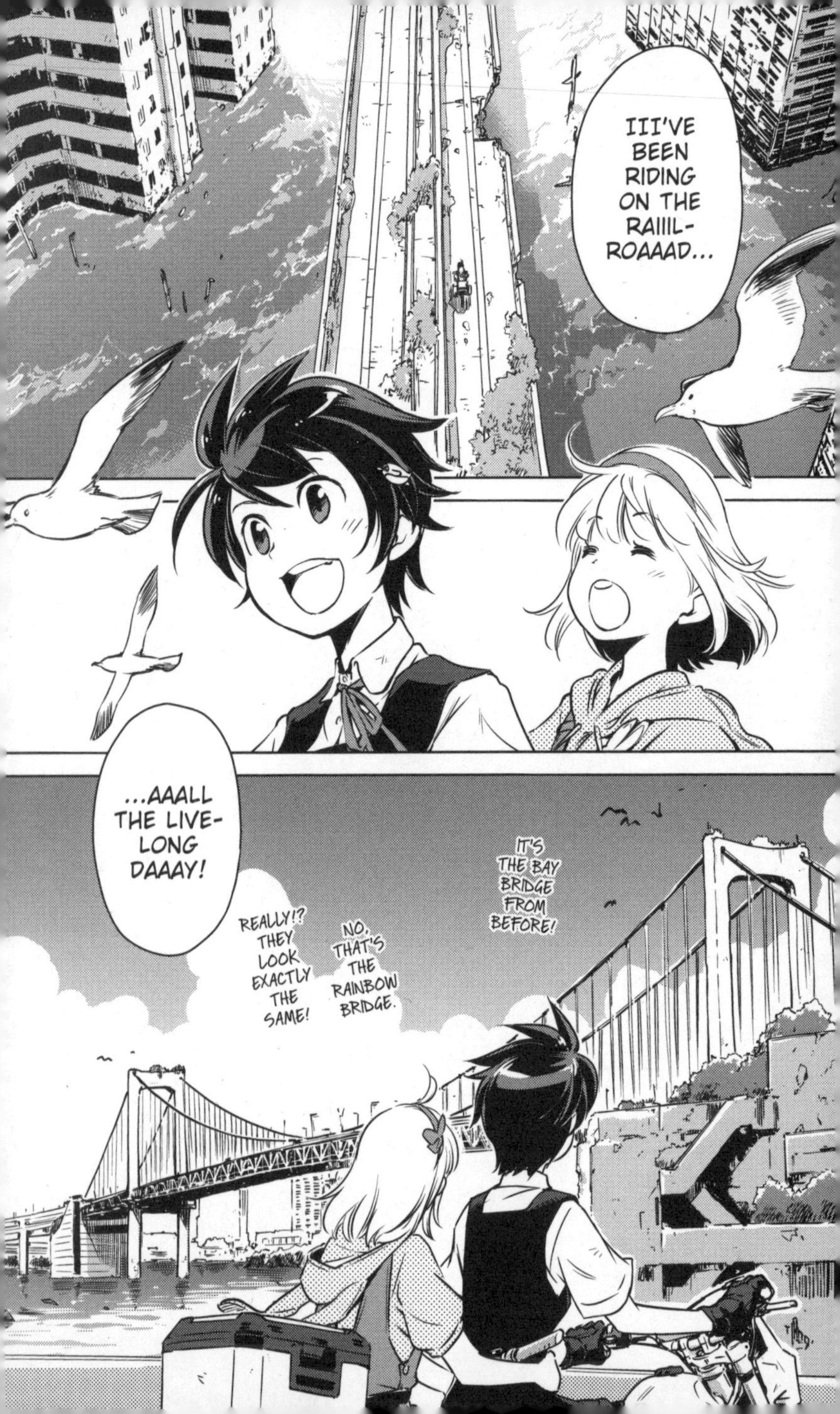
III'VE BEEN RIDING ON THE RAIIIL-ROAAAD...
...AAALL THE LIVE-LONG DAAAY!
IT'S THE BAY BRIDGE FROM BEFORE!
NO, THAT'S THE RAINBOW BRIDGE.
REALLY!? THEY LOOK EXACTLY THE SAME!

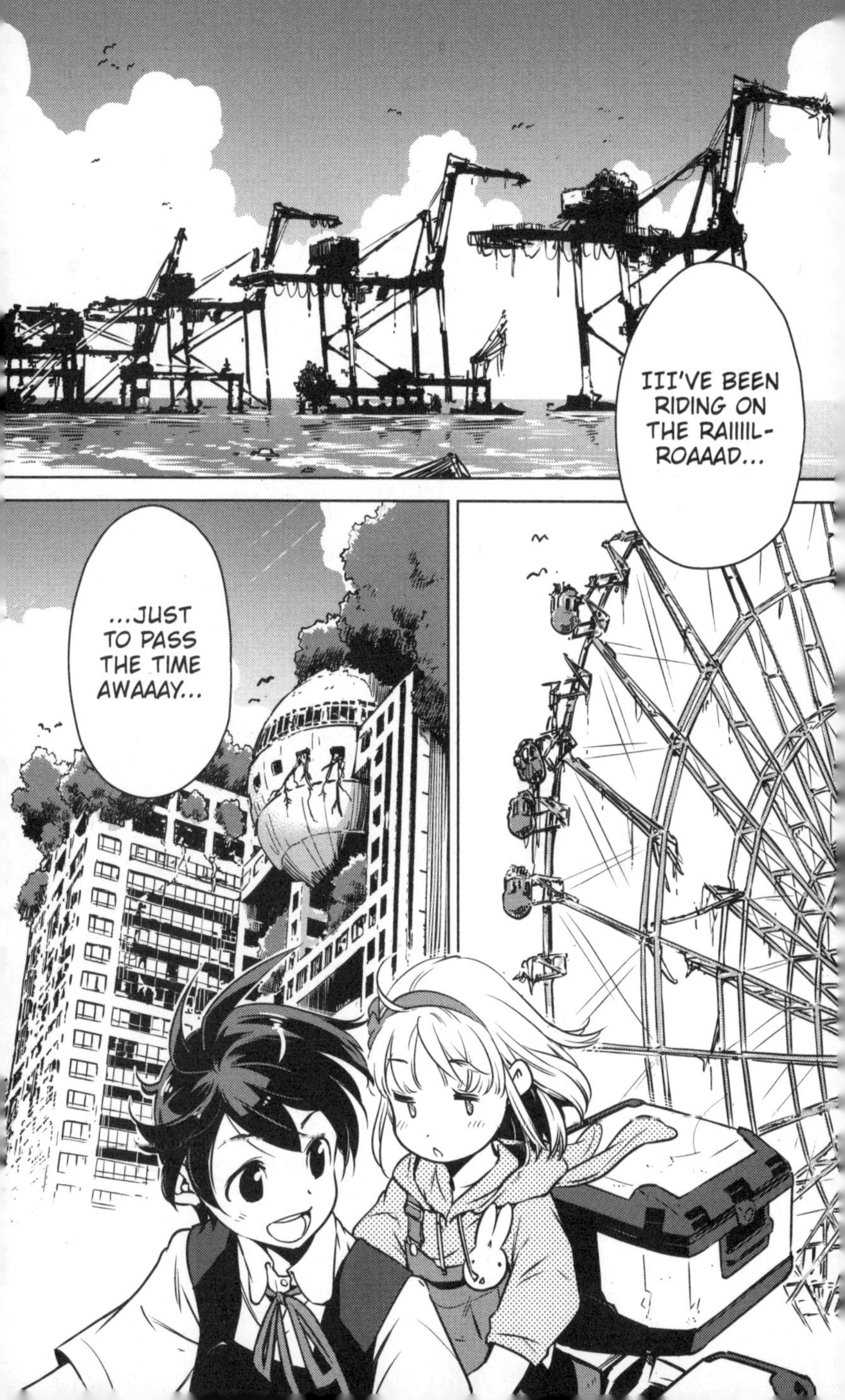
III'VE BEEN RIDING ON THE RAIIIIL-ROAAAD...
...JUST TO PASS THE TIME AWAAAY...

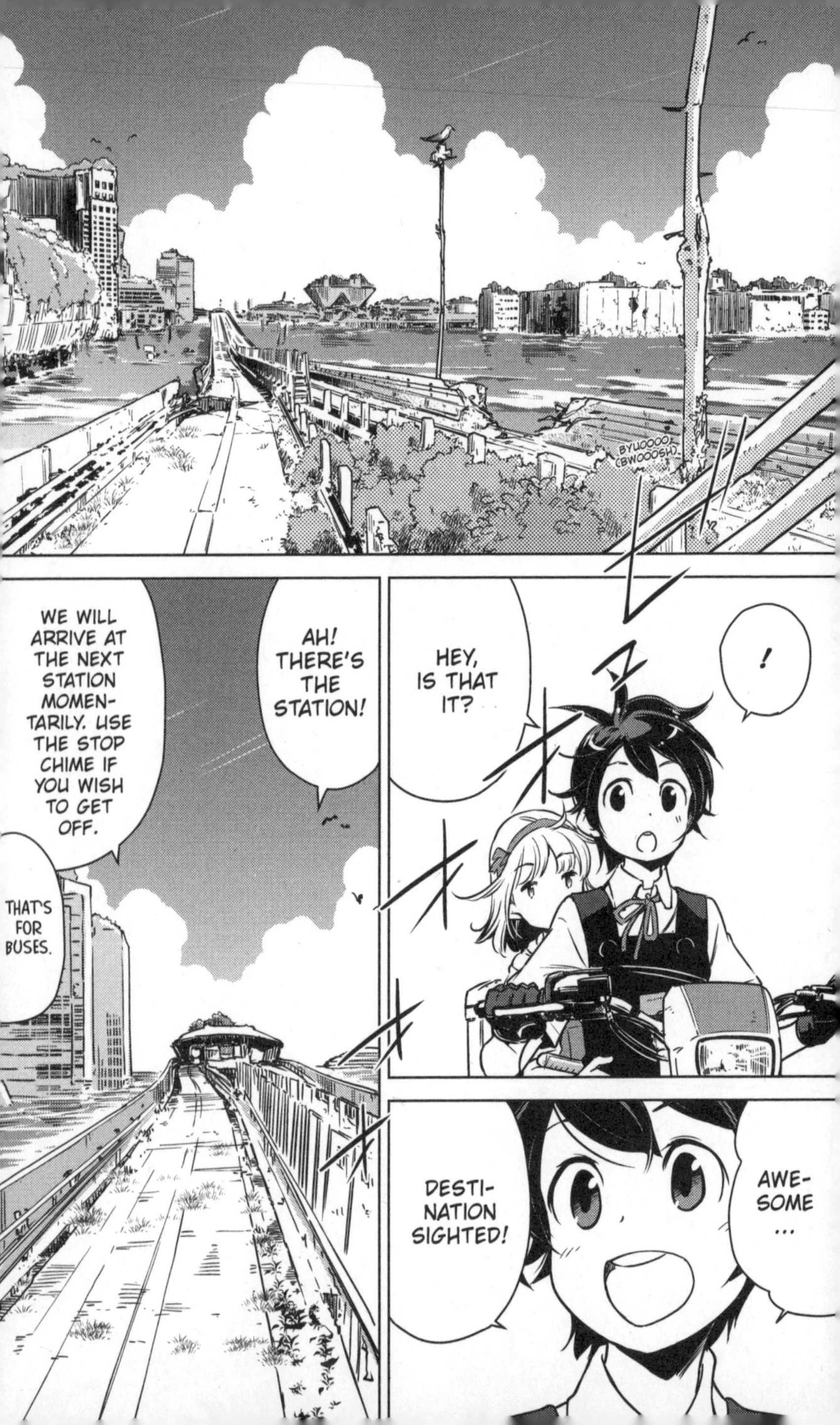
BYUOOOO (BWOOOSH)
!
HEY, IS THAT IT?
AWE-SOME ...
DESTI-NATION SIGHTED!
AH! THERE'S THE STATION!
WE WILL ARRIVE AT THE NEXT STATION MOMEN-TARILY. USE THE STOP CHIME IF YOU WISH TO GET OFF.
THAT'S FOR BUSES.

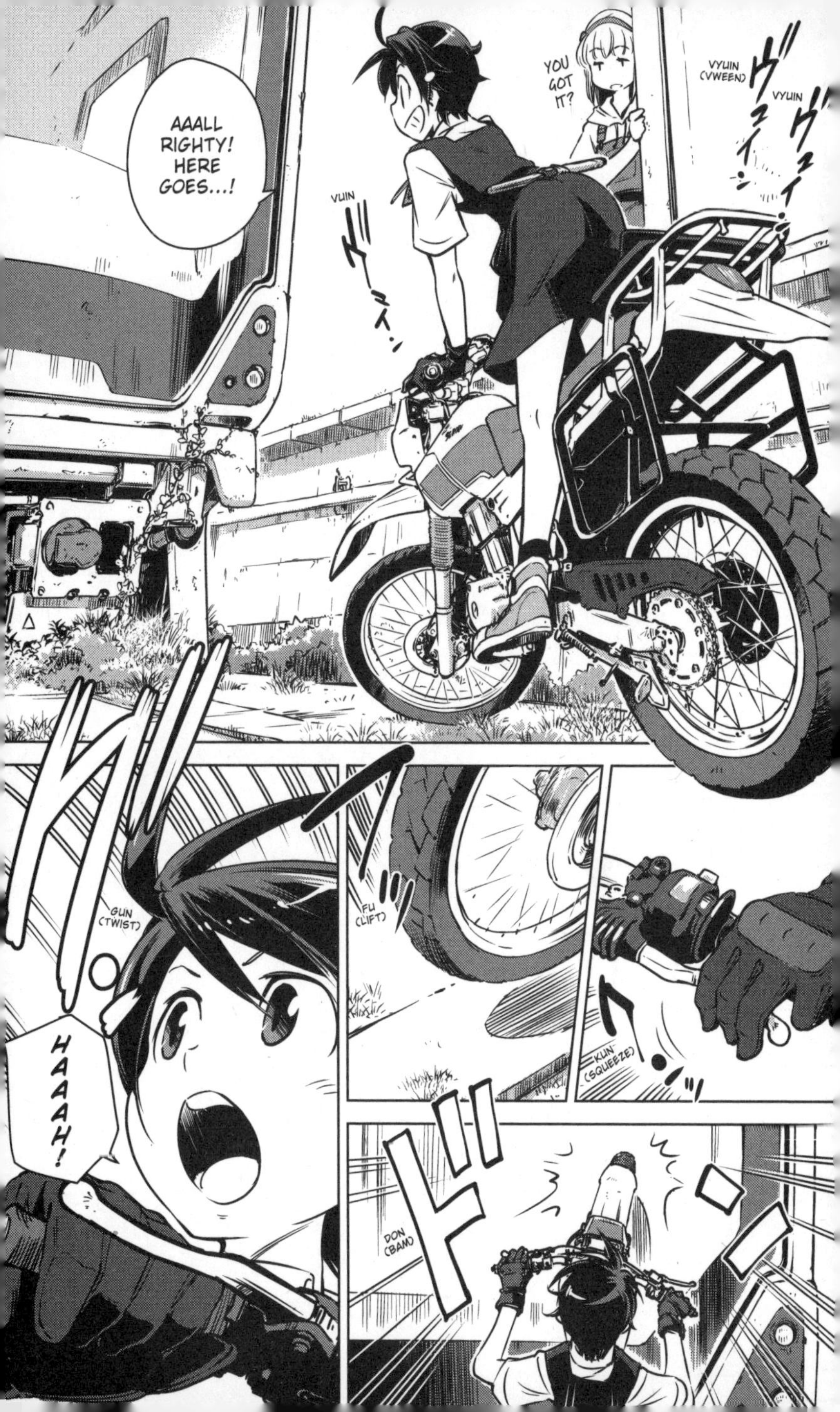
VYUIN (VWEEN)
VYUIN
YOU GOT IT?
AAALL RIGHTY! HERE GOES...!
VUIN
KUN (SQUEEZE)
FU (LIFT)
DON (BAM)
GUN (TWIST)
HAAAAH!

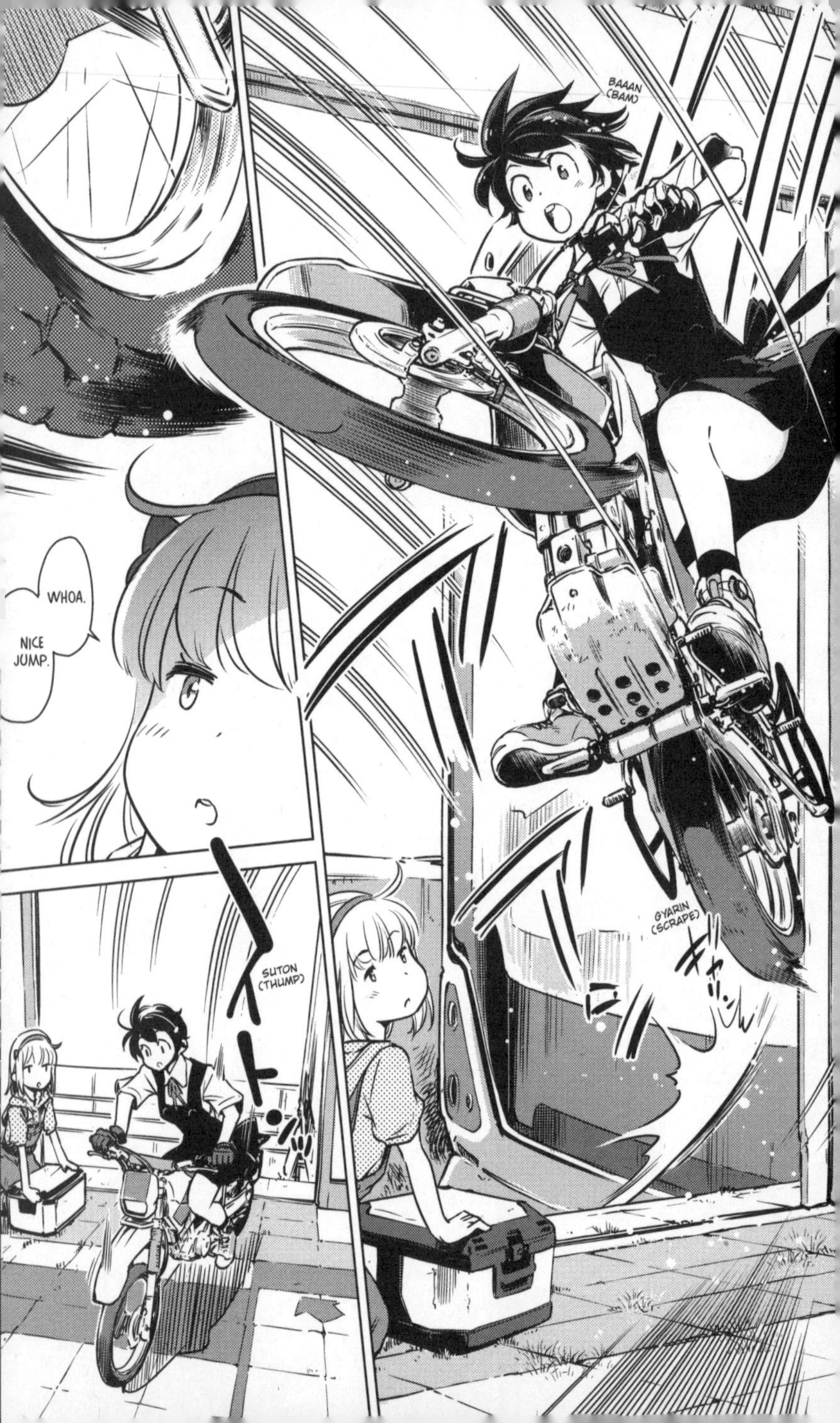
BAAAN (BAM)
WHOA.
NICE JUMP.
GYARIN (SCRAPE)
SUTON (THUMP)

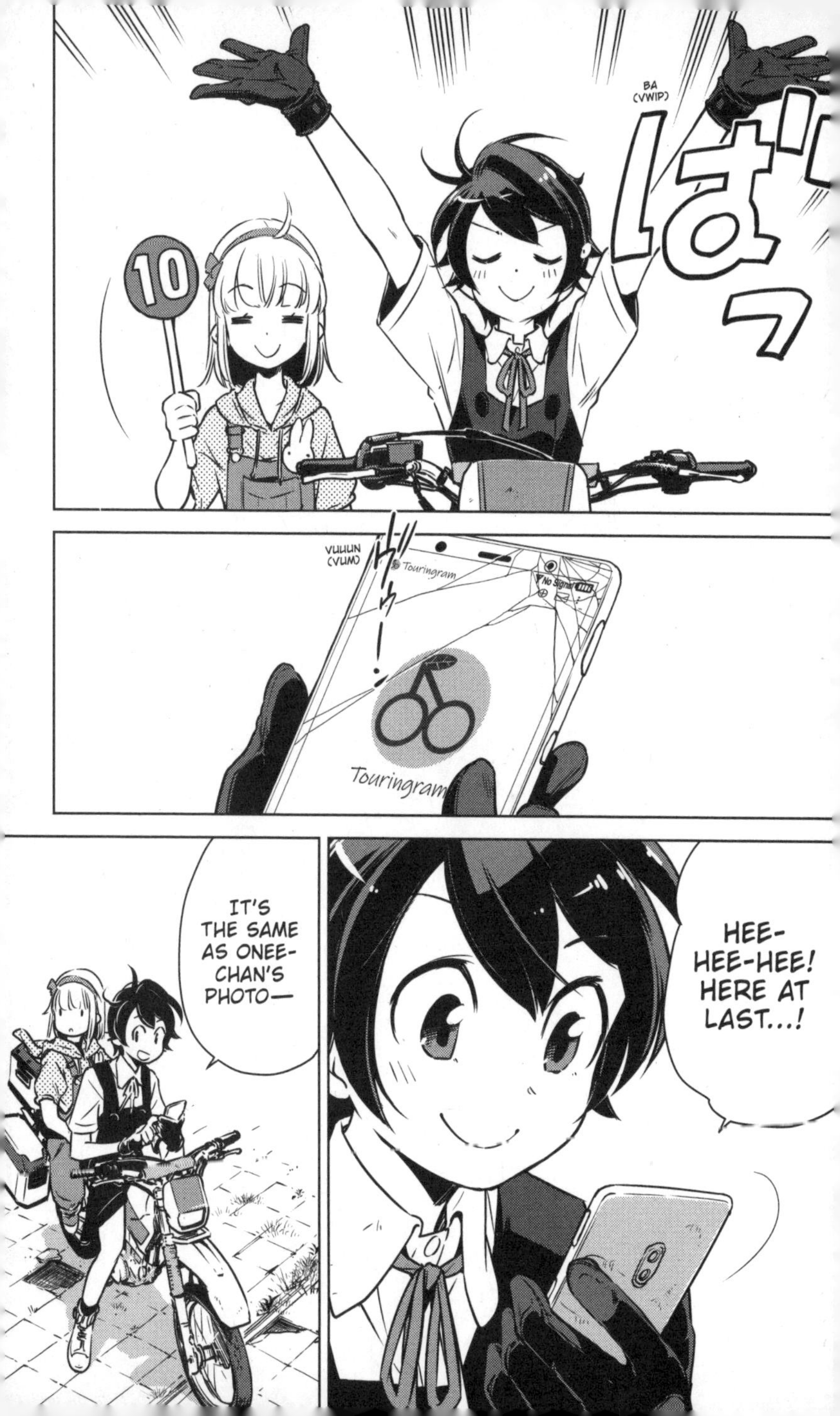
BA
(VWIP)
ばっ
VUUUN
(VUM)
Touringram
No Signal
Touringram
HEE-HEE-HEE! HERE AT LAST...!
IT'S THE SAME AS ONEE-CHAN'S PHOTO—

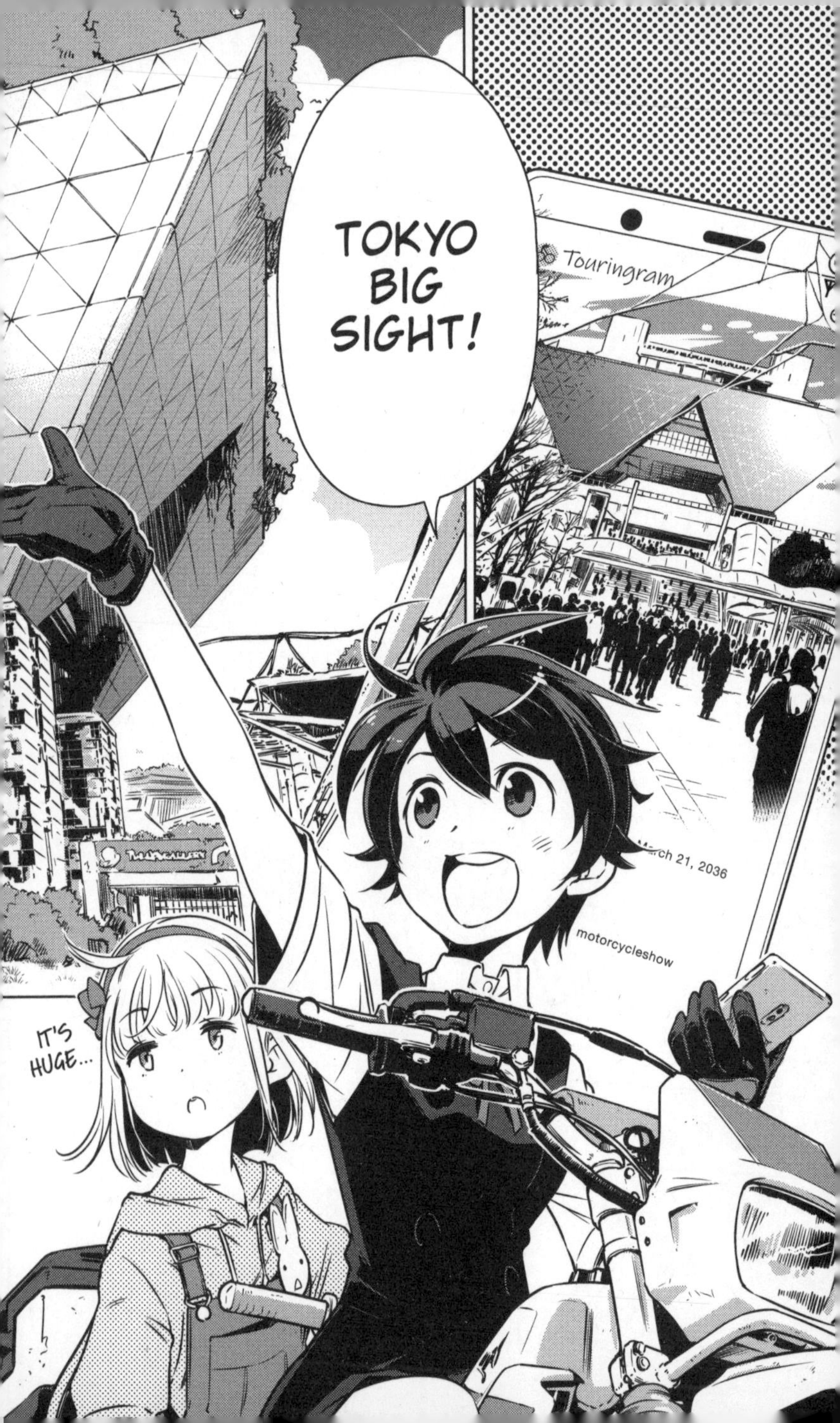
Touringram
rch 21, 2036
motorcycleshow
TOKYO BIG SIGHT!
IT'S HUGE...

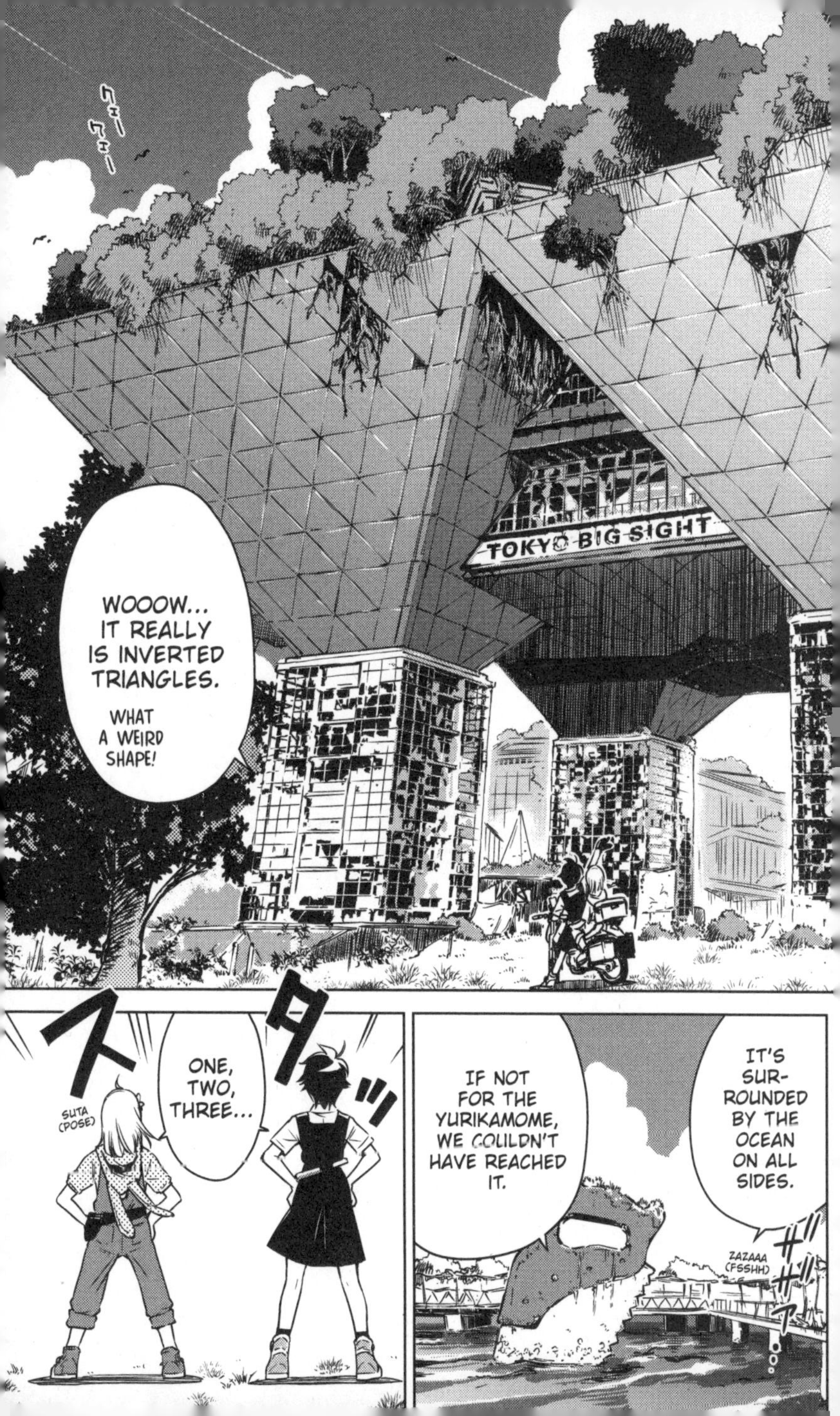
クェー クェー
TOKYO BIG SIGHT
WOOOW... IT REALLY IS INVERTED TRIANGLES.
WHAT A WEIRD SHAPE!
IT'S SUR-ROUNDED BY THE OCEAN ON ALL SIDES.
IF NOT FOR THE YURIKAMOME, WE COULDN'T HAVE REACHED IT.
ザザァ
ZAZAAA (FSSHH)
スタッ
SUTA (POSE)
ONE, TWO, THREE...

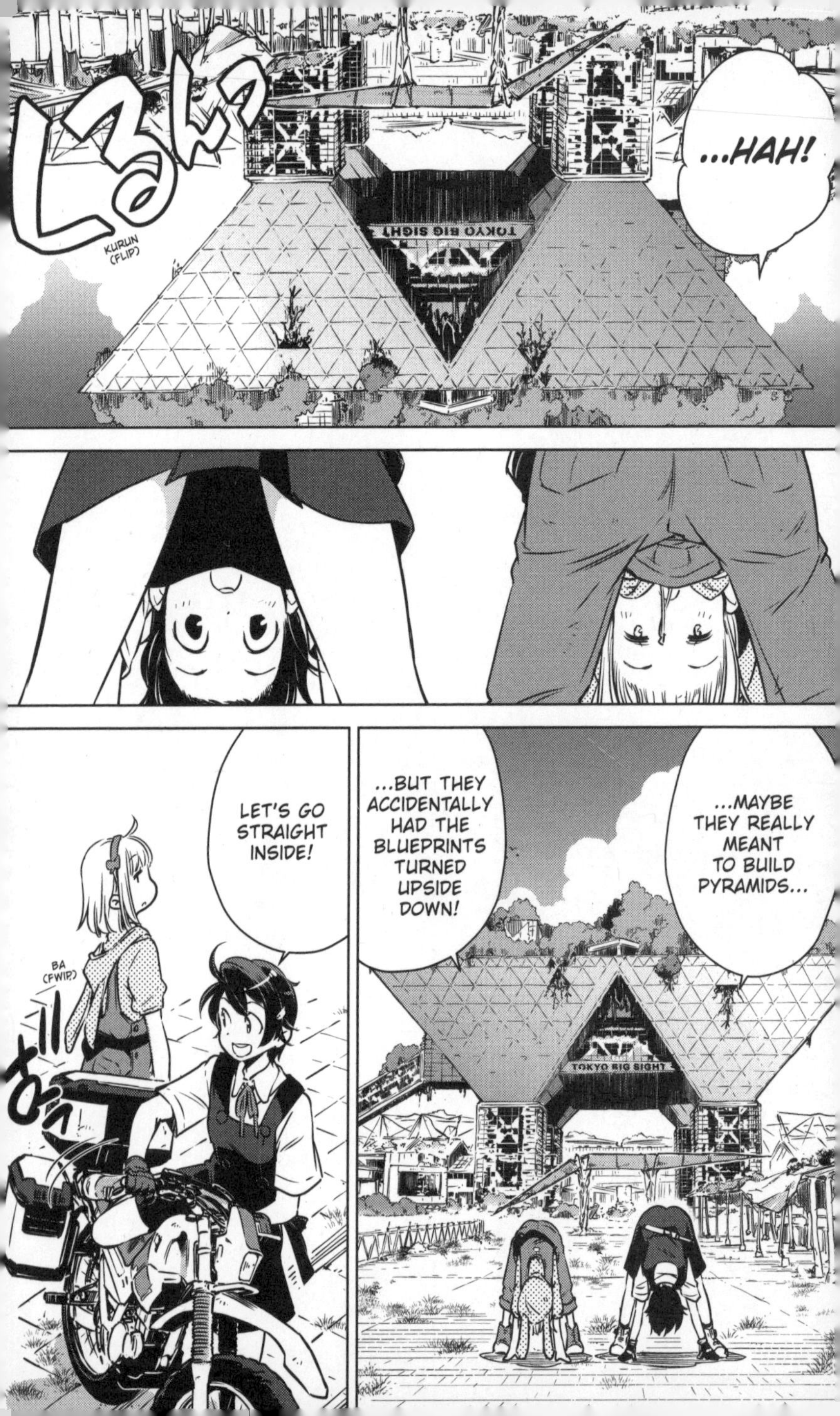
...HAH!
TOKYO BIG SIGHT
くるん
KURUN (FLIP)
...MAYBE THEY REALLY MEANT TO BUILD PYRAMIDS...
...BUT THEY ACCIDENTALLY HAD THE BLUEPRINTS TURNED UPSIDE DOWN!
TOKYO BIG SIGHT
LET'S GO STRAIGHT INSIDE!
BA (FWIP)

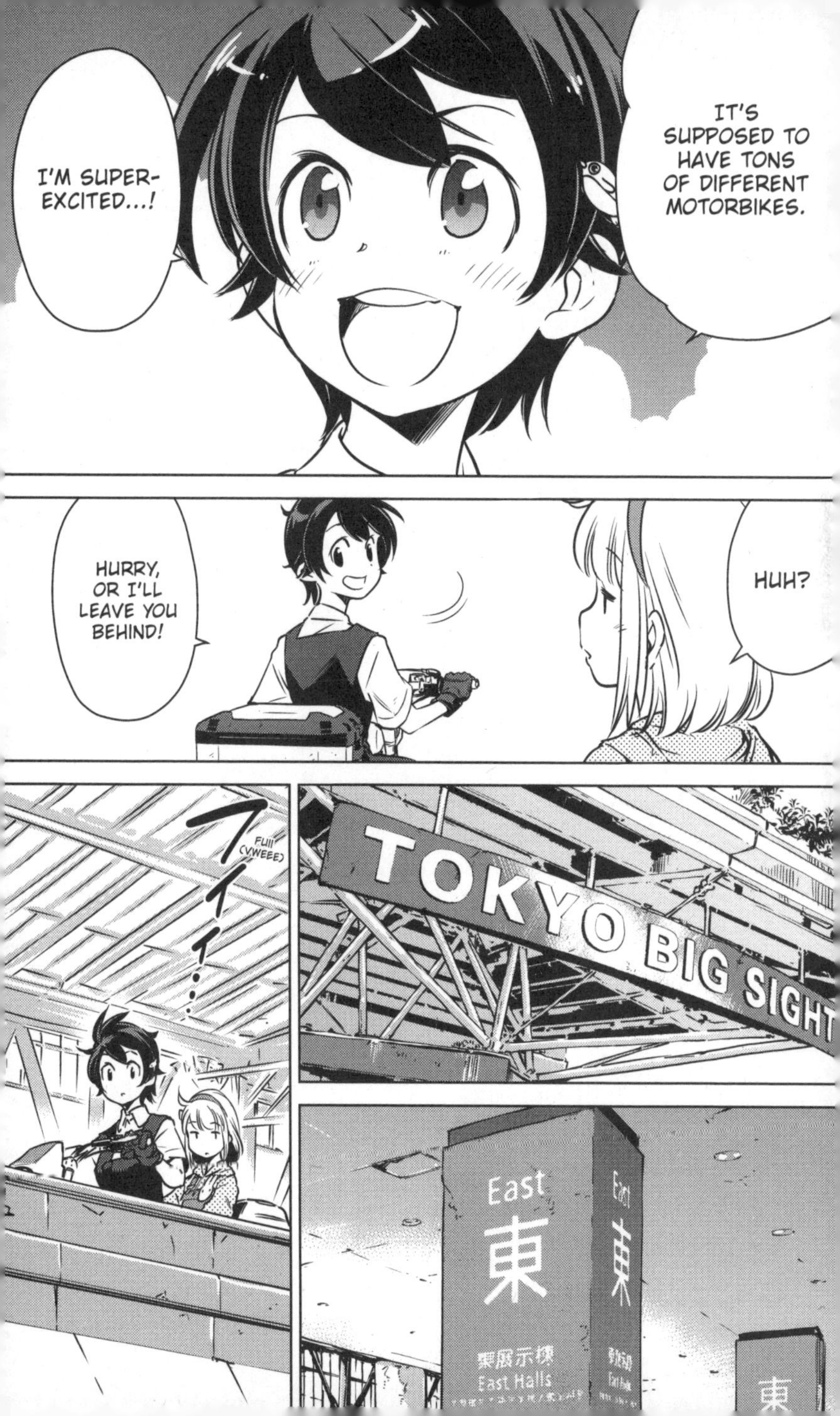
IT'S SUPPOSED TO HAVE TONS OF DIFFERENT MOTORBIKES.
I'M SUPER-EXCITED...!
HUH?
HURRY, OR I'LL LEAVE YOU BEHIND!
TOKYO BIG SIGHT
East
東
東展示棟
East Halls
東
FUII (VWEEE)

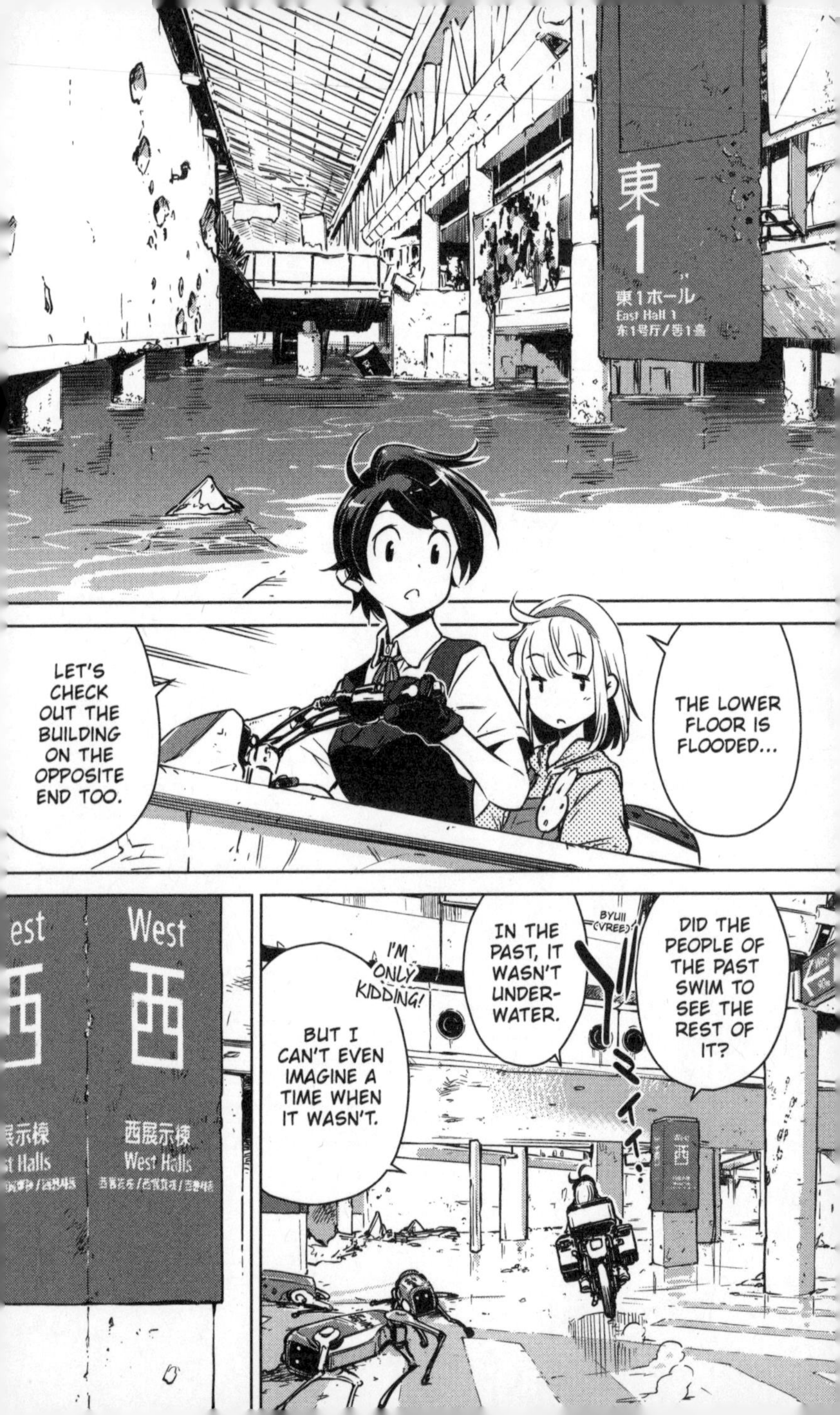
東
1
東1ホール
East Hall 1
THE LOWER FLOOR IS FLOODED...
LET'S CHECK OUT THE BUILDING ON THE OPPOSITE END TOO.
DID THE PEOPLE OF THE PAST SWIM TO SEE THE REST OF IT?
BYUII (VREE)
IN THE PAST, IT WASN'T UNDER-WATER.
I'M ONLY KIDDING!
BUT I CAN'T EVEN IMAGINE A TIME WHEN IT WASN'T.
West
西
西展示棟
West Halls

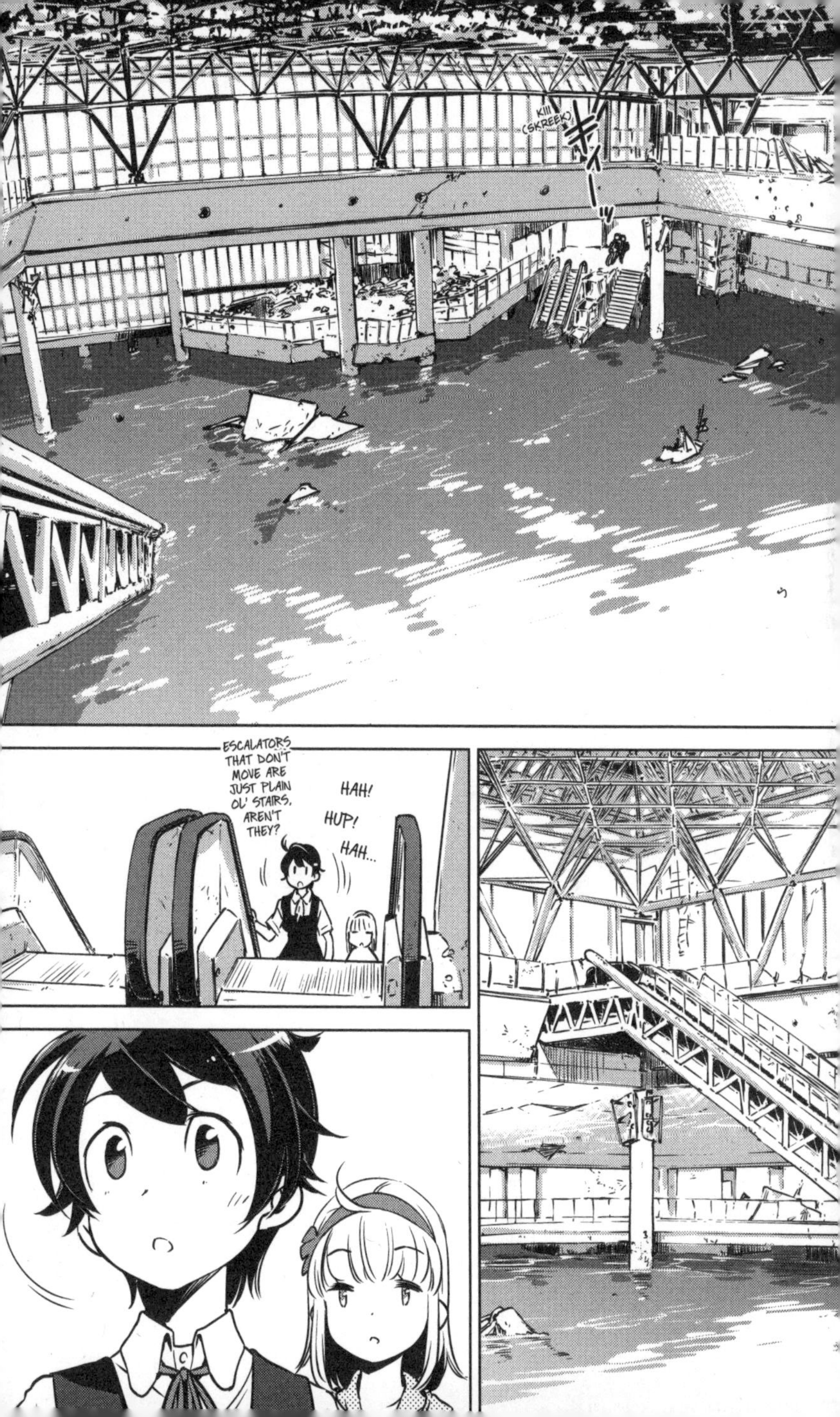
KIII (SKREEK)
ESCALATORS THAT DON'T MOVE ARE JUST PLAIN OL' STAIRS, AREN'T THEY?
HAH!
HUP!
HAH...

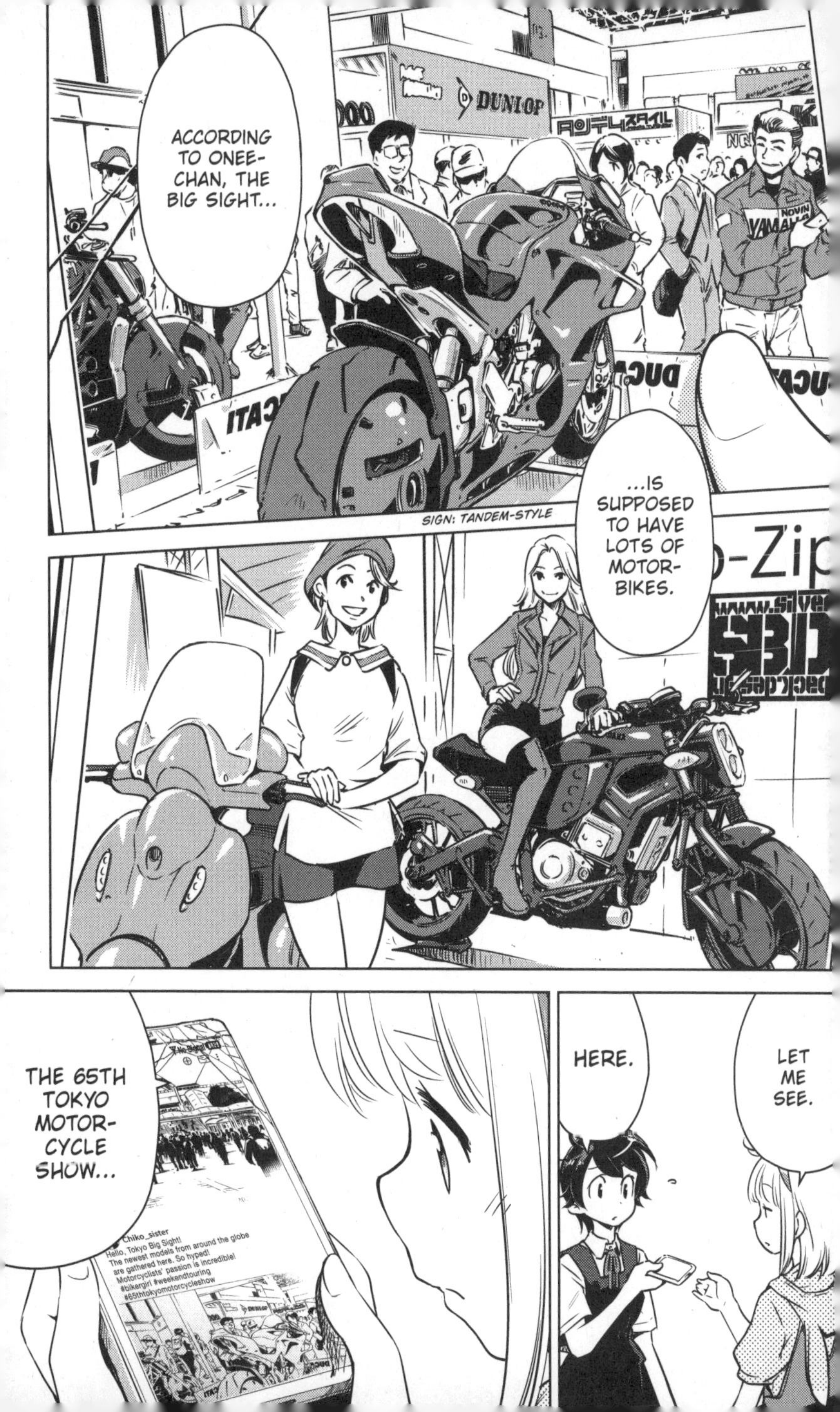

ACCORDING TO ONEE-CHAN, THE BIG SIGHT...
SIGN: TANDEM-STYLE
...IS SUPPOSED TO HAVE LOTS OF MOTOR-BIKES.
LET ME SEE.
HERE.
THE 65TH TOKYO MOTOR-CYCLE SHOW...
Chiko_sister
Hello, Tokyo Big Sight!
The newest models from around the globe are gathered here. So hyped!
Motorcyclists' passion is incredible!
#bikergirl #weekendtouring
#65thtokyomotorcycleshow

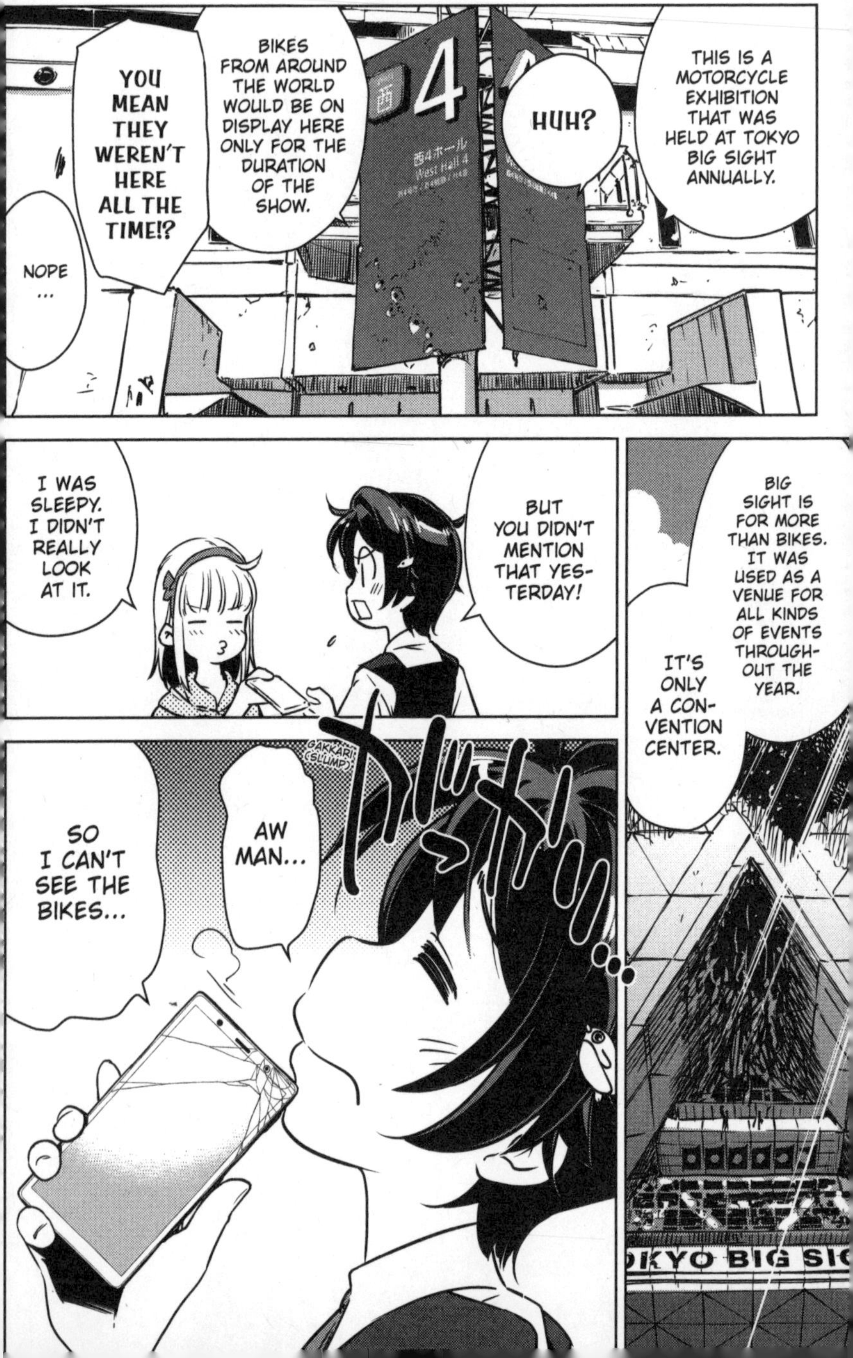
THIS IS A MOTORCYCLE EXHIBITION THAT WAS HELD AT TOKYO BIG SIGHT ANNUALLY.
HUH?
BIKES FROM AROUND THE WORLD WOULD BE ON DISPLAY HERE ONLY FOR THE DURATION OF THE SHOW.
YOU MEAN THEY WEREN'T HERE ALL THE TIME!?
NOPE ...
BIG SIGHT IS FOR MORE THAN BIKES. IT WAS USED AS A VENUE FOR ALL KINDS OF EVENTS THROUGH-OUT THE YEAR.
IT'S ONLY A CON-VENTION CENTER.
BUT YOU DIDN'T MENTION THAT YES-TERDAY!
I WAS SLEEPY. I DIDN'T REALLY LOOK AT IT.
GAKKARI (SLUMP)
AW MAN...
SO I CAN'T SEE THE BIKES...

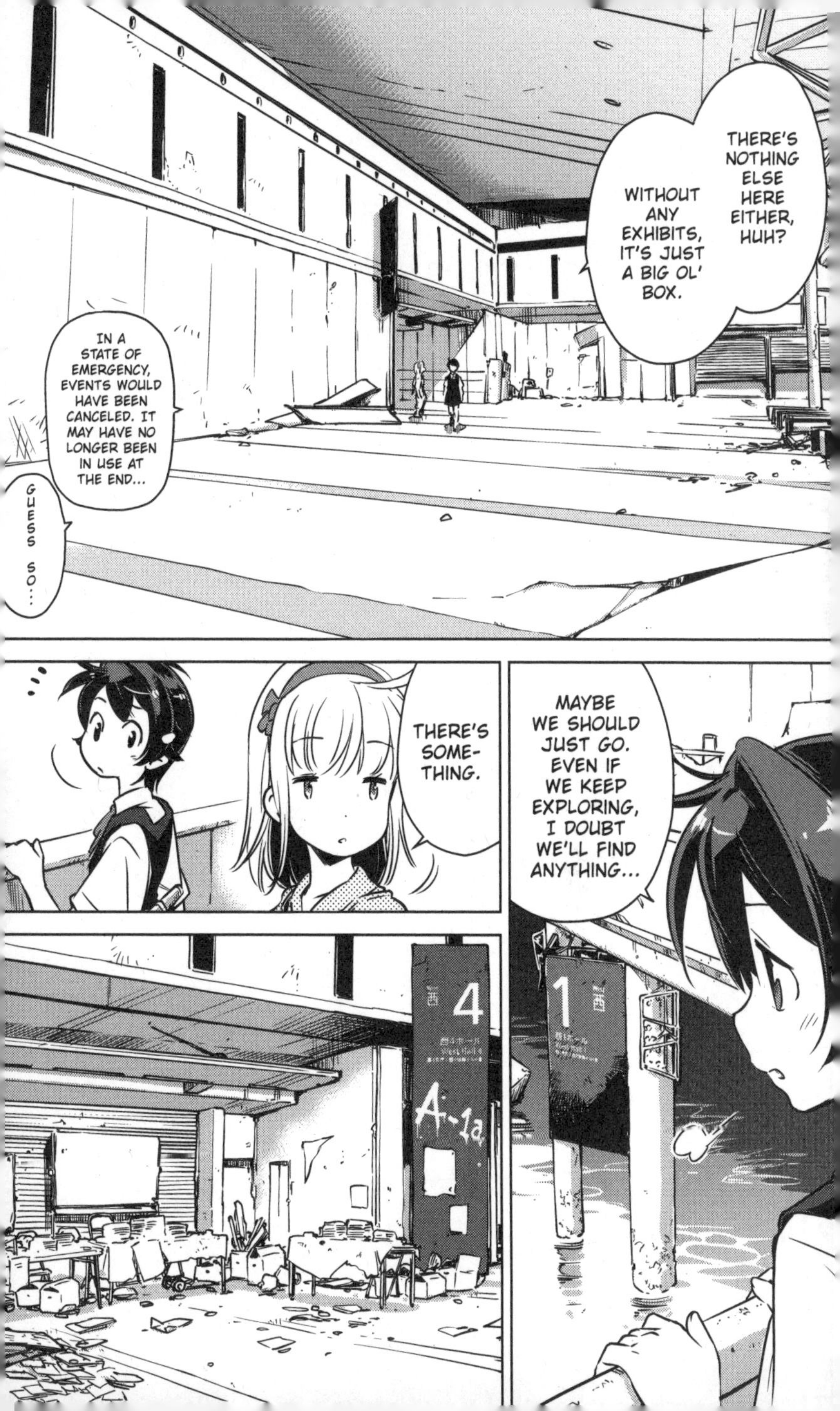
THERE'S NOTHING ELSE HERE EITHER, HUH?
WITHOUT ANY EXHIBITS, IT'S JUST A BIG OL' BOX.
IN A STATE OF EMERGENCY, EVENTS WOULD HAVE BEEN CANCELED. IT MAY HAVE NO LONGER BEEN IN USE AT THE END...
GUESS SO...
MAYBE WE SHOULD JUST GO. EVEN IF WE KEEP EXPLORING, I DOUBT WE'LL FIND ANYTHING...
THERE'S SOME-THING.
4
A-1a
1

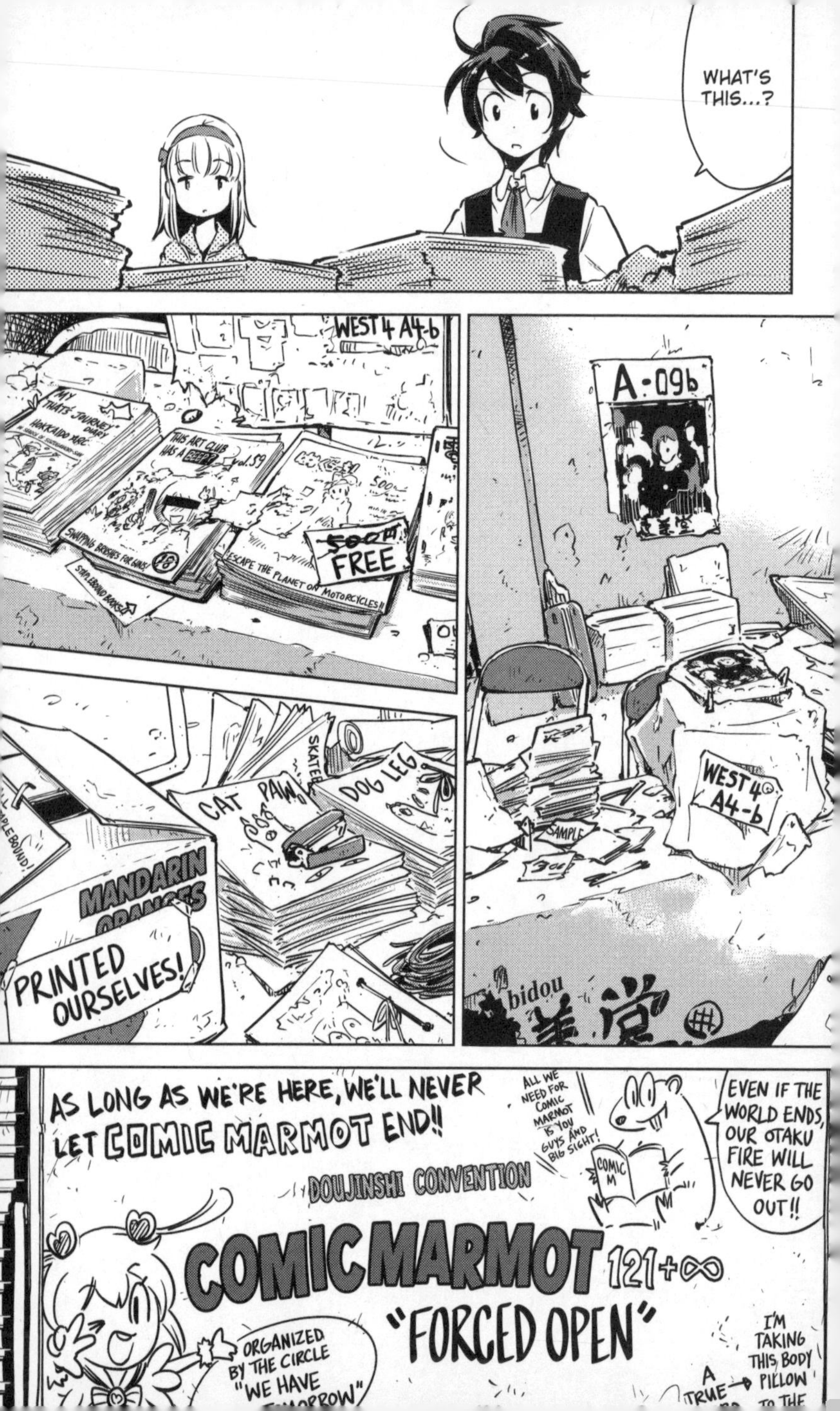
WHAT'S THIS...?
A-09b
WEST 4 A4-b
SAMPLE
bidou
WEST 4 A4-b
MY THAT'S JOURNEY DIARY
HOKKAIDO ARC
THIS ART CLUB HAS A BEEP? vol.59
SWAPPING BRUSHES FOR GUNS!
18
STAPLEBOUND BOOKS
500円 FREE
ESCAPE THE PLANET ON MOTORCYCLES!!
SKATE
CAT PAW
DOG LEG
MANDARIN ORANGES
PRINTED OURSELVES!
AS LONG AS WE'RE HERE, WE'LL NEVER LET COMIC MARMOT END!!
DOUJINSHI CONVENTION
ALL WE NEED FOR COMIC MARMOT IS YOU GUYS AND BIG SIGHT!
COMIC M
EVEN IF THE WORLD ENDS, OUR OTAKU FIRE WILL NEVER GO OUT!!
COMIC MARMOT 121+∞
"FORCED OPEN"
ORGANIZED BY THE CIRCLE "WE HAVE
I'M TAKING THIS BODY PILLOW TO THE
A TRUE

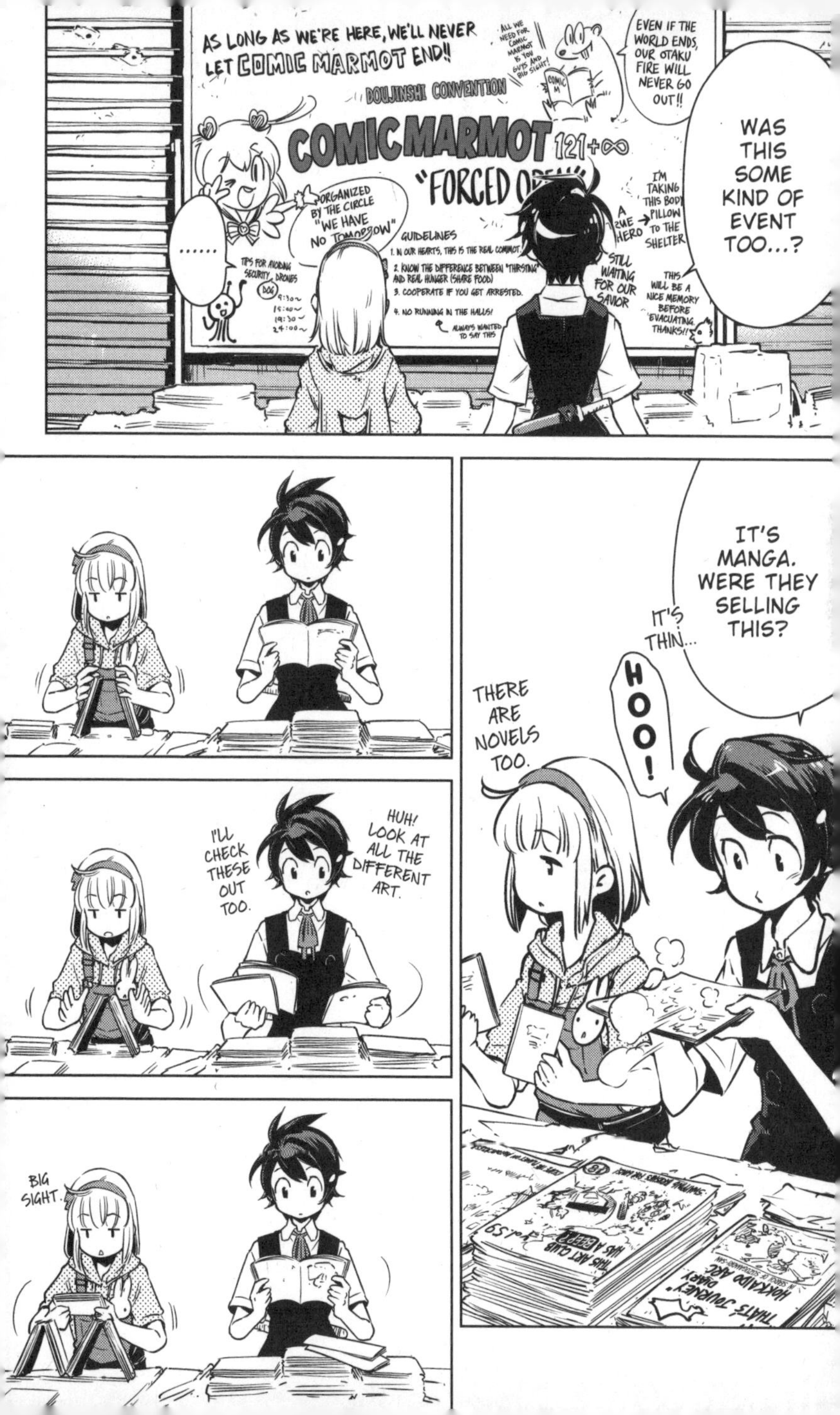
WAS THIS SOME KIND OF EVENT TOO...?
EVEN IF THE WORLD ENDS, OUR OTAKU FIRE WILL NEVER GO OUT!!
ALL WE NEED FOR COMIC MARMOT IS YOU GUYS AND BIG SIGHT!
COMIC M
AS LONG AS WE'RE HERE, WE'LL NEVER LET COMIC MARMOT END!!
DOUJINSHI CONVENTION
COMIC MARMOT 121+∞
"FORCED OPE
I'M TAKING THIS BODY PILLOW TO THE SHELTER
A TRUE HERO
STILL WAITING FOR OUR SAVIOR
THIS WILL BE A NICE MEMORY BEFORE EVACUATING. THANKS!!
ORGANIZED BY THE CIRCLE "WE HAVE NO TOMORROW"
GUIDELINES
1. IN OUR HEARTS, THIS IS THE REAL COMIMOT.
2. KNOW THE DIFFERENCE BETWEEN "THIRSTING" AND REAL HUNGER (SHARE FOOD)
3. COOPERATE IF YOU GET ARRESTED.
4. NO RUNNING IN THE HALLS!
ALWAYS WANTED TO SAY THIS
TIPS FOR AVOIDING SECURITY DRONES
DOG
9:30~
15:00~
19:30~
24:00~
......
IT'S MANGA. WERE THEY SELLING THIS?
IT'S THIN...
HOO!
THERE ARE NOVELS TOO.
THIS ART CLUB HAS A SECRET
vol.59
THAT'S JOURNEY • HOKKAIDO ARC DIARY
HUH! LOOK AT ALL THE DIFFERENT ART.
I'LL CHECK THESE OUT TOO.
BIG SIGHT.

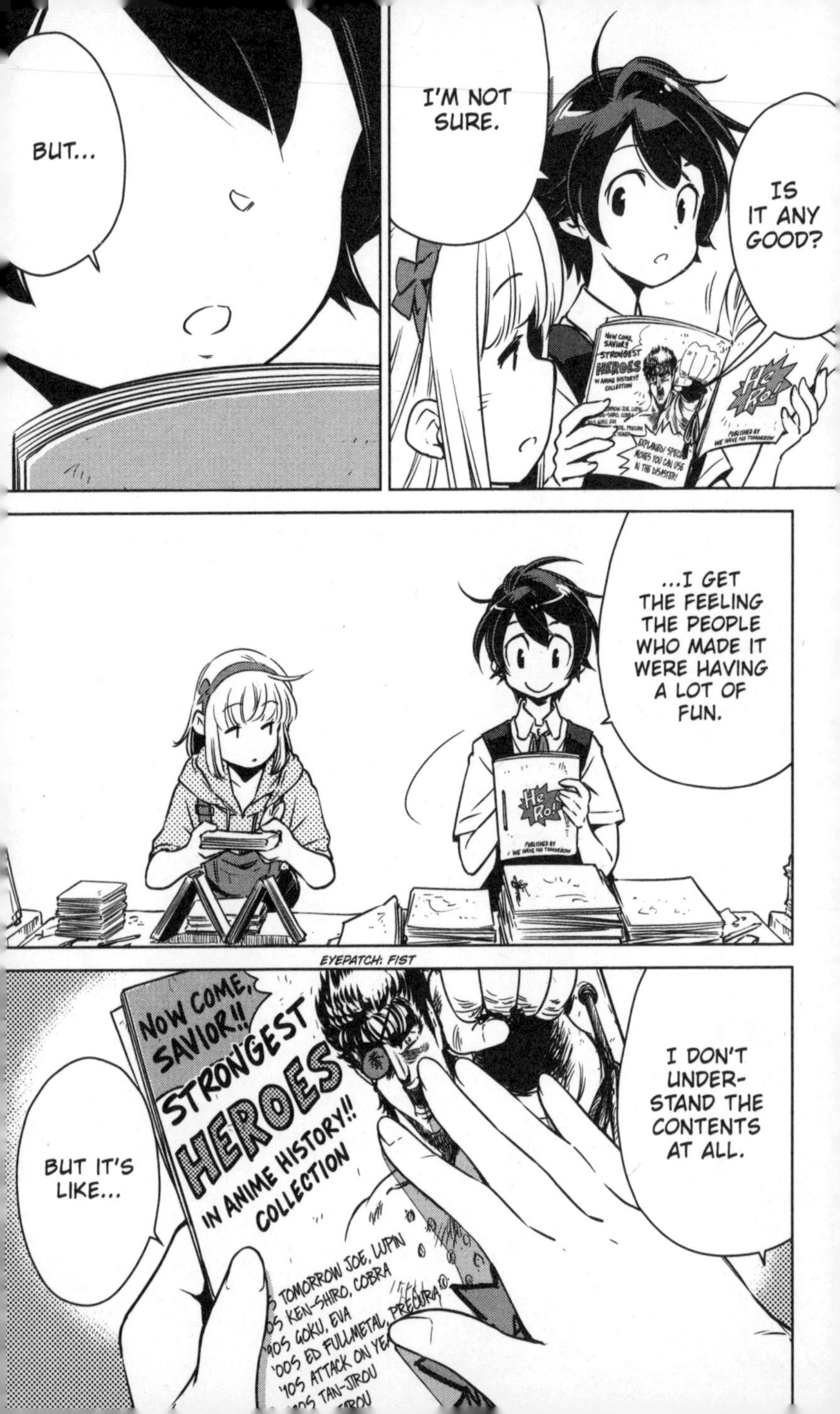
IS IT ANY GOOD?
I'M NOT SURE.
BUT...
...I GET THE FEELING THE PEOPLE WHO MADE IT WERE HAVING A LOT OF FUN.
He Ro!
PUBLISHED BY WE HAVE NO TOMORROW
EYEPATCH: FIST
I DON'T UNDER-STAND THE CONTENTS AT ALL.
BUT IT'S LIKE...
NOW COME, SAVIOR!!
STRONGEST HEROES IN ANIME HISTORY!! COLLECTION
TOMORROW JOE, LUPIN
'80S KEN-SHIRO, COBRA
'90S GOKU, EVA
'00S ED FULLMETAL, PRECURA
'10S ATTACK ON YE
'20S TAN-JIROU

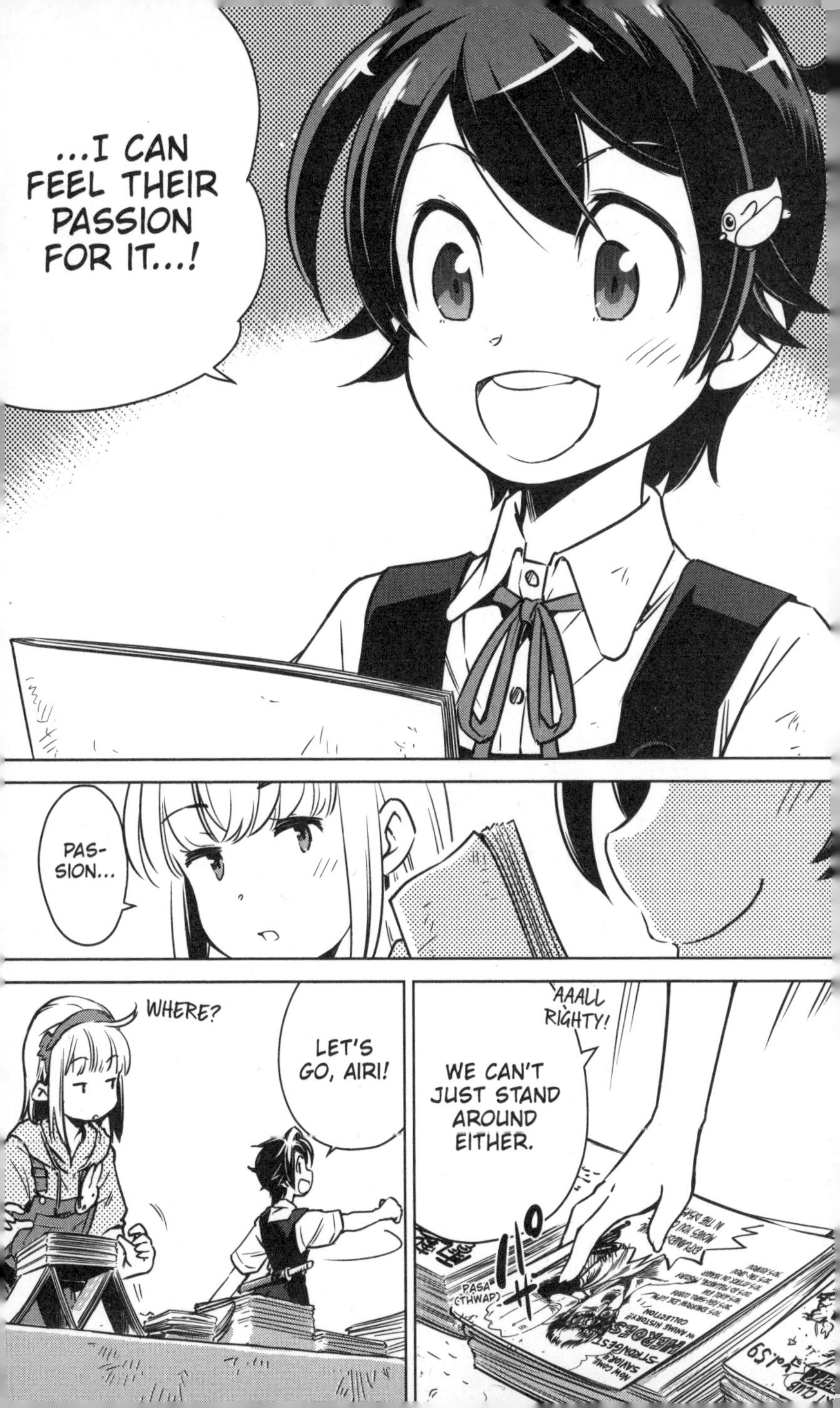

...I CAN FEEL THEIR PASSION FOR IT...!
PAS-SION...
AAALL RIGHTY!
WE CAN'T JUST STAND AROUND EITHER.
PASA (THWAP)
LET'S GO, AIRI!
WHERE?

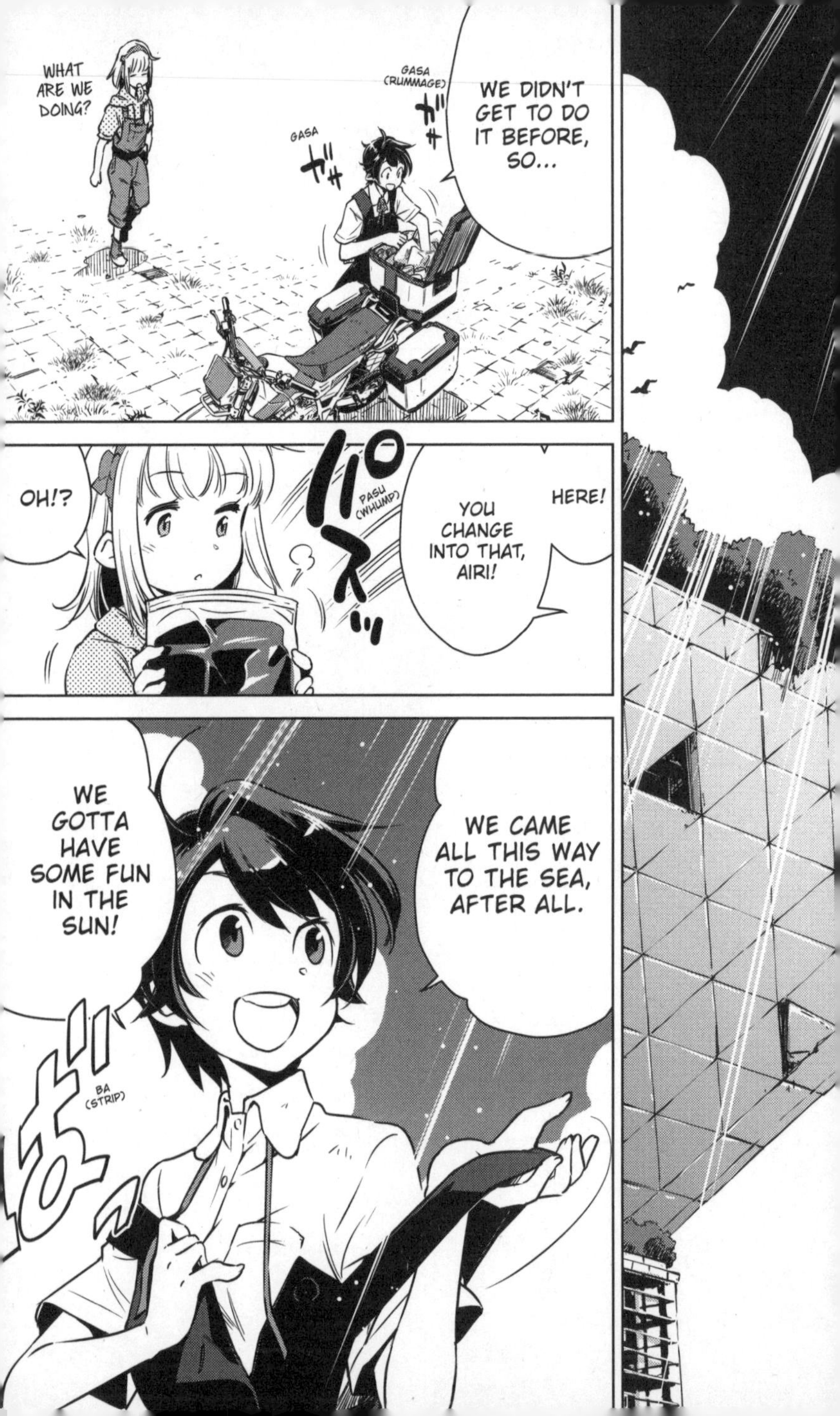
WE DIDN'T GET TO DO IT BEFORE, SO...
GASA (RUMMAGE)
GASA
WHAT ARE WE DOING?
HERE!
YOU CHANGE INTO THAT, AIRI!
PASU (WHUMP)
OH!?
WE CAME ALL THIS WAY TO THE SEA, AFTER ALL.
WE GOTTA HAVE SOME FUN IN THE SUN!
BA (STRIP)

Touringram

No Signal

Touringram

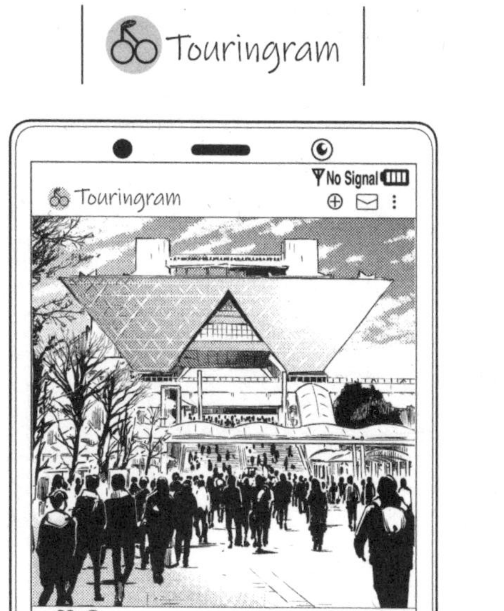

March 21, 2036

Chiko_sister

Hello, Tokyo Big Sight!
The newest models from around the globe are gathered here. So hyped!
Motorcyclists' passion is incredible!
#bikergirl #weekendtouring
#65thtokyomotorcycleshow

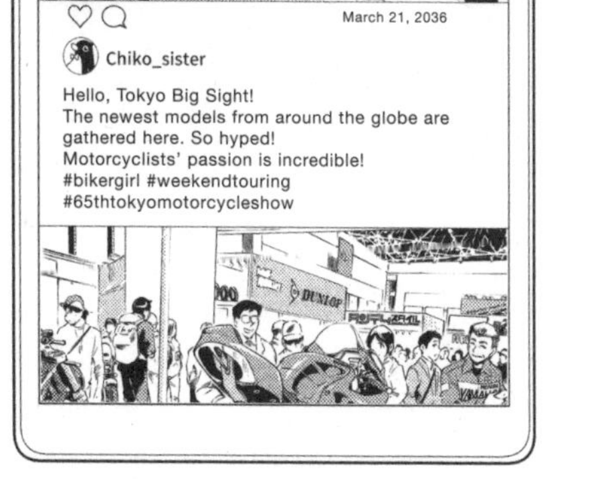
DUNLOP

Translation Notes

Page 3
Youko and Airi are playing *shiritori*, a word chain game where players take turns coming up with words that begin with the last syllable of the previous word. Whoever says a word ending in the syllable *n* loses, as it never starts a word in Japanese. There are several variations, such as limiting valid words to types of food, as is seen here.

Page 5
Mikan are a sweet, seedless variety of mandarin orange.

Page 12
The **Hakone Ekiden race** is a prominent annual long-distance relay marathon race held between Tokyo and Hakone. Over two days, teams from twenty Japanese universities run over two hundred kilometers in ten legs.

Oden is a type of stew consisting of ingredients such as egg, radishes, and fish cakes boiled in a soy-flavored broth.

Page 18
Takoyaki is a popular street food consisting of octopus bits in balls of fried batter.

Page 19
In Japanese, the words for **weekend** (*shuumatsu*) and the end of the world (also *shuumatsu*) are homonyms, creating some fun wordplay in *Touring After the Apocalypse*'s Japanese title, *Shuumatsu Touring*.

Page 32
Airi's "**brace for shock and flash**" is a reference to the first firing of the Wave Motion Gun in the classic anime *Space Battleship Yamato*.

Page 44
One of the central features of the Hakone area is scenic **Lake Ashi**, known for its views of Mount Fuji, which in pre-apocalyptic times can be crossed by tourists on ferries made to look like pirate ships.

Page 50
Yokohama is the port city capital of Kanagawa Prefecture, lying south of Tokyo on Tokyo Bay. **Minato Mirai** is Yokohama's futuristic central business district, and its name means "waterfront of the future."

Page 54
Youko has a towel from **Kusatsu Onsen**, a hot springs resort town in Gunma Prefecture, northwest of Tokyo.

Page 53
Hokkaido is Japan's largest and northernmost prefecture. Agriculture is one of its primary industries, and it produces about half of Japan's milk. **Milk Road** (Route 19) gained its name for being the road that the milk tankers drive down.

"**Art is an explosion!**" is a famous quote by artist Taro Okamoto, who designed the central pavilion of the 1970 Japan World Expo, including the iconic *Tower of the Sun* sculpture, which remains in the Expo Commemoration Park.

Himeji Castle dates back to 1333 and is also known as White Egret Castle for its white exterior.

Page 57
The girls are singing a Japanese children's song called "Umi" ("The Sea").

Page 66
Yakitori are grilled chicken skewers.

Page 69
Suzuki are a type of sea bass common to the western Pacific, but it's also the name of a leading motorcycle manufacturer—and thus why Youko jumps to Yamaha, the maker of her beloved Serow, instead of to another fish.

Page 76
Youko and Airi's new companion introduces himself as Schwar-chan—the nickname for *The Terminator* star Arnold Schwarzenegger in Japan.

Page 77
The **crescent building** (seen earlier on page 63) is the InterContinental Yokohama Grand Hotel.

Page 115
Snake wine is an alcoholic beverage found throughout much of Southeast Asia. Made by steeping the whole body of a venomous snake in a bottle of rice wine, the resulting concoction is said to have medicinal properties and is usually safe to drink.

Page 118
Yakiniku is a style of grilling bite-sized pieces of meat and vegetables on a small tabletop grill.

Page 122
Dengeki Maoh is where *Touring After the Apocalypse* was originally published. *Zatsu Tabi: That's Journey* is another travel manga published in the same magazine, where the main character chooses her destination casually and without planning beforehand, usually via Twitter poll.

Page 129
The **Yurikamome** is a fully-automated transit system in Tokyo that first opened in 1995. It was named for the black-headed gull common in the Tokyo Bay area.

Page 137
The girls are imitating the pointing-and-calling system famously used by Japanese train conductors to reduce errors and accidents.

Page 140
The Japanese lyrics to "I've Been Working on the Railroad" are quite different from the English version it takes its tune from: "the railroad continues forever / past fields, mountains, and valleys." In the original Japanese, Youko alters the second part to "past buildings, waves, and the sea."

Page 156
Comic Marmot is a reference to Comic Market, aka Comiket, the biannual convention focused on self-published *doujinshi* books.

This Art Club Has a Beep? is a reference to another *Dengeki Maoh* manga, *This Art Club Has a Problem!* by Imigimuru.

Suzugamori is the manga artist protagonist of travel manga *Zatsu Tabi: That's Journey*.

Page 157
The **savior** that is repeatedly mentioned is a reference to Kenshiro, the protagonist of the landmark 1980s post-apocalyptic manga *Fist of the North Star*. Here, he's parodied as **Ken-shiro**.

Page 193
Japan's official calendar is divided into eras based on the ruling emperor. The **Reiwa period** began on May 1, 2019, when Emperor Akihito abdicated and passed the throne to his son Naruhito.

Chapter 5

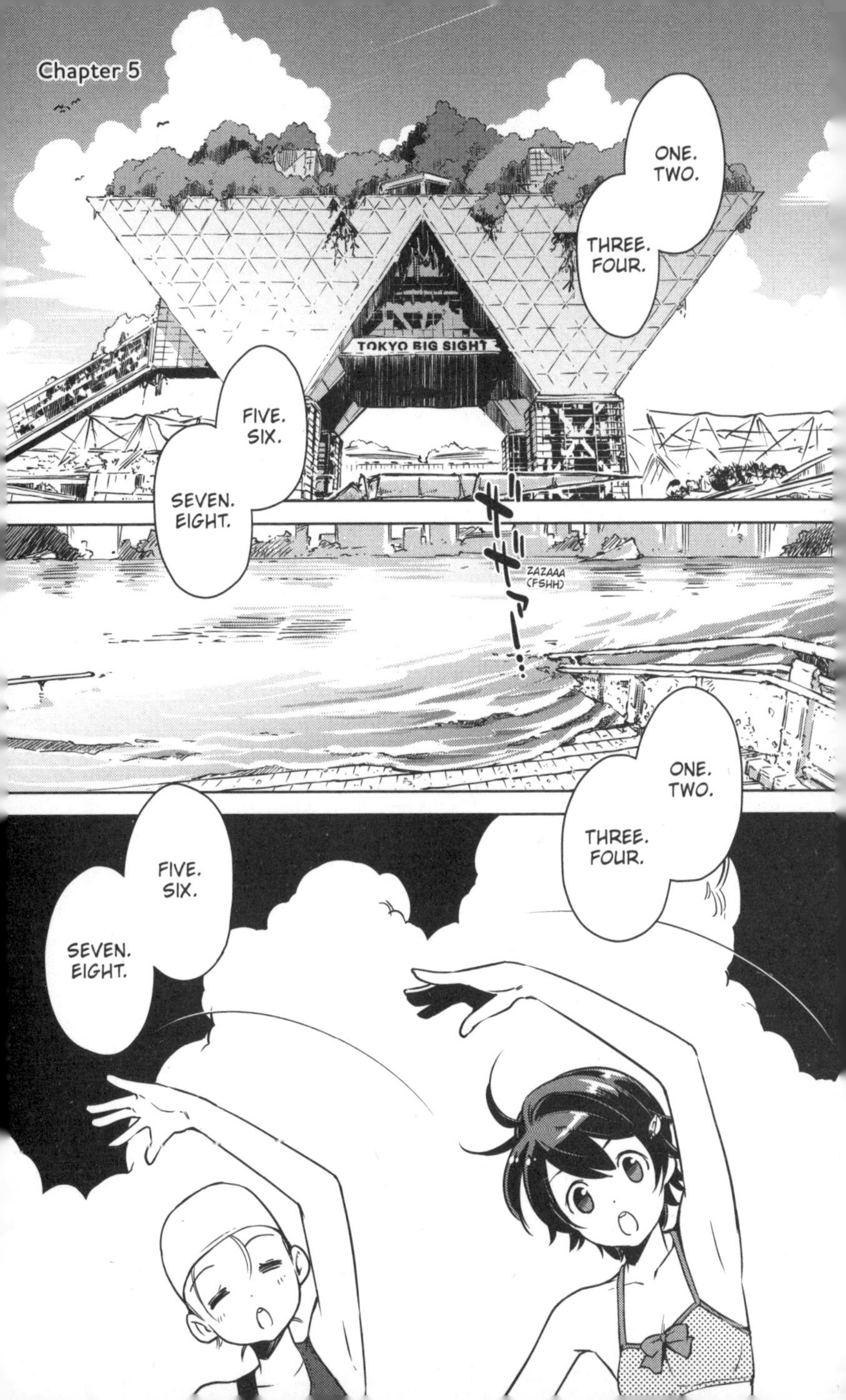
TOKYO BIG SIGHT
ONE. TWO.
THREE. FOUR.
FIVE. SIX.
SEVEN. EIGHT.
ZAZAAA (FSHH)
ONE. TWO.
THREE. FOUR.
FIVE. SIX.
SEVEN. EIGHT.

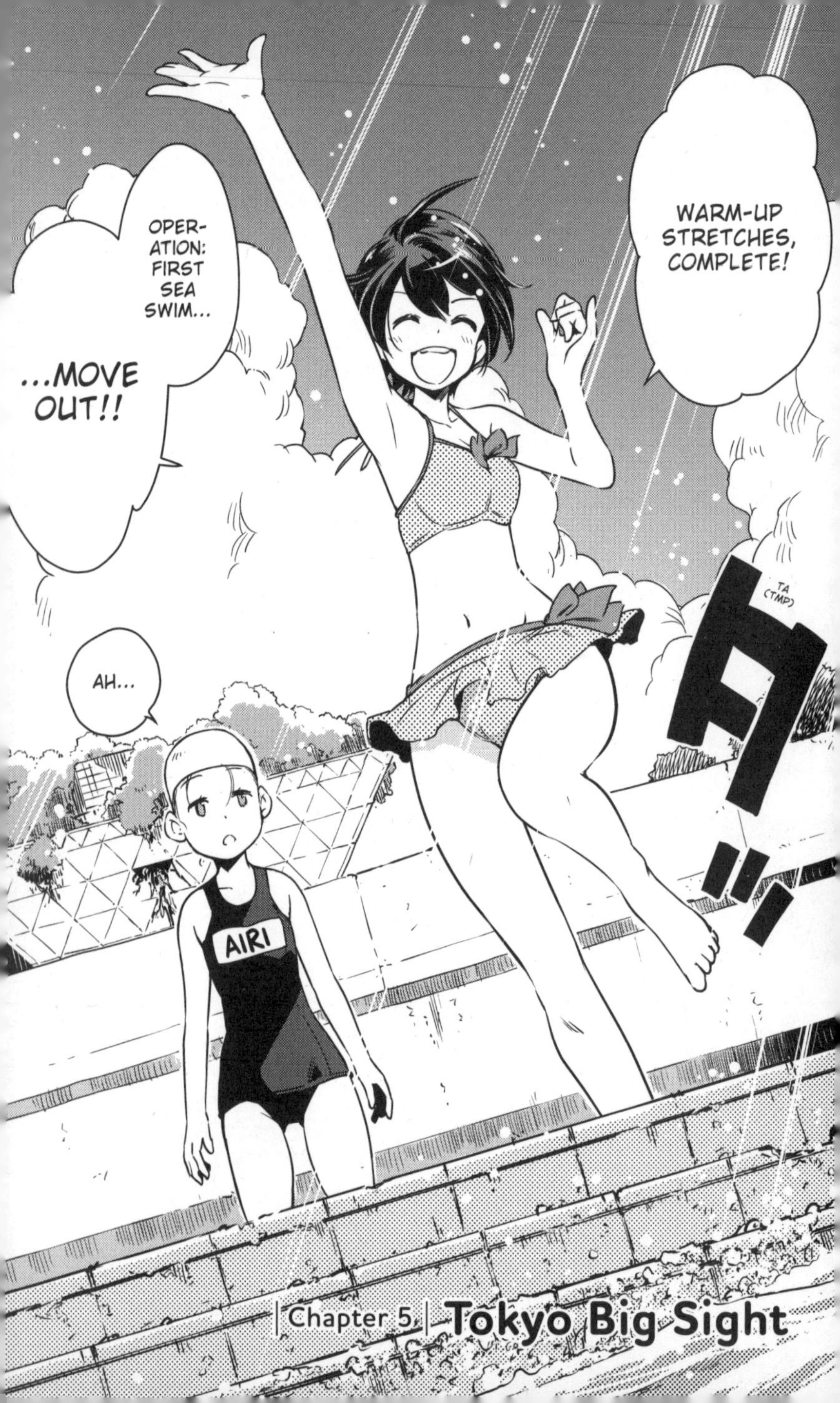
WARM-UP STRETCHES, COMPLETE!
OPERATION: FIRST SEA SWIM...
...MOVE OUT!!
TA (TMP)
AH...
AIRI
| Chapter 5 | Tokyo Big Sight

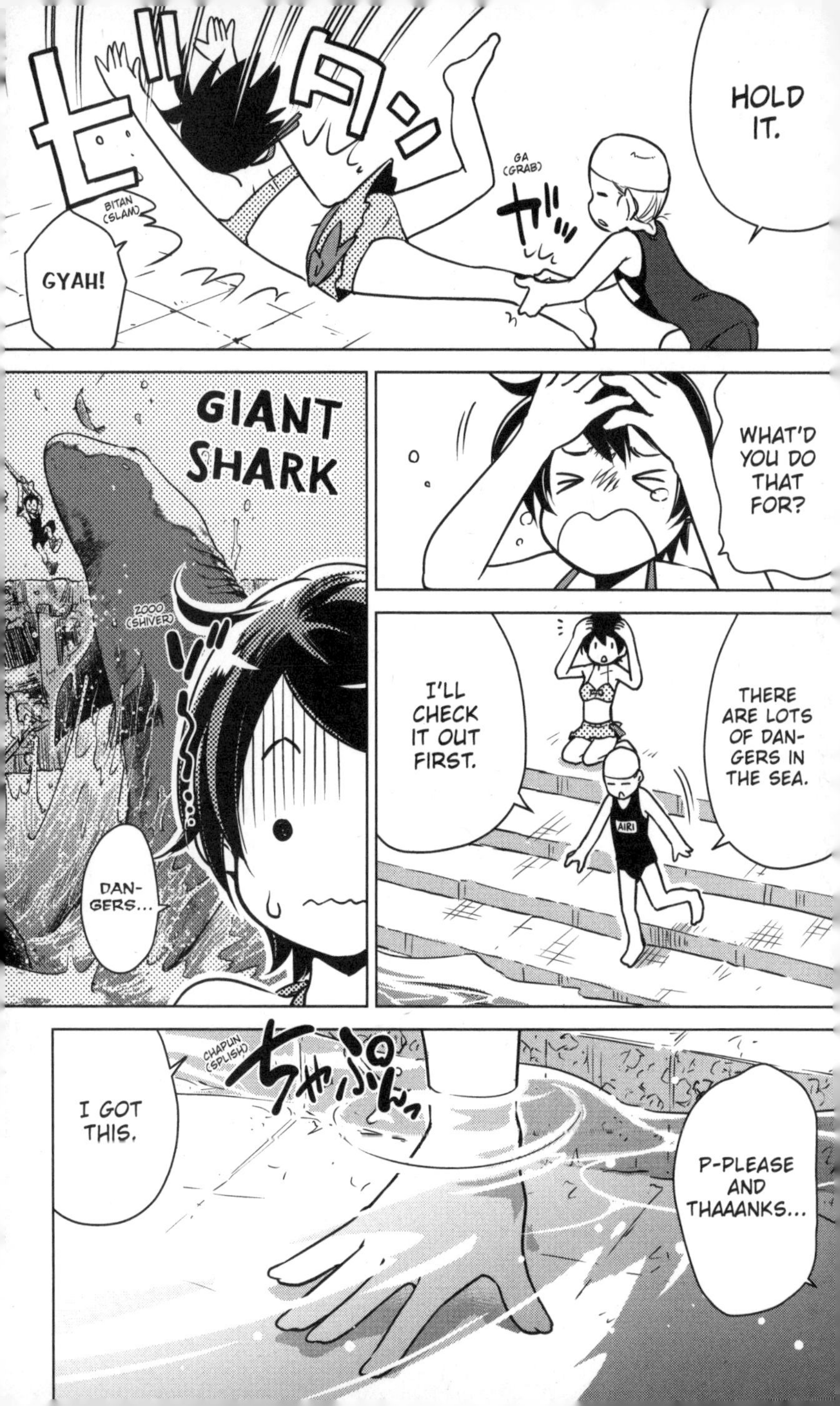
HOLD IT.
GA (GRAB)
BITAN (SLAM)
GYAH!
WHAT'D YOU DO THAT FOR?
THERE ARE LOTS OF DAN-GERS IN THE SEA.
I'LL CHECK IT OUT FIRST.
GIANT SHARK
ZOOO (SHIVER)
DAN-GERS...
P-PLEASE AND THAAANKS...
CHAPUN (SPLISH)
I GOT THIS.

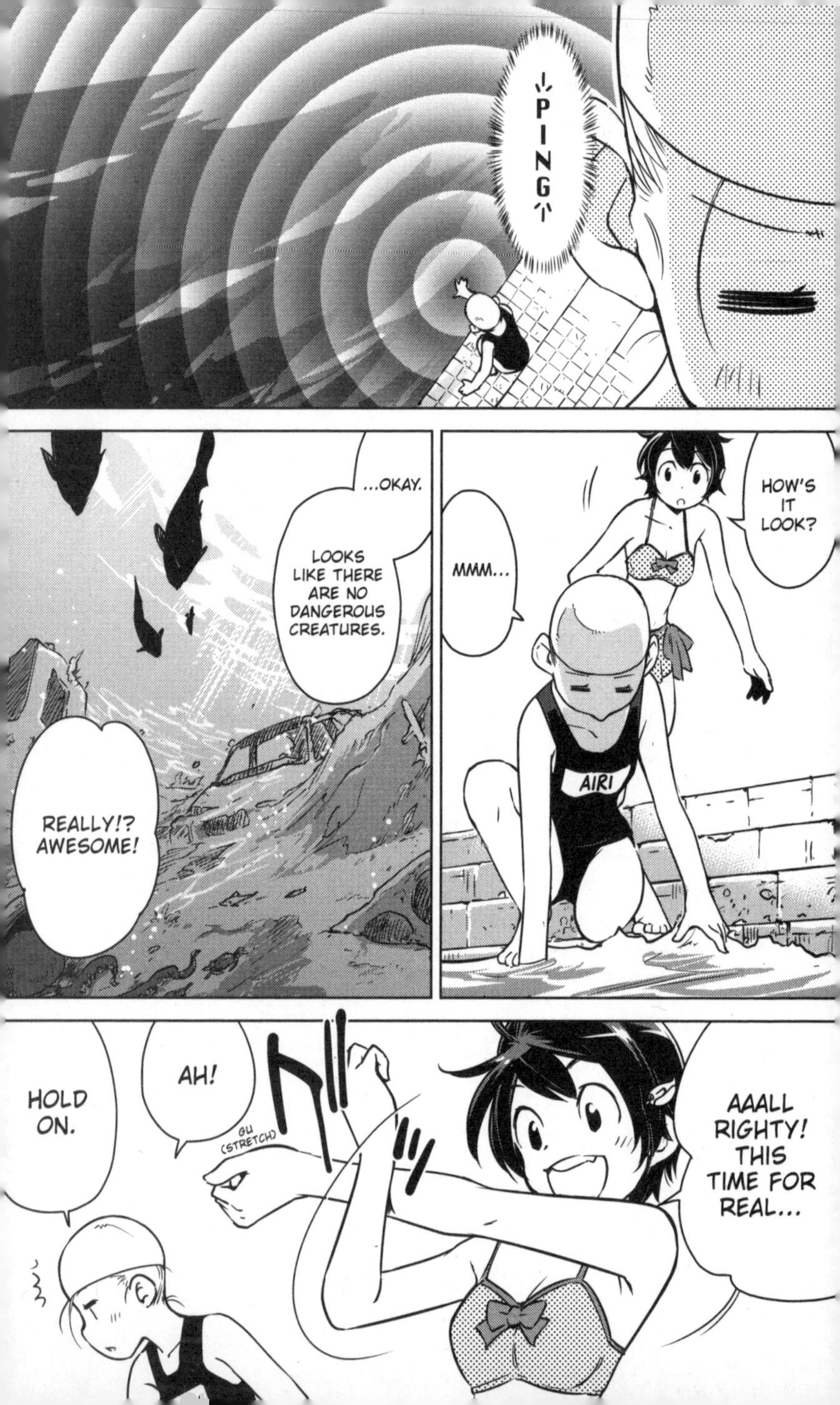
PING
HOW'S IT LOOK?
MMM...
...OKAY.
LOOKS LIKE THERE ARE NO DANGEROUS CREATURES.
REALLY!? AWESOME!
AIRI
AAALL RIGHTY! THIS TIME FOR REAL...
GU (STRETCH)
AH!
HOLD ON.

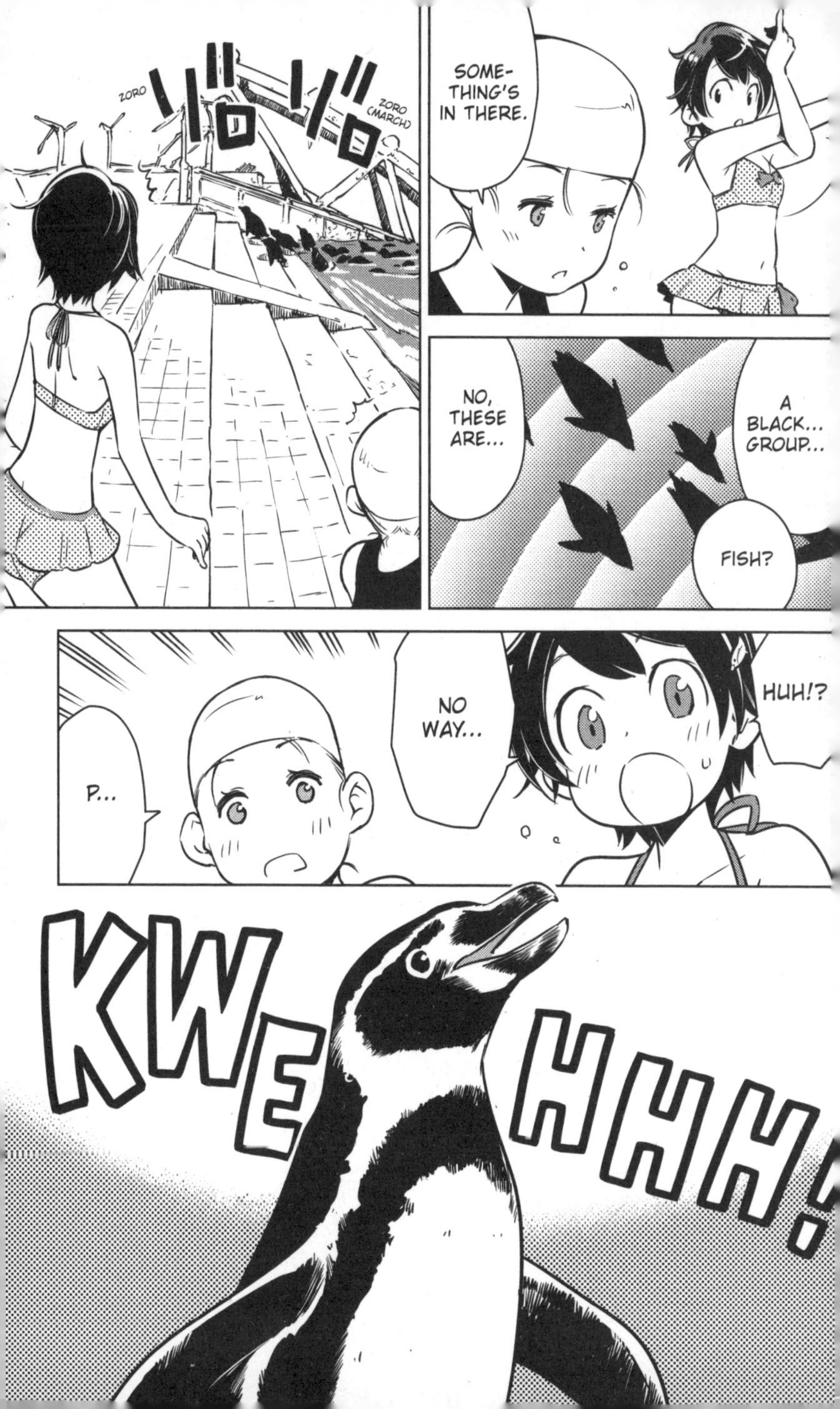
SOME-THING'S IN THERE.
A BLACK... GROUP...
FISH?
NO, THESE ARE...
ZORO (MARCH)
ZORO
HUH!?
NO WAY...
P...
KWEHHHH!!

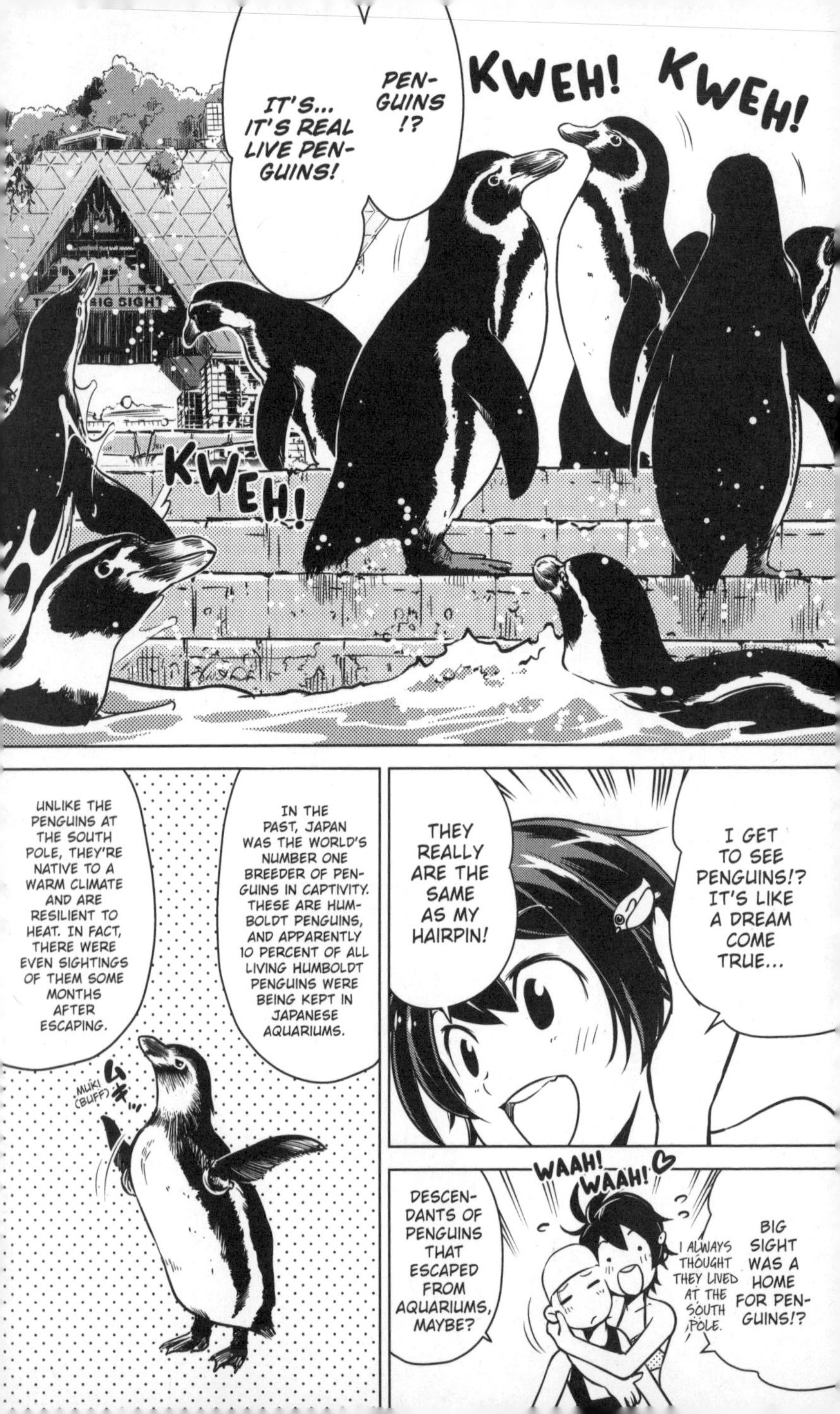
KWEH! KWEH!
PEN-GUINS!?
IT'S... IT'S REAL LIVE PEN-GUINS!
KWEH!
I GET TO SEE PENGUINS!? IT'S LIKE A DREAM COME TRUE...
THEY REALLY ARE THE SAME AS MY HAIRPIN!
WAAH! WAAH!
BIG SIGHT WAS A HOME FOR PEN-GUINS!?
I ALWAYS THOUGHT THEY LIVED AT THE SOUTH POLE.
DESCEN-DANTS OF PENGUINS THAT ESCAPED FROM AQUARIUMS, MAYBE?
IN THE PAST, JAPAN WAS THE WORLD'S NUMBER ONE BREEDER OF PEN-GUINS IN CAPTIVITY. THESE ARE HUM-BOLDT PENGUINS, AND APPARENTLY 10 PERCENT OF ALL LIVING HUMBOLDT PENGUINS WERE BEING KEPT IN JAPANESE AQUARIUMS.
UNLIKE THE PENGUINS AT THE SOUTH POLE, THEY'RE NATIVE TO A WARM CLIMATE AND ARE RESILIENT TO HEAT. IN FACT, THERE WERE EVEN SIGHTINGS OF THEM SOME MONTHS AFTER ESCAPING.
ムキ...
MUKI (BUFF)

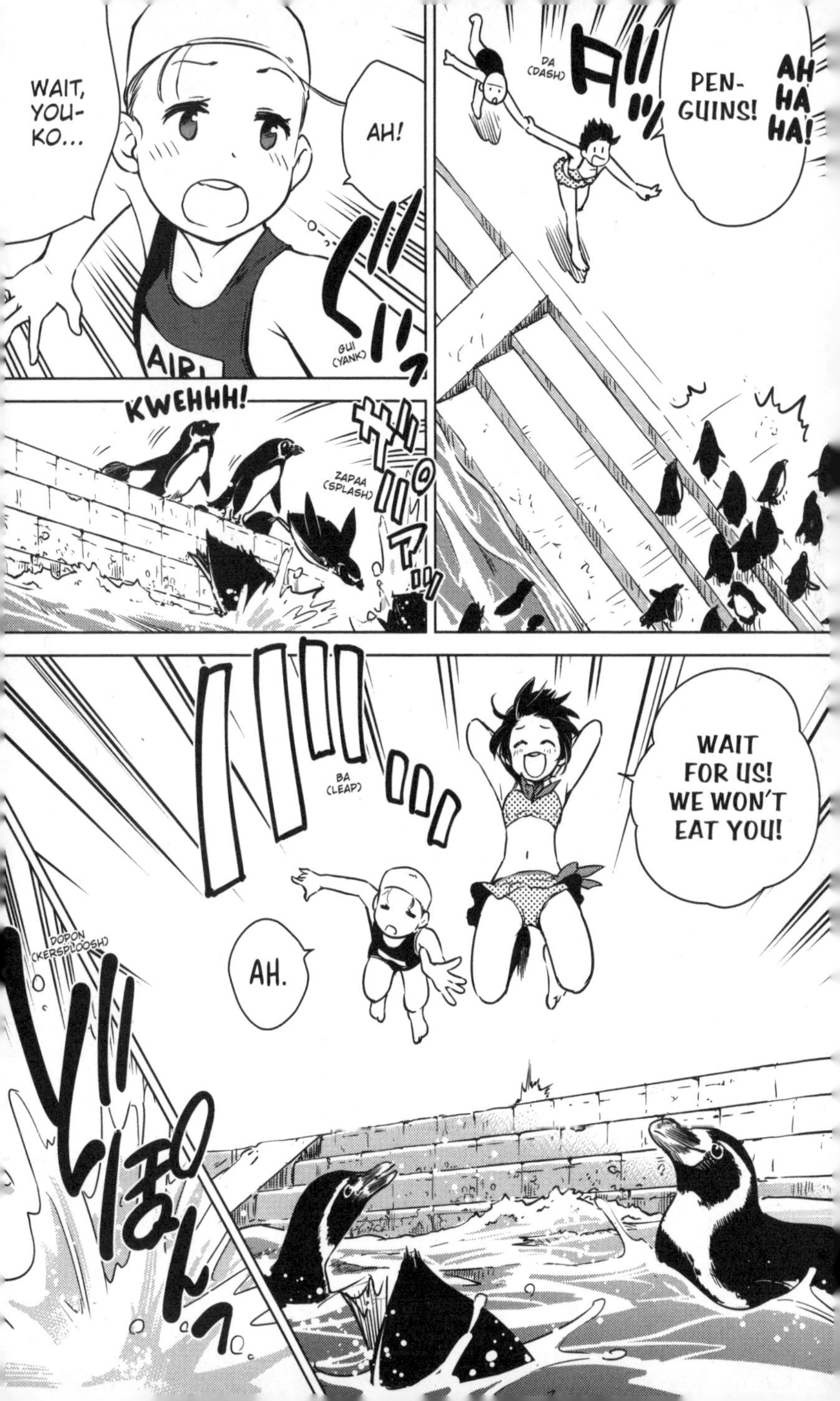
AH HA HA!
PEN-GUINS!
DA (DASH)
AH!
WAIT, YOU-KO...
GUI (YANK)
KWEHHH!
ZAPAA (SPLASH)
WAIT FOR US! WE WON'T EAT YOU!
BA (LEAP)
AH.
DOPON (KERSPLOOSH)

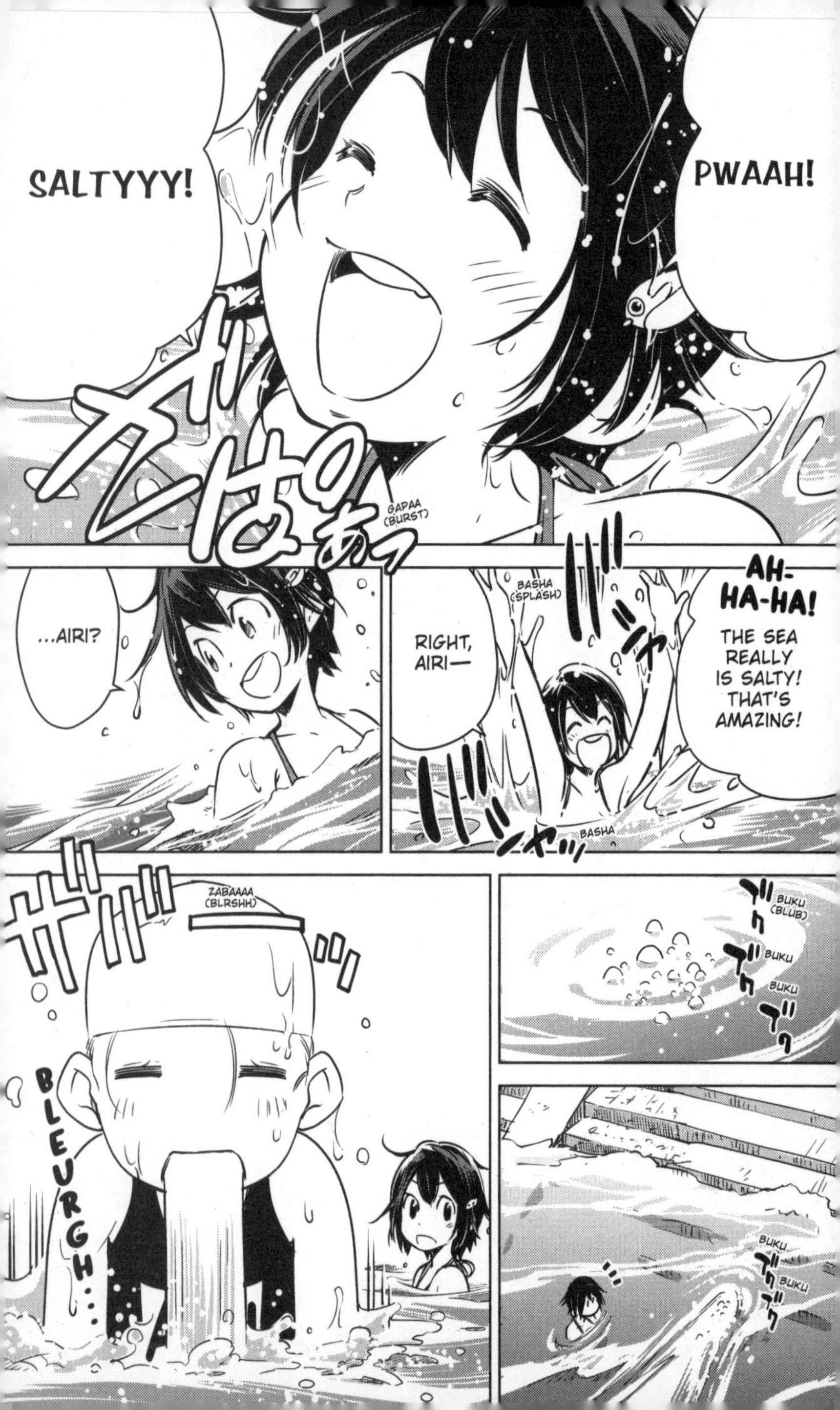
PWAAH!
SALTYYY!
GAPAA (BURST)
AH-HA-HA! THE SEA REALLY IS SALTY! THAT'S AMAZING!
BASHA (SPLASH)
RIGHT, AIRI—
BASHA
...AIRI?
BUKU (BLUB)
BUKU
BUKU
BUKU
BUKU
ZABAAAA (BLRSHH)
BLEURGH...

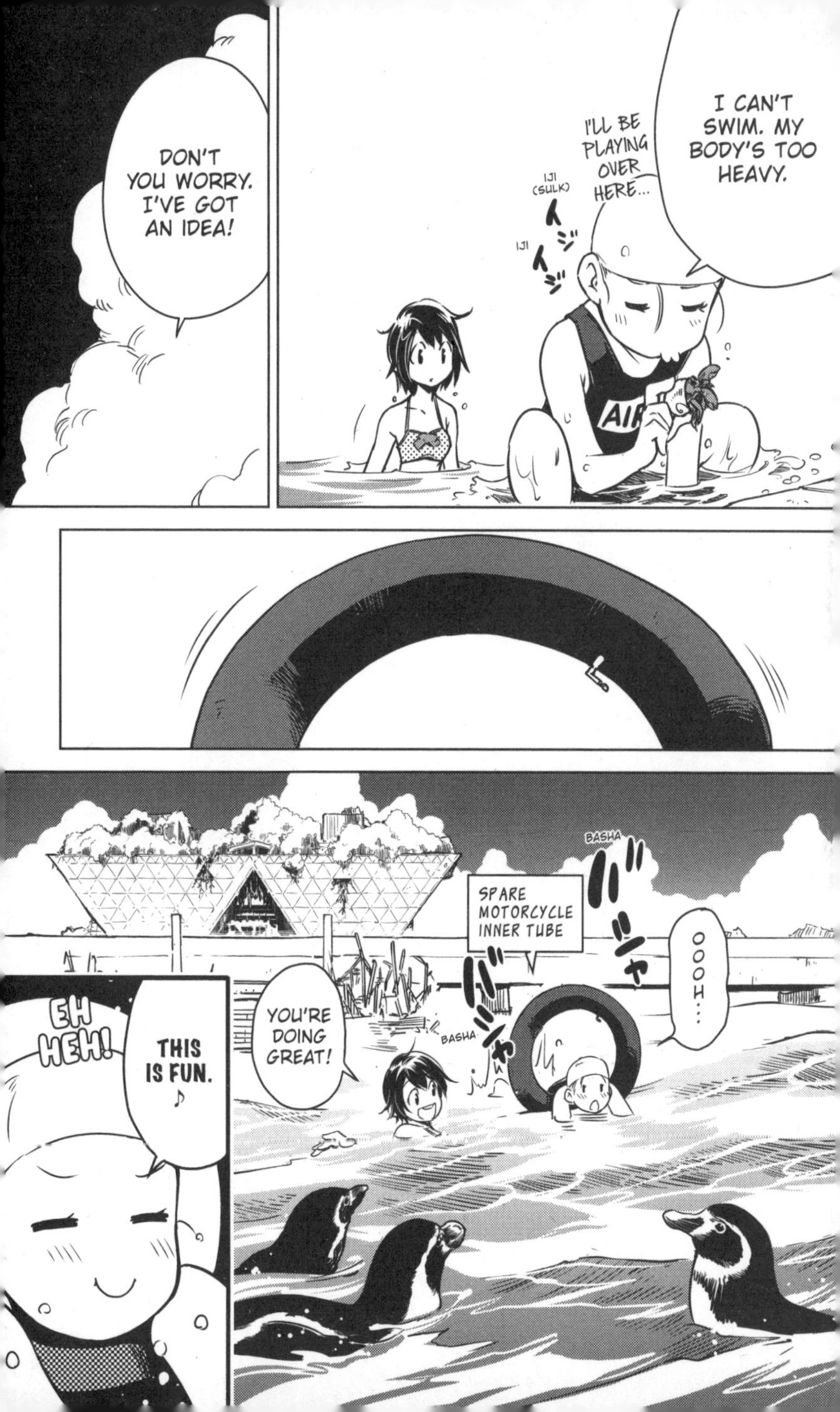

I CAN'T SWIM. MY BODY'S TOO HEAVY.
I'LL BE PLAYING OVER HERE...
IJI (SULK)
イジ
IJI
イジ
DON'T YOU WORRY. I'VE GOT AN IDEA!
BASHA
バシャ
OOOH...
SPARE MOTORCYCLE INNER TUBE
バシャ
BASHA
YOU'RE DOING GREAT!
EH HEH!
THIS IS FUN. ♪

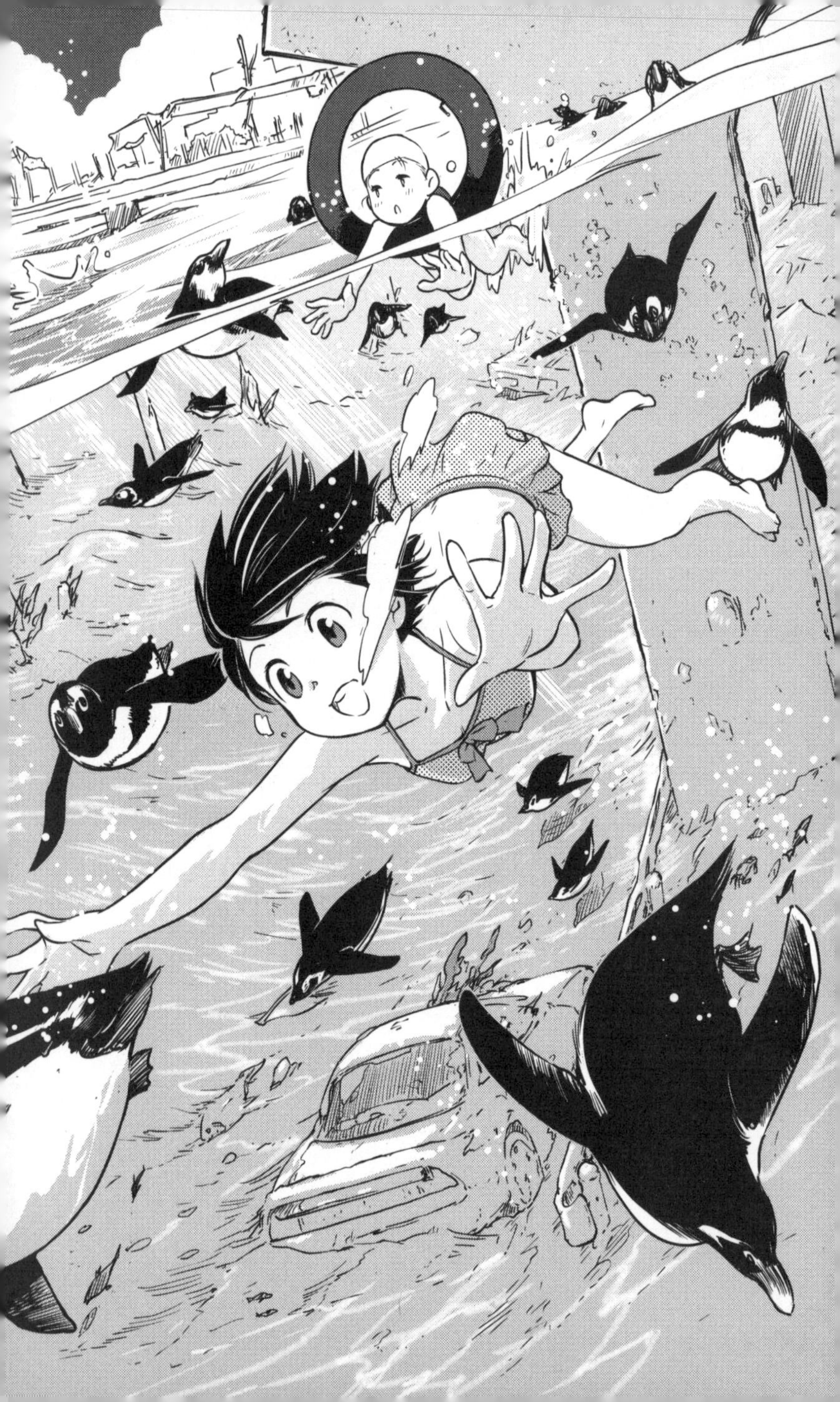

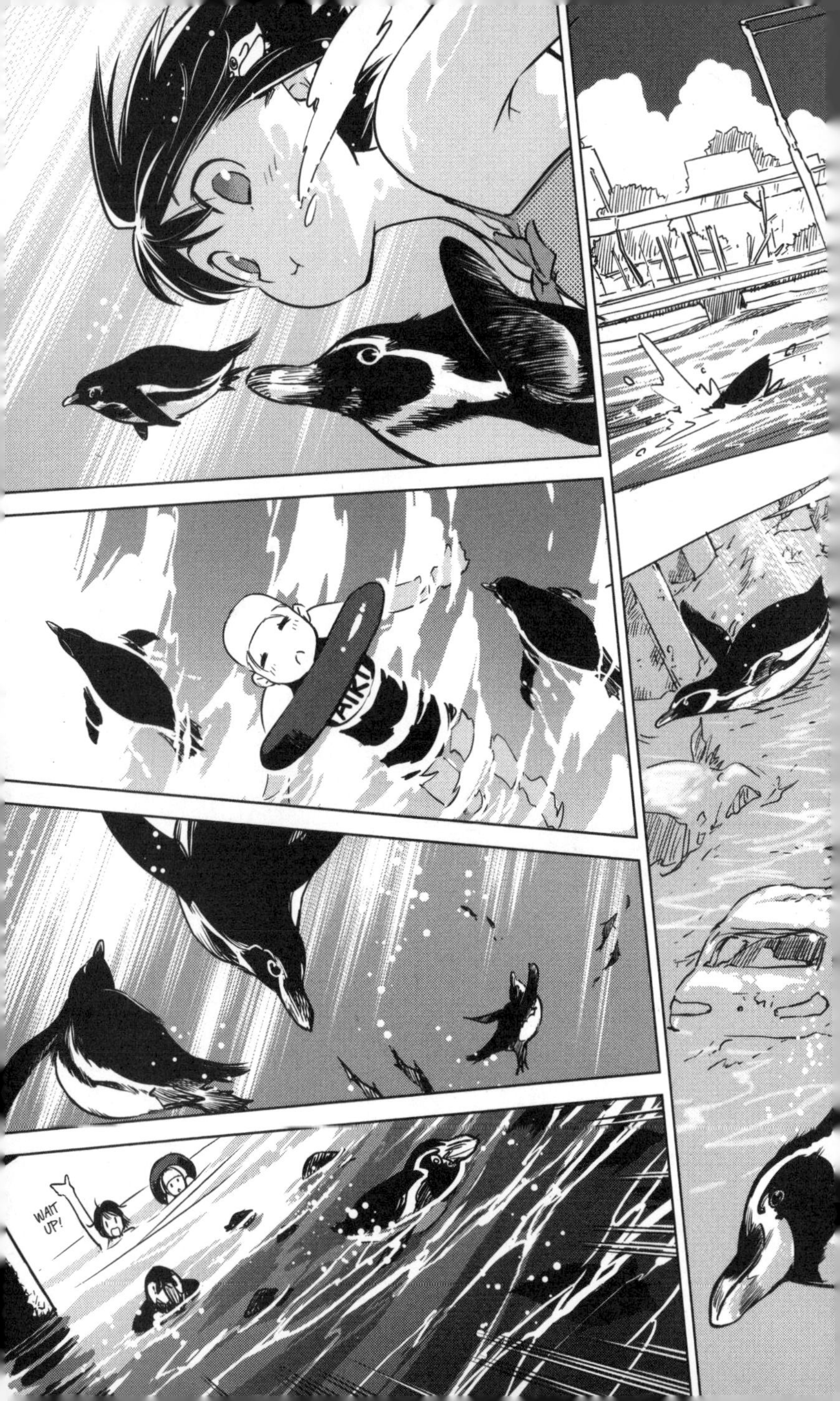
TAIKI
WAIT UP!

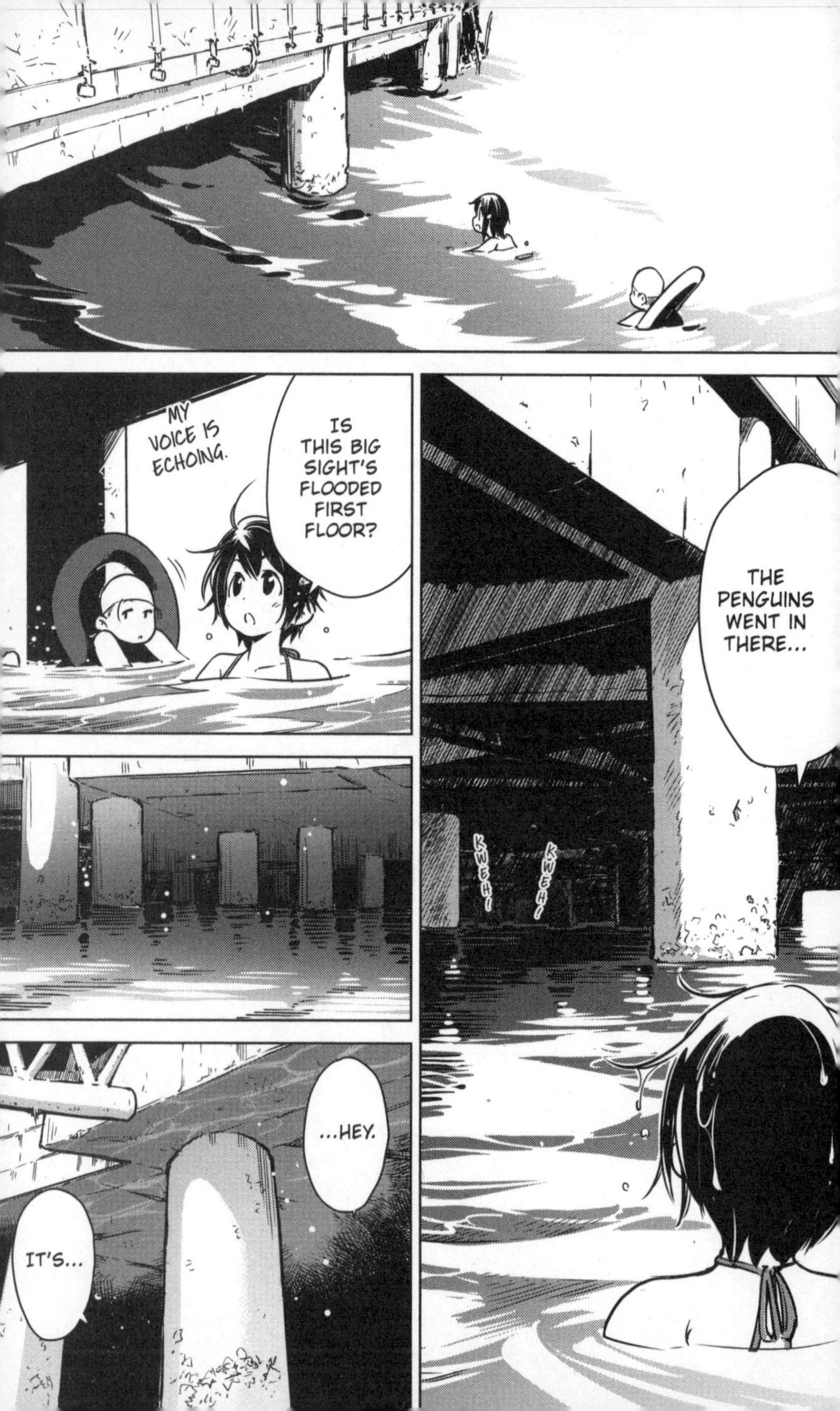
THE PENGUINS WENT IN THERE...
KWEH!
KWEH!
IS THIS BIG SIGHT'S FLOODED FIRST FLOOR?
MY VOICE IS ECHOING.
...HEY.
IT'S...

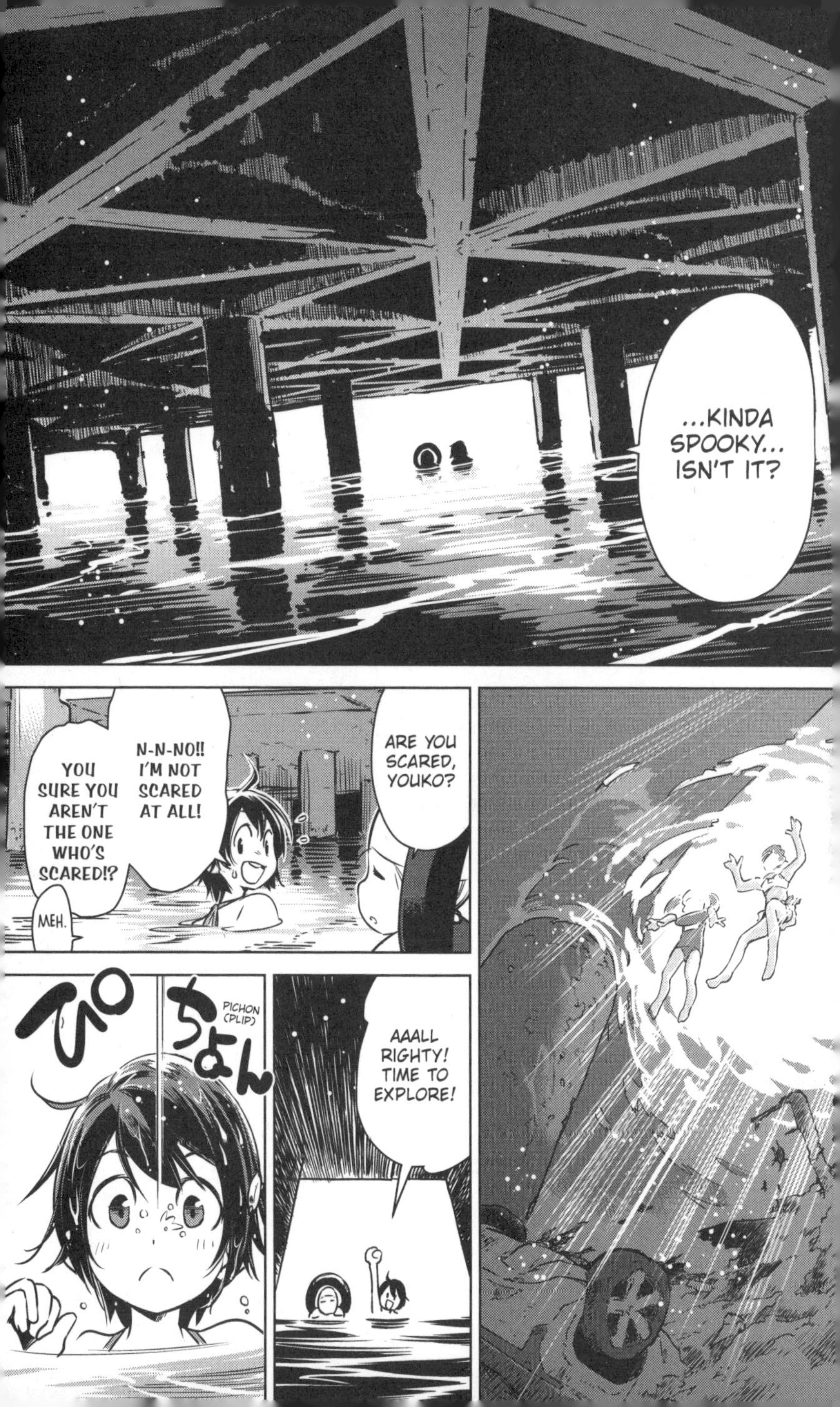
...KINDA SPOOKY... ISN'T IT?
ARE YOU SCARED, YOUKO?
N-N-NO!! I'M NOT SCARED AT ALL!
YOU SURE YOU AREN'T THE ONE WHO'S SCARED!?
MEH.
AAALL RIGHTY! TIME TO EXPLORE!
ぴちょん
PICHON (PLIP)

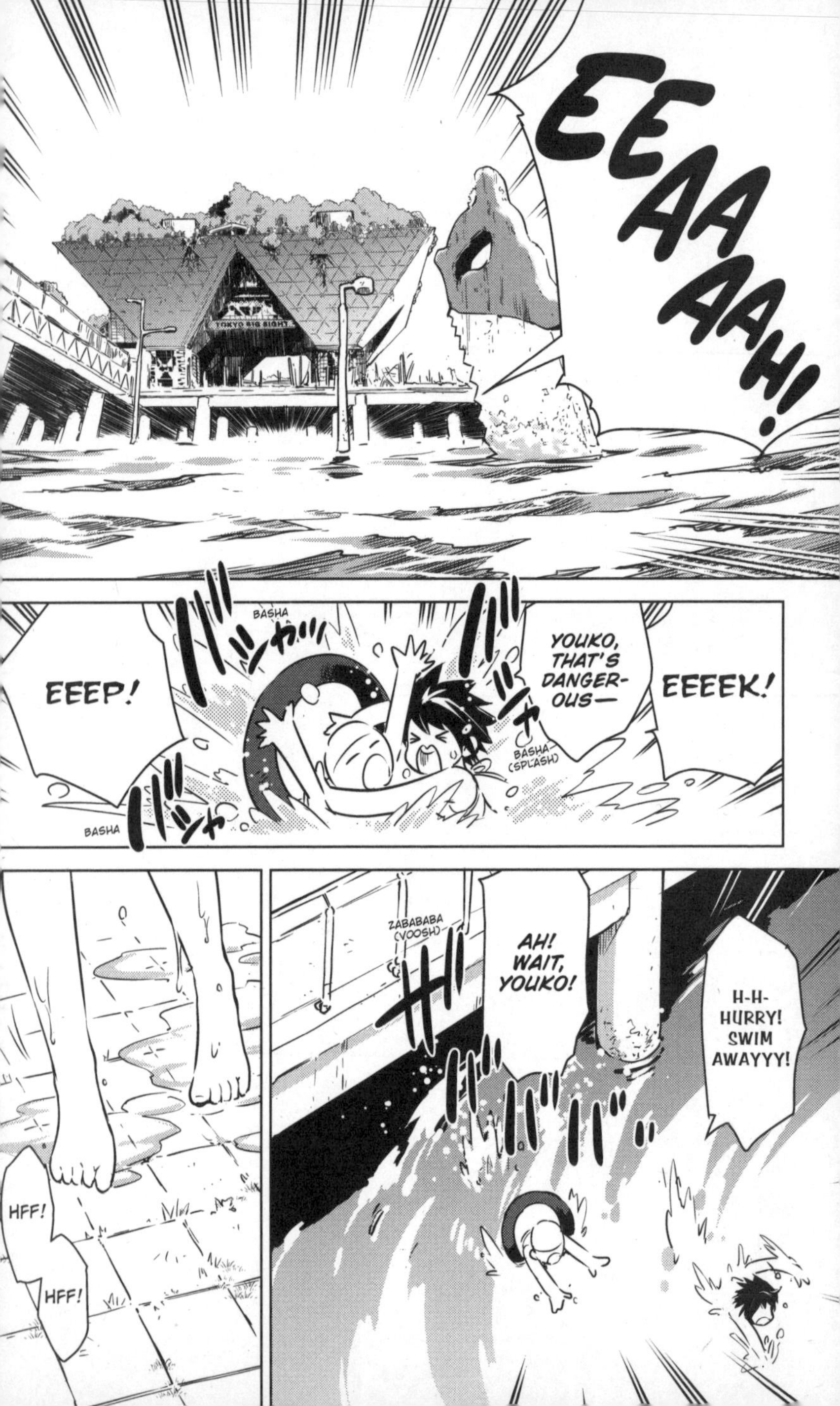
EEAAAAH!
EEEEK!
YOUKO, THAT'S DANGER-OUS—
BASHA (SPLASH)
BASHA
EEEP!
BASHA
H-H-HURRY! SWIM AWAYYY!
AH! WAIT, YOUKO!
ZABABABA (VOOSH)
HFF!
HFF!

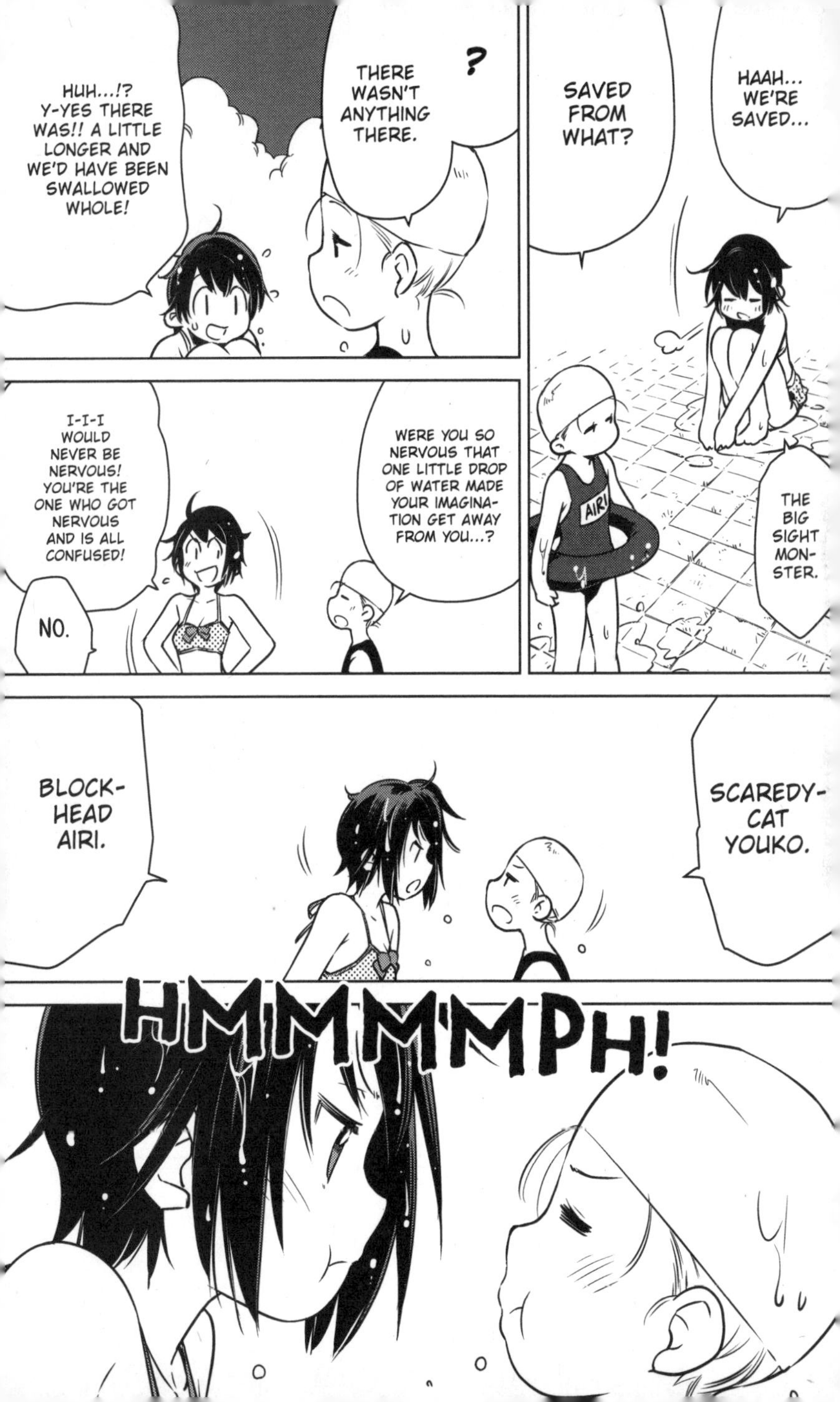
HAAH... WE'RE SAVED...
SAVED FROM WHAT?
THE BIG SIGHT MONSTER.
?
THERE WASN'T ANYTHING THERE.
HUH...!? Y-YES THERE WAS!! A LITTLE LONGER AND WE'D HAVE BEEN SWALLOWED WHOLE!
WERE YOU SO NERVOUS THAT ONE LITTLE DROP OF WATER MADE YOUR IMAGINATION GET AWAY FROM YOU...?
I-I-I WOULD NEVER BE NERVOUS! YOU'RE THE ONE WHO GOT NERVOUS AND IS ALL CONFUSED!
NO.
SCAREDY-CAT YOUKO.
BLOCKHEAD AIRI.
HMMMMMPH!

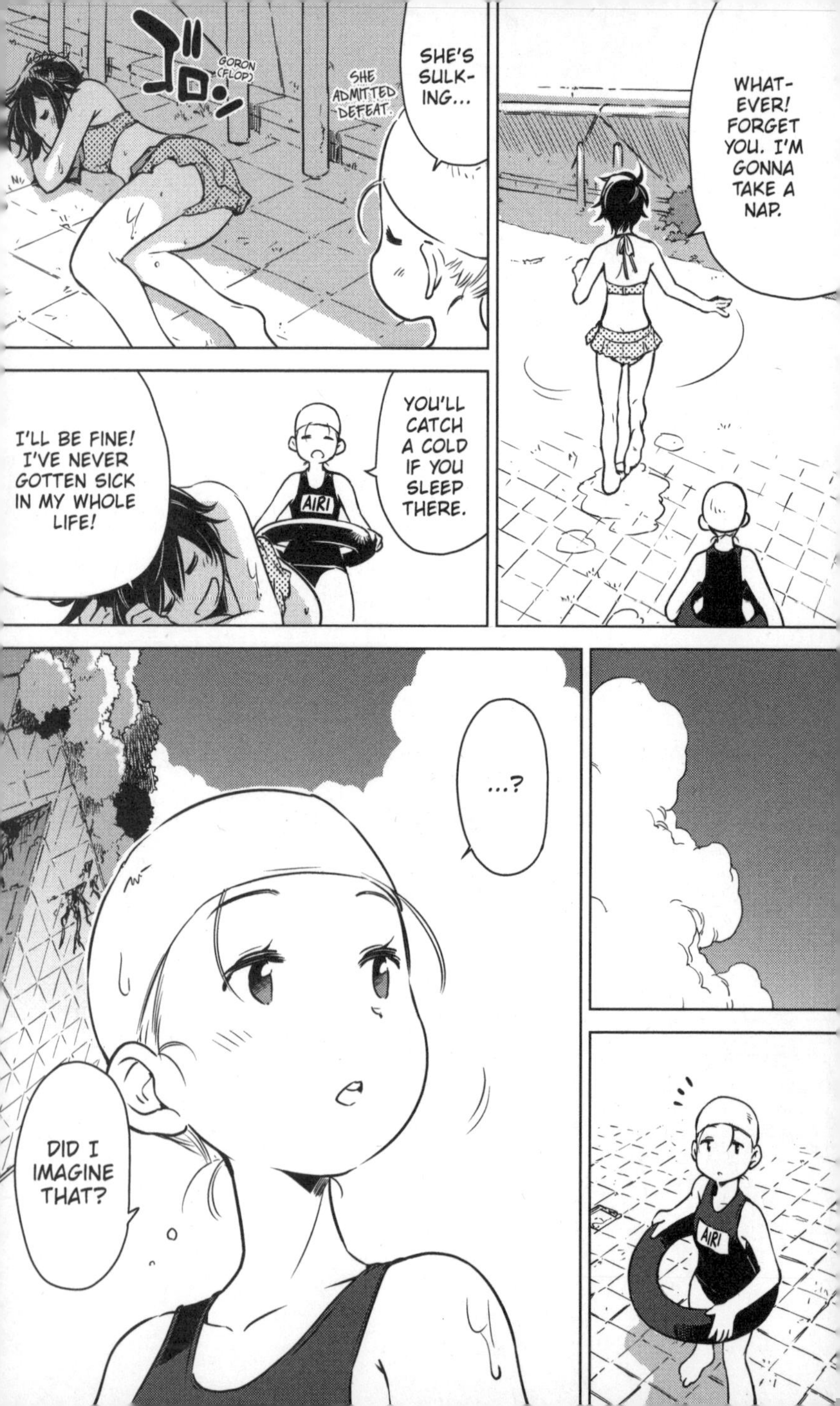
WHAT-EVER! FORGET YOU. I'M GONNA TAKE A NAP.
SHE'S SULK-ING...
SHE ADMITTED DEFEAT.
ゴロン
GORON (FLOP)
YOU'LL CATCH A COLD IF YOU SLEEP THERE.
AIRI
I'LL BE FINE! I'VE NEVER GOTTEN SICK IN MY WHOLE LIFE!
AIRI
...?
DID I IMAGINE THAT?

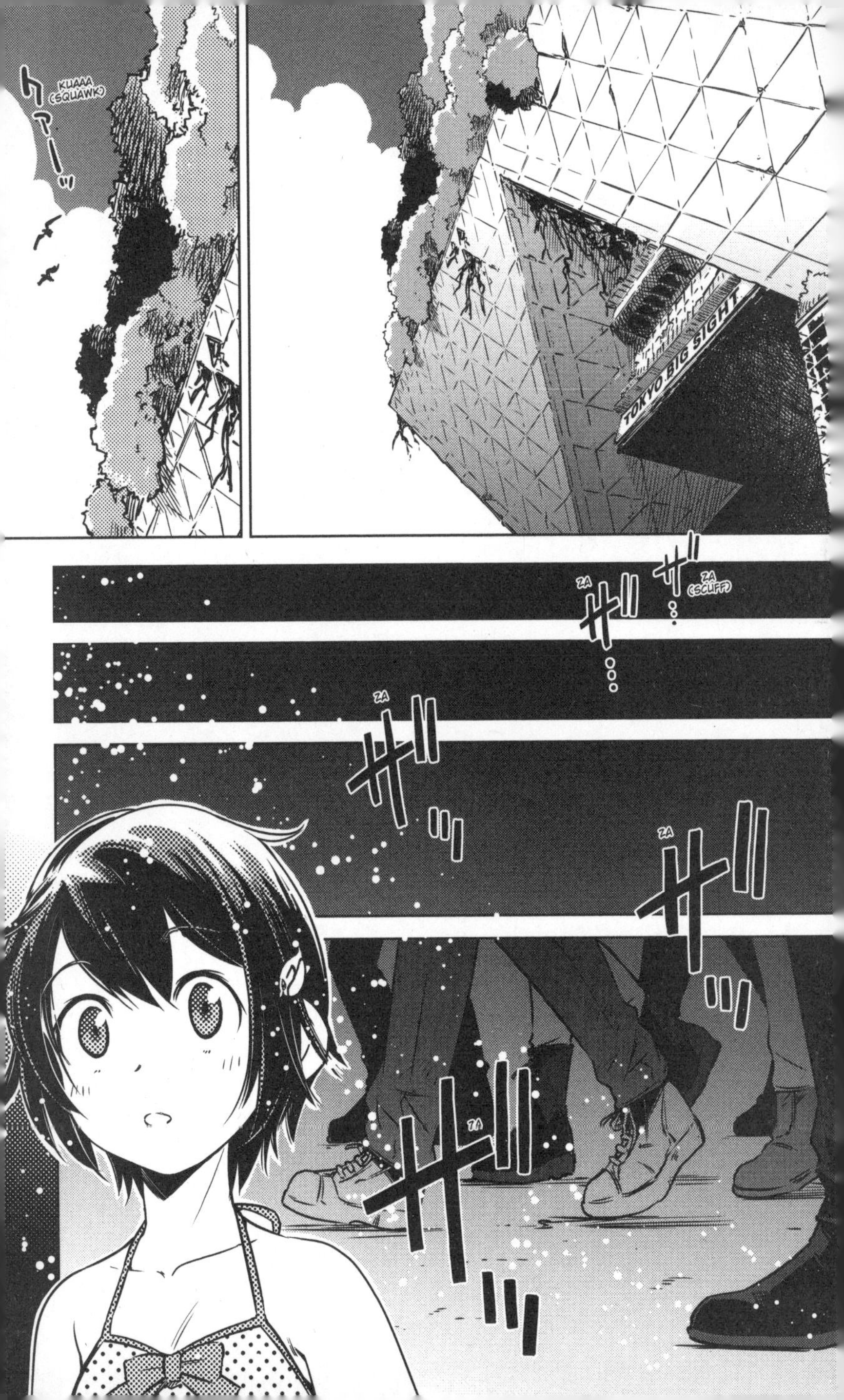

TOKYO BIG SIGHT
KUAAA (SQUAWK)
ZA (SCUFF)
ZA
ZA
ZA
ZA

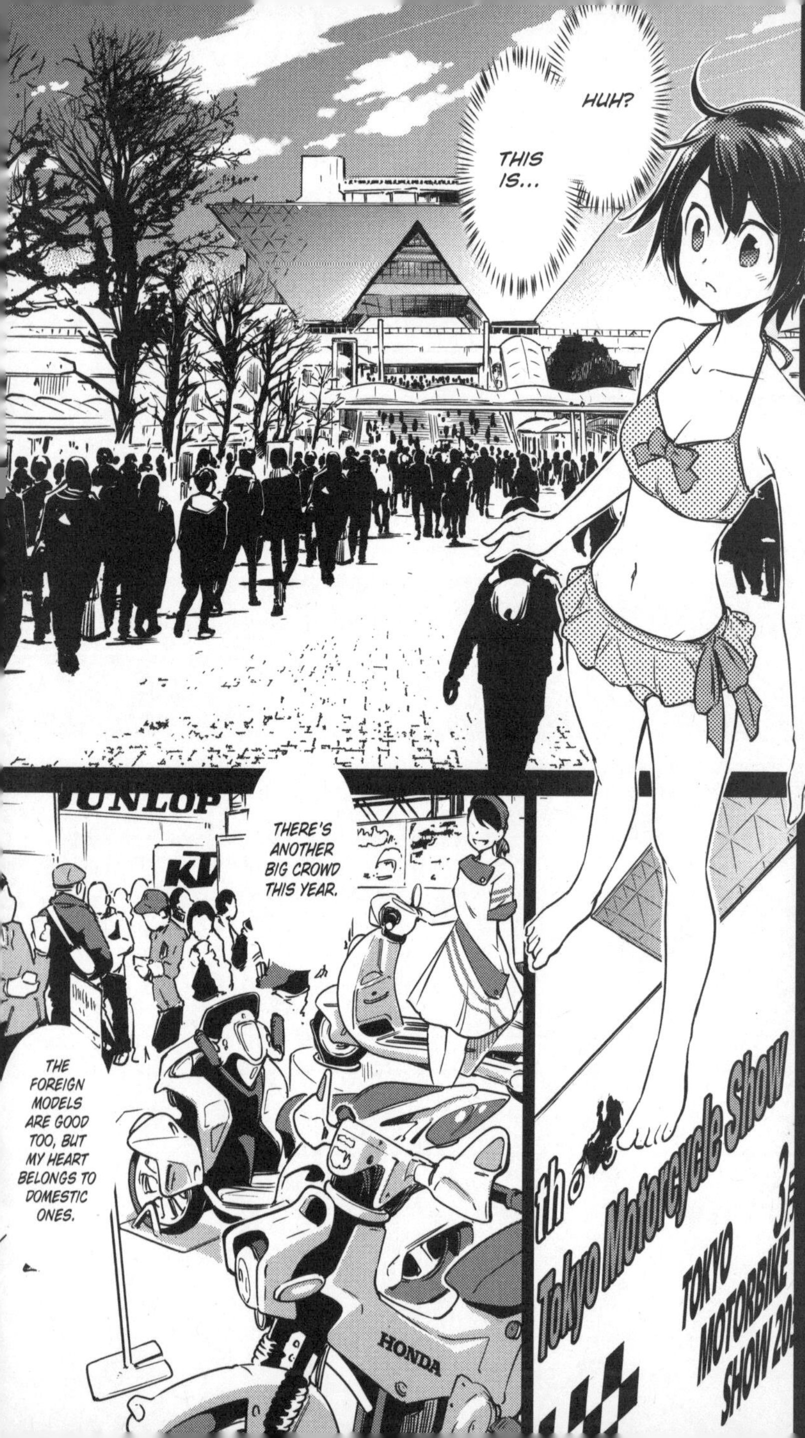
HUH?
THIS IS...
Tokyo Motorcycle Show
TOKYO
MOTORBIKE
DUNLOP
THERE'S ANOTHER BIG CROWD THIS YEAR.
THE FOREIGN MODELS ARE GOOD TOO, BUT MY HEART BELONGS TO DOMESTIC ONES.
HONDA

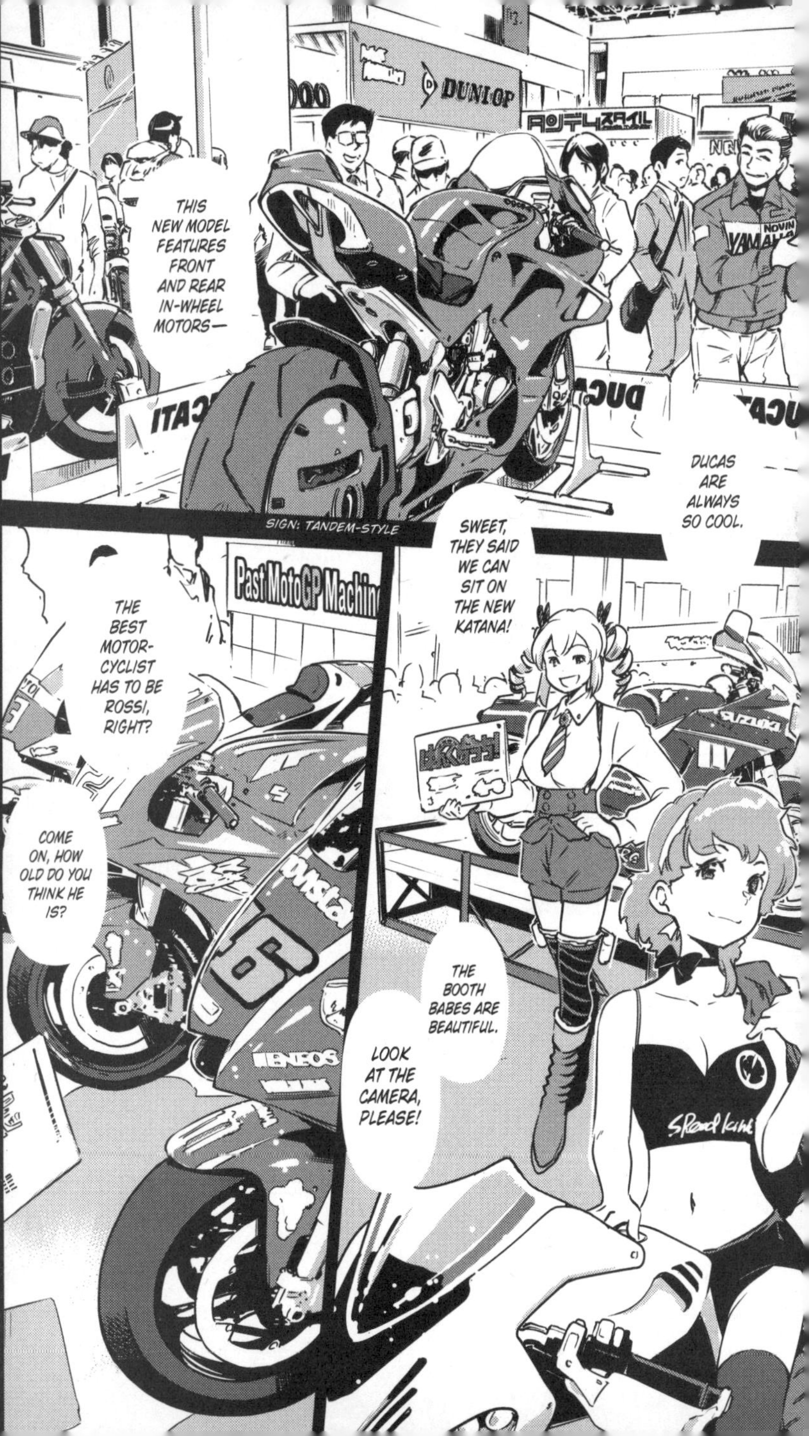
DUNLOP
DUCAS ARE ALWAYS SO COOL.
THIS NEW MODEL FEATURES FRONT AND REAR IN-WHEEL MOTORS—
SIGN: TANDEM-STYLE
SWEET, THEY SAID WE CAN SIT ON THE NEW KATANA!
THE BOOTH BABES ARE BEAUTIFUL.
LOOK AT THE CAMERA, PLEASE!
Past MotoGP Machin
THE BEST MOTOR-CYCLIST HAS TO BE ROSSI, RIGHT?
COME ON, HOW OLD DO YOU THINK HE IS?

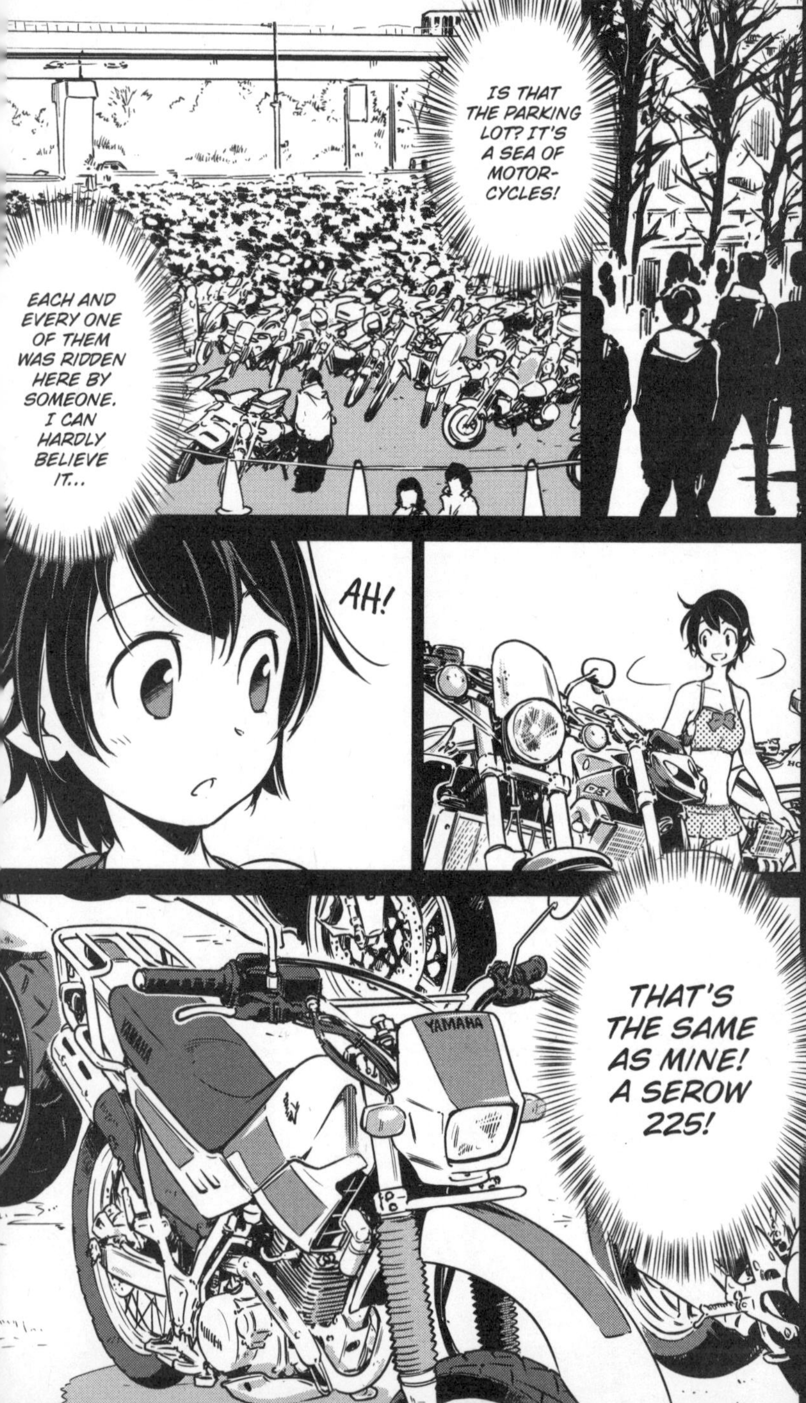
IS THAT THE PARKING LOT? IT'S A SEA OF MOTOR-CYCLES!
EACH AND EVERY ONE OF THEM WAS RIDDEN HERE BY SOMEONE. I CAN HARDLY BELIEVE IT...
AH!
THAT'S THE SAME AS MINE! A SEROW 225!
YAMAHA
YAMAHA

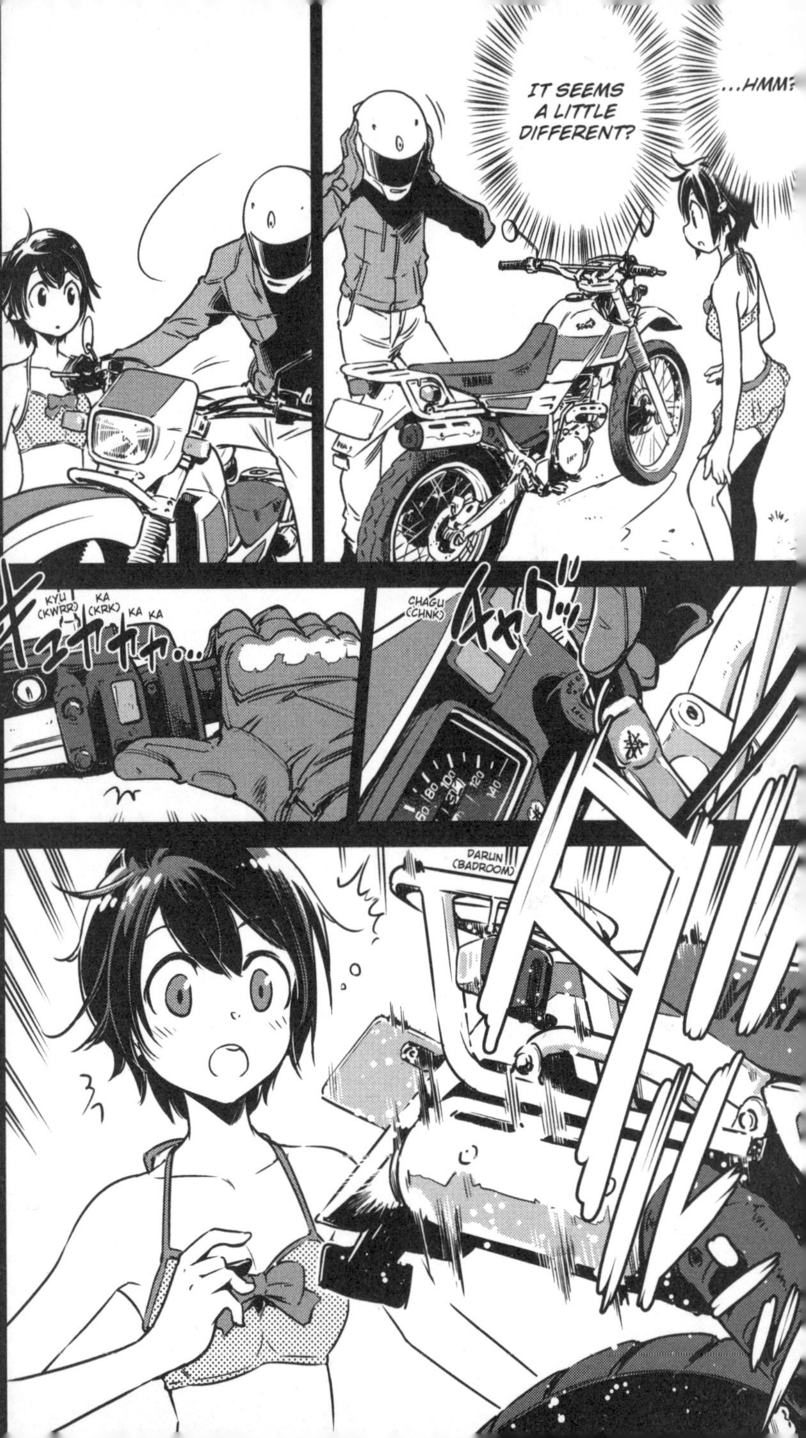
...HMM?
IT SEEMS A LITTLE DIFFERENT?
CHAGU (CHNK)
KYU (KWRR)
KA (KRK)
KA KA
DARUN (BADROOM)

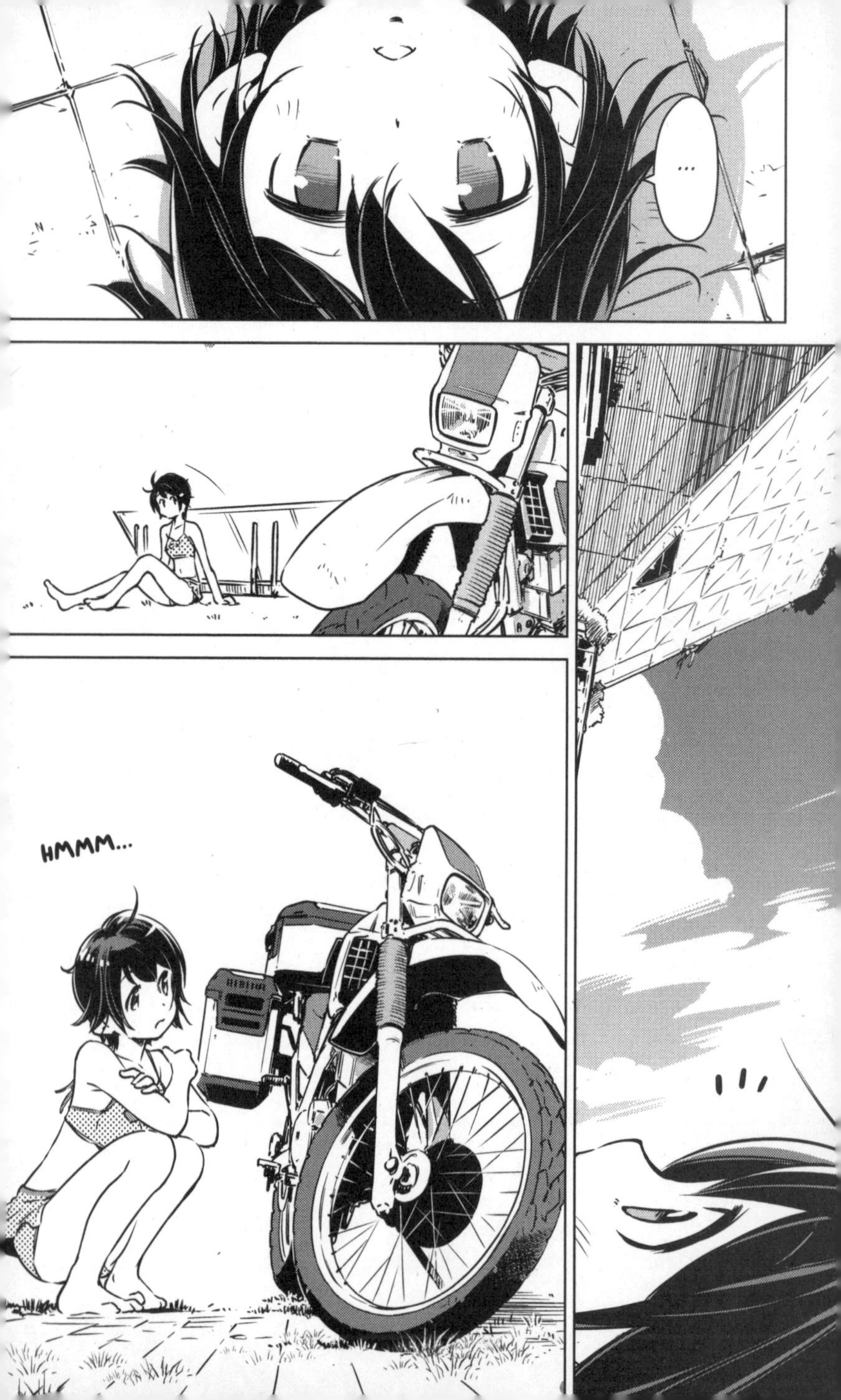
...
HMMM...

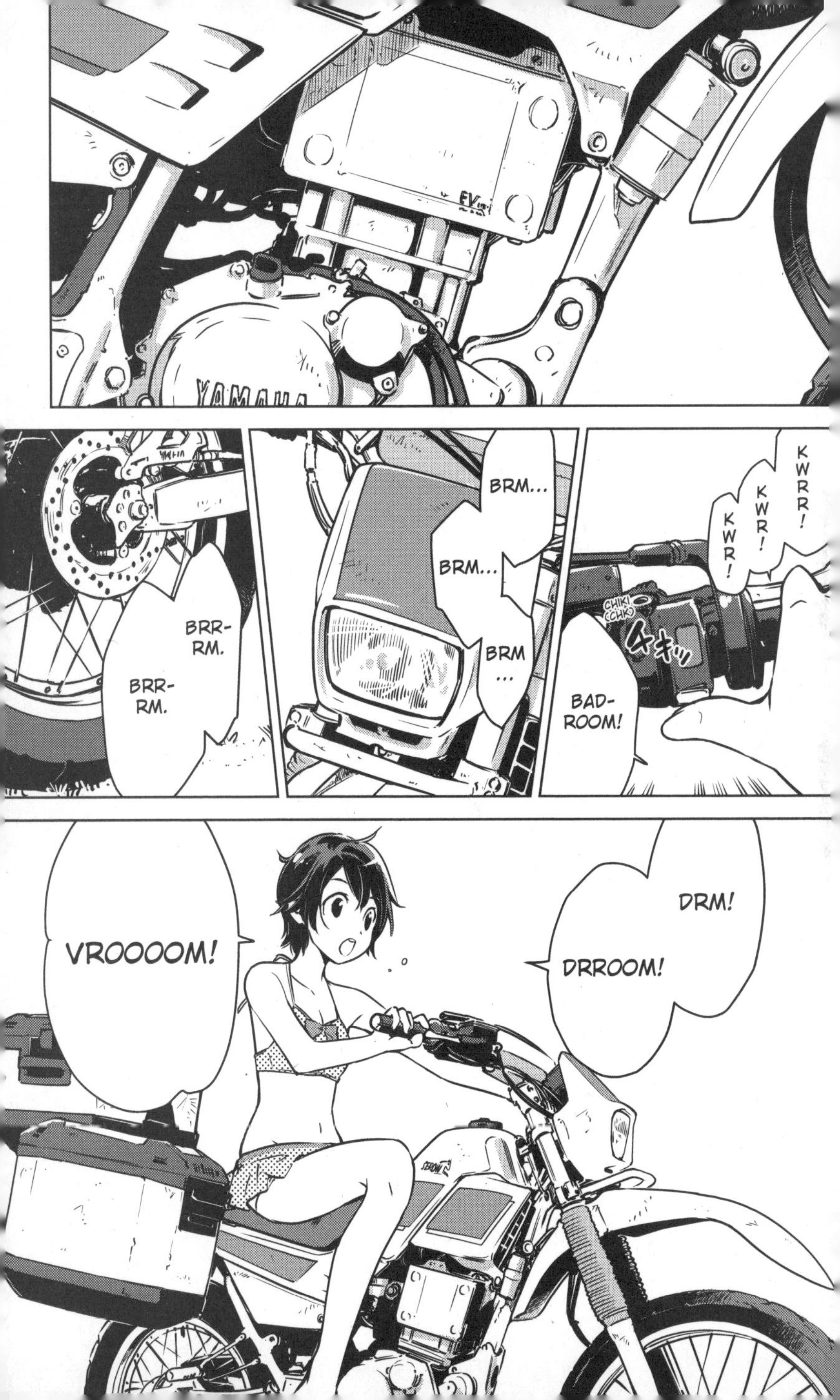
KWRR!
KWR!
KWR!
CHIKI (CHK)
BAD-ROOM!
BRM...
BRM...
BRM...
BRR-RM.
BRR-RM.
DRM!
DRROOM!
VROOOOM!

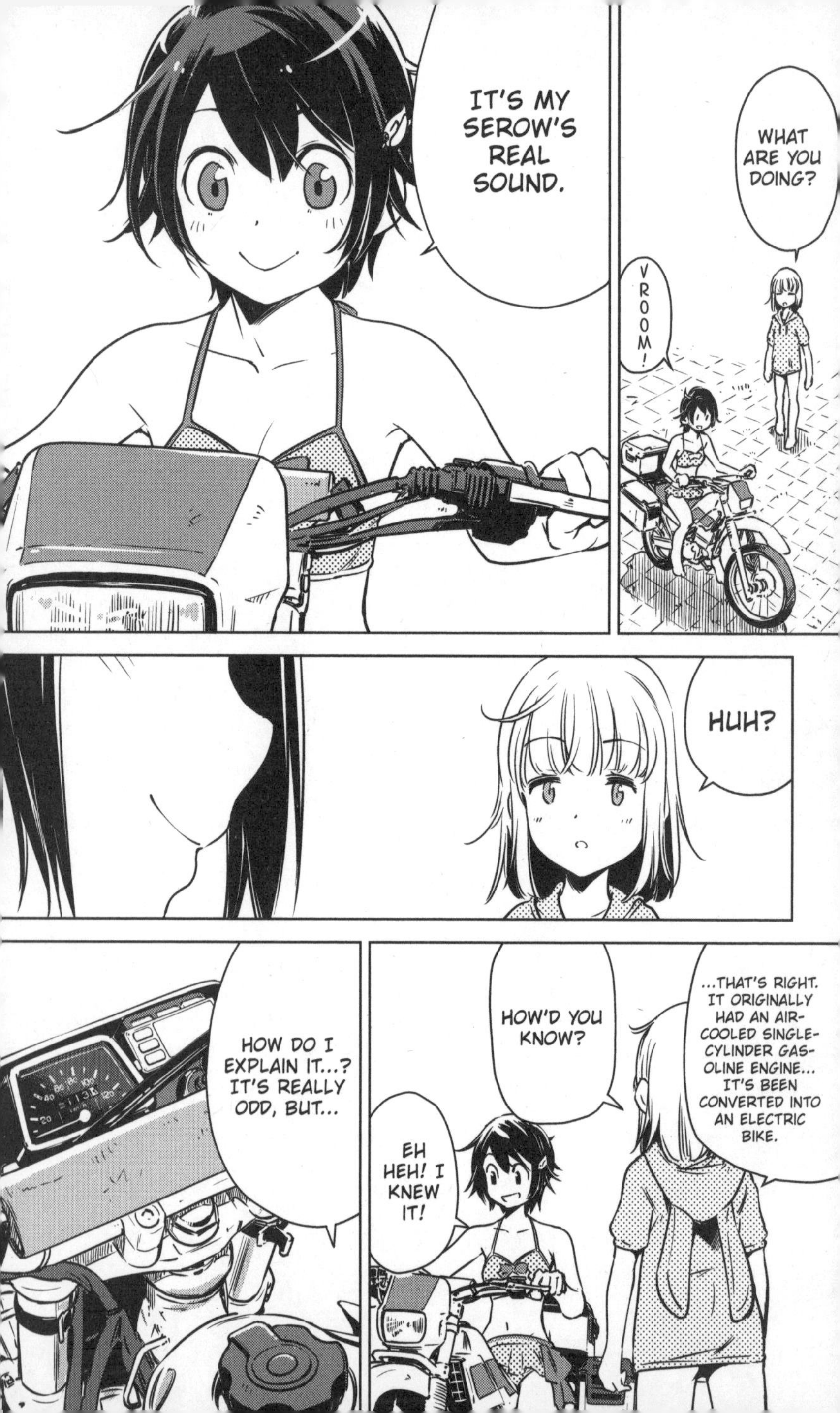
WHAT ARE YOU DOING?
VROOM!
IT'S MY SEROW'S REAL SOUND.
HUH?
...THAT'S RIGHT. IT ORIGINALLY HAD AN AIR-COOLED SINGLE-CYLINDER GAS-OLINE ENGINE... IT'S BEEN CONVERTED INTO AN ELECTRIC BIKE.
HOW'D YOU KNOW?
EH HEH! I KNEW IT!
HOW DO I EXPLAIN IT...? IT'S REALLY ODD, BUT...

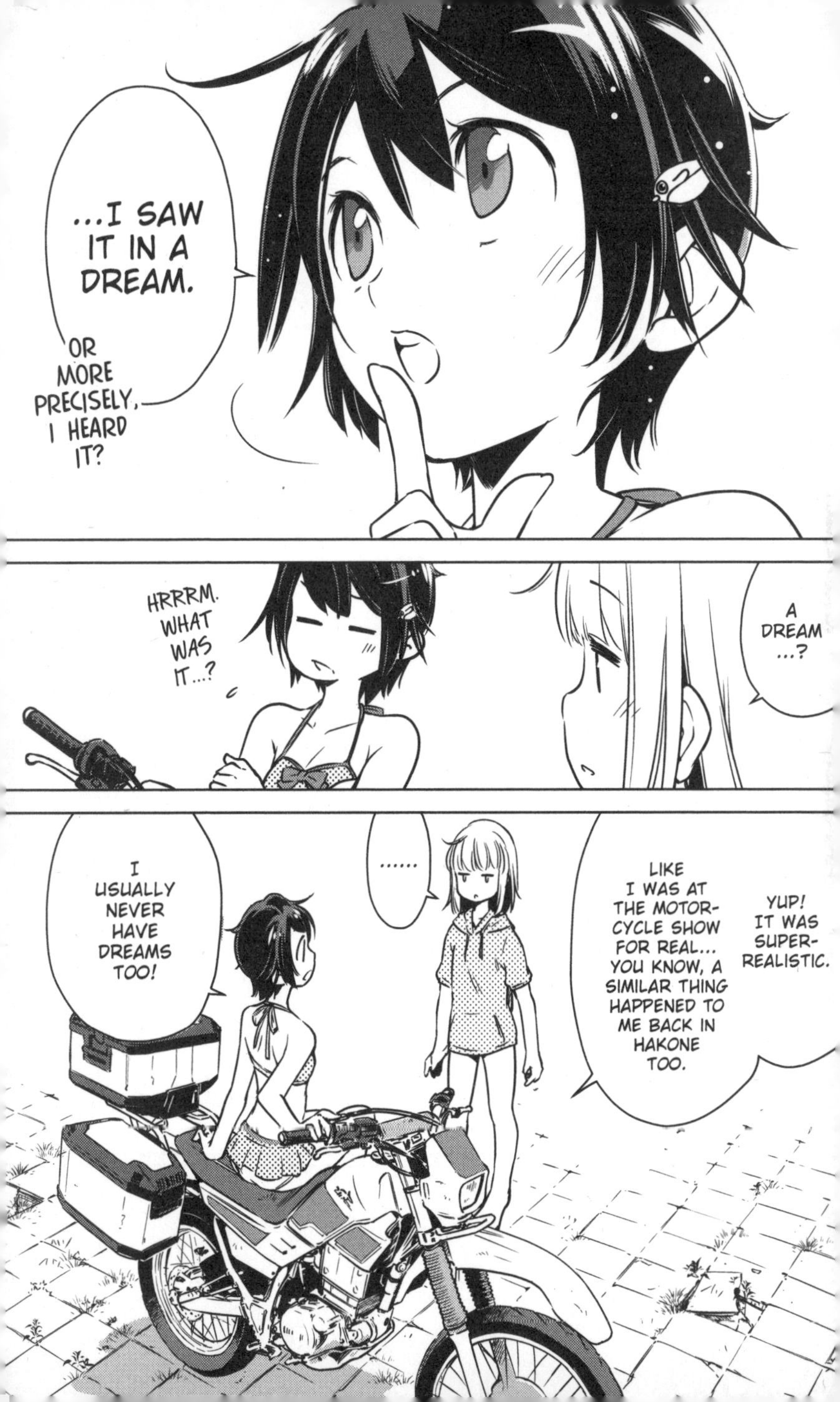
...I SAW IT IN A DREAM.
OR MORE PRECISELY, I HEARD IT?
A DREAM ...?
HRRRM. WHAT WAS IT...?
YUP! IT WAS SUPER-REALISTIC.
LIKE I WAS AT THE MOTOR-CYCLE SHOW FOR REAL... YOU KNOW, A SIMILAR THING HAPPENED TO ME BACK IN HAKONE TOO.
......
I USUALLY NEVER HAVE DREAMS TOO!

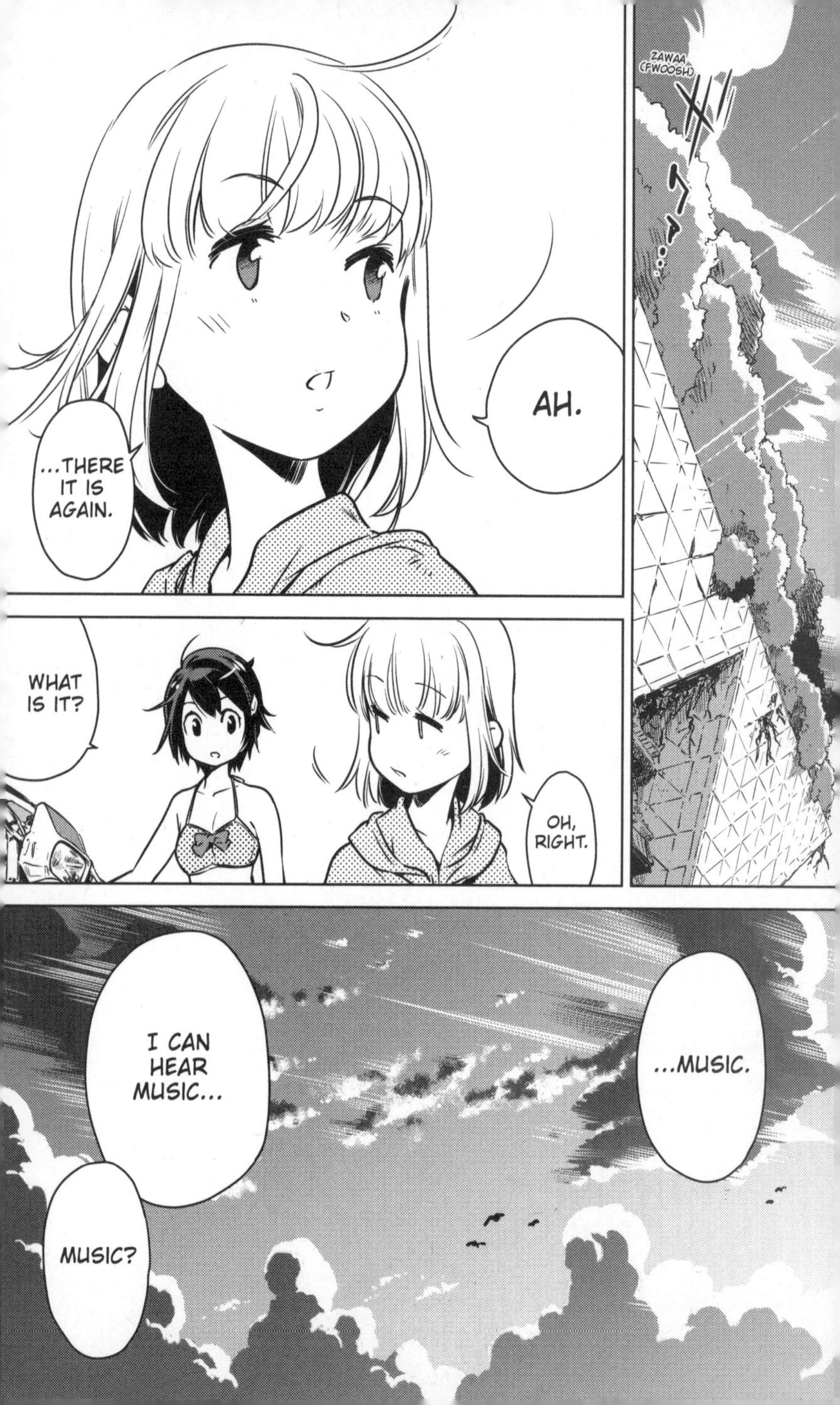
ZAWAA (FWOOSH)
AH.
...THERE IT IS AGAIN.
WHAT IS IT?
OH, RIGHT.
...MUSIC.
I CAN HEAR MUSIC...
MUSIC?

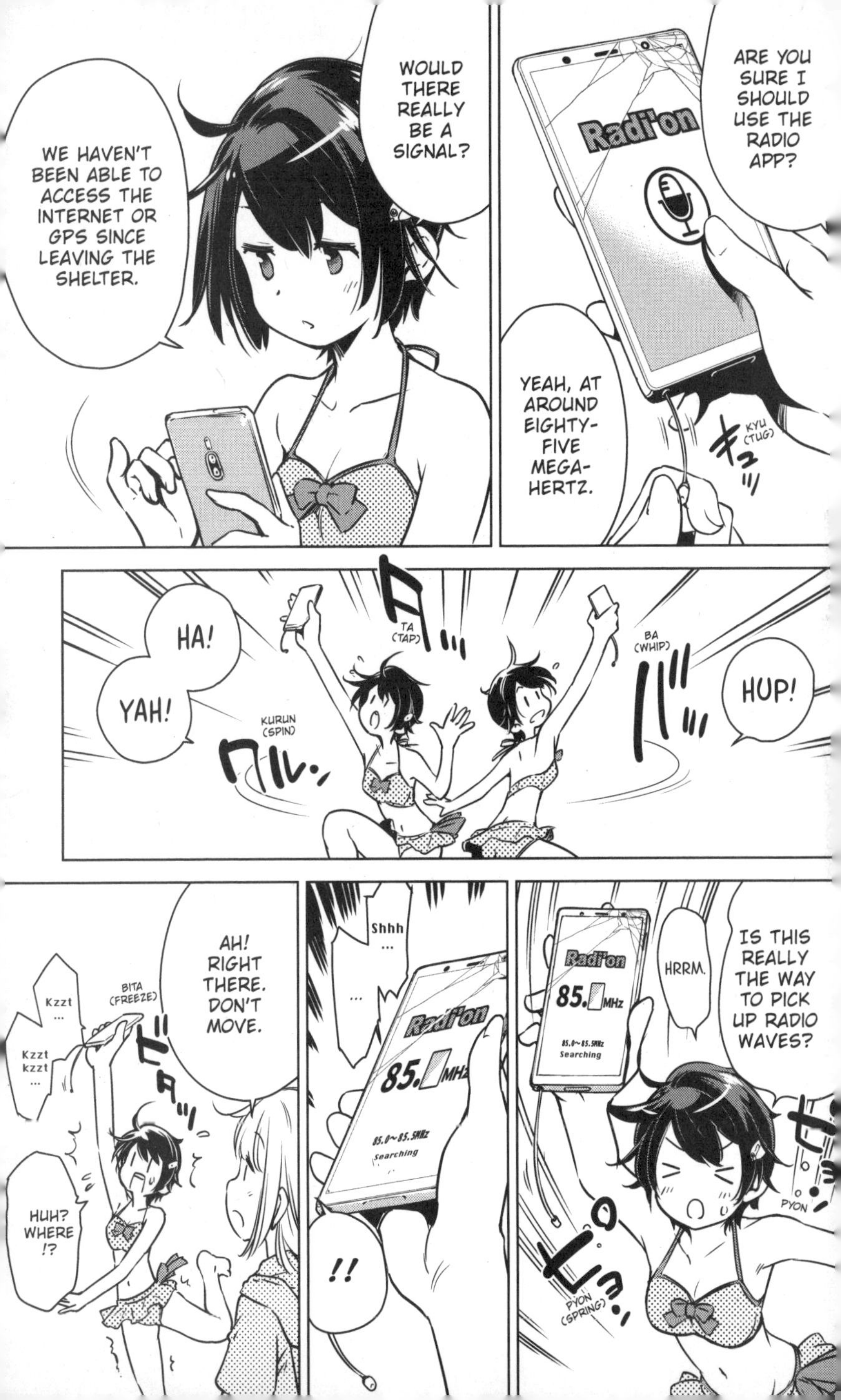

ARE YOU SURE I SHOULD USE THE RADIO APP?
Radi'on
YEAH, AT AROUND EIGHTY-FIVE MEGA-HERTZ.
KYU (TUG)
WOULD THERE REALLY BE A SIGNAL?
WE HAVEN'T BEEN ABLE TO ACCESS THE INTERNET OR GPS SINCE LEAVING THE SHELTER.
HUP!
BA (WHIP)
TA (TAP)
KURUN (SPIN)
HA!
YAH!
IS THIS REALLY THE WAY TO PICK UP RADIO WAVES?
HRRM.
Radi'on
85. MHz
85.0~85.5MHz
Searching
PYON
PYON (SPRING)
Shhh ...
...
Radi'on
85. MHz
85.0~85.5MHz
Searching
!!
AH! RIGHT THERE. DON'T MOVE.
BITA (FREEZE)
Kzzt ...
Kzzt kzzt ...
HUH? WHERE !?

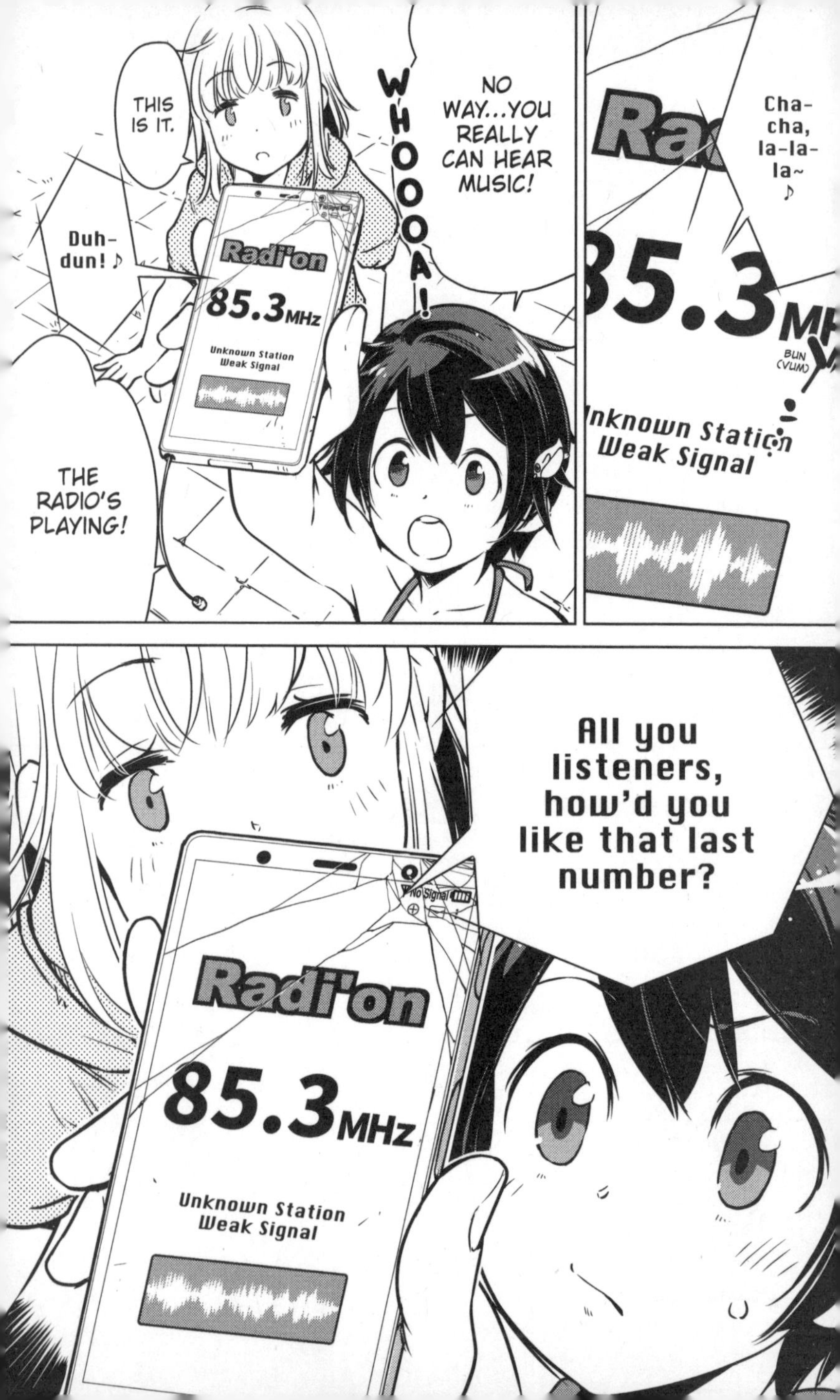
Cha-cha, la-la-la~ ♪
85.3
BUN (VUM)
Weak Signal
NO WAY...YOU REALLY CAN HEAR MUSIC!
WHOOOOA!
THIS IS IT.
Radi'on
85.3MHz
Unknown Station Weak Signal
Duh-dun! ♪
THE RADIO'S PLAYING!
All you listeners, how'd you like that last number?
No Signal
Radi'on
85.3MHz
Unknown Station Weak Signal

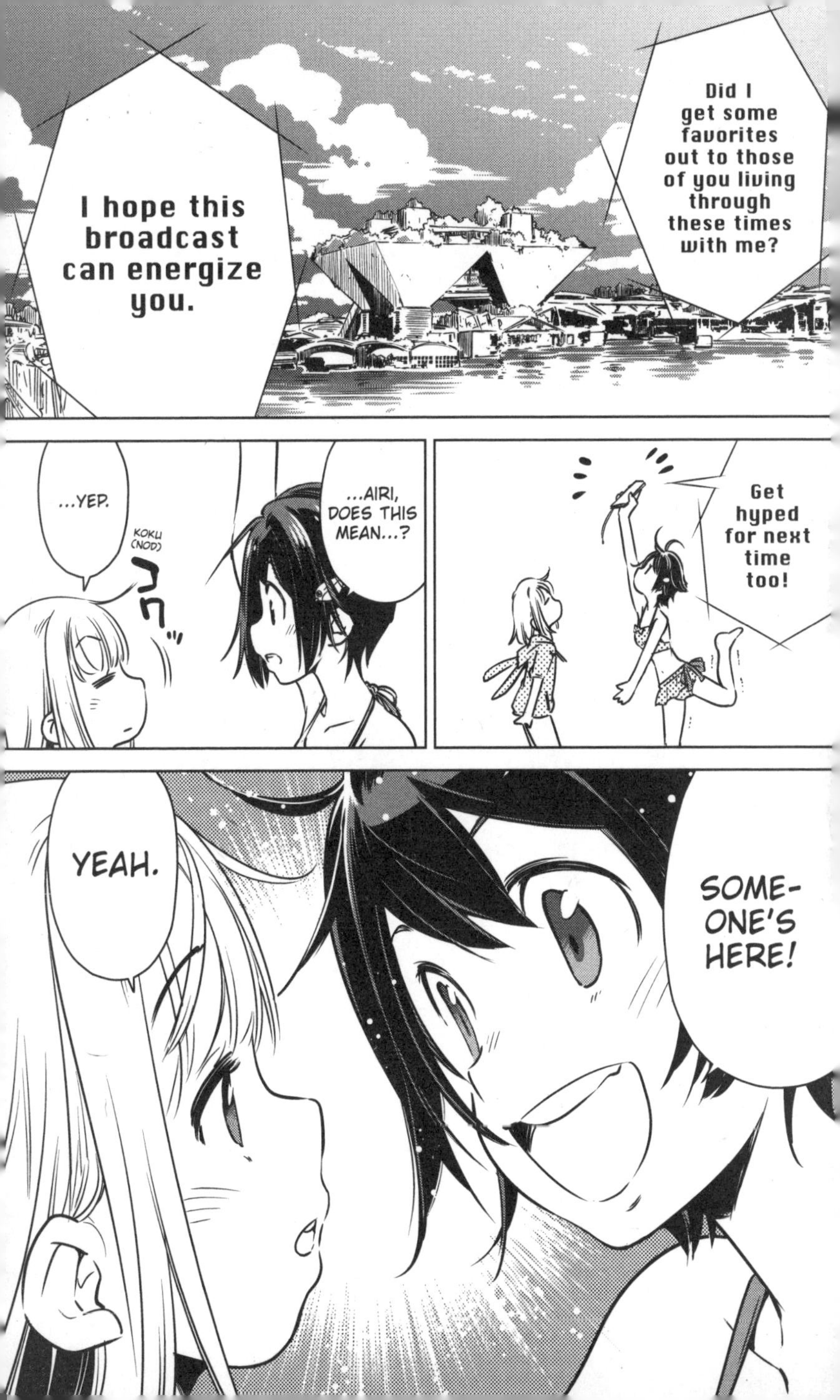
Did I get some favorites out to those of you living through these times with me?
I hope this broadcast can energize you.
Get hyped for next time too!
...AIRI, DOES THIS MEAN...?
KOKU (NOD)
...YEP.
SOME-ONE'S HERE!
YEAH.

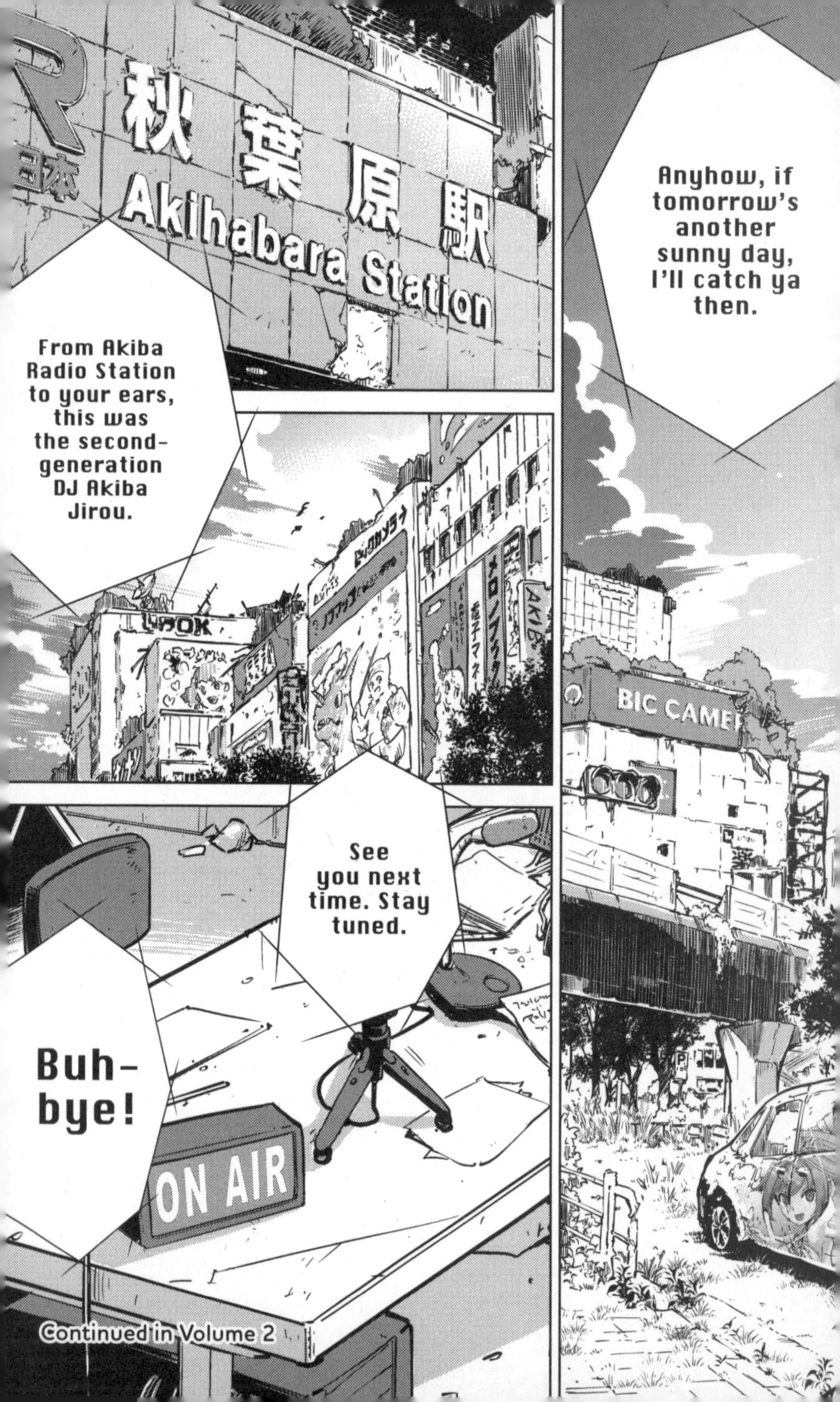
Anyhow, if tomorrow's another sunny day, I'll catch ya then.
秋葉原駅
Akihabara Station
From Akiba Radio Station to your ears, this was the second-generation DJ Akiba Jirou.
See you next time. Stay tuned.
Buh-bye!
ON AIR
Continued in Volume 2

AFTERWORD

Thank you very much for reading Volume 1!
I was born in the twentieth century. As a kid, I always thought the end of the century would be the end of the world. The prophecies of Nostradamus were in the public mind, and post-apocalyptic movies hit the big screen one after another...but here in the twenty-first century, all that is nostalgic at this point, isn't it? *Touring After the Apocalypse* originated from that nervous excitement that blanketed the world back then. I hope that here in the Reiwa period, long past the turn of the century, I can give you a new sense of nervous excitement through Youko and Airi's journey. See you again in Volume 2!

Sakae Saito

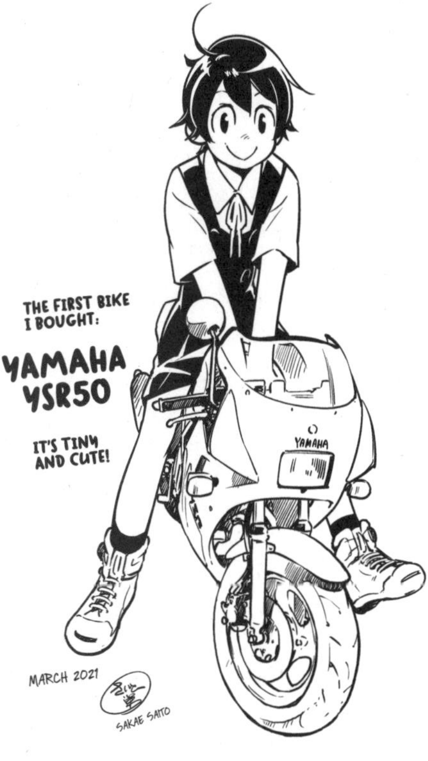
THE FIRST BIKE I BOUGHT:
YAMAHA YSR50
IT'S TINY AND CUTE!
YAMAHA
MARCH 2021
SAKAE SAITO

●Special Thanks
Taki-M

●Materials Assistance
Imigimuru-sensei
Yoshitaka Matsuo

Touring After the Apocalypse [1]

Sakae Saito

Translation: Amanda Haley
Lettering: Phil Christie

SHUMATSU TOURING Vol. 1
©Sakae Saito 2021
First published in Japan in 2021 by KADOKAWA CORPORATION, Tokyo.
English translation rights arranged with KADOKAWA CORPORATION, Tokyo, through TUTTLE-MORI AGENCY, INC., Tokyo.

English translation © 2022 by Yen Press, LLC

Yen Press
150 West 30th Street, 19th Floor
New York, NY 10001

Visit us at yenpress.com
facebook.com/yenpress
twitter.com/yenpress
yenpress.tumblr.com
instagram.com/yenpress

First Yen Press Edition: November 2022
Edited by Yen Press Editorial: Thomas McAlister, Carl Li
Designed by Yen Press Design: Andy Swist

Yen Press is an imprint of Yen Press, LLC.
The Yen Press name and logo are trademarks of Yen Press, LLC.

Library of Congress Control Number: 2022942371

ISBNs: 978-1-9753-4880-9 (paperback)
978-1-9753-4881-6 (ebook)

10 9 8 7 6 5 4 3 2 1

WOR

Printed in the United States of America